PURE
GOLD

PURE
GOLD

Library of Congress Control Number: 2003098037
ISBN 0-9747031-0-9

For more information please contact:

Promontory Publishing Co.
1204 E. South Temple Street
Salt Lake City, Utah 84102

And for a testimony that the things that they
had said are true they have brought
twenty-four plates
which are filled with engravings,
and they are of pure gold.

— Mosiah 8:9

And thou must open thy mouth
at all times, declaring my
gospel with the sound of rejoicing.

— Doctrine and Covenants 28:16

PURE
GOLD

---

*A behind-the-scenes look at
a builder of the Kingdom*

KEITH ELLIOTT GARNER

By Susan Stewart

To President Gordon B. Hinckley, who opened

wonderful doors of service through which President Garner entered.

To Elder David B. Haight, who backed with utmost confidence

Bishop Garner and let him soar.

To Elder Marion D. Hanks, who befriended and

heartened Keith always to be his indomitable self.

To each of them for their encouragement, support,

and help in bringing **PURE GOLD** *to fruition.*

Table of Contents

FORWARD

For the past quarter century, I have worked for, or as my boss corrects me, worked with Keith Garner. The title secretary describes my duties most succinctly; however, after these many years, my resume might also list bookkeeper, receptionist, gardener, sales representative, graphic designer, cleaning lady, interior designer, painter, editor, typist, chauffeur. Needless to say, with my liberal arts background, I have performed better in some of these roles than in others. In fact, my father shook his head every time our conversations revealed that one of my work assignments was to balance bank statements for Mr. Garner's numerous businesses. My father only hoped I balanced bank statements better for Mr. Garner than I did for myself. Initially, it amazed me that my lack of experience and training in particular fields never seemed to deter Mr. Garner from giving me many expansive opportunities for which I often felt unqualified. To assure my success, he always went the extra mile, sometimes in the face of others' criticism, openly exhibiting a confidence in me that I could and would perform. He even printed a business card which made me smile. It read "Susan Stewart, Chief Executive Officer." As exalted as this moniker sounded to me, I had learned many years before that the more meaningful and significant title and the one that Mr. Garner carries in his head and heart and accepts as the universal business card reads "Child of God."

Seemingly endowed from a pre-mortal existence with this infinite, immortal, panoramic vision of life, he quickly internalized the gospel teaching that we are all the spiritual offspring of an Eternal Father and Mother, and, therefore, brothers and sisters. Over a lifetime of reading the Book of Mormon, an eternal view deepened, and particular scriptures touched powerful cords of remembrance and resolve in him, among these the prophet Jacob's counsel.

Think of your brethren like unto yourselves,
and be familiar with all and free with your substance,
that they may be rich like unto you.
But before ye seek for riches,

> *seek ye for the kingdom of God.*
> *And after ye have obtained a hope in Christ ye*
> *shall obtain riches, if ye seek them; and ye will*
> *seek them for the intent to do good--to clothe*
> *the naked, and to feed the hungry, and to liberate*
> *the captive, and administer relief to the sick*
> *and the afflicted."– Jacob 2:17-19*

I would not be surprised to see this scripture framed and hanging on the wall near his desk, but framing and hanging becomes entirely unnecessary because he long ago committed this counsel both to memory and to action.

Perhaps it goes without saying that his application of this gospel perspective benefits my life enormously, and I am not alone. His innovative style, avant-garde thinking, ignoring of conventional practices, and defining of work as an avenue for personal growth has opened up vast worlds of opportunity to many. The only roadblock to success that I have ever seen manifest itself in this generous atmosphere seems to be the recipient's own work ethic, integrity, determination, and imagination.

Today I am privileged to be engaged in another expansive role as his collaborator in preserving and sharing the life experiences of this man whose energies have been enthusiastically and joyfully devoted to the gospel of Jesus Christ. This new challenge is daunting; in fact, his counselor in the Menlo Park Ward bishopric and lifelong friend Hugh S. West commenting on any book written about Keith Garner mused, "However it is written, it won't do him justice." I agree.

Then why attempt writing his story? Assuredly not because Keith Garner is a household name and certainly not because he desires to be one. Although he has served in some high profile Church callings, his seasoned personality simply shuns the spotlight. He purposely avoids the notoriety that for most of his life has been available to him. Nonetheless, his dogged effectiveness, magnified by its unique and cheerful application, defies invisibility. In many circles, some of which extend across the globe, his labors, some recent and others years prior, set a "gold standard" for performance and are so acknowledged. His ingeniousness has deservedly earned him his nickname "rare bird." In fact, for many with whom he has associated, he would be their choice for the *Readers Digest* feature, "My Most Unforgettable Character." Such merited epithets describing Keith's interesting life seem to make an attempt to record his memories mandatory.

When a remarkable story is told, it is unremarkable to hear the comment, "You should write a book." Nevertheless when it is directed to Keith, whose life is a continuous and joyous rendezvous with the remarkable, he cannot easily dismiss this spontaneous plea uttered eagerly so many times over his more than eighty years.

The first time he recalls such a request was upon his completing two years, two months, and eleven days as a missionary for The Church of Jesus Christ of Latter-day Saints in the Hawaiian Islands, a call to serve lasting almost three months longer than normal because of the Japanese attack on Pearl Harbor. Keith returned to San Francisco full of stories and heard "Elder Garner, you should write a book!"

Countless fascinating chapters followed, making this first appeal almost commonplace in his adventurous life. Having flown, sometimes in the midst of enemy fire, in his capacity as president of the Southern Far East Mission around war torn South Vietnam aboard the gun ship affectionately called *Here After*, Keith's commentary was repeatedly met with "President Garner, you should write a book!"

Even the bank manager in Palo Alto, California, after clearing Keith's check, the cuff he had torn from the white shirt he was wearing and issued to a vendor in Tehran for the purchase of an ornately engraved brass disc, amusedly chuckling at his client's resourcefulness, said, "Mr Garner, you should write a book!"

Again, after Keith's journey of discovery to Persia resulted in the pictorial defense of the Prophet Joseph Smith's claim that the Book of Mormon was translated from gold plates and after Keith, holding one of King Darius' gold plates, appeared in Church literature and archeological treatises, many opined, "Bishop Garner, you should write a book!"

To each of these repeated petitions for a book, Keith, after crediting his reply to one of his favorite authors Charles Dickens, recites, "When I go back to the slow agony of my youth, I wonder how much of the histories I invented hangs like a mist of fancy over well-remembered facts." He accurately adds that autobiographical accounts are rendered suspect by their obvious subjectivity.

Keith's reluctance to document his remarkable life can also be explained in a more pragmatic term, time. On a daily basis taking into account only his business ventures, he physically and mentally fills his hours with a myriad of changing tasks: adding three thousand square feet to the pro shop at his Idaho golf course property, developing a new logo and advertising plan for the funeral home he owns, processing plans for approval by Salt Lake City of a new hilltop home construction, and meeting with or telephoning bankers, architects, lawyers, investment brokers, real estate agents, construction superintendents, and accountants. His frequently asked questions at the end of the traditional eight hour work day, "Do you know it's already five o'clock? Where did the day go?" reveal both his pride in the day's accomplishments and his frustration at the scores of uncompleted tasks that he predictably tackles in the evening hours.

The understandable time problem must be conquered to enable the documentation of his extraordinary life because Mr. Garner's oral recollections still mesmerize his listeners and elicit the familiar request for his life experiences to be written. Lifetime associates, referring to Keith's oft-repeated recollections by number when a situation brings the memory to the surface, and new acquaintances, sitting enthralled as Keith entertains them with both his past milestones and his present challenges, reinforce the value of his manuscript when they strongly state, "Yours is a book I would read!"

Yes, Keith Elliott Garner should write a book. With some reticence, he finally agreed to assist in this effort because he has been persuaded that this enterprise is simply an extension of his lifelong service as a missionary, a life of deeds now translated into words.

After he came to this conclusion to record his memoirs, why did he ask me to assist him? First, I am one of those who has strongly requested or, in more descriptive words, pestered him to write this book. I had come to my own conclusion that he is simply too busy and too modest to write about himself. In frustration he asked me, "Why don't YOU write it if you think it's so important?" I accepted enthusiastically, yet with some trepidation, the invitation and energetically proceeded.

As all secretaries can attest, whether it be the well-known Clare Middlemiss, President David O. McKay's constant secretary; Arthur Haycock, secretary to five presidents of the Church; or the considerably lesser known Susan Stewart, secretary to Keith Garner, a secretary is a witness to public and private histories and is, therefore, uniquely qualified to offer at least a firsthand glimpse. My proximity as his secretary has given me the unparalleled privilege of watching his life in action, participating in times of some of his great successes and most bitter disappointments, sitting with him as he shares his recollections, traveling to places of import in his life, meeting his friends and adversaries, and learning from his study and practical application of gospel principles.

In addition, my access to primary source materials has been unlimited. For many of his eighty plus years, Mr. Garner has kept personal notations, all of which I have read. He has an extensive collection of letters that he wrote and received from people with whom he was engaged in Church, business, and social relationships, and some of this correspondence I have incorporated verbatim. A special thanks is owed to Keith's oldest sister Loma, who kept every missive from her youngest brother, along with correspondence from his mother and father and his associates. Almost without exception, the friends, ward members, seminary students, missionaries, Temple Square hosts, hostesses and tour guides, professional associates, and acquaintances I contacted by letter or in person provided valuable insights and experiences. President Gordon B. Hinckley, Elder David B. Haight, and Elder Marion D. Hanks, friends who shared some of the most exciting times in Keith's life, were generous with both their time and their information.

Many of my sources have known Mr. Garner longer than I. In fact, the first time I shook hands with him was from behind the reception counter at the Visitors' Center North on Temple Square in 1974. My initial perception was that of a man whose very countenance radiated warmth, intelligence, and a gentle confidence. From that time forward, I joined a host of others who called him "President."

Today, almost thirty years later, his business office is located a few blocks East on South Temple, and I, from a lasting and strongly held respect for him, still call him president. He flinches at my appellation, even to the point of accusing me of having been mesmerized. I have assured him, as I do the reader, that this simply is not the case. In sharing his memories and others' memories of him and his most precious convictions, I have tried not to intrude, for truly his life speaks for itself.

Elder Hanks, in conversation with Keith regarding his life and the publication of this book, clearly addressed Keith's concerns. Keith had opined that the overall tenor of the book was excessively acclamatory with the words, "Scrud, this book is too laudatory for me to allow it to be published!" Elder Hanks countered with a story about the great baseball player, Dizzy Dean, in which Dizzy, after his brother chided him for enumerating for reporters all his accomplishments, said, "If you done it, it ain't bragging." Elder Hanks then concluded, "Keith, you done it."

Chapter

O N E

Unto the Isles of the Sea

"I live almost in a state of perpetual excitement."
— Joseph Smith, Jr.

      This five foot nine giant's first words to me were, "It's a wake back there." Keith E. Garner referred to the retirement party for President T. C. (Ted) Jacobsen. After nine years President Jacobsen had been released from an unpaid assignment as Director of Temple Square in Salt Lake City, Utah.

      Not unfamiliar with hearing from the First Presidency of The Church of Jesus Christ of Latter-day Saints, Keith, not eager to leave the mission field, felt sad when President Marion G. Romney called and asked him to move from Menlo Park, California, to Salt Lake City, Utah, to assume the duties of president of Temple Square. "Move from the Garden of Eden to the lone and dreary world!" As bishop of the Menlo Park Ward, he cautioned his parishioners from the pulpit not to move to Utah because the center of Church administration often left members disappointed in the lack of perfection they would unwittingly not expect and surprised at the human frailties they often found. In some ways these feelings would prove prophetic, for Salt Lake City might be called Keith's personal fiery furnace.

      Almost as if they were kindred spirits, the Mormon poet Eliza R. Snow penned sentiments in 1876 which echoed Bishop Garner's foreshadowing when she wrote the poem "Think Not When You Gather to Zion."

Think not when you gather to Zion,
Your troubles and trials are through,
That nothing but comfort and pleasure
Are waiting in Zion for you:
No, no 'tis designed as a furnace,
All substance, all textures to try,
To burn all the "wood, hay and stubble,"
The gold from the dross purify.

Think not when you gather to Zion,
That all will be holy and pure,
That fraud and deception are banished,
And confidence wholly secure:
No, no, for the Lord our Redeemer
Has said that the tares with the wheat
Must grow till the great day of burning
Shall render the harvest complete.

Think not when you gather to Zion,
The saints here have nothing to do
But to look to your personal welfare,
And always be comforting you.
No; those who are faithful are doing
What they find to do with their might;
To gather the scattered of Israel
They labor by day and by night.

Think not when you gather to Zion,
The prize and the victory won.
Think not that the warfare is ended,
The work of salvation is done.
No, no; for the great prince of darkness
A ten fold exertion will make,
When he sees you go to the fountain,
Where freely the truth you may take.

For the first time in his life, Keith's response to a call to serve in a Church position reverberated with a half-hearted, "I'll have to get back to you." After struggling for confirmation, his dutiful answer echoed over the phone lines, "Yes, I'll come."

Now he arrived in Salt Lake City, not yet as a welcomed new director of

Temple Square, but as a replacement for a well-known and appreciated overseer. That night after a short greeting, Keith, without deflecting the spotlight shining on President Jacobsen's tenure, left the party. The next morning President Garner returned, as he would almost daily over the next four years, to work in combining the welcoming format of the visitors' center with a place of gospel learning and testimony bearing. This format became the pattern repeated in Church visitors' centers throughout the world.

Keith Garner was not unknown upon his arrival on Temple Square in January 1975. Patrons and visitors to Temple Square, as well as emissaries and investigators of the Church worldwide, recognized his countenance. On the lower level of the Visitors' Center North among explanatory exhibits extolling the principles and programs of the restored gospel, a life-size picture of Keith Garner stood conspicuously positioned. In his hands he held a gold plate excavated from the foundation walls of the Audience Hall of the palace of Darius, the King of Persia, (521-486 B.C.). The picture sparked the curiosity of visitors and led many to explore the claim made by Joseph Smith, the Prophet, that he had translated the Book of Mormon from gold plates delivered to him by one of the book's authors, Moroni, a resurrected being who lived his mortal life upon the American continent and died in approximately 421 A.D.

This was the same picture which appeared prominently in an informational tract distributed throughout the missions of the Church as well as at the 1964 New York World's Fair Mormon Pavilion. Truly a no more expressive picture could be conceived to portray the essence of the man Keith Elliott Garner.

Keith's lifelong embrace of the Book of Mormon began early, and with each passing year, his grasp seems to become firmer. In 1938 he joined with his older sister LaVon and her friends a discussion group in San Francisco referred to as "The

Farewell Dance

GIVEN IN HONOR OF

Elder KEITH GARNER

Called to the Hawaiian Mission

on Friday Eve., December 29, 1939

in the
San Francisco Ward Amusement Hall
1649 Hayes Street

Admission 50c   *Extra Lady* 25c

Refreshments

Just recently upon seeing this memento and noting admission was charged, a colleague remarked "even at that young age he had it figured out."

Elder Garner and his fellow missionaries at the Salt Lake Missionary Home, 3rd from left on 3rd row

Book of Mormon Club." These study gatherings helped him to determine in his own mind and heart that the Book of Mormon contained God's revelations. This serious probe could not have come at a more propitious time, for it prepared him for an imminent mission call. On September 12, 1939, Keith received a call from the President of the Church, Heber J. Grant, to labor without monetary compensation as a missionary for The Church of Jesus Christ of Latter-day Saints in the Hawaiian Islands.

"I remember they asked me where I wanted to go, and I said wherever I'm supposed to go. It was a wonderful experience to be called, and I couldn't have found a better mission in all the world to go to than Hawaii."

His departure date was set for January 1940. This four-month-heads-up and the continued graciousness of his sister and brother-in-law, who provided him free room and board, allowed Keith additional time to save what he thought would be sufficient for his needs over the next two years--a grand total of $600 or twenty-five dollars a month.

His earnings came from working full-time at American Trust Company while studying at the University of San Francisco in the evenings. He and his friend Jack Hargraves alternated shifts as messengers for the bank hierarchy. The bank president, James K. Lochhead, flanked by his two executive secretaries, Theresa Wallace and Jean Chenowith, sat on a raised platform directly across from and to the right of the tellers. To the left on another raised platform sat the nine executive bank officers. Keith stood between the platforms under a separating marble arch waiting to be summoned. He ran between bank executives, tellers, and customers on bank business with deposits and documents. He was also at the disposal of the executive officers of the bank to run personal errands such as obtaining tickets to *La Boehme* at the San Francisco Opera House or theater tickets at the famous Geary Theater. One of the duties Keith enjoyed most was placing crisp, brand new $100 bills, the director's fee for periodic Board of Directors' meetings, in front of each director's chair. Keith walked around the large conference table distributing the bills and chanting, "One for you; one for me!" Touching such large denominations gave him quite the rush of power. Jean Chenowith liked Keith, and he appreciated her mind, her beautiful clothes, and her status, trappings of the glamour he associated with insiders whose wealth moved the world.

The name American Trust Company carried prestige. The imposing building at 464 California Street located in the heart of the financial district between Montgomery and Sansome reflected the ornate architecture of the period with marble floors, arches, and large pillars. American Trust Company would eventually purchase Wells Fargo Bank and later use its name.

Even in this heady environment, Keith was not shy about his missionary plans. No one wanted him to leave. Mr. Kirk, an executive vice-president, and A.T. (Andy) Matthew, assistant vice-president in charge of the tellers, both cajoled, "You have a great future here; you stay and let someone else spend two years of his life proselyting for your Church!"

Keith left, but before he did so, he introduced Jack, his cohort at the bank, to his beliefs, his friends, and his world view. He invited Jack to Church and social activities at the San Francisco LDS Ward Chapel at 1649 Hayes Street, and within a short time, Jack requested membership and asked Keith to baptize him.

The time between his call and his departure for the mission field passed quickly with dinners, dancing parties, and newspaper announcements that celebrated Elder Garner's call to the Hawaiian Islands. The excitement of a new adventure in a new place with new friends and new experiences turned into an excitement for missionary work and an eagerness to be on his way. The magnitude of his upcoming assignment became clear, and he determined early to immerse himself in the work. Keith and approximately

Seeing him off are: l to r: Doris Loosley, Clora Martin, his sisters: Ruth, LaVon and Beatrice; in front: Jack Hargraves

seventy-five other newly called missionaries spent a week at the Missionary Home in Salt Lake City where he completed a "special course of training in preparation for this sacred labor."

The time for departure arrived. At the San Francisco dock, Keith declared to the girl he'd been dating that he wouldn't be writing. He didn't want any diversions. Although he'd enjoyed their association, he thought it would be unfair to ask anyone to focus on him while he was focusing exclusively on missionary work. Besides, turning to his handsome, debonair friend Jack, he concluded that it was obvious there would be plenty of other very favorable dating options over the next two years for a girl left free. Surrounded by his three sisters LaVon, Ruth, Beatrice; LaVon's best friend Clora Martin; his friends Doris Loosley and Jack Hargraves, Keith boarded the *Lurline III* for the five day sail to Hawaii on January 18, 1940.

The *Lurline*, built by Bethlehem Shipyard at Quincy, Massachusetts, for the Matson Navigation Company, was a relatively new luxury liner launched by Mrs. William P. Roth, the Matson president's wife, on July 18, 1932. It held 475 first class passengers, 240 tourist class, and a crew of 359. [1] The *Lurline's* service route was San Francisco-Los Angeles-Honolulu and back. A 1930s brochure lauding the quality of "the Matson liners that dominated the Pacific in the pre-war years," the *Lurline* and her three sister ships, the *Monterey, Mariposa*, and *Matsonia* acclaimed,

> *As the rainbow spans the horizons so Matson liners cross the open seas between to the wonderlands of Hawaii, Samoa, Fiji, New Zealand, and Australia, weaving island pearls into a new pattern of existence. Departures of the Lurline (et al) are as full of thrills and color as the happy collection of ports, countries, and people, the most fascinating section of the universe, for which they set sail. The South Pacific-- lands of unimagined beauty and charm--impossible to define."*

The brochure also described the first class dining room, the dance pavilion, the writing room, the library, the first class staterooms, and deluxe suites with sumptuous superlative scenes of "perfect harmony," unusual "trellised walls," "palm-filled nooks," and "tropical bamboo motifs in luxurious furnishings." The *Lurline* offered every imaginable comfort. For Keith, like many other twenty year old innocents on the Lord's mission, his eyes beheld a new world waiting to be discovered.

Enroute to the Territory of Hawaii, the USS *Lurline III* docked in the port of Los Angeles. Keith, as they were about to leave Los Angeles, dashed off a picture postcard of the *Lurline* to a sister in Utah. He writes, "Gee, I had a perfect send off.

---

[1] "Maritime Matters," 1 [on-line]; available from http://www.maritimematters.com/lurline32.html.; Internet; accessed 20 June 2001.

I certainly have some wonderful sisters! The boat is leaving in half an hour, so everything is in a hurry, sorry. Thanks for taking care of me. I really appreciate it all."

Elder and Mrs. Rollo Dutson and two lady missionaries assigned to the Japanese Mission also headquartered in the Hawaiian Islands joined Keith and his companion Elder Vernon F. Dickman on board. "Out the first day," Keith relates, "I noticed we were two decks lower than the top. Above they were enjoying music and laughing, and I could hear the clinking of glasses. I figured, why don't we get up there and see what's going on. We climbed the stairs. When we got to the top, there was a guard who asked where we were going. I told him we were just going in to watch the dancing. He wanted to know where my cabin was. Pointing to the stairs, I told him

Elders Garner and Dickman.

that it was down there. We were sent downstairs with a polite but pointed explanation, 'That's where you go; this is first class, young man, and you're cabin class.' The first class passengers had paid for all the privileges, and we had paid a lesser amount. Our accommodations were great, but they weren't as great as the upper deck. That's when the practical ramifications of our belief in the Resurrection hit me; there are degrees of glory! The three degrees of glory about which the Apostle Paul speaks and Joseph Smith enlarges in Doctrine and Covenants, Section 76: celestial, terrestrial, and telestial, aren't all of the same order, and there are gradations within kingdoms."

Keith continues, "Interestingly enough a few years later on my way to the Philippines on a troop carrier, we passed the Hawaiian Islands, and I thought of my experience years before going over in cabin class. On this ship I was a commissioned officer. I was on the top deck. I wasn't in with the senior officers, but I was in that environment. The enlisted men were below deck. We used to bring them up for an hour or two, so they could see the sunshine and the waves; other than that reprieve their restrictions were pretty severe. They slept in bunks on three or four tiers; we had regular beds, and we were also allowed to grab a cot and go out on the deck to sleep under the stars. Looking at the vast sky and endless sea, I listened to a young lieutenant, Arthur Holland, whom I met on ship, tell me the stress on the structure of the ship. He was a genius with math. He'd give me the formulas on how all these things worked.

Anyway, the first time I went to Hawaii in cabin class, and the second time I was in the company of officers. In comparison to the first, the second time I felt like I

Elder Garner ready to disembark.

was in the celestial kingdom. I found that within the celestial kingdom there are also degrees. I was a junior officer, a lieutenant, so I didn't have the same status as the majors. Advancement to major, lt. colonel, colonel, or Navy captain guaranteed additional privileges commensurate with the higher rank. Their clothes carried the insignias of office. Their quarters were more comfortable. Their food was prepared better. They received individual attention. Such noticeable distinctions brought the pragmatism of the gospel keenly to my attention."

Upon arrival in Honolulu, Keith disembarked the *Lurline* and set foot for the first time on Hawaiian soil. He was greeted by President and Sister Roscoe C. Cox, their family, and a dozen missionaries, all of whom carried leis which they placed around his neck in welcome.

Today in Keith's mind, the Hawaii of 1940 shines. Waikiki Beach, not yet crowded with resort hotels, could be purchased for a few dollars, but it was at that time a relatively undiscovered Shangri-la. Keith reflects, "Everything felt new." It was a virtually untouched paradise. The climate, the people, the music, the language, the food, the environment blended to created an aura of tranquility. The puffy cumulus clouds enhanced the beautiful expansive sky and showered the islands in the afternoons with cleansing rain that invigorated the earth. The South Sea island breezes blowing in off the encircling blue ocean cooled the sunny beaches. The pervasive, pungent fragrance of a profusion of flowers filled the atmosphere. Without a hint of struggle to make it flourish, the Hawaiian soil was alive with spontaneous growth. Orchids were as common in Hawaii as sunflowers in Utah.

The Hawaiians were a genuine, generous people whose friendly countenances radiated a simplicity. Their universal love of music and the gaiety of life took precedence over any inclination towards more serious pursuits. The words that came out of their mouths, indeed the Hawaiian language, sang with a preponderance of harmonious vowels. The spontaneous *kani ka pila* or strike up the music vibrated throughout the islands. The Hawaiian greetings *aloha kakahiaka* (ka-ka-hi-a-ka) for good morning (dawn to 11 a.m.), *pehea 'oe?* (how are you?), *aloha awakea* for good noon (11 a.m. to 1 p.m.), *aloha auinala* for good afternoon (after 1 p.m.) and *aloha ahiahi* for good evening intoned consonance throughout the day.

On the fly leaf of *The Hawaiian Language*, the book Keith used to learn the language, he has printed "Elder Garner, 1124 Kalihi Street, Honolulu, Oahu, T of H, January 29, 1940", and has had it signed by Chas A. Callis, a distinguished member of the Quorum of the Twelve Apostles. In a section subtitled "Some Peculiarities of the Language," the author Henry P. Judd writes,

> *Every word must end in a vowel and every syllable must end in a*
> *vowel. No two consonants can be pronounced without at least one*
> *vowel between them. There is but one exception to this rule and it*
> *applies to a word introduced by the American missionaries-- Kristo.*
> *Any amount of vowels may be used together... The Hawaiian is rich*
> *in descriptive terms for rains, winds, etc. There are six words meaning*
> *to carry--hali, auamo (on the shoulder), ka'ika'i (in the hands), hii*
> *(in the arms), koi (on stick between two men) and haawe (on the back).*
> *Some expressions are cumbersome; for example in the Lord's prayer*
> *the words, 'Forgive us our debts as we forgive our debtors' is but*
> *nine words in English and twenty-four in Hawaiian."* [2]

Keith's recollections of Hawaii sometimes center on the meaningful words of the musical language he learned. The Hawaiian saints called the proselyting elders *mikanele*, which is a transliteration of missionary. As a comeback to Keith's playful teasing, an older lady on Molokai who ran the Hoolehua Grocery Store smilingly dubbed him *mikanele kolohe* meaning naughty elder. He liked the succinctness of the phrase *au pau au* for I'm finished. To this day one of his favorite utterances is *e like no me au* (I feel the same). Two descriptive phrases *pani i ka puka* (close the door) meaning close the hole and *kalihi moe* which means naughty in bed he finds amusing in their

---

[2] Judd, Henry P., *The Hawaiian Language*, (Honolulu, Hawaii: Honolulu Star Bulletin, Ltd., 1939), 5-6.

Elder Garner's arrival.

literal simplicity. But perhaps the phrase he used most often while in Hawaii during his sojourn there was *hauoli nui nei au* meaning I'm very happy.

The Hawaiian people's life sustenance came primarily from the ocean. They loved fish, squid, crab, and shrimp which were caught almost effortlessly from the depths of the surrounding sea. From the fertile ground grew taro. The root was washed, mashed, and served as one of the staples of the Hawaiian diet, just as rice is served in the Asian diet and potatoes in the American diet. Bananas, pineapples, papayas, and mangos were delectable, picked fresh, not green. The traditional Hawaiian luau linked robust pigs cooked in ground ovens called emus and served with taro, fish, and fruits with music and dancing, thus creating a medley of tropical unanimity.

Shortly after Keith's arrival, he and Elder Stuart Winegar traveled around Oahu for nearly thirty days. During this initial period, he learned of the basic goodness of these people, their living conditions, the simplicity of their lives and their homes. Typical of their graciousness, one family Keith remembers gave him and his companion the key to their apartment. When they would tract in that area, they would luncheon there, preparing their own meals in the convenience of this hospitable family's home. If they wanted to read or if they got tired, they were encouraged by their benevolent hosts to let themselves in and relax. In the first thirty days of his service, the elders actually traveled without "purse or script," living with members of the Church in the area.

Coincidentally, seventy-six years to the day before Keith's birth, May 11,

1843, Hawaiian Church history began when Joseph Smith called the first LDS missionaries to serve in the Sandwich Islands. On December 12, 1850, from a point overlooking Honolulu called Pacific Heights, Elder Hiriam Clark with ten other missionaries dedicated Hawaii for the preaching of the gospel, and two months later, he baptized the first Hawaiian member of the Church. Also interestingly enough, the Hawaiian Temple was dedicated Thanksgiving Day, November 27, 1919, the year of Keith's birth, by President Heber J. Grant, the man who would issue Keith's call to serve there twenty years later. [3]

The Islands' past and present came together for Keith in the person of Brother McGuire, a distinguished, older gentleman and a direct descendant of King Kamehameha, who provided shelter for the missionaries in the Kaimuki District. According to Keith, shelter is just too common a noun to describe their lodgings. "It was a stately mansion, really. He raised orchids, a whole back-yard of orchids interspersed with all kinds of flowers. Brother McGuire loved every type of vegetation. Every plant in his care seemed to know it since he could grow anything."

He stood tall, well proportioned, strong, and bronze with a heavy mustache and dark eyes. He wasn't pure Hawaiian, but part

Brother McGuire's "stately mansion" with Elder Garner's companion Elder Ralph Chalker in front.

haole. His name suggests a genealogy which might include an Irish sea captain. Nonetheless, his bearing was stately as it should have been considering his regal Hawaiian ancestry. Keith's wry smile emerges as he tells of teasing Brother McGuire about his royal ancestry while he cooked for his boarders. "Brother McGuire was a cook by profession and did all the cooking for the missionaries who stayed in his home. He was a very good cook," Keith assesses, and then reports. "One concoction he prepared for himself raised some eyebrows. He mixed strawberry soda with poi,

---

[3] Julie A. Dockstader, "Building on a 'wonderful legacy of service' in Hawaii", *Church News*, 16 December 2000, 4.

put it in the refrigerator to ferment, and when it blew the refrigerator door off, he pronounced it ready to eat. He justified this recipe by saying, 'It is not a violation of the Word of Wisdom (which forbids alcoholic beverages) because I don't drink it; I eat it.'" According to Keith, "He is folklore." Remembering those times, Keith exclaims again, "What a place to go on a mission!"

However, even in Shangri-la he found a few unpleasant distractions. The intoxicating scent of plumaria was a first for him, but so also were the moving legions of cockroaches scurrying across the floor at night as he attempted to find the bathroom.

Food presented another challenge for him, partly because of his own culinary idiosyncrasies. He readily admits to being a fussy eater, especially liking his foods well-cooked. He even reported

Elder Garner and his companion Elder Stuart Winegar taken at Aiea, Oahu, February 3, 1940; "Notice the sugar cane in the background. It looks like corn."

from the ship on which he had sailed to Hawaii, "So far I have eaten every meal and then some. 'Mind over Matter' that means food!" Apparently having exercised considerable will power, he had found the food on the luxury liner *Lurline* a little more than just edible. Unfortunately for him in the beginning of his assignment in Hawaii, he found the tropical menu less digestible. Unused to the Polynesian cuisine, Keith tried to live on bread, bananas, and papaya which raised painful boils on his back and under his arms.

"I didn't enjoy poi at first. After awhile when I learned to eat it properly, then it was interesting. It's like cracked wheat. Some of the missionaries really liked it. One of them couldn't survive the day without having some. I also don't normally like anything that's raw, but I ate fish and crab because it was served." Keith learned from his distress that he must attempt to eat with the people and accept their customs.

Paradoxically, the problem changed from not finding enough edible food to having too much. During the holidays while in Honolulu, Keith and his companion had two or three dinner invitations extended for the same night by prominent members of the Church who enjoyed serving feasts to the missionaries. When this happened, Keith, attempting not to offend the generosity of his hosts, utilized a large empty Diamond Kitchen Match Box which he inconspicuously took from his pocket and filled with the delicious excess from his plate.

Keith worked in Honolulu for ten months. Honolulu proper was middle class America, ninety percent haole. The major districts there were Kaimuki, Makiki, Kalihi, and Manoa, and he worked in each of those four areas. He had two or three companions while on Oahu, and he's sure they tracted the entire city of Honolulu. At that time the Church had few chapels, so with some ingenuity Keith and his companion received permission for the Church members to use the Kaimuki Public School for Sunday School classes.

Bearing half the weight of a self-created stick apparatus from which an old time phonograph and the last "Fullness of Times" records hung, an anxious Elder Garner now paired with Elder Ralph Chalker, "a really good missionary, a good worker," carried (koi) the heavy phonograph from house to house moving the work forward. As people invited them in, they plugged in the phonograph and sat and listened to the story of the Restoration of the Lord's Church, of how the angel Moroni, a messenger, was sent from the presence of God to the boy Joseph.

Keith found great excitement in telling the story, enlarging, and explaining it. He enjoyed bearing his witness to the people. Logically, these investigators always asked, "What happened to the gold plates after Joseph Smith translated them?" In the early days of his mission, Keith responded directly by telling investigators how Joseph had been allowed to translate only one-third of the plates and how he had been given an exquisite promise that the remaining sealed two-thirds would be delivered again at a later date. Accordingly, he reported, "The angel Moroni has taken them for safe keeping, and the plates remain in his possession to the present day."

As Keith told of this event, he watched his investigator's eyes and could read in his expression the thought that these poor young men surely had been duped, even deceived, to believe such a fantastic tale. After he had become more accustomed to the work, Keith replied to this question with this answer. "In Salt

Louise P. Sheldon and Elder Garner on "The Garden Island"

Lake City on Temple Square, there is a little log cabin, and in the corner there is a vault, and in the vault these gold tablets are kept." Then he would wait for their response. He recalls no one becoming excited. They all said in various ways that if their travels ever took them through Salt Lake, they would make a point of seeing the gold plates. After they made that half-hearted reply, Keith would tell them, "No, I was just kidding; the angel had picked up the records and taken them from the boy."

At the time and even today, Keith remains incredulous at this demonstrated lack of curiosity in the gold plates. To him, this lack of interest is startling, even shocking. He muses in amazement. "If a young man came to my home and told me that gold plates abridged by an ancient American prophet, buried in a hill over 1400 years before, delivered in 1827 to a lad of eighteen by a messenger straight from the presence of God could be viewed in a vault on Temple Square, I would immediately leap to my feet and run all the way to Salt Lake City to investigate this evidence, confirming the marvelous story of continuing revelation from God." That not one person responded in this manner is mind-boggling to him. However, that does not mean he did not have success in delivering this message. Hearts and minds of people blessed with faith accepted the good news without needing to examine gold plates.

One such lady Keith taught was Louise Sheldon. She and her husband, the sheriff of the Island of Kauai, were prominent, influential people who lived just down the road from the mission home in Kapaa. She was a tremendous musician and a gifted choir director. Her literary talents were also well-known. A month before Keith's departure she wrote a beautiful poem, "My Garden Island," for him.

"My Garden Island"

The beautiful island setting creates the ideal backdrop for her note of thanksgiving, a note that Keith has kept all these years tucked away among other keepsakes.

Dear Elder Garner,

My vocabulary does not contain the words that can express the gratefulness of my heart and soul for the day that God sent you to me and my home. Words are inadequate so please let this simple line suffice, 'thank you for the knowledge and truth you have cleared up for me.'

Once again, I thank you for considering me a missionary in your heart and action and for so kindly and graciously accepting me in your group on that ever memorable day. A picture, a scene, and an experience that will ever be a flame, a torch of light, that illumination that remain[s] ever fresh in my memory and aid[s] me in reaching that goal for which I am aiming. I have thanked the Lord often for that opportunity and do so yet whenever my thought lingers there in its roamings.

I have never before really had a great desire to study and learn about your religion. I was (rather, sort of) satisfied with the 1/100 part of it I knew, but I do now and strong is the urge to do it thoroughly since that memorable day. Nui loa kou minamina i kou hoi koke. I have admired the convictions you produce and your follow ups on them so much.

Be reassured that your work here has been profitable and not in vain and should that special day come, there are three who I will be longing to be with me. You are the third party. But, my dear friend, before that day comes, I have or you have left a big job on my hands. I am not willing to enter alone and if it is God's will and he is willing, with the little knowledge I now have, I will set to work in the path intended and gradually with the aid of the Holy Spirit clear up misconceptions and misunderstandings. Then hand in hand we'll meet you there. So help me God.

Aside from all the above it has been good to know you. You really have been a source of joy at every turn and I'll miss your laughter and "O.K. Ha! Ha!." I do sincerely wish you all the happiness and joy of this life and also prosperity. Wish you all the luck in the world, success in what you aim to do and succeed in securing the position that is uppermost in your mind now. Thanks again; Good luck, God speed; Bon Voyage in the Air; Aloha Oe a Mai Poina Oe Iau.

Your friend and Missionary Mother,
Louise Sheldon 3/1/42

The details remain sketchy for Keith of the "memorable day" to which Sister Sheldon refers, but the euphoric feeling created by the evening spent at the Sheldon's does not. Keith remembers that walking home he and his companion felt like their feet never touched the ground.

Keith embraced the relaxed, warm Polynesian atmosphere. Serving the Lord necessitated his working diligently, but also entailed participating in other joyful activities such as the Hawaiian holidays of Kamekamehu Day and Lei Day, attending the circus and the play *My Love Came Back*. The saints in Hawaii delighted in Church socials in which the missionaries participated, including the Young Men and Women Mutual Improvement Association's Harvest Ball and Minstrel Show.

In the 1940s, unlike today, mission rules allowed the elders to swim. The exotic, sunny beaches of Oahu and Kauai were Keith's springboards for plunges into the Pacific Ocean. On Kauai he and his companion had all of the white sands and warm water of the beach at Nawiliwila Bay entirely to themselves.

Probably the most unforgettable recreational gala Keith attended and helped plan was a spectacular, authentic Hawaiian Luau with an abundance of fragrant leis, a roasted pig, poi, and native fruits, that were prepared in honor of President David O. McKay, then a counselor in the First Presidency. Following the dedication of the Honolulu (Beretannia) Tabernacle on the 20th of August 1941, he and his wife Emma Ray attended the luau in Laie.

An entry written in his mission record book prior to President McKay's arrival states, "During these two weeks, I suffered from an injured arm, prepared for conference, therefore failed to fill in properly." Keith's obedient and conscientious personality seemed to expand, tempered by a recognizable practicality. He tellingly writes, "I was so busy this month I didn't get time to fill out my report book. This report is making a liar out of a good missionary, but I can't help it. This report is taken from last month's."

Indeed, he was busy. The two months to which he refers in his record book he and his companion spent as the only elders on the Island of Molokai, with Keith serving as district leader. Molokai seemed to be the place to which "undesirable" Hawaiians were consigned. Keith describes his new, bleak environment. "I went from Oahu to the land of desolation, Molokai, where there were no beaches, wind constantly blowing. That was quite a contrast to where I'd been. It was hard to believe I was in Hawaii. Our clothes became saturated with the redness of the soil. There wasn't anything that was indigenous to that place except the wilderness flowers." Yet from this bleakness, he and his companion received the unique privilege of serving the patients confined to the leper colony at Kalaupapa.

Historically, the Mormon congregation on Kalaupapa existed from the late 1800s. In about 1871 Joseph H. Napela, a Mormon elder, came to Kalaupapa as a kokua (helper) for his wife, who was suffering from leprosy. He was appointed president of the Kalaupapa Branch of the Maui, Molokai, and Lanai Conference in

October 1873. He contracted the disease and died at Kalaupapa. [4]

Access to the colony had always been very limited, and Keith found it so now. To reach the village entailed traversing on foot a narrow three mile trail which hugs nearly perpendicular cliffs and descends 1,600 feet from Topside Molokai. The trail became even more challenging with its twenty-six switchbacks that corkscrew in and out of canyons and ravines. [5] "They always knew we were coming because they could see us coming down the trail on the Pali," Keith remembers. This unique Latter-day Saint community looked forward with great anticipation to the visits of the Mormon elders.

In 1941 leprosy or Hansen's disease still remained a mystery, eliciting dread and fear. On one of his first trips to the colony, Keith fell, scraping his arm, drawing blood, and creating a scar which he still carries. The only known way to contract leprosy is through open sores; nevertheless, not surprisingly Keith simply wrapped his wound in his handkerchief and proceeded to the waiting, welcoming patients below.

Missionary Garner

During his mission, Church services at Kalaupapa were held in a small LDS chapel. Upon entering the building, Keith read signs "Unclean" and "Clean," directing those who entered to the appropriate seat. He immediately felt flowing from the congregation a spirit of hope known to those who suffer pain in isolation. He marvels, "The organist played the organ with some of his fingers bandaged and others missing, yet he hit every stirring note."

Because Keith and his companion were the only elders in Hoolehua, the main city on Molokai, he escorted different groups of visiting elders who wanted to descend the Pali to see Kalaupapa. Hanging on to the railings placed at the more precipitous points, they viewed a magnificent valley below. At the bottom of the trail, these young men encountered the disease cured in the New Testament by the Savior and the patients who now confronted life in seclu-

---

[4] "Frequently Asked Questions about Kalaupapa," 2 [on-line]; available from http://www.nps.gov/kala/docs/faq.htm.; Internet; accessed 19 Dec 2000.

[5] "Moloka'i, Kalaupapa," 1, [on-line]; available from http://visitmolokai.com/kala.html.; Internet; accessed 19 Dec 2000.

Missionary Garner

sion. Both pictures, the expansive valley below and the confined, diseased patients,
were potentially life altering for Keith and his fellow missionaries.

Legends of the heroic efforts of a Belgian priest Joseph de Veuster, ordained
Father Damien in Honolulu in 1864, vitalize the mystique of this colony. In the midst
of his work to restore a measure of human dignity to the unfortunate residents
through programs providing water, food, work, homes, medical care, and other basic
necessities, Father Damien announced to his church's hierarchy that he could not be
reassigned, for he too had contracted leprosy. He died in 1889 and was buried next
to his church Saint Philomena at Kalawao. In 1936, four years before Keith's arrival,
Damien's body was exhumed and taken to Belgium.[6] Elder Garner heard the stories
of Father Damien's spirited efforts. It was said that the Father placed human needs
before church politics and relied on the spirit of the law over the letter of the law
when the individual case seemed to merit such a course. This view mirrored a discernment which found expression in Keith's own ministrations.

After Molokai, Elder Garner was transferred to Kauai for the remainder of
his mission. Having already served ten months on Oahu, eight months on Molokai,
and a few weeks back in Honolulu when David O. McKay was there, Keith now
looked forward to serving on his third island. "All of these islands were contrasts, but

---

[6] "Frequently Asked Questions about Kalaupapa," available from
Internet, http://www.nps.gov/kala/docs/faq.htm, 2.

I ended up in the most beautiful of all the islands, Kauai. They don't call it the Garden Island for nothing." His assignment brought leadership opportunities, personal sorrow, and a world at war.

This phase of his mission started rather inauspiciously with Keith's hubris overtaking his humility. The expression "Hawaiian time means whatever time it is" provides the context for this episode. Keith tells the story. "Rarely did meetings start on time because Polynesians simply don't move quickly. Years before, President Cox had served a Hawaiian mission. He spoke like a native, and on this occasion I thought he adopted their method for telling time. When I came in from Molokai to Oahu, I was assigned to Kauai. We traveled primarily between islands on inner island boats. You could board around 5 p.m., go to bed, and the next morning you were docking at Kauai. I just remember President Cox said that he'd go down early to the dock because he had some instruction to give me; he wanted to talk to me. I got there early, and I waited and waited. Just as the boat was pulling away, he drove up. I just kind of waved 'You're late!' The next morning when I arrived a letter was waiting for me. I should have saved the letter. President Cox was a great writer; he had been editor of the Ephraim newspaper, and so he wasn't hesitant or cowardly in using wording that expressed the situation. To have just left was the wrong thing for me to do, but at the time, it seemed like the logical thing to do."

Keith had lived with the Cox family on Oahu for several months during the first phase of his mission, and he had become like a son. President and Sister Cox truly loved Elder Garner, and Elder Garner loved them. While it has been observed that all mission presidents love the elders and sisters with whom they work, this relationship was noteworthy in its depth.

Each shared experience helped to form a lifelong bond. One such incident occurred during a visit by Elder Callis to a conference in Honolulu. Elder Garner found President Cox disappointed. The cause of his distress had arisen after Elder Callis had expressed his disapproval of President Cox's invitation to a Protestant choir to sing at the LDS Conference. Elder Callis thought local LDS members should have been given that opportunity. President Cox confided in his young elder that his intention had been to use this invitation as a missionary tool. Elder Garner, the missionary, thought President Cox's idea brilliant.

Elder Garner and Vaun Cox on Molokai

As far as he was concerned, to have a captive audience of Protestant singers in an atmosphere of worship to whom Elder Callis could deliver his conference address showed his mission president's wisdom. It beat tracting!

After a year of this kind of close association when Keith was transferred to Molokai, President Cox entrusted to his care and instruction his teenage son Vaun. Vaun accompanied him to the Halawa Valley where they tracted together, visited the branches, and generally spent much time in each other's company.

It was a good tradeoff. While Elder Garner taught Vaun many lessons and

First row: President and Sister Roscoe C. Cox, President and Sister David O. McKay, Bishop and Sister Joseph L. Wirthlin; fifth row: first on left, Keith Garner

gave President Cox his loyalty and esteem, President Cox set for him an example of leadership, character, humility, and compassion worthy of imitation. Roscoe Cox was a gifted man who lifted his life by adherence to his favorite scripture. "Be not overcome of evil, but overcome evil with good."[7] Keith quotes President Cox's words to him, "'If one man leads a good life and another hasn't, then the only way for him to catch up is for him to multiply his good deeds so he can balance the ledger.' He explained that when he was younger he wasn't as dutiful as he should have been, something which he regretted, but he was trying to make up for it. He felt that was a part of repentance. 'You've got to do so much more to catch up with the guy that

---

[7] Romans 12:21

never did it in the first place.' He was a great mission president!"

President Cox's wife complemented and helped her husband magnify his position as mission president of the Hawaiian Islands. Keith tenderly describes her as "an ideal lady, a perfect mission president's wife, always friendly and courteous, a good mission mother." In 1977 while president of Temple Square, Keith gave the first speech in the Spring Quarter Friday Forum lecture series when he spoke to the student body at the Ephraim LDS Institute of Religion at Snow College about the role and purpose of Temple Square and the visitors' center. [8] "After I finished, somebody

said, 'Do you want to see Sister Cox?' I drove up to her home. Her red hair had grayed, but her support of her missionaries had not. She had listened to me on the radio and seemed joyful at what she identified as my accomplishments and grateful for our shared recollections." These were exceptional people, and Keith would accept their support and love as he dealt with the upcoming news from home.

Elder Garner and "his mission mother" Sister Cox

---

[8] "Mission President Prepares Friday Forum Address," *Ephraim (Utah) Enterprise*, 24 March 1977, 85:27.

Chapter

T W O

Where is thy Sting?

"Precious in the sight of the Lord is the death of his saints."
— Psalms 116:15

On the 8th of October 1941, Benjamin Franklin Garner, sixty, died at Thomas D. Dee Memorial Hospital in Ogden, Utah. At his funeral service, each speaker referenced his great love of missionary work. Alma T. Flinders remarked, "I believe it is the mission of Brother Ben to teach the gospel. Brother Ben and I were sent out on a home mission. Brother Ben's testimony to those who were not those of our faith aided them in seeing the true light. In the end, he brought many to the Church who accepted our faith." Adam A. Bingham added, "I have never heard any man who could thrill me more than when he was before the public. He was an ardent and fluent speaker, but he was never called on a mission, but his greatest desire was to fill a mission. He even asked for a mission, but he didn't get the call. Now he is where he can preach the gospel to the millions."

Brother Bingham, who had given Keith his patriarchal blessing, remembered Keith to the assembled congregation in these words, "That poor boy in the mission field, I feel sorry for him. I pray that God will bless and help him in this great sorrow that has come to him at this time."

For Keith as a loving son and a missionary, the death of his father was a singular experience. Ben's particular love of missionary work made his passing while Keith served unique. Keith had felt this fatherly influence throughout his youthful years. When Ben Garner traveled by train between Ogden and San Francisco as a machinist for the Southern Pacific Railroad, he occasionally took his youngest son Keith and some of Keith's siblings along. He took advantage of this chance and every other one imaginable to strike up a conversation about the gospel with any interested party. In doing so Keith's father embarrassed his youngsters, but he also set an example which Keith adopted. Thus, Ben's missionary son's jovial conversational pull toward subjects of seriousness and substance came early and not in a vacuum.

Keith knew of his father's great desire to serve a mission. He wrote weekly to his father and mother of the marvelous experiences he was enjoying in the mission field. He felt that although his father's dream of serving a mission remained unfulfilled, Ben was rejoicing that his son had been given the opportunity to serve. Keith regretted deeply that he would be unable at the completion of his mission to return home, sit with his father, relate his reminiscences, and fervently bear his testimony of the gospel of Jesus Christ.

A letter to Keith penned by his mother as she sat at her husband's bedside expressed the tender feelings of a united family full of love for one another at this painful time.

> This is the third night I have sat by his bed. I sleep a little but I can't leave. Bea, Orvell and Delbert [Keith's siblings] all talked to me last night on phone. They were all at Bea's. You, Keith, by the time this letter reaches you your father will be home. Dr. said he wanted to keep him here 10 days any way. Don't worry dear. You know he was so sick when you left, then again in March and April of this year and he is going to get well from this. Doctor just came in and injected some medicine in the vein of his arm for his heart.
>
> Here it is Friday evening 5 o'clock. I can't see any change in your father but doctor said it would take time for medicine to take effect. LaVon and Kay [Keith's niece] came this morning. She said she called Ruth [Keith's younger sister] up at office and they sent her home. She was crying so much. She wanted to come with LaVon so she will leave there tomorrow. Delbert and Orvell, Bea are going to call tonight so we can tell them how he is. He still is under the tent. Hard for him to breath even there but doctor thinks that will clear up in a few days. Mrs. Hansen phoned and said there was a letter down to house from you. So LaVon and Loma have gone down to get it. Your father raised and said a letter from Keith.
>
> Keith, I haven't written any more and here it's Tuesday morning. All the children got here at 1 am Monday morning. Doctors are surprised that he has lived this long. I have been

here night and day a week ago Tuesday. Del, LaVon up with me last night and Orvell, Ruth night before. He is getting weaker all the time. We have had prayers and administered every day. I just feel like I can't stand it. O why! He says, 'Mae, don't let me go.' They keep him asleep, comes out of it about every three hours. When he saw Thelma [Orvell's wife] he said have the children all come. Then to sleep again.

Third day he was sick I was writing this letter and he said, Mae, what doing. I said writing to Keith and he said, O let me write so I opened the tent and gave him my letter to write on, his hand dropped when he wrote this much.

Hello, darling son. But within a short time I've got to get out of here. All the nurses and doctors are sure very nice to me.

Mary Selina Carr Garner and Benjamin Franklin Garner in front of home on 32nd Street in Ogden, Utah

On the now yellowing note paper appear Keith's reflections, "These are father's last writings. Doesn't seem possible."

It is noticeable that the two traits evident in this cherished father's last hand-written thoughts are a growing impatience for productivity and his gratitude to those who were serving him. Keith is his father's son in both of these qualities.

President Cox received the news of Keith's father's death with a heavy heart. He had been expecting a cablegram from the Presiding Bishopric in Salt Lake City approving the purchase of tickets for all the missionaries returning home between then and the next April in order to escape a price increase slated for the next day. He had just come from a meeting with five new elders when Elder Waldron handed him a cablegram, and he said, "So they sent an answer? Good." It was not the news he expected.

He penned two exquisite letters, one to Keith and one to Keith's mother. In his letter to Keith, he wrote, "We did not know your father and now we shall never know him in this world. But we know his son and we love him and appreciate him. You can be sure that you have the love and sympathy of all the elders and sisters in our mission at this time. We all join in the prayer that this sorrow will be short and that it will prove a strengthening event in your life. Aloha nui and God bless you."

The one to Mrs. Garner also expresses his deep love for her son.

Church of Jesus Christ of Latter-Day Saints
Office of Hawaiian Mission
1121 Kalihi Road
Honolulu, T.H.

Office of   Telephone 8602
Mission president   P.O. Box 3228

October 9, 1941
Mrs. Benjamin F. Garner
3105 Del Paso Blvd.
Sacramento, California.

Dear Sister Garner:

It was a distinct shock when I was handed a Cablegram yesterday and opened it to read: "Kindly advise Keith Elliott Garner his father died this morning. Extend sincere sympathy. First Presidency." That is the third such message to come to me during my stay in the Islands as one mother and two fathers of missionaries have been called away. How I dislike to relay such a message on to one of our missionary sons and contemplate the hurt it is sure to give him. And yet I think there is no place in the world where a young man is better prepared to hear such a message than in the mission field. I recall the days in France back in 1918 when I received word of the death of a soldier brother. How it saddened me and filled my heart with hate and other evil emotions. How I wanted to get in action against those Germans. Then a buddy of mine, a big-hearted Texan, received word of the death of his lovely little sister. How he sobbed and sobbed. He was almost completely overcome and asked for the day off. He had no hope, to say nothing of faith, that he would ever see that lovely girl again.

And then there was Elder John B. Jones here in Hawaii. The word came of his father's passing and was relayed on to his district president. The latter with a group of other elders went to break the sad news. They found Elder Jones and his companion out tracting and taking census. They all went to the elders' room and there, tactfully, the district president broke the news. There was a sob, a flow of tears, and then all knelt in humble prayer. A few more minutes and all left the home, the visiting missionaries to return to their branches, Elder Jones--smiling--and his companion to continue taking census. He KNEW his father lived and that he would meet with him again.

And so, yesterday, when the cablegram came I called Elder Garner's district president, Elder Ray L. Halverson, a capable and sincere young man. He was to go and, in the most fitting and most sacred way he knew how, break the sad news to your son. It was a hard assignment. Your son is greatly loved and it hurts all of us to have such a misfortune and such sadness come to him. I am sure that every missionary in Hawaii, as the sad news gets around, will join in prayer that Elder Garner's grief may be assuaged and that he, like Elder Jones, may return to his work with a smile and forget his sorrow and grief in doing good to others.

Will this change in conditions affect Elder Garner's stay in the Islands? Will he be needed at home? Will his remaining here longer work a hardship on you or other relatives?

Quite naturally we are anxious to have him stay with us his full two years but realize this privilege must depend on home conditions. He is one of the most outstanding elders and is slated for an important position the last of this month to continue until he leaves to return home. We will, of course,

adjust our plans in case it is going to be impossible or impracti-
cal for him to remain longer with us. Your interest will be
our interest, your desires our desires, in this matter. Your
wishes concerning your son's staying on for a full two years or
returning home at some time before then, will be completely
respected. Please write me freely and frankly concerning
the matter.

I hope you will let Sister Cox and me join with the many
others in extending to you our sincerest sympathy and good
wishes at this time. May your present sorrow be rapidly displaced by more pleasant memories of the past--of courtship
days, of little children in a happy home, of first time the first
child went to school, of struggles and triumphs in raising the
family--. And may there also be an assurance of the future as
clear and definite as the memories of the past but with a beauty far greater than anything you have yet experienced in this
world of work and sweat and love and trial.

If a mother is to be judged by her son, then no human
pedestal is too high for us to place you in our estimation. We
love your son deeply and sincerely and to you now we express
our gratitude and appreciation for providing us with such a
worthy son to do missionary work in these Islands.

Again accept our good wishes and a greeting of aloha
from this lovely land.

Sincerely your brother,
Roscoe C. Cox
Mission President

These letters gave comfort and solace, and most importantly, the assurance
that the doctrine of the Resurrection was not just an ethereal concept preached by
young missionaries to the world, but a truth embraced by believing sons and daughters in the crucible of reality. Keith grasped the efficacy of the plan of salvation, and
he held it unyieldingly. Facing the reality of the loss of his beloved father, he com-
posed his own words of comfort, solace, and reassurance. Out of the sorrow of sepa-
ration came two letters he penned from Kapaa, Kauai, which summarize in heartfelt
words his tender reaction. One is dated October 18, 1941, a little over a week after
the news of his father's death had been delivered to him.

Dearest Mother:

I don't know why I have hesitated so long in writing. I
have thought of you and prayed for you every day, almost every

minute. I can't imagine Dad being gone. I just can't believe
it's true and probably won't feel that it's true until I return
home. Joseph wrote and told me that you took his passing
away splendidly like a true and faithful wife that you are. I'm
so proud of you and the wonderful life you and Dad lived.
Imagine Dad isn't suffering now, but in the Paradise of God
fulfilling that mission he so longed for. I picture him in my
mind sitting at this table with me, encouraging and watching
over me as he always did. Often during my mission, I have
pictured myself home sitting by his side and relating my experiences. I wanted him to meet me at the boat, so I could
throw my arms around his neck and kiss him--Well, he won't
be there physically, but I know he will spiritually. He lived a
beautiful life, one worthy of emulation. In his letters he never
forgot to tell me how wonderful his dear wife was and how she
stuck by him through so many years of trials and disappointments. Mother, just think, we'll see him again. His boat has
gone, and somebody (his mother and father and friends) are
meeting him on the other side. You and I and all of us will be
privileged to take that boat someday. Oh, what a reunion that
will be! Be brave, Mother. He's with you all the time. Even
death can't separate the love Dad had for you, nor yours for him.

I was planning on returning this month, but I got a letter
from Loma and Joseph (and it was such a comforting letter)
telling me to finish my mission. I know you really want me to,
and I know Dad does. I was out of money, but Joseph said he
would send me $50.00. I had to take it. I know they need it
plenty, but I'm between two barrels. LaVon, Vaun, Loma and
Joseph have surely been generous to me. But I'll pay them
back just as soon as I possibly can. I am moving over to the
other side of the island tomorrow and will be there until
January 13th. President Cox wrote and told me that he has
passage for me on the Matsonia January 23rd, so I'll be in San
Francisco either the 29th or 30th.

I'm still doing the same things. I'm glad for the transfer.
I will do my best as a District President. While I was D.P. on
Molokai, I didn't have thirteen missionaries to take care of, but
I'm thankful for the experience, and I'll do my very best.

All my love,
Keith E

The other letter is written to his sister in Syracuse, Utah, a few weeks later, and it is she who must be credited for the preservation of these moving firsthand accounts.

Dear Loma and Joseph:

These last few weeks have been the busiest of my mission. The day I was officially notified through President Cox of father's passing I also received a letter from him telling me to move over to Kapaa and take Elder Halverson's place. Since then I have had a full program, consisting of cottage meetings, transfers, bookkeeping, and a million other finite things that turned up. (I'm thankful that I have been kept busy. It takes care of those idle minutes that are usually spent in reminiscing.)

I surely appreciate the fine letters you sent informing me of Dad's passing. It was the first time that death had entered the family; consequently, I never dreamed that anything like that would happen. I have never been so shocked and lonesome in my life. He was such a wonderful father. When I left to come into the Mission Field, I was so young. I never really sat down and had a chat with him. During the last two years, I have often thought of my return home and the subsequent evenings spent with Dad relating my missionary experiences. He always longed to go on a mission, and I know he would have been immensely interested in just what a mission consisted of. I know that when I return home, I will miss him more than ever. Well, Loma, he lived such a wonderful life and has graduated now from all pains and sorrows. We know that we shall see him again. Boy, am I grateful for this beautiful Gospel. Imagine death without a faith that we shall see our departed love-ones again? It's void and ridiculous to the nth degree. I hope that Mother fully recovers from this ordeal. Do you think she will? They loved each other so much and were together so long it will prove a real test to overcome.

I surely hate to take your money because I know you need it. I pray God to bless you abundantly for your faith and kindnesses. I know He has blessed you, and He will continue. I hope Delbert and Orvel awaken from their long sleep and start to live really good lives and honor their priesthood. I think of them so often. Here I am trying to tell others to live righteously, and my own brothers aren't going to church nor giving a damn about anything. I pray that they have changed.

Benjamin and Mary Garner's family: Front row l to r: Mother Garner, Loma May Cook, Beatrice May Waltz, May LaVon Pollei, Ruth Mildred Kimball; Back row: Delbert Franklin Garner, Orvell Morcell Garner, and Keith Elliot Garner

Dad surely tried. Maybe I shouldn't talk; I'm not so good myself. Thanks again for the money, and I promise to put it to good use.

I received a letter from President Cox today, and he mentioned that you wrote to him, but that was all. He surely has been good to me ever since I came into the field. Sister Cox told me that they considered me one of the Cox family. While I was laboring on Molokai, their son Vaun came over and stayed with me a week. Now President Cox wrote and asked

me if he, Vaun, might come over here and stay during the
Xmas vacation. I think Vaun's about 16.

That picture you sent me of Dad is so good and natural.
He almost talks to me. What will home be without good old
Dad? I often think of the night I left Sacramento for Hawaii.
There was Dad, deathly sick, not capable of bidding me goodbye but just lying there looking up into my eyes, and his eyes
seemed to say: "Darling boy, do the best you can and leave the
rest up to the Lord. You'll be home before you know it." If his
life isn't worthy of emulation, none are.

I had a thrilling experience today. I'll enclose a copy of
the letter I received from P. Cox and that will explain it. I
haven't the slightest idea who it is.

He wrote me several days ago that he had me booked to
sail on the 23rd of January. These two years have surely flown
by. It just seemed like the other day that I left you at the station in Ogden. Just imagine that was two years ago. Auwe.

I'll write more just as soon as I get settled. Elder
Halverson is leaving Tuesday, and then it will be easier to sit
down and accomplish a few of my unfinished tasks. Thanks
again for all your kindnesses. I am so proud of Brother and
Sister Cook.

All my love,
Keith E.

P.S. Aloooooha to all the children from Allen down. Do you
think I will be able to recognize them? Bye.

Perhaps this sorrow even strengthened Keith's already firm resolve that sharing the gospel was the most important work one can do with one's life. Throughout
his life these missionary tugs would inspire him to cross the street and the globe to
share this precious message.

He had been informed by both Joe Cook and President Cox that the money
necessary for him to complete his missionary service would be forthcoming, fulfilling
his desires to honor his father and his mother's wishes for him to serve the entire two
year term of his mission call. The Lord truly does provide and sometimes from more
than one source. As Keith noted in his letter, his hard earned $600 was nearly gone.
He knew with his father's passing his mother would need all the resources at her disposal. However, Loma and Joe had already informed President Cox that family funds
would be made available as Keith needed them, so he could finish his mission. His
distress in having to accept his sister and brother-in-law's generosity is made clear in
his letter to his mother. Having no other choice, he gratefully accepted their kindness

with the promise that he would "pay them back just as soon as I possibly can."

President Cox who was moved by the Spirit unexpectedly learned of another helpful backer for Elder Garner and shared this news in a letter to Keith written on October 23, 1941.

> Elder Keith E. Garner
> Box 33
> Kapaa, Kauai
>
> Dear Elder Garner:
> On Tuesday I was standing on a corner on King Street talking with a man from Kohala when I saw a church member I knew across the street. I broke off my conversation with: "There's a man I want to talk with," and away I went.
> I didn't have anything in particular to talk with him about so it was weather or something while he drank his orange juice and then we went up the street. He said there used to be an elder working in the Makiki-Manoa district who seemed to be quite an outstanding young man. He had heard this missionary speak once in Waikiki and was very much impressed by him, he said. I asked if it could have been Elder Garner. It could.
> This brother then said he had heard a rumor that you might have to go home early on account of finances and asked if that were so. I told him you had spent all of your earnings and that now your father had died. He was very sorry to hear that. I said you had written that you had received word from home that you could stay until the end of your regular time and that I had that day received a letter from your sister, Mrs. Cook, containing the same news. He was happy to hear that.
> Then he asked what it cost a month for a missionary to remain here and I told him about $32.00 to $35. He said you were one missionary he would like to see stay your full time and an extra month if possible and so desired. He then opened his wallet and handed me $35--the same bills herewith enclosed----and asked that I send it to you but not to tell who had given it. He once was on a mission and said he knew how it was to have funds run out. I told him I would tell you who gave the funds the day you sail for home. (Remind me to do so.) He preferred that his identity remain a secret between him and me. Then he turned and went back the way he had come, having walked a block and a half out of his way.

Why did I feel I wanted to talk to him? I am sure you and I know why it was. I know you will use the money probably better than any other elder in the mission would or could use it. God bless you in your good works.

Sincerely your friend and brother,
Roscoe C. Cox, Mission President

This fortuitous encounter solved what was a then unknown future need brought on by an unexpected episode looming on the horizon--this one delaying Elder Garner's scheduled return home by a few months.

C h a p t e r

T H R E E

Days That Will Live in Infamy

*"I fear all we have done is to awaken a sleeping giant
and fill him with a terrible resolve."*
– Admiral Isoroku Yamamoto
as quoted in the 1970 movie *Tora, Tora, Tora*

In his missionary record book, Keith writes, "The Japanese attacked Pearl
Harbor December 7, 1941. I was laboring on the island of Kauai at the time. We saw
little or no action on this island but since have heard of several submarines being sunk
near our shores. There are twenty missionaries on the island now--January 12, 1942,
ten Hawaiian Mission, ten Japanese Mission. We are waiting to be called out--at least
a few are going. President Cox is in Honolulu,--hope he writes soon and relays some
news. The missionaries are anxious to know of their status." As events transpired,
President Cox passed them on to Keith, but through it all, his counsel always
remained the same, "In the meantime go to work!"

Unmistakably the aura of working in a peaceful, tropical paradise gave way to
occasional feelings of unsettled anxiety. Rumors of Japanese planes crash landing on
Kauai, of submarines off the coast poised to disembark Japanese troops, and of the
island's imminent evacuation swirled on every corner. Yet even the direst of rumors,
most of them exaggerated, some of them untrue, and all of them unrealized, could
not compare to the devastating event which had just happened a mere 110 miles as
the crow flies southeast on Oahu. In a stirring account of what President Franklin D.
Roosevelt called "a date which will live in infamy," Edward Oxford writes:

On the flagship *Akagi* Commander Mitsuo Fuchida, who would lead the aerial attack, reported to force commander Admiral Chuichi Nagumo and announced his readiness for the mission. The admiral rose from behind his desk and shook Fuchida's hand replying, "I have every confidence in you."

...The vista was tranquil and picture-like. Fuchida's enjoyment of the scene would have been complete had not his observations confirmed reports that the strike force's most coveted targets--the three aircraft carriers of the U.S. Pacific Fleet--were not in port...

Ford Island Naval Air Station--a patrol plane base, aircraft repair facility, and home for the fleet's carrier aircraft when those ships were in port--lay right in the middle of Pearl Harbor. At 7:55 a.m. Lieutenant Commander Logan Ramsey, standing near a window in its command center, heard a plane dive low overhead.

"Get that fellow's number," Ramsey called to the station's duty officer. "I want to report him for about sixteen violations!"

Looking out the window, the officer surmised that the offending pilot was a squadron commander--because "the plane had a band of red on it."

Seconds later an explosion rocked the base.

Elder Garner's District on Kauai: Front row, l to r: Don Halvorsen, John D. Richards, Dean Larsen; Back row, l to r: David J. Evans, Irving Dana Muir, Newel Washburn, Keith E. Garner, J. Melvin Glade, Kenneth N. Gardner, Glen W. Clarke, and Ray Hill

"Never mind; it's a Jap!" Ramsey exclaimed as the realization finally set in. He ran to the radio room and dictated a brief message: "air raid, pearl harbor. this is not [a] drill." At 7:58 a.m. Ramsey's historic alert, transmitted in plain English, went out on all frequencies...

On the fantail of the *Nevada*, moored alone at the opposite end of Battleship Row, a twenty-three man Navy band and a Marine color guard stood at attention as eight o'clock approached, waiting to raise the colors. Out of the corners of their eyes the men noticed aircraft diving at the other end of Ford Island. Then they heard explosions. The only sensible explanation was that some sort of Sunday practice attack--by U.S. Navy or maybe even U.S. Army planes--was taking place. Promptly at 8 a.m. the bandsmen struck up "The Star-Spangled Banner," and the Marines began to raise the American flag.

The musicians barely saw the Japanese torpedo plane flash in low over the harbor from the direction of the Navy Yard. The aircraft dropped its torpedo, then swept overhead. Its rear gunner fired at the men, missing them but shredding the flag. Maintaining remarkable discipline, all held their positions through the final notes of the National Anthem. Then they ran for cover...

By about 9:50 a.m. barely two hours after the attack began it was over. The Japanese planes withdrew, diminishing into specks as they moved over the horizon. In a final act of deception, they flew off in several directions, confusing the Americans as to whence they had come.

To look at Pearl Harbor--to consider what the Japanese had wrought--was to witness a scene of incomprehensible devastation. The *Arizona*, her back broken and superstructure aflame, sat on the harbor bottom, as did the *West Virginia*. The *Oklahoma* and *Utah* lay capsized. The *California* was sinking, the *Nevada* aground. The *Pennsylvania*, *Tennessee*, and *Maryland* all showed damage from bomb-hits. The *Raleigh* was barely afloat; the *Honolulu* and *Helena* were both damaged. The *Oglala* lay on her side; the *Vestal* was beached. The *Curtiss*'s deck was smashed. The *Shaw*, her bow gone, shouldered in her half- submerged drydock. The *Cassin* and *Downes* were both shattered. The *New Orleans* and numerous other ships were perforated by shrapnel.

Hangars on Ford Island blazed, and remnants of dozens of

aircraft lay in charred heaps. Oil, debris, and bodies floated in the harbor.

Elsewhere along the shores of Oahu, plumes of smoke rose from the battered airbases.

Eighteen American warships sunk or seriously damaged-- eight of them battleships; Japan lost five midget submarines.

More than 160 American warplanes destroyed and nearly as many more damaged; Japan lost twenty-nine of her attacking planes.

More that 2400 American sailors, soldiers, fliers, Marines, and civilians killed and more than 1170 wounded; the number of Japanese dead estimated at sixty-four. [9]

On that sunny Sunday morning, Elder Garner and his companion Elder Don "Kid College" Halvorsen, who had just arrived, began their eight mile walk from Kapaa to attend Church services in Lihue. As they neared Lihue, they heard planes in the distance, and Halvorsen who had earned his nickname because he had a conversational familiarity with most subjects speculated on what type of aircraft they might be. Halvorsen's casual classification did not elicit any alarm, for when they arrived at Lihue and were told of the surprise attack still in progress, the two missionaries were almost as astonished as the servicemen who comprised the Pacific Fleet at Pearl Harbor. Elder John Richards remembered, "We got up, and my companion had a radio, and we were listening to KSL out of Salt Lake City. It came over the radio from Honolulu. 'This is not a sham battle; those are real bullets.' Elder Muir said to me, 'That's a lot of baloney; I lived in Honolulu. That's a sham battle.' This Halvorsen (Keith's companion) he got up on the church, top of the church, and was looking, in spite of the radio announcers telling everyone to get off the buildings, get down, and get undercover, get off the streets."

Although Kauai was not the target of the Japanese assault, the island's proximity created potential danger for its population. Immediately following the attack, the beautiful Garden Island became an armed camp. With the approval of President Roosevelt, Governor Poindexter relinquished his political power to Lt. General Walter Campbell Short who declared martial law. He ordered a blackout on Kauai, and sentries patrolled the beaches off the Kaulakahi Channel.

Emotions ran high, and fear turned to hatred of the Japanese perpetrators. Even before this act of war, native born persons of Japanese ancestry felt and were

---

[9] Edward Oxford, "Turning Points: One Sunday in December," *American History*, December 1998, 3,5,7,11,19-20 [journal on-line]; available from http://www.tampabay.rr.com/mspusf/pearlharbor.html.; Internet; accessed 20 June 2001.

viewed at best as dual citizens, owing loyalty to both Japan and the United States and usually in that order. Following the attack, discreet discrimination turned to outright bigotry with a supposed basis for justification. How did one explain this crushing attack on the United States of America except to point to an easily recognizable enemy? Hawaii was particularly exposed to this malady. The census of 1940 recorded the islands' population as made up of 37% Japanese. The population of Kauai was 35,818 of which 43.2% or 15,470 were Japanese. The Church of Jesus Christ of Latter-day Saints having already responded to this actuality had two missions on the Hawaiian Islands: one, Japanese and the other, Hawaiian.

Elder Garner found himself planted in the middle of these two cultures. His feelings ran the spectrum: shock and anger at the cowardly surprise attack carried out by young Japanese pilots caught up in a frenzy of hatred and revenge, grief for the 2400 defenders of freedom resting in watery graves, and compassion for the loyal Americans of Japanese ancestry living in Hawaii. Most of Keith's feelings of empathy for the Hawaiian Japanese residents came to him firsthand. In contrast to the restrictions imposed today, Keith and his companions were regularly allowed to use the public schools during after school hours to teach gospel classes. It was Keith's custom as he diagramed the plan of salvation on the blackboard to turn and look at the students seated before him. Among the class he always saw young, eager students of Japanese ancestry listening to his important message. He portrays them in gentle words, "These Japanese boys and girls on Kauai, and for that matter, wherever we met them on the islands were dedicated, good people, eager for an education. We had great classes and enjoyed their earnest questions. It was a wonderful experience to teach a group who were so responsive to us and to our teaching of the gospel." Out of these student groups emerged Adney Y. Komatsu and many other men and women of his caliber who would play major leadership roles in strengthening Church governance.

Keith often tells a story President Komatsu shared with him while each was serving as president of an Asian mission during the 1960s. In this context it provides some clues to the impact Pearl Harbor had on Japanese Americans a generation later. "Adney Komatsu was raised in Hawaii. He was called to preside over the Japanese Mission. He accepted and moved his family to Japan. After his children had attended their first day of school in this new land, one of them flatly announced to his father that he wanted to go home. He did not like it, he did not want to be in Japan, he did not appreciate that he'd been moved and had given up his whole way of life, and he was getting out of there. Adney invited him to sit down and talk with him about what he had said. President Komatsu took a piece of paper, divided it in half, labelling the columns pros and cons. He began, 'The advantages of being here, number one. You are Japanese.' The astounded child answered incredulously, 'I am?'"

These groups of Japanese Americans with whom Keith felt honored to associate had none of the overwrought fervor of the Japanese kamikaze pilots. Keith explains, "In the later months of the war when the Japanese knew they were defeated, they elected to destroy our ships by using kamikaze pilots. These were young men who were willing to give up their lives by diving their planes into large concentrations of troops or into our destroyers or aircraft, any target that would be worthy of their life or plane. It was almost a religion with them. The emperor of Japan had more volunteers than his generals had planes to fly. In our time we see this same dogma in the terrorist order. Children, really, willing to give up their lives, believing a greater heaven is promised for that gesture of suicide. The Japanese had the same feeling of being a chosen people; therefore, they believed they were conducting missions of cosmic import. Based on these consuming ideas, a joke made the rounds. I don't know where it originated, but its telling was widespread and is still told. It is the story of the Japanese kamikaze pilot who was engaged to a sweet little Japanese girl at home. He wrote her a letter in which he revealed that he was a kamikaze pilot. Although he had volunteered, he assured her with the words, 'I'm involved, but I am not committed, so keep the ring.'"

Elder Garner, unlike the kamikaze pilot in the joke, was both involved and committed. His commitment to missionary service was not to the culture of death practiced by kamikaze pilots but rather to the culture of life, eternal life. However, meshing all the sentiments swirling through his head into a rational whole required an intelligence forced to function in an inexplicable world. Keith made the adjustments to an event which compelled him to change from missionary to civilian soldier overnight.

As the district leader on Kauai, he received his first taste of a pseudo World War II command. He continued to oversee the missionary work on Kauai, but now his duties also called for his oversight of the missionary-civilian effort to patrol the beaches. "I remember we were concerned that they were going to land troops on Kauai, and we walked the beaches." Most of the Mormon elders were put on sentry duty. They watched all the bridges. In addition to patrolling the beaches, they would stay at night at military posts and listen for the telephone.

An island-wide blackout made missionary cottage meetings in the evenings impossible. Again resourcefulness prevailed. The missionaries and the island population started putting black tar paper in the windows, preventing any inside lights from being seen from the outside. Even so, Elder Richards recalls, "One night we were out too late. We were coming up from Koloha Beach, I think, and boy, we heard this fellow yell out to us, 'Identify yourselves,' and we took a few more steps, and there he was with a gun. They were guarding everything."

Elder Richards continues, "We didn't see any action on Kauai at all except for one or two of these small two man submarines that would come in, and they'd fire their shells. They set a few cane fields on fire. A national guard unit, made up of one hundred barefoot Polynesians, was there to protect us. They plowed up all the fields and the grass in front of the hospital at Lihue, and they blocked off any vacant place where a plane might land. We were restricted; we'd go out in the daytime, but they had a curfew at night."

Keith, along with others, heard of downed Japanese planes on Kauai but never saw any. In fact, there were none. There was a landing by an American pilot flying to Ford Island from the aircraft carrier *Enterprise* who finding himself in the middle of Japanese zeros, high-level bombers, and dive bombers quickly retreated landing in a meadow on Kauai. He was so visibly shaken that he was immediately taken to the hospital at Waimea. Paradoxically, if he had landed at Burns Field, he would have been greeted by First Lt. Jack Mizuha, an officer of Japanese ancestry who was in charge of John Burns Field, a post he relinquished when the Army demoted him to executive officer.

A Japanese pilot on his return from the bombing of Pearl Harbor did crash land on the adjacent small island of Niihau and survived the landing. Believing that Niihau was uninhabited, the Japanese had designated it as the landing place for aircraft unable to return to their carriers.

The Japanese battle plan relied on submarines to carry out outlying missions. The "I" submarine carrying a seaplane and midget submarines launched the midgets which were to slip into Pearl Harbor before the bombers and after the attack launch their torpedoes. Stationed on the periphery of the Harbor, the "I" submarines were responsible for damaging any ships trying to escape from Pearl. In addition, one of the "I" submarine's missions was to rescue the pilot of any downed or damaged aircraft landing as instructed on Niihau. And so one author writes of the downed fighter pilot Naval Airman 1st Class

"This is Elder Garner in action" January 16, 1941

Shigenori Nishikaichi watching assuredly for a submarine to rescue him. [10] Almost every Hawaiian missionary of this period narrates differing accounts of what happened to Nishikaichi. That story's facts even after all these years remain shrouded in medals and myths. In an effort to settle decades of speculation and based on his considerable research, Allan Beekman wrote *The Niihau Incident*, a reputedly trustworthy account of this episode.

A short seventeen and one-half miles from Niihau and alerted to the imminent possibility that Japanese submarines were off the coast poised to land troops on this undefended island, Elder Garner, Elders John D. Richards, Don Halvorsen, and J. Melvin Glade of Salt Lake City, Utah; Glen W. Clarke and Ray Hill of Ogden, Utah; Kenneth N. Gardner of Delta, Utah; Irving Dana Muir of Pocatello, Idaho; David J. Evans of Shiprock, New Mexico; Newel Washburn of Pasadena, California; and Dean Larsen of Wales, Utah, kept their eyes open for this feared occurrence, while trying to keep their gaze firmly fixed on spreading the missionary message.

Four months later Keith's passage home was secured on the RMS *Mauretania* (2). Her namesake was the sister ship of the famous *Lusitania* which the Germans sank in World War I. By design, this first ship built for the famous Cunard lines under the name Cunard-White Star was a smaller but no less luxurious liner holding 470 first class passengers, 370 cabin class passengers, and 300 tourist class passengers, meant to appeal to those who wished first class service in a more intimate setting. Shortly after its launch in 1939, it had been converted into a troopship at Sydney, Australia, in 1940, [11] and it would be the troop ship, not the luxury liner, that awaited Elder Garner at the dock.

On April 4, 1942, Keith Elliott Garner was honorably released from his labors in the Hawaiian Mission.

Church of Jesus Christ of Latter Day Saints
Hawaiian Mission

Elder Keith Elliott Garner
San Francisco Ward, San Francisco Stake

This certifies that you are honorably released from your appointment as a missionary to this Mission.

No greater service can be rendered than to labor faithfully

---

[10] Allan Beekman, *The Niihau Incident*, (Honolulu, Hawaii: Heritage Press of Pacific, 1982).

[11] RMS *Mauretania* (2), 1-2 [on-line]; available from http://www.trainholidays.com/pages/mauret2.htm.; Internet; accessed 11 June 2001.

for the salvation of the souls of men. The gratitude of those
who have been the beneficiaries of your voluntary, generous
labors will ever be a source of satisfaction and inspiration to you.

   May the joy that comes from the conscientious performance of the duties of this high calling ever abide with you
and inspire you with a constant devotion to the Gospel of
Jesus Christ.

Roscoe C. Cox
Mission President

President Cox, as promised, did not forget to reveal to Elder Garner the
name of his admiring, benevolent benefactor, George Knapp. Knapp represented the
stalwarts of the Church in Hawaii. The Knapps, along with the Mussers, Woolleys,
Clissolds, and Christensens were prominent, well-to-do members of the Church, who
for the most part, had earlier served their Church missions in the Islands and then
returned. Brother Knapp's affluence was tied to a savings and loan in Honolulu which
he owned. Scrooge he was not. Elder Garner joined others who Knapp, throughout

a long life and on most occasions
anonymously, blessed with needed
resources and other acts of thoughtfulness.

   President Cox's farewell
also included the reminder to Keith
that he was still a missionary of the
Hawaiian Islands, and so mission
rules applied until he reported to
his stake president in San Francisco.

   He boarded the RMS
Mauretania II with other passengers,
many female civilians, trying to
return to the mainland following
Pearl Harbor and the outbreak of
war. No dating, of course, was one
of the mission rules, so for the
duration of the sail home, he left his
white shirt, dark suit, and traditional tie hanging on his bedpost for
one of the Navy men to wear to the
ship's nightly entertainment, dancing,
and social activities.

Elder Garner "a hui hou" (Until we meet again)

Keith sailed, having uttered "mahalo nui loa" (thanks very much) and "a hui hou" (until we meet again), outfitted with behavior patterns which would last a lifetime, many polished in the heady days of missionary service at the hands of generous Polynesians, faithful mission leaders, and steadfast companions; he leaped into the world of 1942 with testimony, ambition, patriotism, and determination.

Chapter
FOUR

The Fight for Right

"Duty, Honor, Country"
— West Point Academy Motto

      Already affected by the bombing of Pearl Harbor and after military service in World War II, Keith's responsibilities as president of the Southern Far East Mission placed him in Vietnam during the war years 1965 to 1968. Notwithstanding this reoccurring proximity to deadly conflicts, he would not have put the armed services on any list of career choices he might consider. This lack of military inclination is not indicative of a lack of patriotism or of a waning love of freedom; in fact, no inheritance could be or ever would be more precious to him. At his direction and evidencing his appreciation for the United States of America, the Stars and Stripes waved proudly over every ministorage complex he built from Redwood City to San Jose and over many other properties he developed and owned, including his South Temple office and his Arlington Hills home. This seems appropriate since Old Glory represents the sovereignty which had allowed him the very real chance to give his talents expression, to succeed in his chosen pursuits, and to live his life freely.

      Though the unexpected actuality of service in the armed forces of his country was unchosen and seemingly should have brought into conflict two of Keith's defining personality traits, his pragmatic temperament and his independent spirit, it did not. Pragmatically, he recognized that he, as a soldier, must be disciplined and obedient in order to accomplish the objective of winning World War II, one of the most crucial team missions ever successfully attempted. The accomplishment of this mission would

Keith during his years at Washington school

define a generation and ultimately be referred to as a watershed in the preservation of free agency--the eternal tenet over which the war in premortal heaven was waged, the democratic idea that Jefferson immortalized as a God-given right, and the very principle which let Keith's independent spirit flourish.

Military life for him was not a snug fit, but his presumably contesting characteristics worked together, complementing each other in interesting ways. All factors considered, he enjoyed his World War II tour of duty, and the instruction he received armed him with intelligence that he would use to his advantage throughout the years ahead. In a lighthearted vein, he acknowledges that the perks received from wearing the uniform of his country were not bad either.

Much earlier the benefits of military participation, especially when performed in a safe setting, had become clear to him. At Ogden High School, he joined Company "D" of the ROTC as a private, and during his junior year, he found very appealing the possibility of qualifying to be a ROTC cadet captain in his senior year. If selected, he could choose any young lady as his "sponsor." He refers to this period of his young life as "arrival." In one of his more whimsical attempts at recording his story, he dashed off rather melodramatic recollections and intemperate generalizations of those years growing up in Ogden.

Keith writes, "I was born in Sugar City, Idaho, on May 11, 1919, the sixth child and the last boy in a family of seven. The World War I Armistice was signed in November of 1918, so I was on the way before the termination of hostilities.

I really don't remember my years in Idaho; in fact, my whole life is shrouded in vague showers and isolated remembered experiences. In the very early years, the family moved from Idaho to Ogden, Utah. I've never been sure whether my father was a farmer or lived on a farm and worked at the sugar factory. Perhaps he attempted both, but hard times came as they usually did in those early years, and we went to

Ogden where Dad went to work for the railroad as an engineer. I've heard some conversations in the past that when the railroad strike began he went out on strike with
the workers. In this case the unions lost, and my father lost his seniority. When he
went back to the railroad, all he could get was work as a machinist. When I grew up,
I remember Dad as a machinist.

We lived at 315 32nd Street between Washington Boulevard and Grant
Avenue. It was in the low income area, I'm certain; in retrospection, there were
lower income areas of hobos and tramps. I never related to this lower strata, yet I was
conscious of the higher and more affluent sector of our drab city.

I attended Washington School for ten years. I was always the smallest kid in
the school. I always felt I was staring at somebody's belly button. My teeth were
large and out of proportion to my face. I was really an ugly, underdeveloped kid. I
never enjoyed school, for I was sub-average and really never learned to study. I played

Royal Coal Baseball Team; Keith front and center

marbles, tops, and baseball. I loved baseball above all sports and actually excelled in
it. These recreational activities took all of my time. I was never prepared when I
attended school; therefore, it was always poison. I lived in fear of being called on to
participate, and the hands on the clock in the classroom never moved, so I suffered
through ten years of school at Washington. (Keith's mother's recollection is that 'he
started at the Washington School in first grade. He didn't do very well until the third
grade. I was so worried about him. When he got into the third grade, he had a

teacher who thought a lot of him, and he just came up a flying from then on--just went right through his grades.') There is an expression in the Book of Mormon that describes my early years. I think Jacob related their trials and suffering in the new land, and then he writes, '...thus we lived out our days.'

I wouldn't want to leave the impression that I wasn't happy because I was. Our home life was difficult because we lived in a 1200 square foot home with only one bath, and I had four sisters, and I remember they had priority in the bathroom, especially during the busy hours of the day.

Our cars were usually Essexs. I remember Dad dug a pit in the garage and spent a number of evenings in that hole working on the cars that were continually breaking down. He asked me to hold the light for him during these evenings, but he wasn't very successful since I detested the menial operation. The garage was cold, and

Mary Lou Humphris

lying on the ground under the car was a boring and tedious operation. Many of the cars during this era were not dependable. We were really in an experimental stage of building cars; therefore, they had flaws and defects that made certainty in driving questionable.

The year that I left Washington and headed for Ogden High a new world came into being. I felt suddenly that my mournful probation was coming to an end. Achievement in class through preparation for the next day's assignment gradually began to form in my mind. I was committed but unable to dedicate my devotion to it primarily because I lacked a workable knowledge of *how to do it*.

It was during these critical days that I met Maren Eccles and Mary Lou Humphris. I sat next to Maren, and I marveled at her beauty, her wealth as demonstrated by her wardrobe and car, and her smart head. I enjoyed chatting with her because she represented the class in our society that were secure, knowledgeable, and, therefore, enjoyable to be around. Mary Lou was a beautiful blonde, and during the year I mustered up enough courage to visit her at her home on several occasions although I never accumulated enough dollars and courage to take her out. Naturally there was no car. I was afraid to borrow Dad's because it was substandard, so the

Keith in Officers Candidate School

alternative was just to visit her and dream of better times.

In ROTC training I observed early that if I were selected as a cadet captain I would pick a sponsor, a young lady, so I exerted every effort to win an appointment for my senior year. As I look back on this accelerated pace and realize that I really just came out of the bush, the thought of being a ROTC captain was remote. I never knew whether I made it or not. During the summer, Dad lost his job in Ogden, and Lee Fife, a friend and master mechanic living in Sparks, Nevada, gave Dad a job in the Sparks Railroad Roundhouse. So I left the possibility of becoming a high school ROTC captain and Mary Lou behind. She sent me a picture and wrote on the face of it, 'To Keith, with love, Mary Lou.' I hadn't been rejected again. I had arrived. I guess that is why I've always kept the picture because it represented success, arrival, a new era in my life. Amazing what that photograph did for my future ego. After I received the picture, I never talked to her or wrote her a letter."

Mary Lou's gesture, such an insignificant yet pivotal event, instilled a confidence in Keith which might have ebbed and flowed as the years passed but which has never left him.

Keith continues, "Sparks was the very best thing that happened to me. I guess this was the real beginning of a beautiful life. I excelled in all my classes because I studied, studied, and studied. The drama teacher befriended me, and I participated in Shakespeare plays and debates and loved every minute of it. I even tried out for the varsity basketball team and would have been a needed player if I had been taller. As it was, I was #1 on the second team, and we played Reno, Carson City, Fernley, etc. and were champions in our terrestrial sphere.

I graduated from Sparks High in 1937. Although sixty-seven graduates is rather a small graduating class, that graduation represented the most productive year of my life. To a degree I had 'come of age' and had resolved to make the best of my life. In the fall, I registered at the University of Nevada, a great little school in Reno."

At the university Keith did not take ROTC because all that was offered was ROTC-Infantry, and infantry meant bivouacking. Open air military or even Boy Scout encampments were not, nor would they ever be, on Keith's list of favorite activities. The boy scouts that he and other leaders accompanied to Boy Scout camps during the fifties might be surprised to learn that periodically after "lights out" he would quietly sprint to his parked car, make a beeline for the nearest motel, spend a comfortable night, jump into the shower, arrive at camp refreshed, and then encourage the boys to get out of their sleeping bags and meet the day's opportunities with zest. With his eyes twinkling, he would yell, "Okay, out of the sack!" He is sure he never really fooled any of them; he reveals that one of the camp competitions seemed to be to guess the name of the motel where he would be staying.

Lieutenant Garner and his mother

Post Pearl Harbor, April 1942, with a year's university studies in Reno, a Hawaiian mission completed, and now enrolled again at the University of San Francisco, Keith's options were either to enlist or to wait to be drafted. He chose to enlist. His strong preference was to become a naval aviator. Having the minimum two years of college training required and with the following letter of recommendation written by A. T. Matthew, the assistant vice-president of American Trust Company, he entered the Navy's recruiting station in downtown San Francisco.

> Bearer of this letter, Keith Elliott Garner, was originally employed by the American Trust Company in 1938. At the expiration of two years he left us to become a Missionary for the Mormon Church in the Territory of Hawaii.
>
> After the expiration of his voluntary service as Missionary he was again employed by the American Trust Company.
>
> During the time Mr. Garner has been with us he was almost continually under my supervision and I cannot speak too highly of him. His integrity, loyalty and up-standing character was all that could be desired. I have no hesitation in stating that given the opportunity he would be a worthy representative of the United States armed forces no matter what branch of the service he is acceptable to.

The naval recruiter took his application, asked him a few qualifying questions, and proceeded to a preliminary medical evaluation. He told Keith to stand over in the far corner with his back to him and place his finger in his left ear. He tapped a quarter and a dime together and asked him to quantify the number of taps. With his finger in his left ear, he responded correctly, "three." Then the recruiter instructed him to put his finger in his right ear, and he began to tap. "I thought he'd left the room," Keith exclaims. "When I turned around, he had moved from the other side of the room and was now standing right behind me tapping the coins together." His directive to the disappointed recruit was "Sorry. Pick up your application." With regard to this incident Keith even now shakes his head and mutters, "For the first time in my life, I found out I was deaf in one ear."

While not the duty or branch of the service he preferred, he enlisted in the Army on July 24, 1942. His Army serial number read 19119973, a number he, like other World War II veterans, recites sixty years later without missing a digit.

Keith's World War II stories are docile when compared to those who saw combat in the European or Pacific theaters. His stories are ones of lessons learned, ingenuity utilized, friendships established, hubris exercised, and destinations discovered. He already had under his belt maturing experiences which made enlisting as a private not the spirited choice it became for many young men, some under draftable age. Keith approached his duty deliberately. His service was mostly spent in the preparatory phases of warfare prior to the dramatic events told in moving anecdotes of friends lost in combat, of battles fought along the front lines, of

His mother wrote on the back of this picture: June 17, 1943, the day Keith left for Army, taken in LaVon's back yard at 748 19th Ave, San Francisco.

climactic victories, and of devastating defeats. Yet he, along with others whose World War II days were spent stateside, played necessary if unheralded roles in the lofty mission billed as the preservation of Western democracy.

While still continuing his studies at the University of San Francisco, he entered the University ROTC program. On January 18, 1943, in a letter sent to his mother, Colonel Alva F. Englehart writes in part:

Your son, Keith, was selected after careful consideration
of his academic grades, ROTC work and his officer-like qualities to be a contract student in the Advanced Course, ROTC,
at this University.

Entrance upon the advanced course provides for the
granting of deferment from Selective Service during the time
he is enrolled in the advance course. Successful completion of
ROTC training and any future training prescribed by the War
Department entitles him to attend the Officers' Candidate
School, and upon its successful completion a commission as a
Second Lieutenant in the Officers' Reserve Corps.

Since one of the requirements for completion is that
the candidate be in excellent physical condition, it is important
that all advanced course students maintain themselves in
proper physical condition through the medium of proper
diet and exercise.

When he was called to active duty on June 7, 1943, he was sent to Camp
McQuaide for Coast Artillery Basic Training. Camp McQuaide, named for Father
Joseph P. McQuaide who served in World War I as an Army Chaplain assigned to the
250th Coast Artillery, was located six miles west of Watsonville, California. Camp
McQuaide was awash in beautiful eucalyptus trees and the waters of Monterey Bay,
a perfect setting for training in coast defenses.

ROTC student Garner found that the most exciting course of study was
learning how to fire 155mm cannons. He and his classmates were taught to apply
with precision the principles of trigonometry to calculate an accurate trajectory.
They were taught how to load the cannons, how to pull the lanyard, how to zero in on
moving targets. The noise level prompted him to say, "If I hadn't been deaf before,
I'd have been deaf after. When you'd pull a lanyard, those things would make a lot of
noise. We were just kids, and I don't remember any one of us having the sense to put
anything in his ears while we fired." During this training he and his fellow basic training soldiers watched men who didn't appear to have a death-wish take a target out to
sea on a barge, put a long tow rope on it, and drag it up the Pacific Coast. Then they
would see if they could shell the target. "The secret," according to Keith, "was to
shoot one over, one under, and the third one should hit the target dead center." Not
surprisingly he muses, "I used to always marvel at the guys that used to get in those
barges and pull the targets because although we were all university boys, this was a
new science."

Entering the USF-ROTC-Coast Artillery program had sounded like a good
option, especially when one imagined himself guarding the San Francisco Bay from the
famous landmark Mark Hopkins Hotel atop Nob Hill! But America realized when the

Japanese did not attack Singapore in the way expected, that fixed gun positions were a poor defense. The British had their guns set for an attack from the sea; the Japanese marched down the Malaysian Peninsula. Unable to move their guns, the British allowed the Japanese to take Singapore "with a song, really." So the Coast Artillery Corps at the University of San Francisco was scrapped. Keith and sixteen of his USF Coast Artillery buddies were given a choice between the paratroopers or the infantry. They were offered fifty dollars more a month to jump--a very attractive incentive, especially when weighted by the worth of the dollar in the '40s, but Keith categorically states, "Not one of us took the paratroopers."

Because of the change in military strategy and even after having successfully completed their Coast Artillery Basic Training program, they were not commissioned. In fact, all of these would-be Coast Artillery soldiers had to start over. This meant an additional two months of Infantry Basic Training and four months at Officers' Candidate School-Infantry, both at Fort Benning, Georgia. This turn of events triggered Keith's observation. "Well, look I'm infantry, and I hate it, but I'm destined for it...." Typically he decided that he would try in his own atypical way to make the best out of the situation. There was no better place than Fort Benning, Georgia, to test his resolve.

Georgia, although lush with vegetation and dotted with clear lakes, is also uncomfortably hot and humid. This heavy oppressive air intensified the severity of the training. As harsh as the experience may have seemed at the time, the seriousness of the mission for which these cadets prepared justified the rigorous discipline, physical challenges, and intellectual demands. Keith pulled himself through the mud on his belly, climbed over walls, navigated water hazards, marched for miles, shot at targets, studied mathematics, bayoneted German and Japanese dummies, and played war games; and in the process, Corporal Garner learned more than one valuable lesson at Fort Benning. One lesson remained with him for the rest of his life.

Early in his training, the inspecting officer found the condition of Keith's rifle unacceptable. When asked about his rifle, he defensively argued, "Sir, I didn't have time." The officer queried, "Soldier, what were you doing between ten last night and six this morning?"

Over the years when Keith's inquiries about lack of performance were answered similarly, he has said on occasion and thought on many more, "Soldier, what were you doing between ten last night and six this morning?"

Keith followed the orders of those over him in the chain of command, if sometimes, like most other inductees, reluctantly. On one seemingly insignificant matter, he good-naturedly tussled verbally with the officer in charge. The subject in question was shaving gear. No one ever thought a description of Keith should portray him as the grizzly, outdoor mountain man who shaved himself with his hand-sharpened pocket knife. Keith's refined masculinity and his practicality made him far more compatible with the image of the well-dressed, meticulously manicured, clean-shaven male whose use of modern amenities causes the rudiments of life to become easier. In other words, he had never shaved in his life with a razor blade, and he didn't intend to start now!

He questioned, "How am I going to shave when I'm out on bivouac or in combat?" Keith answered his own question by rigging up a large walkie-talkie battery used for communication purposes and plugging in his reliable Sunbeam electric razor. Once while he was out on bivouac shaving, the commanding officer, a captain or major, came by and inquired, "Lieutenant, what are you doing?" Keith said, "I'm shaving." The officer observed, "That's a lot of noise." "Right, but it gives me a good shave" was Keith's response. He warned, "If you get into combat, you're not going to be able to use that razor." Keith half-seriously teased, "Well, I'm not going into combat then." As he watched the rest of those guys pulling whiskers off with cold water from their canteen, he just thought, "That's for the birds."

This conversation between Keith and the officer in charge could have been right out of Irving Berlin's World War II all-soldier revue. It was the perfect backdrop for Keith's commanding officer to erupt with the lyrics of Irving Berlin's "This is the Army, Mr. Jones."

A bunch of frightened rookies
Were list'ning filled with awe,
They listened while a sergeant
Was laying down the law.
They stood there at attention,
Their faces turning red.
The sergeant looked them over,
And this is what he said:

This is the army, Mister Jones--
No private rooms or telephones;
You had your breakfast in bed before,
But you won't have it there any more.

This is the army, Mister Green--
We like the barracks nice and clean;
You had a house maid to clean your floor,
But she won't help you out any more.
Do what the buglers command:
They're in the army and not in a band.

This is the army, Mister Brown--
You and your baby went to town;
She had you worried but this is war,
And she won't worry you anymore. [12]

Coincidentally, adjacent to the basic infantry school was a paratrooper school. Keith recalls, "We used to watch those young recruits. They had a tower over there; they'd jump off the tower with a parachute. It was quite a sight to see those young kids jump, and in a few cases, as I remember, the parachute did not function properly. We never knew why those chutes occasionally malfunctioned. We were just happy we were digging holes instead of jumping off towers. As tough as infantry was, I thought it was a lot better than the paratroopers."

At Officers' Candidate School, there was a far more frightening alternative than paratrooper training. Keith's heightened motivation to pass his OCS courses is understandably attributable to the always present alternative, a one-way ticket to the front.

Finally graduated from OCS-Infantry at Fort Benning in September 1944, having received the Expert Rifleman Award, and now assigned to the 125th Infantry Division, Keith spent the next year training troops. With three of the original sixteen USF boys, Herm Schlesselmann, Ed Casey, and Bob Riordan, he was stationed first at Camp Maxey in Paris, Texas, next Camp Gruber in Muskogee, Oklahoma, and then Camp Rucker in Ozark, Alabama.

Keith, himself only twenty-five, instructed youngsters, mostly teenaged boys, who had enlisted or been drafted. "Training troops meant I taught them to assemble a rifle or pistol, taught them techniques of house to house fighting, taught them how to dig and how to protect themselves in a fox hole, taught them how a peripheral defense works. The main thing was, I guess, I taught them everything there was to know, at least that I'd been taught, about the rifle. They were riflemen, and they had to be able to take a rifle apart blindfolded, put it together at lightning speed, and fire it accurately. On the firing range, we put up targets, and they qualified for marks-manship ratings of Sharpshooter, Expert Rifleman, or other designations by demon-strating expertise in holding and shooting a rifle properly."

Keith's prowess with a rifle was acknowledged even by himself; yet some other necessary characteristics of the good soldier he lacked, illustrated in his account of the following incident. "We were out as usual on bivouac, having spent most the day either on the rifle range or on grenade throwing detail. We officers took turns taking over the company of young recruits. At the end of the day, I was given the

---

[12] *The Complete Lyrics of Irving Berlin*, ed. Robert Kimball and Linda Emmet (New York: Alfred A. Knopp, 2001), 358.

assignment to take our company back to camp. I was doing great and on course until I got into the rows and rows of barracks, and those buildings all looked the same to me!" He used his head and was able to find the company's living quarters without showing his ineptness by barking out the order, "First Sergeant, take over the company." He stepped up; Keith moved along with the troops, and they completed the return in good form. He quickly understood that acquiring the art of delegation is an integral part of success in life. Of course, he also learned that the trick to its productive utilization is to be wise, sufficiently informed, and spiritually reliant to know to whom to delegate.

Keith concludes in reference to this incident, "I've often said because of my sense of direction or lack there of it's a good thing I didn't lead anybody into combat. If I'd gone to Europe, the company I led would have been mistakenly behind German lines most of the time."

With experiences like this and others yet to come, Keith knew he was not cut out to be a soldier in the traditional sense of the term. In fact, every so often he manifested that he was not delighted with this rough environment at all. "I remember on one occasion I was away on leave after I was commissioned and I didn't return to the base until way late in the evening. My company was all out on bivouac, and I thought here's a real chance for me to go to the barracks and get a good night's rest." Foiled again! "When I got there, the company commander was waiting for me with the greeting that he didn't want me to lose the opportunity of sleeping out in the bivouac with my company. I was amused that he was there. He certainly had my number and knew my energy would be concentrated on avoiding the roughing-it exercise, and so he had made a special effort to insure I'd be participating. I yielded to rank, got in a jeep with him, and we went out, and I slept with the rest of them. I don't remember whether it was a ground operation or whether we had some kind of a mattress; I do know I didn't look forward to it. I made up my mind if I ever went on leave again, I would come back at a time of my selection rather than at the eleventh hour."

The rank of second lieutenant, which Keith and all graduates held following OCS, constitutes the lowest rank in the officer chain of command. Often in the initial stages of any second lieutenant's service, the higher ranking officers barely tolerate these men with a single gold bar on their shoulders. Noncommissioned officers and privates enjoy more regard than second lieutenants; it is an undisputed fact in Army circles that sergeants having risen through the ranks are militarily smarter than second lieutenants. This attitude emerges in most cases because a second lieutenant is still inexperienced and has no service upon which a reputation or credentials can be based. In Keith's case, the fact that he had gained his commission, not at West Point but at Fort Benning in a ninety-day-war-accelerated program, earned him an additional measure of disdain. His group of second lieutenants was commonly referred to as the "ninety-day wonders!" Of course, among the commissioned officers, a second lieutenant is always in the subordinate position. Second Lieutenant Garner found himself laden with all these negatives when he walked into the command post and was met by a first lieutenant. He recounts, "I greeted him in what I felt was the appropriate manner with a simple good morning, sir." For whatever reason, he rebuffed the greeting with a curt, "Lieutenant, when you come in here, you salute." Keith knew that military etiquette did not require an officer to salute higher ranking officers when inside a building unless reporting for a formal evaluation. Lieutenant Garner was not there for that purpose. He didn't say anything; he just let it go. However, the next time he went into the same office a couple of days later, he again greeted this officer like a gentleman with a cheery good morning, sir. "I remember that he became really upset that I hadn't followed his instructions; he wanted to be saluted. I felt his demand was outside regulation since we were under cover, and I felt its only purpose was to embarrass me and place a brand new second lieutenant under his thumb. I had also come to know him a little better by then, and I thought he was a little arrogant. As a result of not saluting, I found myself with extra duties, officer of the day, more times than my normal assignment."

Lieutenant Schlesselmann remembers, "When the 125th Infantry was moved from Texas to Camp Gruber in Oklahoma in December 1944, our Company Commander was First Lieutenant ____. When we reported in to him, it was clear he was definitely in charge, expected us to 'look alive.' The word going around was that he was aiming for promotion to captain, and I'm sure he didn't look kindly on any of his junior officers who failed to carry out orders to his expectations. For those who, for whatever reason, didn't measure up in this category, punishment in the form of unpleasant duty assignments would follow. I don't know whether or not he was ever promoted. Luckily we left him behind when the regiment moved to Camp Rucker in Alabama."

For Keith, unpleasant duty assignments did follow. As he notes, "There was always one officer labeled 'officer of the day' on duty to whom everyone reports simply because nobody else is around." Having received this designation on more than the usual number of days, Keith enjoyed the liberty it gave him to make unmonitored decisions. He often used his extra-duty assignment to give the troops for which he was responsible a small break from their specified janitorial duties. He remembers, "I had the assignment on one occasion for making sure the officers' quarters were cleaned properly. The floors needed to be scrubbed and polished, and even today I can picture those little kids, eighteen-year-old peachy cheeked boys, over at the officers' quarters doing that menial work. I told them to just take off and enjoy the evening. I let the kids go and gave them another evening's leave. These youngsters were going overseas; they were infantry. I knew that wasn't the easiest assignment in the military; in fact, at the time I thought it was probably the most dangerous. I had a lot of concern for them, and while trying to prepare them for the rigors of a war they too soon would face up-close, I also tried to lighten burdens of less consequence. I really wasn't a disciplinarian when it came to commanding."

The seriousness of the situation in which Keith and others found themselves rarely left the surface. With little or no warning, units were called up, individual soldiers were transferred out, and orders were posted for overseas assignments. This uncertainty constantly invaded the training camps.

Keith wrote to his mother, "Boy, was I surprised to learn the other day that Wardell, Poggi, Kendrick, and Rice have gone over seas--'Europe.' So out of the thirteen of us--only seven of the group are still here, five of us here at Maxey--two at Camp Howze, Texas.

My regiment is moving next week. The destination hasn't been officially announced, but I do know it's within a close proximity of here, perhaps two hundred miles. Either Texas, Oklahoma, or Arkansas. Personally, I don't mind moving for I do want to see as much of this world [Keith crossed out the word *world*] mean U.S. as possible before leaving. To date, I've had the gravy train but that won't last too much longer. They'll have to put me out in the field eventually. And I need the experience in the worst way. Of course, I'll get plenty of that before long so no complaints."

Always present was the precarious verity that he had been trained and was now training men in preparation for the preservation of their own lives in defending truths for which they might be required to die.

Whether consciously or merely subconsciously, Keith held onto a inner assurance that he would never see combat. He did feel unprepared to command a platoon on a life/death mission, and lacking that confidence, he knew he could never ask another human being to follow him into battle. His lack of a sense of direction precluded such an assignment. Perhaps more noteworthy, his stamina for conquering the mud and rawness of life on the battlefield made him too fragile a warrior for a combat mission. Keith remarks, "It is incredible I was not killed. I watched as wave after wave of soldiers stationed for training at camps Maxey, Gruber, and Rucker were sent to the battlefields. I should have been in the Pacific or in Europe. Had I gone, I feel I would have been a casualty of war. I was not called up. I survived."

The calmness brought on by this unexplainable surety that he would not be a combatant came from a boyhood event. When he was eleven, Keith remembers attending the picture show *All Quiet on the Western Front*, a re-creation of World War I, which had concluded only a decade earlier. He ran home right down the middle of the road, instead of using the sidewalks, because of a previously unexperienced fear precipitated by the terrible events he had just witnessed on the big screen. He burst into his home and poured out his feelings about the horrors of trench warfare, the blood, the anguish, the sorrow to his father. His dad prophetically and comfortingly reassured him. "My dad told me I'd never experience combat like that and so not to worry about it. So I didn't." This simple statement of Keith's confidence in his father's assurance speaks volumes about the strength passed from this steadfast father to this loyal son. And, in fact, Keith never did worry about it!

Neither he nor his University of San Francisco Catholic buddies rejoiced in

Garner with improvised belly tank showers in background on the Pasiq River in Manila

the prospect of having to take the life of an adversary. Few soldiers did. Accessing the courage for battle was not the issue. Keith's psyche, now trained to shoot in defense of duty, honor, and country, not to mention his own life, recoiled at the coarseness of combat, and luckily he never had to experience it.

By August 14, 1945, the world knew the war was over. All that remained was the signing ceremony. General Douglas MacArthur representing the United States aboard the Battleship *Missouri* in Tokyo Bay on September 1, 1945, made it official, and September 2nd was declared VJ Day. August 16th Keith left Camp Roberts in California via Fort Ord with orders stationing him in the Philippines. With his location for the next year already in the military pipeline, the flicker of hope that he would not be required to fulfill a tour of duty in the Philippines or any other overseas post was squelched.

He protested. "The war was over when I left. I really put up a complaint for sending me over there when the war was over, but nobody listened." Keith strongly identified with George M. Cohan's stirring anthem "Over There." He could sing the line, "The Yanks are coming and they won't come back until it's over over there," with bravado. However, the part of the lyrics which resonated most loudly for him and which he found applicable to his circumstances was the phrase "It's over over there!" Nonetheless, his tour of duty to the Philippines with the military commenced on September 4, 1945. Keith set sail from Los Angeles and after three weeks on the seas docked in Manila Harbor. "When we arrived in Manila, armed personnel were carting out of various buildings the bodies of dead Japanese soldiers who had been shot prior to our arrival," Keith recalls.

While post World War II historians would later attempt to estimate the horrendous cost in lives lost, the United States already had learned from World War I the enormous cost economically of bringing military supplies back home. Some politicians asserted that it had contributed to the Great Depression of 1929. So in an attempt to prevent history from repeating itself, a mopping up operation was gearing up when Keith arrived. Freighters in the Manila Harbor bulged to overflowing with supplies amassed for the invasion of Japan. Keith remembers, "As far as the eye could see, food, clothing, jeeps, tanks, ammunition, and all kinds of armaments of war were stacked up one, two, three stories high for miles." Addressing the lessons learned from World War I, the military brass had created jobs designed to dispose of this buildup of materials. As part of this task, Lieutenant Garner was detailed from the 125th Infantry to Headquarters Second Major Port, Water Division as a gear or general supply officer. As one of the affectionately named "Flying Manhole Covers," his main job was to assist with the unloading of these freighters. "It seemed like there were hundreds of freighters. I was put in charge of supervising a number of Filipinos. I had an easy job really. I had lots of freedom. It's the kind of job you'd like to declare as your pension days." Tankers and other military equipment were unloaded onto flat bed barges, secured with chains at the four corners, and fastened to the

Keith and Army buddies walking down a street in Manila

barge. "While the barges were being towed into the harbor, if there happened to be some large waves caused by other ships going by, occasionally, being courteous to the military, GIs loosened the supports and lines. When the barge hit this backwash, the tank or other armament would just tip and fall over into the water; having delivered the load to the bottom of the bay, the detail would go back to the freighter and put another load on the empty barge. I didn't see a lot of that, but I saw some of it." As wasteful as this sounds, the equipment had lost its value because of the restrictions imposed forbidding its return to the United States. Additionally, warehousing in the hot sun would have rendered it rusted and useless. Keith suspects a diver into Manila Harbor today would find much debris from World War II.

Assigned to the port command in Manila, Keith's lodging, in what he calls "quonset huts," was located in a parking lot bordered by the Pasig River. Again ingenuity transformed meager quarters into accommodations with a view, complete with a luxury, although not a private, bath. "We all wanted showers, and so we rigged up a couple of belly tanks, gas tanks. These fuel tanks were used by the Air Force, and after the fuel was spent, they simply dropped them. We got a couple of them, put up a support, filled both of them with water, put shower heads on the bottom end of them, and built an enclosure around them with a little dressing area and a shower area. We had real hot water heated by the sun. Cold days don't exist in the Philippines, and so perpetually hot days meant the tanks were always heated. We had nice hot water all the time I was there."

Like other self-taught capitalists, Keith's entrepreneurial flair surfaced as unsought openings materialized. Though it has been many years, Keith recalls the perks and opportunities trading cigarettes for more desirable goods gave him. "The non-smokers in the Philippines at the time had real economic advantages. We used to get rations of cigarettes, so many per soldier or officer. I've forgotten the number, but whatever the number when you pick up the habit, you want more than you are allotted. Art Holland and I had more friends than we normally would have had because we had all our rationed cigarettes to trade. We could choose to deal with anyone we wanted. We had a real business going." Even discounting the obvious health benefits, their abstinence from cigarettes was worth their while.

Keith saw no combat during his stint in the military, not that he had an overwhelming desire to do so. In fact, the only shoot-to-kill combat he would ever see was from the air over Vietnam. Nevertheless, many soldiers would undoubtedly join with Keith in suggesting that basic training should be defined as combat, without being shot at with live ammunition.

Keith reminisces, "The closest I ever came to combat occurred on a pier where some GIs tried to block my exit because they coveted my jeep. It was a beauty!"

Since Lieutenant Garner had fifty or more Filipinos working under him and since they had demonstrated their proficiency in many tasks, he

Two young entrepreneurs: Lts. Art Holland and Keith Garner

took advantage of expertise General Motors might have envied. He commandeered a surplus jeep and put them to work. "I took the nice leather seats out of an old ambulance and replaced the jeep's little seats with these two beautiful leather seats. I replaced the tires with balloon tires. I enlarged the gas tank in the back; it was necessary for me to fill up maybe one time the whole time I was there. I really dolled it up. These Filipinos had it fixed up for me all the time. I should have taken a picture of it.

I used to drive around the long piers, flanked by freighters being unloaded onto barges. Every enlisted man, I'll use that term reservedly, who saw the jeep, coveted it. They would have loved to have had it. I went out one time; it was later in the evening, and I drove down the pier. I just happened to glance in the rear view mirror. I saw these guys, American troops, maybe five or six, and they were putting a barricade up so I couldn't get the jeep out. I had a .45 in a holster. I turned the jeep around quickly, put my foot on the throttle, my hand on the horn, and pulled out my .45. I knew how many rounds I had. I shot two or three up through the top of the jeep. I had guys leaving the barricade and diving into the water on each side. That was the closest I ever got to combat…from my own troops. Well, what they wanted was the jeep. I never even took a picture of it. It really gripes me that I didn't." Keith may not have saved his country on the battlefield, but he successfully defended his prized jeep.

On one of his leaves, he and three of his buddies decided they wanted to see Yokohama. They secured a DC-3 and flew the approximately 1,858 miles from Manila to Yokohama, landing only once to refuel in Okinawa. Keith never saw any Japanese who were still breathing during the time he was in the Philippines. Of course, he did in Yokohama. Taking a tour of the area, they found it sparse, bleak, and marred by war. In spite of the war having ended only months before, these GIs felt secure. They were greeted with smiles and waves from the Japanese whom they saw, mostly women, children, and elderly people.

The most exciting part of their junket occurred on the return flight. As they left, the navigator put the map on his lap, and they headed southwest. They had traveled some distance when the navigator concluded that Okinawa, the island where they had refueled on the first leg of their trip, seemed to have disappeared. Perhaps the strong winds blowing off the Pacific had altered their course. Nerves became slightly frayed, fuel was getting low, and no land was in sight. All they could see was water. "That's a lot of ocean," Keith said, stating the obvious. With the caveat, "I'm an infantry soldier, and not even good at that," he emphatically suggested, "For the life of me, I know China is pretty big, and if we're going south, let's just go right, and we'll find something." They did. After what seemed like a couple of hours flying, they found an airstrip in all probability on either Formosa or the small island of Matsu and landed there safely. The Chinese graciously offered them the use of one of their huts as lodging for the night. The next morning Keith's party welcomed a long line of Chinese personnel carrying five gallon cans of gasoline that they placed on the plane's wings and with which they systematically filled the nearly empty tank. The lost crew thanked them profusely with gestures and bows and with great relief took off for Manila. After returning safely after such a frightening incident, they all felt grateful to be standing on firm ground. Keith had bargained with the Lord over the Pacific and promised "If you get me through this one, I won't fly again unless I'm forced to!" As the events of his life unfolded and he found himself airborne of necessity, he on several equally ominous occasions renegotiated this promise.

About halfway through his duty in the Philippines, he received a promotion. The casualness of the following exchange reflects a drastic lessening in the seriousness of the mission and consequently an easing in the formality of relationships. Colonel Evelyn, his commanding officer, without any apparent provocation said, "Keith, how long have you been a second lieutenant?" Keith said, "Oh, quite awhile." Colonel Evelyn followed up offhandedly with the question, "You want to be a first?" "Sure," he replied. The colonel invited him in and proceeded to make Second Lieutenant Garner a first lieutenant. Keith observed that not much changed, but it did mean he got twenty dollars a month more income. He left the Philippines and his last active duty as a first lieutenant.

Keith makes it very clear that at that time and in those circumstances none of his reporting officers viewed him as a particularly prime candidate on the fast-track to promotion. Captain Nathan A. Hall's comments on the Efficiency Report covering 16 September 1944 through 31 December 1944 regarding Keith's performance as a Platoon Leader, Anti-Tank Company, 125th Infantry Regiment, Not Combat read: "A serious, unassuming officer of ordinary mentality, who has a neat appearance and a mild disposition. Sometimes appears eccentric. Quite idealistic in his thinking, but is well informed on world and professional affairs. He is industrious in his work."

Captain Travis A. Sanders comments in a report covering the period between 1 January 1945 to 30 June 1945, "The officer's old weakness was a lack of confidence and an opportunity to demonstrate his ability which he has overcome in a splendid manner. An inspiration aids him greatly. The officer has definite possibilities of being superior material in the future."

Despite Lieutenant Garner's lack of recollections of Church and missionary activity during these war years, both Captains Hall and Sanders must have observed his Mormon traits, for they included some of them in their reports. Perhaps these peculiarities emerged in noticeable actions like his carrying an obviously well-used Book of Mormon in his duffle bag, his not imbibing, not using unseemly language, not gambling, not smoking, and not drinking coffee--the very same standards Mormon boys of courage and conviction stationed worldwide were living. The only real temptation Keith experienced happened every time they were out on bivouac. Keith loved the smell of coffee brewing and the warmth emanating from a filled cup as soldiers wrapped their hands around it on cold mornings. "We always knew when the coffee wagon was coming because the aroma preceded the caravan. The caffeine in coffee is a real inducement, and I can understand why people drink it. It was a very welcomed treat for the soldiers, and I often thought if I'd just shut my mouth I could have had a cup of coffee."

His not drinking coffee started a great friendship. Dr. C. Elliott Richards recalls, "We met at Camp Maxey in Paris, Texas, and came into contact with each other when we attended our first officers' dinner. Across the table from me was an officer who was also not drinking coffee or anything. So immediately afterwards we rushed to each other and said almost in unison 'You must be Mormon.' The Church at that time was not very widespread."

In a letter to his mother from Camp Maxey he writes describing Thanksgiving spent with the Richards, "All in all we had a great day, and it felt wonderful to be with some good old Mormons. It always does!" Then he writes about an incident involving one of his USF buddies. "Incidentally Casey came running up to me the other day and informed me that he just received some Mormon boys and they insisted on having LDS put on their dog tags instead of 'P' for Protestant. He asked me if they could do it? I asked him how he'd like to have a 'P' put on his instead of the 'C' for Catholic. So they'll have 'LDS.'"

These obvious indicators drew attention and may have accounted in part for Captain Hall's and Sanders' notice. Perhaps it was his believing heart quietly manifest in less noticeable but even more powerful ways.

Lastly, Lt. Colonel A. Evelyn issued Keith's final report covering 1 July 1945 to 31 December 1945 on his role as a gear officer and comments, "This officer has displayed aptness and ability in learning a new job and is doing a good job on this assignment."

It might be concluded that Keith's demeanor, goals, and the value that he placed on his and on others' free agency left him uncomfortable and therefore unsuited for the higher echelon of military command. However, it is apparent from these reports that he served well and that the Army appreciated his service.

Honorably discharged April 19, 1946, Keith received the standard letter sent to veterans from President Harry S. Truman. Although widely issued, the meaningful words remind readers of the intrinsic contribution made by those men and women who served in World War II, as well as those who serve today in preserving precious liberties.

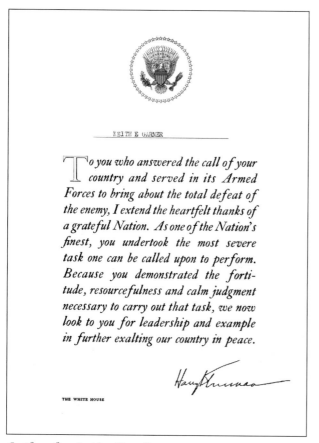

Certificate from President Harry Truman

KEITH E GARNER

To you who answered the call of your country and served in its Armed Forces to bring about the total defeat of the enemy, I extend the heartfelt thanks of a grateful Nation. As one of the Nation's finest, you undertook the most severe task one can be called upon to perform. Because you demonstrated the fortitude, resourcefulness and calm judgment necessary to carry out that task, we now look to you for leadership and example in further exalting our country in peace.

Harry Truman

THE WHITE HOUSE

Herman J. Schlesselmann, in reference to receiving his discharge papers, wrote to Keith in 2001, "I think for all of us that was a very happy day." Keith concurs, echoing the sentiments he heard expressed at an LDS sacrament meeting in

Vietnam by an officer completing his eleven month duty in Vietnam. "I approach this moment with mixed emotions--joy intermingled with happiness."

Unlike MacArthur, Keith had no intentions of returning to the Philippines; however, he, too, would return.

Chapter
FIVE

Building the Kingdom; Building a Career

Leaders are movers, shakers, original, inventive, unpredictable,
imaginative, full of surprises that discomfit the enemy in war and
the main office in peace. Managers, on the other hand, are safe,
conservative, predictable, conforming, organizational men,
team players dedicated to the establishment.
— Hugh Nibley

Keith's return to the Philippines would not occur for another seventeen years. In the meantime he opened other chapters in his life, all filled with an array of options. His pursuits, many and varied, make pigeonholing Keith impossible. Indicative of this fact, returning from a family vacation to Tijuana, Keith found one of the questions the American border patrol officer asked him slightly perplexing and unexpected. He answered easily the questions posed about possession of fruits, vegetables, and souvenirs. The uniformed guard leaned on the car and read through the rest of the usual list of queries: name, address, citizenship, destination. When he got to profession, Keith amusedly shrugged his shoulders and silently inquired "What day is it today?" as if the answer would help him determine how to respond. Punctuating the bemused silence came a voice from the back seat, "Dad, what is your profession?"

Keith usually defaults to the general title, land developer or to the more specific title, builder. Over the past fifty years, his instinctive talents for acquiring, financing, developing, and selling properties permitted his adventurous and mercurial nature to soar. The money he earned for his own account gave him freedom to be his own boss, his own servant and the independence to pursue other fascinating spheres, some related and others completely new.

However, he did not begin as a land developer with this treasured emancipation. His exposure to this field came almost as a fluke, a fluke upon which a willing Keith seized. His readiness, instinctively secured by the immovable foundation of the gospel of Jesus Christ, gave him a vantage point from which he could confidently explore the world.

Truman G. Madsen in an address to students who were being recognized for their academic achievement at Brigham Young University reminded these scholastically competent young men and women that the gospel of Jesus Christ is the solid foundation which frees one to pursue without fear any theory taught in the universities of the world. He spoke about fellow students he met as he qualified for his own degrees and how some who spent years mastering the intricacies of their particular discipline were bitterly disappointed, almost as if their whole world had evaporated, when new theories explaining the universe materialized leaving the old ones dashed on the rocks of supposedly better hypotheses. Dr. Madsen's conclusion based on his own experience seemed to stimulate in these students the desire to embrace with exuberance the gospel of Jesus Christ without stifling the intellectual quest.

Keith never needed such a reminder. His attitude based on absolutes allowed him to unlock various vocational doors. His early pursuits included lawyer, banker, Army chaplain, and life insurance salesman.

Immediately after his military service, he was admitted to the University of San Francisco School of Law without having received his undergraduate degree. The university program designed for war veterans awarded both the Bachelor of Arts or Sciences and the LLB upon graduation. Keith immersed himself in classes titled Constitutional Law I and II, Contracts I and II, Criminal Law I and II, Legal Ethics, Practice, Agency, and Torts I, earning B grades in most of these classes and an A in Constitutional Law II. Notwithstanding, in his pursuit of a law degree, he found frustration. His perception of advocacy conflicted with the accepted system of a judiciary tied to precedent. He chaffed at the function of the United States legal system, unquestionably the best in the world, to interpret and enforce laws passed by democratically elected legislative bodies. Keith preferred a simple consideration of what is right, what is wrong, what makes sense, and what is fair. Pouring through centuries of case law to construct legally viable and persuasive arguments left this law student unsatisfied and a little annoyed at the exercise. He never completed his bachelor's degree, and Keith E. Garner, Attorney at Law, never hung on his office door.

For Keith, life in San Francisco prior to World War II and now post World War II meant not only school at the University of San Francisco but also work at American Trust Company. Happily he opened those large ornate glass doors again. The recollection of his days spent inside the bank building at 464 California Street prior to his Hawaiian mission filled him with cheer, especially the distinct personalities which made the work environment come alive. Who could forget Archie Darling? Not

Keith. Mr. Darling, colorful as his name, headed the bookkeeping department. Years before, after Keith served his apprenticeship as a runner for the president of the bank and his two secretaries, he worked as a bookkeeper under Mr. Darling. Keith describes him. "He was medium build with red hair, a debonair dresser. We used to kid him about whether or not he wore Oxford suits. In response he would open his suit coat to reveal the prestigious Oxford label. We teasingly passed the word around that he bought his clothes at Weinsteins, a Kress/Woolworth operation, and then got labels from Oxford and the fashionable men's clothing store Hastings, cut out the Weinstein label, and put in Oxford and Hastings labels." Into this amicable atmosphere, Keith stepped anew; however, he would come to question whether it was a step up.

At the bank he found relative security, a state most workers find comforting. He enjoyed the work and his growing responsibilities; yet he found the exploration of life exhilarating and never closed his eyes to the new, the untried, the possible.

Exciting new openings seem to be right in front of Keith, or maybe it only appears so to others because he has the amazing ability to recognize them and seemingly without much trepidation embrace them. He recalls, "I became acquainted in the San Francisco Ward with a fellow by the name of Wolford, E. V. Wolford. He was a vibrant fellow, a great golfer. When I had to go down to the bank one evening to stuff statements to mail to the customers for whom I was responsible, he joined me. As we stuffed bank statements, he said, 'Keith, you should go into the insurance business. There you are not confined to hours. You can just sell. You are free, and your time is your own.'

At the bank I worked in a department with a guy that I had known during my work there before leaving on my mission. He was one of the department heads; I have forgotten his exact title. Anyway, one day as we were balancing bank statements, we had a little extra time. I called him by his name and said, 'How long have you been here?' He said that he'd been there for a long time. I said, 'Do you make good money?' He said, 'No, but I have security, and I like my work.' Well, I'd just started there again. In my early years at the bank, I made fifty dollars a month. In the military as an officer, I was making $275.25, which I was startled to find was more than this man was making. I realized if I stayed at the bank I'd have the same attitude that he had, except I wasn't built like he was. I thought silently, 'This seems ridiculous for me,' and stated too bluntly and out loud, 'You mean you've been here all these years and you only make that kind of money?' He said, 'Yeah.' I yelled out, 'I quit!' and that was my last day of employment as a banker.

I don't know whether I had the security of the insurance offer or not, but it didn't make any difference to me because in a free society you don't have to worry. You just go out and go to work somewhere."

Keith often speaks of the conflict between security and freedom. He reads with understanding about the war in premortal heaven described throughout the Bible [13], Book of Mormon, Doctrine and Covenants, and Pearl of Great Price, most especially in the book of Abraham. Lucifer offered his brothers and sisters a certain future after mortality. Christ, presenting the Father's plan, offered them eternal life, the chance to become like the Father. They would have all the aids necessary to guide them back into the presence of their Heavenly Father, including the universal gift of the Spirit of the Lord and through baptism and confirmation the gift of the Holy Ghost. They would have available to them the Lord's redeeming and atoning sacrifice to cleanse their sins, making it possible for them to return in glory, heirs to all that the Father has.

The choice between the two plans presented to God's children in the premortal counsel in heaven replays itself over and over day after day here on earth. It is the same choice, a choice between guarantees of a lesser amount and the risk and rewards of a higher value. Keith usually selects the risks which bring the more valuable rewards.

Predictable, which is not an adjective which comes to mind as descriptive of Keith Garner, is applicable to his choice to sell life and disability insurance. His beliefs, while secured by spiritual witness, are essentially practical. While it is not possible to protect what are ultimately only worldly worries, the insuring of life, assets, and partnerships for beneficiaries is one way to evade the unanticipated. Of course, the freedom selling insurance offers the salesman in terms of his time and effort is the point that sparked and held Keith's attention. He told Wolford he was interested in the freedom E. V. had described to him while they stuffed statements into envelopes reflecting others' often substantial bank balances.

Keith recounts his launch into the insurance business. "E. V. introduced me to Wallace Allred, long-time bishop of the Mission Ward in San Francisco. He was the supervisor for the Hunter & Hunter Agency which was the Kansas City Life Agency in San Francisco. I liked him from the beginning; he was a charming fellow, a great salesman, and so I started selling life insurance."

Keith quoted and applied the old maxim that selling, any kind of selling, is a numbers game. If a person has ten conversations, he is better off than if he has just five. He agreed with Pete Grimm, a yet-to-be-met friend's optimal thinking when he told him during one of Keith's many visits to the Philippines, "I'd like to sell a pair of socks to every Chinaman."

Keith never sold to billions, but he revisits his finding fruitful application for the numbers principle. "I thought I've got to find where potential clients are cloistered, where I can get a lot of them instead of just making appointments on an individual basis throughout the evening or trying to interrupt their business during the day. Having a military background, I thought the best grouping that I know of

---

[13] Revelations 12:7

prospective buyers is out at the Presidio. I told Red Wolford, 'Let's go out to the Presidio. There are a lot of GIs out there, and a lot of them are career military. They are going to stay in for life rather than giving a few years.' We went out there. I introduced myself to the company commander and told him I was a first lieutenant in the Reserves. I think I was reserve at least for a couple of weeks until I realized I'd have to go to meetings, and then I gave that up. I told him that I was there to supplement his soldiers' earnings by giving them an endowment that would cash out at the end of ten, fifteen, or twenty years. In the meantime if anything happened to them, their families would get the proceeds. The officer in charge liked it and introduced me to the sergeant. The sergeant would call ten or fifteen enlisted men at a time into formation. I would talk with them, explaining the program. Almost invariably when I concluded my presentation, they stood in line to purchase these ten, fifteen, twenty year endowments. I sold in this fashion at the Presidio for weeks and weeks, day after day. Each day I stayed out there until my arm was too tired from writing applications to do it any longer."

Before Keith left the Presidio, having sold an insurance plan to almost all the available personnel, he realized that he had not approached the man who had escorted these applicants all these weeks, the top sergeant. Keith said, "Sarge, I think you and I ought to sit down. You had better take one of these forced savings plans."

This man had been in the service for Keith guesses a decade or more. He had hash marks from his wrists up to his shoulder blades, a rough fellow who fit the stereotype of an Army sergeant of the 1940s and '50s.

He said, "Nah. I put my money in houses and lots." Keith warned, "You don't want to put everything you have into real estate." He queried, "Who said anything about real estate? I'm talking about houses of prostitution and lots of whiskey."

Even Keith had one who got away!

Keith details his next opportunity. "Then somebody told me about Hamilton Air Force Base up near San Rafael. It was a staging area for sending officers, primarily officers, overseas. They were there for just a short time, and then they shipped them overseas; unlike the Presidio, it was a fluctuating situation. I said, 'Well, that is the place to be.' I went up there. I took E. V. [Red] Wolford and Clark Hamblin with me."

As was his custom throughout his life when Keith discovered opportunities upon which he was able to capitalize, he spoke up and invited others to give it a try. A few of Keith's friends accompanied him to Hamilton over several years; some were more successful than others.

On the first visit to Hamilton Air Force Base, Keith, E.V., and Clark found their way through the maze of buildings and the layers of personnel in order to make the right contacts. Keith explains his plan. "Most of these people were officers, pilots enroute to overseas assignments incident to the Korean War. Many of them were married, and all they had was $10,000 GI insurance; I had an opportunity to supplement that with additional insurance at a low premium.

I primarily focused on savings, forced savings without interest. I told them it was better to have the principle than to have nothing. They would go through the money otherwise. This way if anything did happen to them, there was a reward for the family, and at the end of their service, they would have the money."

Keith and his two associates became acquainted with the officer in charge of the allotment section at the base and made arrangements with him for premium payments to be automatically deducted from the serviceman's pay. This accommodation benefitted both Keith and those to whom he sold. It made unnecessary the sending out of a premium notice and gave the purchaser the option of having this payment taken directly out of his paycheck. He found that most of them liked the program. They would sign an authorization card, Keith would turn it in at the paymaster's office, and they would process these allotments for the officers and soldiers.

Because most of them were basically waiting for deployment, Keith identified two advantages to his being able to make the sale. First, Kansas City Life policies had no war clause exclusion. Second, the airmen had both the time and desire to listen to him. In fact, at their request he made himself available to them during their off-hours. At the base they would tell him that if he would meet them in San Francisco, then they could converse in a more relaxed setting. So he spent much time at hotels in San Francisco, often the Mark Hopkins or the Sir Francis Drake, talking with them about insurance. One can be certain insurance was not the only topic of discussion. Keith's military background and wealth of storytelling talent probably interested some of these prospects at least as much as the intended subject of conversation.

"They had a need, and I was there! As I reflect on it when I was going through Fort Benning in earlier years, I took a life insurance policy from a salesman that came out. I know he had an easy time selling me because he was offering something desirable at a good price with a convenient payment plan."

Maybe that recollection in the midst of all this success as an insurance salesman spurred Keith to investigate the possibility of becoming an Army chaplain. Maybe his sense of adventure emerged, or maybe it reflected the punch line from the famous Amos 'n Andy story. Keith replays the broadcast as he remembers it. "As part of one episode of the popular radio program *The Amos 'N' Andy Show*, Kingfish and his wife are in the kitchen having an argument. He picks up the frying pan, hits his wife over the head, and runs into the woods. Hauled before the judge and asked to state his defense, Kingfish explains, 'We were arguing, the frying pan was handy, her back was turned, and the back door was open. It seemed like the logical thing to do.'"

Whatever the reasons, Keith, qualifying himself for participation in the chaplain corps, was transferred from inactive to active reserve on 18 January 1951. He filled out the obligatory paperwork and received the necessary endorsements. Over the next year, a series of letters between Army and Church authorities and Keith reveal the investigative process in which he participated.

He was advised by a January 24, 1951, letter signed by the counselors in the First Presidency J. Reuben Clark, Jr. and David O. McKay, "We have given our endorsement of your application for appointment as a Chaplain in the United States Army." In a letter dated January 30, 1951, T.A. Rymer, Director of General Commission on Chaplains, Washington, D.C., wrote to Chaplain Roy H. Parker, Chief of Chaplains: "At the request of the proper authorities of the CHURCH OF JESUS CHRIST OF LATTER DAY SAINTS, the General Commission on Chaplains forward the ecclesiastical endorsement of The Rev. Keith Elliott Garner, 822 Sunnybrae Boulevard, San Mateo, California, who has made application for appointment as a chaplain in the United States Army."

On May 8, 1951, Colonel Patrick J. Ryan, Chaplain of the Sixth Army, head-quartered at the Presidio informed him by mail:

> On a recent visit to the general headquarters of the Church of Jesus Christ of Latter Day Saints at Salt Lake City, your name was given to us as being available for commission-ing and extended active duty with the Chaplain Corps…
>
> The Office of the Chief of Chaplains has directed us to bring twelve Latter-Day-Saints Chaplains to extended active duty at once. Your name will be submitted to Department of Army for assignment within the Sixth Army area as soon as you have been commissioned as a Reserve Chaplain. We cannot promise that you will be stationed in the Sixth Army area but at least that will be our recommendation.…

Later that year on October 2, 1951, Colonel Ryan's assistant wrote Keith:

> According to information which we have just received from Mr. Bruce R. McConkie of the L.D.S. Servicemen's Committee under day of 27 September 1951, you have been granted Ecclesiastical Indorsement for the Chaplaincy of the U.S.A. May we congratulate you upon the receipt of this favor. It is good to be thus highly regarded by your Church.
>
> Judging that you are interested in securing a commission as a 1st Lieutenant in the Chaplains' Corps, may we suggest that you make immediate application to the Office of the Chief of Chaplains, Department of the Army, Washington 25, D.C. The necessary forms will then be mailed to you for your prompt attention.

PRESIDENT'S CLUB *Notes*

KEITH E. GARNER
1948 Club President

as reported by
F. W. BOYCE, *Club Secretary*

D. L. STITT
L. C. Mersfelder
Qualified September 28

Twelve New Members Added to 1949 Roster Of President's Club By October 8

O. E. DURHAM
L. C. Mersfelder
Qualified September 29

CALEB B. ELLIOTT
J. T. Allen
Qualified September 29

KEITH GARNER
Hunter & Hunter
Qualified September 29

GLEN E. PORTER
J. T. Allen
Qualified September 29

JOHN WAGAMAN
Missouri–Kansas City
Qualified October 4

FRED MITCHELL
J. T. Allen
Qualified October 5

W. W. BUTLER
Missouri–Kansas City
Qualified October 6

CARL JORGENSEN
J. T. Allen
Qualified October 6

J. E. MILLIGAN
L. C. Mersfelder
Qualified October 6

HERBERT W. RICE
Bayard Judd
Qualified October 8

STILL NO PICTURE!

KENNETH R. WEEDIN
Missouri–State
Qualified October 8

10

LIFETIME *for November 1, 1948*

From **Lifetime** *for November 1, 1948*

While this available service opportunity coupled his missionary verve with his military training, he concluded that even its apparent perfect fit could not overcome the obvious disadvantages he identified. "It was a new adventure, but it would not have been a wise decision for me at the time. I had only been married a few years, had two children, and was heavily involved in the present. Accepting a changing and evermore certain overseas assignment in war-torn Korea would have interrupted my life course again." Keith distinguishes the determining factor in his declining to take the remaining steps to secure an appointment. "I had already been in the infantry long enough. The chaplain corps is similar in many respects to the infantry corps; they are often on the front lines." Even so, he kept this option open until November 10, 1952, when he received an honorable general discharge from the Army of the United States and from his membership in the active reserve, an event which happened almost simultaneously with his call to be bishop of the Menlo Park Ward.

Thus, Keith's profitable pursuit of premiums as a life insurance salesman defined his career throughout his early working years. A national report singling out the Hunter & Hunter Agency reads: "Fifty-three agents wrote business during September [1948] to run up a total of over $900,000 and place the Hunter and Hunter Agency at the top of the list (with the exception of Missouri) in written business for the month... Leading the entire agency was **Keith E. Garner** of the northern California division, followed by **Greg Mahakian** ...Placing third in the agency and first in the Salt Lake division was **Junius Romney** Northern California: **Clark Hamblin** ranked third...."

Keith's production received rightful recognition. He recalls, "I became president of the Kansas City Life President's Club for 1948. I believe the convention that year was held at the Chateau de Frontenac in Quebec City. I remember I had to give a speech." E.V. Wolford states, "Keith rehearsed his speech all across the country as we traveled to Quebec City." Keith modestly replies, "I remember getting up there and talking to them about something. What could I have said to these pros which would have been instructive?!"

The audience to which Keith spoke consisted of the company's most productive insurance professionals. With his insurance license in his wallet, he obviously fit into this group since that year he outsold everyone else in the company nationwide. However, his accomplishment reflected the unique opportunity he found at the Presidio and Hamilton Air Force Base. His picture published with eleven others in *Lifetime*, "President's Club Notes," announcing "Twelve New Members Added to 1949 Roster of President's Club" attests to his atypicalness; he appears as a handsome, young man with a full head of curly hair and an ear-to-ear smile among a group of distinguished older men with a range of receding hairlines and more serious demeanors. Keith puts into words his reluctant pride in taking his place among these top sellers. "I really wasn't a bonafide salesman in the sense that most of the salesman in Kansas City Life and all companies were, the kind that sell executives, fathers on a one-to-one basis."

Even though reportedly his words were well received, he still expresses his ambivalence. "So my being the top salesman wasn't a great achievement because I was able to sell these groups of military a lot easier than the typical insurance salesman sold individuals. Yet it was an achievement because I did go there, start it, and make it work. Clark made a lot of good money, and E. V. Wolford did. For guys that are just starting out, it was a real opportunity for us."

He recalled, as he, first among equals, dined with this elite group of insurance salesmen, how early in his insurance career the head of the agency had invited him and another inexperienced salesman to be his guests for lunch. The only directive from that business lunch he remembers is W. G. Hunter pointing to the least expensive meals and telling them to order from that side of the menu. Keith would never find himself in that position again, and if he ever gave a similar instruction to anyone with whom he shared a meal and for whom he picked up the tab, a common activity so typical of what many have called his generous nature, it would also be in jest.

Much of his success in the insurance industry and later career choices is attributable to his adherence to principles he discovered and naturally embraced. Keith worked hard, worked smart, worked creatively, and worked freely. The key word he emphasizes is *work*, the eternal principle which the Lord tethered with glory. "For behold, this is my work and my glory – to bring to pass the immortality and eternal life of man." [14]

Work is a word Keith's father helped define for him by his actions. As a child Keith witnessed his father compromised by poor health arise in the morning, work when he could hardly do so, use every fiber of his combined faith and work to be self-reliant, come home in pain, and fall on the floor exhausted. Keith's mother then eased his discomfort by rubbing his back.

Amid the heartache of seeing these trials, Keith also saw joy, an uplifting byproduct of work, as his father sat on the front porch in the cool of the evening strumming his guitar, lifting his rich tenor voice in strains of popular songs of the 1920s and stirring anthems from the Church hymn book, thereby entertaining the whole neighborhood. A joyful noise seemed to follow the Garners wherever they went, from Grandfather Fred's band to the quartet made up of his father and uncles to young Keith, dressed in a white shirt, blue bow tie, white pants trimmed with a blue stripe, and a beanie circled with blue satin ribbon, beating his own snare drum as he marched down Washington Boulevard with the eight "man" elementary school drum corps in Ogden patriotic parades.

The definition of work in Keith's dictionary never included sitting on the sidelines watching the parade pass him by. Rather he is the personification of the speedy

---

[14] Moses 1:39

cartoon character the road runner. He seems to be always on the run, uttering the cautionary warning, "beep, beep." On a daily basis, he physically and mentally darts among a myriad of tasks.

Tevya's statement, "…we always wear our hats," spoken in the Norman Jewison film *Fiddler on the Roof* is true for Keith as well. The declaration, "Our forefathers have been forced out of many places at a moment's notice," which elicited Tevya's observation, reminds one both of Jewish forced exoduses over centuries and the Mormon migration from Nauvoo, Illinois, in 1847, an event in which Keith's ancestors participated. However, unlike the forced movement associated with the Jews and the Mormons, Keith's head covering represents a readiness to take on a multiplicity of chosen pursuits at a pace with which most cannot keep up. With a twinkle in his eye, Keith also admits that he relishes the symbolism of being coifed with the hat of a mover, perhaps partly, as a repudiation of John F. Kennedy's turn against tradition in the early 1960s when the President of the United States rarely wore a hat and in so doing set a fashion trend.

Whether the hat was his drummer's beanie trimmed with satin, his Royal Coal baseball cap, his first lieutenant's hat, his banker's green visor, his Stetson dress hat, his gardener's straw hat, his Stoneridge Country Club golf cap, his superintendent's hard hat, all these hats fit Keith, for he is always on the move animated by his work ethic.

Keith ascribes to the French writer and philosopher, Voltaire, a statement he can often be heard quoting. "The further I advance along the path of life the more so

Keith, center, created a "joyful noise," even while saying, "I was always the smallest kid in the school; I always felt I was staring at somebody's belly button."

I find work a necessity. In the long run it becomes the greatest of pleasures and it replaces all one's lost illusions." Working hard does seem to be one of Keith's most invigorating and revitalizing activities.

Although Keith also believes much can be said for instruction through example, he still feels even perceptive observation falls short of active participation. Obviously, no coaching and no classroom instruction can stand proxy for education acquired on the field of play.

Nevertheless, one seemingly inconsequential observation Keith made while working as an insurance salesman for Dean Zahn reaped abundant applications. Keith explains as he retells the story he has told many times when the occasion screamed for this needed guidance. "I worked for a general agent named Zahn. I think his office was in San Mateo. It was a great experience. I watched my contemporaries in the business; most of them were always preparing to sell, but they never quite made it. When they did talk about a sale, they talked about volume instead of premium. I learned early that an insurance salesman doesn't make any money on the volume of the sale, but on the amount of the premium. That's where the commission comes from."

Keith emphatically punctuates this story. "You just can't sit around!" He continues, "Dean was rightly complaining as the general agent; he was always trying to support those who weren't working. They left home and went to the office where they spent their time ever organizing. I never felt I had to organize; I just had to work. Work substitutes and is the means of making a living, not lining up clients on a piece of paper on the desk in the office."

Further illustrating the same point, he, with some bewilderment, tells of the fellow looking for employment who proudly made it known that he had his resume out to forty employers. This seems noteworthy, except that he just sat idle waiting for one to respond. Keith emphasizes, "He needs to get on his feet and get to work!"

Spending unproductive time organizing carries little force as a tool of work for Keith. Another tool, preparation, he weights heavily. Maybe it goes back to his teenage days as an assistant scoutmaster in Ogden, Utah, where he led his troop in the Boy Scout oath. This pledge resides in his memory and more importantly in his day-to-day habits, especially the familiar "Be Prepared!"

Sometimes it is seemingly the most insignificant and easiest preparation that matters most. He rarely, if ever, lets the auspicious moment pass because he is unprepared. A rudimentary example from his present may suffice to illustrate this point. Having placed in front of him a stack of checks for his signature, I found myself without a pen. As I excused myself to retrieve one for his use, he whipped a pen out from his shirt pocket with the verbal punctuation, "I'm an old insurance salesman; I always have a pen."

"Work hard" easily embraced "work smart" as it had earlier for Keith when he sold to the military, and the dynamics of this duo of directives found use as he balanced an expanding customer base. Keith shares his approach. "I discovered the sale had to be made whether the prospect had one dollar or one hundred dollars. I began to concentrate more on people who had money. If I'm going to spend the time on the sale and if they say I'd like to take it but I don't have the money, that's a waste of time. So I was more selective. I presented my plans to men who had larger incomes. I could sell them a larger premium and make more money with my investment of time than if I spent it on smaller sales. Right in the beginning, I decided to look over my dollar and my time, and I realized it is prudent to find the field that promises results of the greatest worth. I picked that up from Elder James E. Talmage of the Quorum of the Twelve. He talked about it in either *Articles of Faith* or *Jesus the Christ*. Simply stated he said that it behooves a man in this world to search out and find the field that gives him the greatest results for his time. Talmage said that the greatest results are found in the gospel of Jesus Christ because if one follows that program he is blessed in this world and in the world to come."

The guiding concept to which Keith refers is found in James E. Talmage's book *A Study of the Articles of Faith*.

> **Importance of Theological Study** In the short span of mortal existence it is impossible for man to explore with thoroughness any considerable part of the vast realm of knowledge. It becomes, therefore, the part of wisdom to direct our efforts to the investigation of the field that promises results of greatest worth. All truth is of value, above price indeed in its place; yet, with respect to their possible application some truths are of incomparably greater worth than others. A knowledge of the principles of trade is essential to the success of the merchant; an acquaintance with the laws of navigation is demanded of the mariner; familiarity with the relation of soil and crops is indispensable to the farmer; an understanding of the principles of mathematics is necessary to the engineer and the astronomer; so too is a personal knowledge of God essential to the salvation of every human soul that has attained to powers of judgment and discretion. The value of theological knowledge, therefore, ought not to be underrated; it is doubtful if its importance can be underestimated."[15]

When Keith is asked as he often is "To what over everything else do you attribute your success?", he consistently offers this controlling concept of time man-

---

[15] James E. Talmage, *A Study of the Articles of Faith*, (Salt Lake City: The Church of Jesus Christ of Latter-day Saints, 1942), 4.

agement for consideration.

Two other core principles Keith embraced early in his career pursuits can be seen utilized throughout every aspect of his life. "Work creatively" and "work freely" were for Keith naturally fitting truisms. Being first or a close second to give life to a new idea infused his psyche, not because it satisfied a competitive edge, but rather because it colored his day with excitement. Creative expressions whether original to Keith or whether appreciatively adopted by him animated his already lively persona. An early illustration, relatively inconsequential when compared to his later land development firsts, occurred when he left one insurance company to sell for another basically because the policies offered by the new company had more style.

He explains, "After a number of years, I left Kansas City Life and went to work for Occidental, Girardian, and Franklin Life insurance companies. I sold for all three. Occidental Life had attractive term policies. Girardian offered a more appealing commission structure. Franklin had a program I liked better; I thought it more inviting. The presentation of the policies, one called a PIPP and another a JISP, had a lot of panache."

Like Keith his father had exhibited a propensity for making himself available to exciting avenues of expression. He bought 1000 shares of stock in the Gold Gulch Mining Company, shelling out a few coins to be part of a potentially profitable venture. This small investment valued at one cent a share evidences father Ben's adventurous spirit. The stock certificate #29, dated 29 January 1934 and signed by President Frank Eastmond and Secretary Thorpe B. Isaacson is still in Keith's possession.

Reflecting his father's flair for the possible and his own creativity and free spirit, Keith tells how he discovered a mother lode of gold, nestled between the San Francisco Bay and the Pacific coastal range, on the streets of Menlo Park. He also quarried neighboring lucrative veins running across the whole peninsula named San Carlos, Redwood City, Portola Valley, Palo Alto, Mountain View, Cupertino, and San Jose.

"I moved to Menlo Park. I was still selling life insurance. I met a successful real estate broker on Santa Cruz Avenue. He was a great guy with a big family. I sold him a large policy, and in the course of the conversation, he said, 'I have some property over on Coleman; how about you taking the property as the premium? Then you'll have property, and I won't have to come up with the cash.' I said great, and so he paid his premium with the property."

Keith's inventive instincts were reinvigorated. Before he moved to Menlo Park, he had for the fun of it built a spec home on Parrot Drive in Hillsborough, Bing Crosby's neighborhood. After he moved to Menlo Park, rather than renting office space, he and Taylor Peery, who had retired that year as vice-president of Bank of America "to pursue his life long hobby--real estate," joint ventured a one story structure with eight store fronts at 635 Oak Grove Avenue where Keith set up shop to sell insurance. The Application for Building Permit #3950 dated January 14, 1955, discloses that it was a new construction on a 32' X 125' lot, to be built using a concrete foundation, concrete block for exterior and interior walls, tar and gravel roof, valued at $30,000. He was charged a two dollar permit fee and a sixty dollar building fee.

Notwithstanding his having already dabbled in building, this unsought introduction stirred his imagination, and acquisition of the Coleman parcel began for Keith a vocation which spanned the last half of the twentieth century and continues into the twenty-first century with little sign of his ever retiring. His stationery reads, "Retired Offices of Keith E. Garner," which he says should be changed to "Tired," but the truth of the matter is that neither he nor his offices have retired. In fact, recently Diane Dunford, who worked with President Garner on Temple Square, inquired whether he had yet retired. She seemed unsurprised when the answer was "No." Her wonderment at what it ultimately would take for him to retire was reflected in her comment, "He'll probably retire only when he slumps over the shovel while digging his own grave!"

Procurement of this parcel on Coleman also came with a problem a more experienced man would have vetted prior to the handshake cementing the deal. Keith explains, "When I got involved in the mechanics of the deal, I learned it wasn't free and clear as I remember. It had a cloud on it, second mortgage which was due and payable."

Stock certificate of Gold Gulch Mining Company

Remaining undeterred and having resolved the existence of the surprise second mortgage, Keith hired Stan Mattson to design apartment units for construction. He acquired additional vacant land along Coleman Avenue and built 119 apartment units within three years. At this juncture a strong case could have been made for renaming the street Garner Avenue.

Though not an architect, Mattson designs had his recognizable signature written all over them--an aptitude for the artistic, necessary elements laid out in new ways with stylish accouterments. As much as Keith relishes the new and has to dig deep to appreciate the old, he pays Mattson the ultimate compliment. "Stan's apartment designs are the best, and driving around Menlo Park, Palo Alto, Mountain View, Cupertino, San Jose, all over, even Salt Lake City, all these years later, the appeal of his designs has lasted." Keith further adds, "Stan Mattson, a graduate of Annapolis, was a talented draftsman. He was a hard worker, punctual in his promises, and full of life."

This comradeship of appreciation was illustrated in a rather unique way. Leaning over a desk and looking at plans for a new construction, Stan noticed Keith's watch on his outstretched arm. He simply said, "I sure like that Rolex watch you have." Keith unexpectedly replied, "Great, you can have it." His observations made in Hawaii surfaced in his own action. He had learned there to be very careful in his expressions of admiration because the Hawaiian people gave cheerfully and spontaneously.

In Stan's case, Keith's gift was not as flighty a gesture as it may seem. Keith felt Stan had merited it. After all, Stan had been there from the beginning.

Pat Farrell, one of Keith's superintendents whom he treated similarly, writes in a letter dated January 15, 1987:

> The other day as Betty and I were vacationing in Hawaii and reminiscing about our past and present, your name came up as you were very important to us in our forming years. I still drive around Menlo Park, Palo Alto, Mountain View and see the good and the not so good buildings that we erected. Those were the fun, carefree years. Today life is so much more complicated. Mainly, because we have more to worry about.
>
> The reason for this letter is to let you know how grateful I am for your generosity. Too many times we forget those who helped us along the way and do not acknowledge it. You gave us the down payment on our first home ($2,500.00) on Wilkie Way, Palo Alto, and numerous bonuses and the experience to build many complicated buildings. These experiences I have put to good use and made a very comfortable living...
>
> Sincerely,
> Patrick Farrell

Throughout the years Keith would hire skilled designers, architects, and builders who filled important roles in helping him bring his ideas to life. In fact, in the process of giving form to his first solo venture, he did not forget about the carpenter he had met on his first visit to the Coleman property. "I went over to look at it. While there I met Art Whitely, a framing journeyman, who was working for a company constructing a building on a nearby lot." Talking to Art and having seen the product of the tools he carried on his belt probably raised Keith's excitement as he proceeded. "I hired Art Whitely. He was a great superintendent and a great builder."

With these two craftsman, Keith started building multiple units, and a new American success story began. "Because of that experience and the energy and the excitement of it, I left the life insurance business and went into construction and land development. It wasn't planned, but it eventually became part of my program. It seemed like it was a better investment of time and talents."

A number of determinants converged, catapulting Keith with a stick of dynamite in hand to the top of a gold mine: California's exploding growth, her burgeoning industry and prolific job creation, the vast amounts of open space available, and a little luck.

In Keith's case it was not "dumb" luck. There was nothing dumb about it or about him. Lacking a college degree and straight A grades, one might expect him to dismiss book learning in favor of street smarts. Not so. He is a man who quotes favorite authors from memory, grasps political nuances, and engages the "best and the brightest" in the world and the Church in stimulating conversations. He becomes a learned man through his efforts. He reads voraciously. It is said he writes a book every time he reads one. When he lends a book that he has found stimulating to a friend, the recipient often notes that Keith's commentary written in the margins is as good as, if not better than, the text and often more thought provoking. His questions to the author scrolled on the pages, his encrypted dictionary definition of words whose meanings were either unclear or unfamiliar to him, his underlining, his summaries, and his references to other works evidence his simple dictum, "There is no use reading unless I understand it." A book lost containing his musings cannot be replaced.

Always engaged in learning, Keith, in 1970, after many of his notable commercial and service successes, inquired into completing his law degree, not so he could hang a diploma on the wall but because he is a student, someone who loves discovery, and completing his law degree appeared to be one way to nourish those yearnings.

Learning for him, however, does not happen only in the ivy halls of academia. Learning for Keith happens by paying attention to life, and in this learning he has a Ph.D. in street smarts. Possessing both academic and life learning, he is unstoppable. Stan Mattson's observation is correct. "When he decided to do something, it might take him awhile, but he got it done."

His Carnegie-like rise to success sounds so simple when Keith tells the story that one not in the know might default to luck for an explanation. "I just thought I could provide a habitat for the nomads that were coming from the East. I liked to build. I think it's fundamental to our society. I went into apartments and office buildings rather than single family homes. With apartments and offices if the builder can't sell them, he can always rent them out. If he builds homes and can't sell them during a lean period, they sit vacant while he pays property taxes and mortgage payments. The income renting a home produces comes with problems. Too many times renters ruin the home. So after the builder surmounts the ordeal of repossession, he has to refurbish the whole thing.

On the other hand, it was an easy write off to build apartments and office buildings. I built, then sold them, and built some more to take care of my income tax problems."

Keith's statements sound as if he had carefully thought through his move into construction. He indicates differently. "What did I think about these things? I didn't. I fell into it, and I enjoyed it. It gave me lots of freedom and opportunities."

Roger Evans, who worked in the Building Department of Salt Lake City, may have singled out the reason Keith was so drawn to land development when he told him, "Most people think you should be called Mr. Spic & Span or Mr. Clean because you're such a dapper dresser, but those of us who know you think you should be called Mr. Dirt." Keith loves digging, dumping, and distributing dirt. Supervising the massive excavation equipment he leases, he climbs up the tractor to the cab and moves the operator over so he can take the controls. When missing, he can usually be found on the road in search of dirt laden semi-trucks, trying to get the driver to dump the dirt at or move the dirt from his construction site.

Keith largely passed on the opportunity to construct residential homes because of the burdens he had endured building the spec on Parrot Drive. He says, "It's easier to build a city than a home for a woman!" One of his admired mentors, Claude Lindsay, did not pass on home construction. Claude, having started in the San Francisco Bay area during World War II, had made his reputation and earned his resources as a prolific, quality home builder. Viewing any one of his residential subdivisions summons the comment "What a beautiful place!" Keith, like many others, applauds and is quick to mention qualities synonymous with Claude Lindsay's building methods. "His constructions were always high quality, well-built, and appealing."

One building venture particularly attracted Keith's attention. Claude had developed Linfield Oaks, an attractive residential subdivision in Menlo Park. In 1965 Keith purchased from Claude a lot on Willow Road in this development and built a forty-six unit luxury apartment house which he named the Caroline Apartments. His sister LaVon and her husband Charles lived there as resident managers and grew very attached to their luxurious surroundings. When Keith, never at home in a management role, reluctantly sold this premier apartment house which necessitated LaVon's moving, she was very sad. Reacting to his sister's unhappiness, Keith deeded one of the elegant, exclusive condominium units in another one of his constructions, the Menlo Towers high-rise, to her.

The number of constructions, the costs of construction, the variety of construction, which Keith built for his own account is impressive if not astonishing. His developments are found in the Western states of California, Utah, Idaho, and Arizona. A recently updated general experience resume with a beginning date of 1956 extending into 2003 offers some data. It lists 3000 apartment units ranging from four-plexes to a 196 unit apartment house, eighteen office buildings, twenty-five houses, three commercial buildings, thirteen ministorage constructions, two high-rises, two motels, four shopping centers, 368 lots in two subdivisions, two office building purchases, an office building conversion, three condominium ventures, one apartment house to condominium conversion, a funeral home, a crematorium, 2190 crypts, 1100 niches, and three resort complexes.

Exhaustive as this listing may seem, especially when one absorbs the amount of work and effort represented, not every project appears on this referenced inventory. Keith's unreported enterprises include a 363 apartment condominium conversion in Salt Lake, the Twin Palms Miniature Golf Course in Palo Alto which he named for the two palm trees flanking the entrance and which was a course he played more times than his eighteen hole golf course in northern Idaho, and the hillside property in Palm Springs which can only be accessed by helicopter. Keith divulges his affection for the Palm Springs property when he describes it as "the only place where lizards carry umbrellas."

The total actual cost of construction is over one hundred million dollars, and that, too, is short by several million dollars. Missing data can be partially explained by Keith's very un-Harvard-like business style. A reluctant manager who was more interested in the experience than in tracking his accomplishments, his exposure, or his risks, Keith bought, built, and sold. Even on the minor matter of automobile purchases and sales, he drove office personnel and insurance agents crazy. Finally, he opted for a suggested general liability policy to solve the nuisance problem for himself and his employees.

Keith's decidedly different business style caught the notice of a Stanford business student in pursuit of an advanced degree. Research for his paper included a forty-five minute interview with Keith. He went away informed and intrigued by how a man so free wielding could garner such success. A read of that analysis would be fascinating and probably would conclude that Keith never ignored the risks of doing business in such a free way but considered other more traditional programs B O R I N G.

Attractive as it may sound to any number of business executives, sitting back in a comfortable chair clipping coupons never enticed him. Seizing an amazing adventure interested Keith, and unquestionably his adventures all had the MADE IN THE

USA FOR KEITH E. GARNER tag attached.

Keith's preferences expressed in the following statement make even the time frame in which these adventures happened look custom ordered. "I'm just grateful I was born after horses and before computers."

He did not completely escape either riding horses or using computers. Working for his brother-in-law on his farm in Syracuse, a young Keith, mounted bareback on a horse galloping back to the barn of its own will, found himself catapulted through the air after the horse stopped unexpectedly and suddenly. Luckily landing in an irrigation canal, he was only bruised and soaked. Keith never acquired a liking for horses employed in work or recreation. He was glad he had been born when transportation meant jumping into a car instead of onto a horse.

He fared much better with computers. Convinced a fax machine was a basic necessity, he purchased one and marvelled both at its ability to transmit a document and the immediacy of the process. Pleased with this new toy, he leaped again into the unknown when in 1985 he authorized Sherman F. Anderson to install a "new fangled" computer system with accounting, inventory, receivable, and other programs. He also signed up for the Internet and used it to locate people, products, information, and even to advertise his funeral home [www.garnerfuneral.com]. He obtained an e-mail address and wrote to, among others, "The O'Reilly Factor." It is uncertain he ever shared by e-mail the following joke, but he certainly got a bigger kick out of the speed of the Internet than he had out of the horse's speedy retreat.

Whether he sent it by e-mail or Pony Express to the *New York Times*, it is likely they would not have appreciated the story, but Keith the "compassionate capitalist" did and with relish shared it with others. "They tell the story of the Pope coming to Washington to visit with President George W. Bush. The President takes the Pope out on the presidential yacht *Sequoia* for a sail on the Potomac. A wind comes up and blows the Pope's miter off his head and into the water. Secret Service agents are aghast but without means to retrieve the Pope's hat. President Bush reassures them, 'Don't worry; I'll take care of it.' So the President lowers himself over the side, walks out to the hat, picks it up, walks back, and gives it to the Pope. The next day the *New York Times* headline reads **Bush Can't Swim**."

Thirty years before and even to this day with computers enhancing his office, Keith measures his achievements by applying the basic principles of successful salesmanship: number of customers, volume, and premium. Almost immediately in his insurance career, he had realized that the value was not in the volume but in the premium. He found the premium in land development came not only in cash but also in the interesting personalities with whom he dealt and in the seasoning experiences which seemed to materialize whenever he walked around the corner.

On the corner of Valparaiso and University Avenue in Menlo Park stands Menlo Towers. The anecdotes told of Keith acquiring the land, obtaining the permits and the financing, starting construction, and selling the individual units incident to the construction of the high-rise is the narrative with some variations of his building career.

His wonder at how all the elements came together is palpable to his listeners as he tells this story which spans ten years. "I bought this property before I went to Hong Kong as a mission president. Five or six single family homes stood on the property; I've forgotten exactly how many. I bought the homes with the intention that I would eventually put a high-rise there. It was a gamble, but I held the property for the three years that I was in Asia. When I returned, I had Arnold Fluckiger, A.I.A., design a nine-story condominium high-rise for that corner. He did a great job. I remember I had to have the building designed leaving out one lot on Valparaiso since the owners had lived there for many years and didn't want to sell."

Under **BUSINESS & FINANCE**, one of the Bay area papers ran a picture of the proposed construction titled **Menlo's first high-riser**. "This is a model of the proposed 10-story [nine-story] garden apartment building Encinal Park Inc. wants to build on an acre and a half lot at Valparaiso Avenue and University Drive in Menlo Park."

Keith had named one of his first apartment complexes, a forty-five unit built on Encinal Avenue and San Antonio Street in Menlo Park, Encinal Park Apartments. He liked the name, derived from combining Encinal Avenue and Menlo Park, so much he chose it for his construction company. Therefore, Encinal Park, Inc. appeared in the newspapers and on the city records, chronicling Keith's climb up nine stories as well as his other Garner projects.

Keith's audacity, evident to many in his high-rise proposal, brought some strenuous opponents to the planning meeting. Keith recognized that getting the necessary approvals might be an uphill battle, and it was very difficult. "The height restriction in Menlo Park, I think, was forty feet, and my proposed building stood over twice that high. There was no other building in Menlo Park that was over forty feet, and here I was going to put in a nine-story."

How he secured approval from the city still is a question asked by uncomplaining Menlo Park residents, to say nothing of the more than one curious California businessman, including Taylor's son Richard Peery, who wanted to know how Keith ever managed to pull it off. No other building in Menlo Park, an upscale community distinguished by its farsighted planning, rises so far up into the sky. Keith is the only person who can claim to have accomplished that feat. The funny part is that he did not attend the crucial meeting with the mayor and city council, so his recollections are not based on personal knowledge. "Luckily it passed the planning commission and city council primarily because it was right across the street from Menlo College and not Atherton per se" is his explanation. That definitely was a factor; however, his representatives at the meeting witnessed the unusual activities and were eager to relay the good news to him.

The mayor of Menlo Park, William Lawson, Keith portrays as "a salty good guy." He turned out to be the key player in the episode. "At one of the meetings, those that were opposed to my building going up, several were opposed to it, accused the mayor of making a side agreement with me or inferred that I'd influenced him in some underhanded way. He listened to that for awhile, and I heard that he finally said, 'I was opposed to this building, but now I'm in favor of it.' And they approved it."

Keith emphasizes, "I wasn't there." Leo Handley, writer for the *Tribune*, was and filed the following story which appeared on December 18, 1968, in the *Redwood City Tribune* under the headline

Tentative Plan Approved: Critics Can't Halt High Rise Approval

In the face of bitter criticism from several Menlo Park residents the City Council Tuesday night approved tentative plans of a high rise apartment dwelling and voted 3-1 to introduce the necessary ordinance amendments.

Second reading and possible approval of the amendment was set for the council's Jan. 14 meeting.

The proposed nine-story apartment structure, which would be the first high rise dwelling in the city and one of the highest on the Peninsula, would be built at the corner of Valparaiso and University Avenue by Encinal Park, Inc. of Menlo Park.

Apartments in the 60-unit dwelling would rent from $500 to $1,500 per month, depending on the number of bedrooms and amenities. Cost of the structure has been estimated at up to $3 million.

About 40 persons were in the council chamber, although some came to hear other matters on the long agenda.

William D. Wagstaff, 1055 Valparaiso, charged the high rise plan was proposed by certain city pressure groups and interests for their own profit and not necessarily for the best interest of the community.

Mayor William R. Lawson demanded to know what special interest Wagstaff was alluding to and said, "I don't appreciate your attitude.

"I have heard more innuendoes tonight than I have in 16 years on the council. You are biased and prejudiced and the only objective person to you is someone who agrees with you. Now will you please sit down."

Several other persons said they questioned whether a high rise apartment and the others that probably would follow on the precedent would be contrary to the best interests of Menlo Park as they saw them.

William H. Kennedy, 847 Valparaiso, declared the matter
to be a simple decision.

"The people in Menlo Park do not want high rise -- any
more than they do in Atherton or in Carmel. We can prove it
to you if you give us time."

Wagstaff, during a less controversial part of his presentation, asked for a council delay on its decision until after the
first of the year. He said many people could not attend the
meeting because of Christmas shopping, illness and other obli-
gations.

Councilman Donald Horstkorta, the lone dissenting councilman, termed the decision one "of paramount significance"
and questioned whether the council should not defer a decision
to further study by the planning staff.

Mayor Lawson said the population of the city is likely to
double by 1990 and high rise developments are the only way to
conserve the land "and some of the amenities" and not become
another sprawling Los Angeles with the attendant problems.

Councilman Michael Balangie was in the hospital."

At the council's January 14th meeting the Amendment passed by a margin
of 4-1.

Having jumped such a giant initial hurdle, Keith's challenges were not all
behind him. On Monday, January 11, 1971, two years later and following months
that saw new ordinances enacted and building plans drawn, finalized, and approved,
Keith, confident he would secure financing, went ahead and began clearing the houses
off the land. Obtaining financing required considerable skill and also happened over a
period of many months. Impatient with the slowness of the process, Keith moved
ahead at his always more accelerated pace. "I got a bid on taking the dirt out for the
basement and then a bid for how much it would cost to fill it up again in the event I
was unable to get financing."

Keith identifies one of the impediments to his securing funds. "I contacted
Fox & Carskaddon and Coldwell Banker, reputable real estate firms in the area, about
the reality of selling the condominiums. Both said it wouldn't work and tried to dis-
courage me from building it. The banks were reluctant when they heard that several
of the large brokerage houses wouldn't even consider selling the units for me."

Keith's journal entries describe his perseverance and his progress. Wednesday,
May 26, 1971: "Actually started digging on high rise; no final decision on financing 'til
Friday, June 4." Tuesday, July 27, 1971: "Worked on hi rise financing; rather close."
Thursday, July 29, 1971: "Interim loan $3,000,000 on hi rise received today."

Keith describes his financing roller coaster ride. "I had a verbal commitment.

Then I didn't have a commitment because I didn't have it in writing. I'm not sure I even had it. I went ahead and started the building. The financing came. It wasn't enough, and so the bank gave me more money than I'd asked for originally."

On Friday, July 30, 1971, a few days after the construction loan was funded, Keith writes, "Steel strike pending; railroads on strike." Keith walked by his construction sites and visited with the men carrying strike signs. It was just another obstacle he conquered, and there had been many.

What was he thinking during these challenging days? Unable to acquire all the lots desired, he built around the unavailable lot. Aware that his idea did not conform with city specifications, he got the necessary approvals to go ahead. Without financing in hand, he tore down the existing homes and excavated the underground parking garage. Unsuccessful in convincing well-known real estate brokers to sell the units, he found other marketers. Keith reveals his mind set in an entry jotted down on March 29, 1971. "Working now on 94 unit in Cupertino, office building at 505 Hamilton Road, Palo Alto, still debating 9 story High Rise in Menlo Park. It is difficult to know which way on the condominium. Sincerely hope the Lord guides me. It's vital; much good can come from it."

Nearly a year after he began clearing the property, Wednesday, November 24, 1971, a milestone was reached. "Finished pouring 1st floor on Menlo Towers."

Though reaching this point had been labor intensive, Keith's joyful creativity continued to flow as he watched the building inch toward the sky. Having already met the city's requirement for parking spaces, he settled on an innovative idea attractive to buyers because of the convenience offered. Car lifts installed in the underground parking garage made it possible for two cars to use one car space.

He selected eminently qualified interior designer Frances Badger to recommend the colors, the wallpaper, the lobby decorations, the hall lighting, and the carpeting for the common areas. Characterizing Frances' know-how, Keith says, "She was great at interior design. I had already used her volunteer services at the Menlo Park chapel, and she had done a great job. She had also decorated many of my apartment houses for me, especially all the ones where I wanted some expertise. I enjoyed working with her." Because Frances' contribution to the Menlo Towers was as much a part of the structure as any of the fundamental features, the residents, some who had lived there from the beginning, wondered decades after its completion what Frances would think of the condominium board replacing her verdant greens with neutral hues.

Intrigued by the design and amenities some well-known potential purchasers made inquiries. Willie Mays, the San Francisco Giants baseball legend, showed an interest, but his desire to have two units combined into one nixed the deal. Another star athlete Frankie Albert, the great Stanford and San Francisco 49ers' quarterback, bought a unit. The prominent owners, at least those who were football fans, enjoyed bragging about their illustrious neighbor.

Keith moved in too. During March and April 1974 prior to his departure in

December for his Temple Square assignment in Utah, he moved his family from 955 Westridge, Portola Valley, to the penthouse suite where they resided for a few months.

Though the move may have been precipitated by his really having "never been satisfied with the home in Portola Valley," he had expressed even stronger feelings about the first home they lived in upon his return from Asia in 1968. "The Atherton rental was a mansion, but I would have sooner had a small, tiny house with a view than this palace hidden away in the trees with fences and gates and hibernation in it."

He did not face that difficulty atop the Menlo Towers. He had a spectacular 360 degree view of Menlo Park, Atherton, Palo Alto, and Redwood City. He could turn one way and rest his eyes on the signature Hoover Tower and the Stanford University campus. He could turn another way and gaze in the direction of Half Moon Bay on the ocean side. In fact, he could turn in any direction and see tree-lined streets, beautiful foliage, elegant gardens, making Menlo Park the ideal location for *Sunset* magazine's headquarters.

Withdrawing from this magnificent vantage point when exiting the penthouse, he stepped into an elevator for the nine-story descent to the parking garage. The elevator normally stopped on its way down to collect other residents. The good morning's Keith exchanged were pleasant, but with a few, Keith felt like a sitting duck being pelted with recommendations for improvements. He didn't really mind the suggestions; rather, it was the inescapable confinement which made him feel uncomfortable.

When these bothersome encounters happened, Keith thought of the story told about the acclaimed architect Frank Lloyd Wright and was tempted to mimic the words reputed to have been uttered by him. "An owner of one of the untraditional, totally unique homes he designed confronted him complaining about the roof leaking onto his grand piano. Wright simply told him without hesitation or apology 'Move the piano.'"

Keith might say he would have been more content with his living arrangements in the penthouse if a private elevator had been available for his exclusive use, but judging from the way he runs his office, he would not have meant it. His office door is rarely closed. Unlike other prosperous businessmen, Mr. Garner is readily accessible. He rarely takes advantage of the choices available for guarding his privacy: unlisted phone numbers, directions to secretaries to screen his calls, an office secured like Fort Knox, or a scheduler to handle his appointments. He is his own private secretary.

The uniqueness of his management style surprises most of his employees. Keith fully and confidently allows his employees the freedom to perform their jobs without interference. For example, Fred and Joan Latu, resident managers of Menlo Terrace Apartments in California, as part of their duties collect and send the rent checks and the invoices for maintenance and repairs to Mr. Garner's office in Utah for deposit and payment. They note that other than observing that the FedEx letter they send to him once a month has arrived, Keith never voices any concern. Having not heard from him for a while, Joan will sometimes call to check in. Keith merely responds to her with "If you don't see me, you know everything is going well." Without having to do something to attract his notice in a negative way, Joan must wonder what it will take to get his bright smiling face there for a visit. In fact, she and Fred volunteered to transport to Salt Lake from Yerba Buena Gardens in San Francisco four large Robinson Alexander iron landscaping pots that Keith had purchased for placement at the Garner Funeral Home so they could see him in person.

Donna Brown, retired manager of Stoneridge Country Club, gives some observations about working for Keith Garner. She writes:

> "The first time I met Keith was quite awhile after I began working for him in Blanchard, Idaho. My immediate supervisor was the company manager, and Keith was in Utah; I had spoken with him briefly by phone, but having not met him in person, I formed a visual image of the man.
>
> He finally came to Idaho to visit the project site, and I was able to only spend a few minutes with him at that time and was very surprised by his mild nature and kind spirit. Because of employers I had known before, I expected a person who would come into the office, evaluate the efficiency of the operation, make critical suggestions, and possibly discuss improvements that were needed. As I learned then and grew to know through the years, this was not Keith. He became much more than a 'boss.'
>
> Keith Garner is a supportive, affirming good friend. He looks for the potential in a person and takes an active role in helping him/her to a point of achieving that potential. Many times during my years of working for him, I saw Keith help others strive, be it physical, emotional, spiritual, or financial, toward a goal. He has a desire to promote good character traits in others, putting them in a position of gaining experience and knowledge.
>
> I appreciate the opportunity to have worked with him and greatly respect his kind nature and the humble generosity of his spirit, willing to share his gained wisdom with each encounter. I count Keith Garner as a very dear friend and am blessed to have spent a few years working with him."

Donna echoes many employees' sentiments. He is the boss, but there is something in his nature that makes him much more; he is a mentor, a friend.

The strength and weakness of his life-affirming administrative style is a seem-ingly inborn directive that makes his forgiving seven times seventy an imperative for how he lives his life and conducts his business. On too many occasions for his office staff's liking, Mr. Garner has, even at his own peril, given second chance after second chance to the "undeserving," those whose dishonesty, disservice, and disdain were insufferable. Even the disassociation came not at Mr. Garner's hands, but as they cre-ated circumstances where to offer the 491st chance passed wisdom and even Keith's compassionate character.

Sometimes he finds himself in the shoes of the Arab merchant in the story reportedly told by Elder B. H. Roberts. Keith tells it this way. "A merchant was out in the desert with his camel. As they traveled, the scorching sun shone down on them until it was excruciatingly uncomfortable. The merchant pitched his tent. Desiring to give the poor camel some relief from the heat, he allowed the camel to put his nose in the tent door. The camel looked around, liked what he saw, lumbered into the tent, and planted his carcass. Finding the tent only big enough for the camel, the mer-chant, dripping in sweat and very aware of his mistake, found himself outside looking inside."

In analogous disconcerting situations, Keith relates with the merchant and may relate with the sentiments of the older lady in this joke he also tells. "An elderly lady trying to cross the street stepped off the curb. A driver, traveling at excessive speed, careened around the corner, almost hitting her. She jumped out of the way and back onto the sidewalk. The reckless driver screamed, 'Watch where you're going!' She yelled, 'Are you coming back?'"

In Keith's experience some camels tried to muscle him aside and reckless drivers always came back. Nevertheless, yelling is not really part of Keith's leadership methodology. That is not to say that he never raises his voice. His anger even erupts. In more than one setting, his temper has been set off. When Keith was President Garner, president of the Southern Far East Mission, one of his missionaries reports, "President Garner was very kind, but he could take the skin off too when necessary." Another observer recounts having seen him seated in the front row of the Delta Center watching a Utah Jazz game "politely" offer his spectacles to the referee.

Of course, in some situations when tempers normally vent, Keith's remains in check. Stephen J. Swift, now a judge in the U.S. Tax Court in Washington, D.C., tells his story. "On an Aaronic Priesthood trip to Disneyland for which Bishop Garner paid, I was flirting with some girls; there's a pattern here. I got back too late to the rental cars that we had. Because of that we rushed to the Los Angeles airport but missed the plane. Keith took it all in stride without any demonstration of anger or impatience in contrast to a couple of other leaders. I've always appreciated that."

Keith's impatience manifests itself according to the qualifications of the offending party. A teenage boy was granted a reprieve whereas a capable, trusted employee was not.

Duane A. Lee relates, "We had two drawers filled with thirty or more check books. Keith would come in and say, 'How much money is in such and such account?' I'd grab that check book, look, and tell him the balance. I remember on a couple of occasions he'd say, 'That isn't right!' He would know if I was right or not just off the top of his head. I'd look again, and sure enough I'd forgotten to add in a deposit or something. He told me once, 'I can keep better track in my head than you can on paper.' And he was right. I don't ever remember him being wrong. He was just amazing; in his head he could keep track of thirty check books and know within a few dollars what was in each one."

Even though Duane found him a little intimidating, he liked working for Keith. He tells why. "He didn't expect anything of others that he did not expect of himself. He set high standards for himself, even though I don't think he ever realized how high they were. In doing so, he made us reach deeper inside ourselves for talents we didn't even know we had."

Keith was lucky enough to find a few able associates like Duane who were loyal, honest, and smart, whom he seldom put on the spot, and who often felt his great kindness and returned the same. It can be truthfully said that it is unnecessary whatever the situation might be for him to transform, elevate, or reduce himself into something he's not. Renae Hancock, his go-the-second-mile housekeeper over several years, speaking intuitively shared, "If I had been President of the Church, Keith would have treated me no differently."

It is not just past employees who hold Keith in high regard. Jenet Mills, a secretary in his office, wrote on the card she presented to him on his 84th birthday, "Thanks for being such a great man. You are very thoughtful, giving, caring, and most of all a great joy to be around." He unobtrusively invites by an active participation in life and lives such deserved affection and respect.

Another of his unique leadership qualities, this time his practicality, is illustrated in his finding a highly adorned office less functional than one equipped with basic, utilitarian equipment namely "Orange Crate" over French Provincial, Georgian Court, Early American or British Classic.

Duane voices what he and others discovered. "I remember I walked into the offices of a company with whom we were involved, and it knocked my eyes out. I had never seen such a fancy office. I thought 'holy smokes; this is unbelievable.' After completing my task, I went back to our offices." The office to which he returned did not resemble the one he left. Duane continues, "When I first started working for Keith, we were officed in a house up on East Capital Boulevard in Salt Lake right next to his house; he had a desk in the living room. When we moved to the mausoleum, we had our offices in a little house in which the caretaker had previously lived."

He explains. "Keith has never been much on spending on big showy stuff. He essentially said, 'Give me two orange crates, and I'll run the business more efficiently than guys that spend thousands of dollars on elaborate furnishings'."

Keith bought the McIntyre Building, renovated, and sold the floors individually to businesses. That was a new concept in the Salt Lake market, maybe in other
metropolitan areas as well. Certainly he was one of the first to convert office buildings to office condominiums. For a while he had his office on the second floor overlooking Salt Lake's Main Street, but in reality he just used whatever office was available at the time. To attract buyers with more expensive tastes he added a luxurious
penthouse office suite on top of the building, featuring high ceilings, twelve foot ceiling to floor doors, and wool carpeting from Ireland. Frank Muschik, the finish carpenter who also did the work on his Chandler home, crafted exquisitely beautiful cabinets for it. His staff, though they should have known better, thought in creating this
spacious office setting that his intentions might include a permanent office space for
himself in the manner to which he should have been accustomed. Rumors that his
penthouse office suite was really going to be a bowling alley made the rounds, and
Keith, a guy who rolls strikes, would have enjoyed it more if that had been its function.

Duane adds, "I remember when we were in the McIntyre Building. He didn't
want the penthouse office that he built, the one with a beautiful view of downtown
Salt Lake. I think we finally got him to move in there, but you always felt he would be
just as happy with an orange crate as having some fancy desk somewhere. He's very
humble, nothing flashy about him. He didn't need to spend tremendous amounts of
money, money he had, to impress people."

Keith did occupy those elegant offices briefly, but he never considered making
it a permanent move, probably because he thought if he sat down in such lush accommodations for too long he would become too comfortable and lose the desire to
work. Of course, with his makeup, that would have been impossible.

Better known for investing in the structure rather than the furnishings, he
appreciates form and design, and in 1974 so did the City of Menlo Park. Arnold
Fluckiger, who did most of Keith's office buildings, reads from the plaque he was
given, "City of Menlo Park presents to Arnold B. Fluckiger a design award for professional administrative architecture, 800 Oak Grove Avenue, 1974." It is signed by
Mayor Ira A. Bonde who awarded the prize at a city ceremony.

At the award-winning Oak Grove Office Building, Keith, following his pattern, put his offices in the new building until it sold. George Ressel and Betty
Walpole worked there. "George, my father-in-law," he says, "supervised the managers
and collected the rents at the various apartments, motels, and ministorages. He had
previously worked as my bookkeeper. He was fast, dedicated, busy all the time,
the epitome of the perfect office manager. During this period he collected the rents,
and then he delivered them to our secretary Betty Walpole."

Betty enjoyed George's coming into the office carrying his collections under
his arm and with a friendly smile on his face. The managers and renters also enjoyed
his coming. In fact, anyone who knew him would have recommended him highly as a
par excellent public relations representative. Keith remembers, "He enjoyed the

work. I never heard him complain about anything. I never heard anything but positive statements come out of his mouth."

Keith also passed out deserved compliments when he would tell Betty what a wonderful job she was doing. "She was a great gal." Eugene L. Kimball, Keith's brother-in-law, a certified public accountant, the man in whose hands he left his business for the three years he was in Asia, and with whom Keith joint ventured many projects when he returned, agreed and would often say to her, "Betty, you're a good girl," to which she would reply, "But there's no demand."

Gene Kimball is a man of few words, but the few words he used to describe Betty and the words he uses to define Keith are sufficient. "He's the best money man I ever saw." Keith's concise response was, "He's the best CPA I've ever known."

Pacific Union Bank leased the bottom floor at Oak Grove and eventually purchased the building in which he had his offices. Notwithstanding, Keith never moved very far away from bankers. Most of his office buildings had a bank on the bottom floor. Although he did not build the First Security Bank Building on Fourth South in Salt Lake, he did so much business with the bank during those years that the branch manager Marlin Andrus set up an "office" for him comprised of a desk, telephone, and nameplate. With bankers Ed O'Brien, Gil Haynes, Rhees Ririe, Glen Mowry, Wayne Hintze, Sterling Harris, Curtis Harris, Stephanie Wallace, Lamont Tingey, and many others, Keith found associations full of warmth. In an unmatched and particularly unforgettable act of kindness, Kathy Beilfus, the loan officer at West One Bank, made a successful attempt to secure for Keith a needed signature on a loan document by talking her way onto an already boarded and departing plane in order to obtain it.

Keith, in an unscheduled visit during 2000 to Union Bank of California in Palo Alto, dropped by to visit his banker friend Vice-President and Manager Dee Tolles. Their conversation started when Keith, walking into the bank and spotting Dee in his office surrounded by men in suits and ties, directed, "Clear the decks!" Dee said, "It's King Kong." The men circling his desk responded, "We're out of here."

Dee, smiling at his unexpected visitor, said, "Here comes trouble. Garner, you turkey, where have you been? Give me a big hug, you rascal. You get younger every day."

Keith announced, "I'm in my eighties."

Dee countered, "You'll always be in your forties. I am just delighted to see you looking so well and without any Jack Daniels," and then inquired, "You still running the Mormon Church?"

Addressing the bank employees and customers, he said, "This is one of the great guys of this area. We go back over thirty years. I started listing some of the projects we worked on. Then I started thinking about it. Gosh, we did a lot of stuff--the bank building, the high-rise, the first ministorage ever done."

Keith credits his partner Mitch Hunt with the germination of the ministorage idea. "Mitch, knowing how possessive we are, brought the ministorages from Texas.

Americans are pack rats; almost everybody is. They don't want to throw anything away. The government, whether federal, state, or local, was requiring more paper work and more taxes. People weren't going to have enough storage in their offices to take care of all that was required, so ministorage was the logical program to adopt."

Dee shared with Keith his version of the story. "You went to San Antonio, met a Jewish guy by the name of Robinowitz who'd built a mini down there. You came back with this cockamamie story of mini warehouses. I didn't know a mini warehouse from a toad pole."

Interjecting, Keith volunteered, "Before I came to see you, I had already bought four pieces of property to use for ministorages."

Dee continued, "No bank had ever financed this. I waltzed into the loan committee and told them about this crazy Mormon guy Garner, who didn't know his left foot from his right elbow, who wants to build mini warehouses. They said, 'What's that?' I said, 'It doesn't matter. His maxim is we don't pay more than a dollar a foot for land on the freeway.' That was your rule, the best rule anybody ever had. I tell everyone, and they laugh at me. Now it's gone to thirty or forty to fifty dollars a foot on the freeway."

Listeners taking in Mr. Tolles next tale would have had a reason to laugh in disbelief. Dee proceeded in his dramatic, exaggerated, entertaining way. "We would get in that room and yell and scream and carry on. Keith was as emotional as I was or worse. You know, we'd argue over interest rates. Oh, I mean it was awful. It was a love/hate relationship for thirty years. When we did that high-rise, it got really tough. It took a long time and was really heavy construction. It was the biggest building. It took forever to get his entitlements. It turned out to be the best building he ever did; of all the millions he's made, that was by far the best one that he ever did."

Dee turning his attention to another Garner building unequivocally stated, "The prettiest building in Menlo Park is still your old office building. No question about it. It is absolutely gorgeous. The landscaping is terrific the way you did it, and the bank has kept it up. You just did a really, really great job."

As Keith and Dee strolled arm and arm towards the front door, Dee told onlookers, "All the beautiful buildings in Menlo Park Mr. Garner built, and we financed. And it went on from 1970 until…"

Keith interrupted, "We sure tell a story, don't we? It isn't scripture, but it's good!"

Gene Kimball tells about Dee's calling him about an overdraft and suggesting, "First the deeeee-posits and then the checks," and then asking, "Why don't you guys ever have any cash?" To which Gene answered, "You supply the cash, Keith builds beautiful things, and then he returns your cash with interest."

The names Keith selected for those "beautiful things" he built in California evoke images of inviting lodgings. Some refer to the cruise liner on which he first sailed to Hawaii; others reflect the lush environs of northern California; and still others were created out of pure whimsy: Sea Breeze, Shadow Pines, Toko-Ri, Park Lane, The Manor, Coleman Arms, Woodland, Briarwood Manor, College, Arbor, Laurel Grove, Manhattan, Tiki Inn, and Glass Slipper Motel.

The Glass Slipper's design was as whimsical as its name. "I put a roof on it with towers so it looks like a glass slipper." He did not lapse into fancy for long. Behind the motel he added a number of apartment units. "I tied those right into the Glass Slipper so that people if they wanted to come stay longer my manager could put them in an apartment. I worked it both ways."

On the same visit to Menlo Park which had included his visit with Dee Tolles, Keith stayed the night in another motel he had built, the Tiki Inn, now renamed the Stanford Inn, located adjacent to Stanford University. Though he usually chose to stay in San Francisco at the Hyatt Regency, he exclaimed the next morning, "This is as lovely as any hotel I've ever stayed in. Of course, that's why they charged me $150 a night."

No doubt Keith must have wished he could have relaxed in a room at the Tiki Inn or the Glass Slipper after a day's work in Park City, Utah; Blanchard, Idaho; or Pinetop, Arizona. His resort property locations thrust him back into a bygone era.

In Park City, Utah, an old mining town, Keith purchased 175 acres of land. He brought the past to life, combining historical notions with modern amenities. Originally designed to augment university off-campus retreats, Prospector Square housed a conference center with a 330 seat auditorium/theater and twelve lecture/meeting rooms. In addition to its proximity to Park City Ski Resort, golf courses, and biking trails, the athletic club that he constructed with four racquetball courts, a swimming pool, basketball court, tennis courts, a barbecue pit, and game area gave visitors a wide variety of recreational on-site offerings. He also built 323 units: hotel rooms, studio/kitchenettes, and three bedroom condominiums, to which owners/guests could retire.

Sidewinder Drive led to Prospector Park subdivision, where Keith gave buyers their choice of Victorian house plans named for U.S. presidents Theodore Roosevelt, James A. Garfield, William Henry Harrison, and Ulysses S. Grant. These period homes lined streets named Buffalo Bill, Wyatt Earp, Doc Holliday, Butch Cassidy, Belle Starr, Annie Oakley, and Cochise.

Keith left little out. When he returned in 2003, he moseyed on over to the Grub Steak Restaurant, a facility he built in 1976. Not much had changed. Encircled by artistic touches of prairie flowers, wagon wheels, bridles, spurs, pikes, lassos, wanted posters, and mural walls of dance hall girls kicking up their heels, cowboys on horseback, and miners prospecting for gold, he and probably every other patron must have looked to the door expecting Harry Alonzo Longabaugh [The Sundance Kid] or one of his compadres to enter.

Leaving the Old West, Keith took the day's drive from Park City to northern Idaho, stopping in Blanchard, Idaho, a small community between Spokane and Coeur d'Alene settled by French trappers. In 1978 Keith had purchased 1400 acres including Lake Sans Souci and become an absentee owner, a circumstance he has never recommended. The translation of *sans souci* (carefree) set the mood Keith tried to create. Duplicating many of the design features of Prospector Square, he built 114 condominium units, an administration building with a small theater, and an athletic center with a swimming pool, exercise room, and restaurant. Later he added Carefree on the Green Restaurant, an expanded pro shop, and snack bar serving in addition to other fare Par Three Omelettes, Hole in One Muffins, Bogey Burgers, and Eighteenth Hole Sandwiches. He constructed a 50' X 56' recreation building with an exercise/weight room, Par-Tee Golf featuring the famed golf courses Pebble Beach, Doral, Saint Andrews, and Coeur d'Alene Resort, a multi-purpose center with pool table, and a glass enclosed 76' X 50' swimming pool, deck and whirlpool covered by a retractable roof. He later added three luxuriously appointed four-plex units and a tennis court.

He formed the 202 platted lots comprising the Lake Sans Souci Subdivision into Lake Sans Souci Property Owners' Association and built an executive home on the seventeenth green. He created a private water and sewer system, consisting of a 330,000 gallon holding tank, two wells pumping 750 gallons per minute, and a sewer treatment plant.

The drawing card of his Stoneridge development was, of course, his eighteen hole golf course written up in a *Journal of Business* "Special Report" dated April 22, 1999, entitled **Top Golf Courses of the Inland Northwest.** Stoneridge Country Club headed the list. Keith loved surveying his property while buzzing around in a golf cart. In fact, one might say it became his preferred means of transportation. Unfortunately, Keith played his course no more than a half a dozen times over a ten year period. Whether he mastered the eighteen holes at Stoneridge is a matter for speculation, but he made an impressive showing at the Eaglewood Course in Bountiful, Utah, on one of his golf outings with his brother-in-law Gene. From out of the rough, from below the green, and without a view of the cup, Keith, also known as Tom Watson, made a miracle shot. Walking up to the putting green, he wondered where his ball had landed. In amazement Gene pointed to the hole.

Keith indulged in another absentee-owner acquisition when he bought eight acres in the White Mountains of Arizona. Having worked at the roundhouse in Sparks, Nevada, as a teenager, Keith had become familiar with the railroad term. So when he acquired a fledgling timeshare project named Roundhouse Resort with an existing twenty-four unit hotel, restaurant, and sales office in the town of Pinetop, he saw the picture. He incorporated both the train theme and the Indian motifs from the nearby reservation into the sports center he constructed. He sweetened the available amenities with a large indoor pool, whirlpool spa, complete exercise room, racquetball and basketball court, and multipurpose room featuring a ping pong/pool table. He also built three buildings, two with twelve units and one with eight units.

The rough and tumble of the settling of the West presented itself in an unexpected way in the 1980s at Roundhouse Resort. "I always tell everybody I faced down a guy with a gun for Keith," reports Duane Lee, Keith's resort manager. Apparently a disgruntled timeshare purchaser displaying a derogatory sign pulled up to the resort entrance blocking traffic. Duane asked him to leave. The fellow informed him that he was armed, reached under the seat, and pulled out a hand gun. Duane withdrew and called Keith. Keith gave his shaken manager a solution upon which he acted, thereby restoring calm to the usually peaceful setting.

No one ever saw Keith rest by the roaring fireplace in the lobby and enjoy the surroundings except to engage in his favorite relaxation technique, talking business in new innovative ways or sharing doctrinal interplay on the Book of Mormon. He and his friend Julian Smith, a salesman for *Encyclopedia Britannica*, spent one evening seated comfortably looking up admiringly at the large display pictures of Indian chiefs which Julian had provided for exhibit on the second floor inside balcony and visiting about these latter-day descendants of the Book of Mormon Lamanite nation.

Although Keith cannot claim to be nineteenth century gold miner George Hearst, trapper Jim Bridger, cowboy Wild Bill Hickock, or railroad man Leland Stanford, he approached land development with the same spirit of adventure, and he broke new ground with the same free spirit.

Keith branched out into several entrepreneurial investments, including, but not limited to, body fat measurement machines, perfume dispensing vending machines, multi-functional screw drivers, courier services, knock off perfumes, and long distance telephone service from Las Vegas hotel rooms. Also Keith, joined in this investment by Gene Kimball and others, was one of the money men behind Kieth Merrill's 1974 movie *Great American Cowboy*. Though not a rousing moneymaker, the feature documentary narrated by Joel McCrea won the Oscar at the Academy Awards. In truth, most of these escapades ended up being experiences rather than profitable ventures.

Children, dreaming of what they'll be when they grow up, used to skip rope chanting "Tinker, tailor, cowboy, sailor, doctor, lawyer, Indian chief." Sometimes it seems that Keith never made a choice, or rather chose to keep all the innocence and adventure granted to a child in front of him. Having pursued or invested in almost the entire gamut of professions when he moved into his offices on South Temple in 1989, it appeared at this late date in his life that he might have to return to school to become a doctor. He had purchased the one-story office space from a doctor who had used it for his offices. Keith gutted the interior and turned the small medical cubicles into several rooms with high ceilings--spaciousness and expansiveness being Garner trademarks. When the city informed him that his recent purchase had only been approved for use as a doctor's office, he cheerfully toyed with entering medical school.

When faced with this issue and others over the years, Keith, still disheartened by the system, might have thought his being a lawyer a useful alternative profession.

It certainly became more and more apparent to him that legal fees are simply a cost of doing business. Keith's disputes, though emotionally taxing, brought a cast of characters and a complexity of issues which made them all interesting, most surprising, and a few comical.

Keith relates one episode that borders on the absurd. "I was sitting in my office a few days ago. A process server knocked at the door and served me as a defendant in a case filed in California. It seems a young woman had been raped in an apartment I built in 1969. Apparently the intruder gained access through a window he opened in the kitchen. I built the apartment house in '69, sold it in '71, and she was raped in '89. She was claiming in '93 it was my fault because of the type of window I had installed in '69."

Another case ended in an amusing settlement conference. A business entity purchased a building from Keith. The company fell behind on the agreed payments. During the resultant foreclosure, Keith found that ten or more of the apartments were rented to personal associates of the buyer. At the conference the buyer wrote on the chalkboard what he considered the pros and cons of coming to a settlement. The first one he wrote in large letters under pros was "[His full name] loves Keith." Further details revealed the proposal gave the buyer's friends an additional twelve months rent free to vacate the premises. Malcolm Misuraca, one of Keith's California attorneys, perhaps having visions of Keith wearing cement shoes, strongly advised, "Take it." When Mal represented Keith in Utah on other matters, he had the dubious honor of being called by opposing counsel Keith's "hired gun."

Mr. Misuraca expressed his feelings on many occasions to Keith both in private and public. A significant few written in 1983 follow.

> "I would like you to know how I really feel, totally without exaggeration, about the work that I have done for you for these past almost fifteen years.
>
> First, your work has often challenged me to the limit, not because you have created problems for yourself, but because you have generated complex and very interesting business over the years. For keeping me entertained and challenged, I thank you sincerely.
>
> Second, you have never, not once, asked me to do anything of which I have had the slightest shame. I have never felt vaguely uncomfortable to ask for anything that you felt was yours, and I have never once sensed that I demanded of any of your adversaries anything that was not fair but tough. __'s caricaturization as "tough but fair" is a high compliment not only to me, but to the client who permits the lawyer that great luxury of simple justice.

Third, I have never been more cordially received, been given more concern and interest, or been better supported than by you. My trips to Salt Lake City have always begun with anticipation and pleasure, which is not a universal feeling for the people I have worked for and the places I have been. I count Salt Lake City as a place that generates each time new memories of success, accomplishment, and most of all personal satisfaction.

Finally, I want you to understand how grateful I am for you personally. A professor of mine once told me that I could count on the fingers of one hand, and probably not exhaust them, the people in my life who truly enriched it and made it possible for me to get beyond some of my own shortcomings. I am sure that, because I remember what he said, it had an effect on me, but I could not have dreamed what he really meant until the experience itself proved how wise he was. I have learned from you not only a large part of my craft, witnessing how the marketplace really works, but a spirit and formula of success through generosity that has made me a better person, whatever I am as a lawyer. For as much as I appreciate your economic support, particularly in some pretty dreadful times, I value even more what the economists would call the "unpriced goods" that have come from working for you. In my terms, these are the priceless parts of any existence, and for those I thank you sincerely."

Keith's cases ran the gamut from partners who wished to participate only in profits and not losses to joint venturers who blamed him because the venture didn't reap the desired financial return.

Keith muses, "The cases Mal handled for me, that's another book; one I don't have the expertise to write, but one law students might find fascinating as they rummage through the past not only for legal precedents, but for riveting scenarios."

Merlin L. Lybbert of Snow, Christensen, & Martineau also represented Keith. Every witness who met with Merlin in a pre-trial interview remembers him saying as he evaluated the other side's case, "When you have the law behind you, you pound the law; when you have the facts behind you, you pound the facts; and when you don't have either, you pound the table and we're going to see a lot of table pounding today."

For one of his own anecdotes, Merlin had an appreciative audience in Keith whose disinterest in wading through page after page of legal contracts elicited his saying, "I should own a paper mill." Merlin, in advancing the point, told him, "After I graduated from law school we bought a house. My wife and I went to the bank to finalize our home loan. After I signed all the signature pages, my wife a little non-plussed said to me, 'You are an attorney. Aren't you going to read the documents?' I told her that if I had read them I would not have signed."

None of the men who represented Keith were lightweights. Arthur H. Nielsen, Keith's attorney early on and the one who handled Keith's most ill-fated case, was a luminary in the legal community in Utah. Elder Jeffrey R. Holland of the Quorum of the Twelve, called upon unexpectedly by President James E. Faust of the First Presidency to speak at Arthur's funeral held on December 13, 1997, describes extemporaneously in words of praise his association with Arthur.

It was late in Arthur's life and much, much too late in mine that I came in touch with Arthur and Vera. Elder Joe Christensen and I had actually known them when Arthur defended the Church in a released time seminary issue in the 70s. So when President Faust thought 'I wonder if Arthur and Vera would go to Jerusalem,' I was ecstatic. I thought there was no one in the world who could help us more and could do more. You have to understand the legal help that we had on site. We had two attorneys. You have to do everything in Israel with two attorneys. We had a Jewish attorney, who was the former Attorney General in the State of Israel, Joseph Kokia, whose family had been in Jerusalem for eleven generations, four hundred years. He had immense presence and stature in the community as a member of the Israeli cabinet. Our Palestinian attorney, our West Bank attorney, was Foud Shehedeh, the most prominent legal figure in all of Palestinian West Bank, Jordan. So we had good legal help, and we still weren't having a lot of success. The lad from Fairview rode into town and it was like E. F. Hutton when Arthur spoke Joe Kokea and Foua Jahadi listened. They listened lovingly because they had a great relationship, had formed a great team. Arthur Nielsen is the man who brought home to the Brigham Young University, for all intents and purposes, the LDS Church's Jerusalem Center. He brought those forces together, he brought those legal minds together, he brought the competing and challenging forces of the day together, which was remark-able. Maybe unlike anything we've had in recent Church histo-ry. May have been something that matched it in earlier Church history, but not much lately where we had such a mountain to climb. Arthur Nielsen performed that miracle in the name of the Lord for the good of the kingdom of God in that marvelous, modest, wonderful, slightly impish way that's conveyed on that here displayed photo.

President Faust had introduced the subject with these words.

> About fifteen years ago we were struggling to build the Jerusalem Center of the Brigham Young University. Most expensive building which had been built in the Church at that time, a building to be worthy of the Holy City, a building to be worthy of the Church, a building to be worthy of the Savior. You can't imagine the difficulties and struggles that we had, and there's not time to chronicle them. But our district president had received death threats over the telephone. Sometimes construction was disrupted, and we were being pilloried in the newspapers. We looked over people in our acquaintance in the whole Church, who could go to Jerusalem as Special Counsel for then President of the University, President Holland, and do two things. One was to get the long term lease signed and second to get us possession of that magnificent building.

Arthur accomplished both.

Keith had expressed his regard and affection for Arthur pre-trial as they stood together waiting for the elevator at the offices of Nielsen & Senior. He assured Arthur, "However this case turns out, I am glad to have you as my attorney." The case to which Keith alludes did not turn out favorably for him. After a long and distinguished career as a true believer in the ability of the legal system to mete out justice, Arthur found the outcome heartbreaking. Keith's words were genuine; he meant it, and though Arthur is likely trying his next case in a heavenly court and Keith hopefully still has years before his departure, theirs will be a grand reunion.

Keith said of another good man, Alan V. Funk, whom he met in another legal battle, "This good man's integrity and business acumen are above reproach. His credentials in his selected field are impressive, and his accomplishments as an investigator and reliable witness in regard to his discoveries are worthy of any man's attention and respect. He is very modest but confident and courageous in defense of right. His conclusions in any investigation could not be more accurate and rewarding to the cause of justice."

Alan writes.

> I became acquainted with Keith Garner in approximately 1981 or 1982. I was directed by a partner in my accounting firm to meet with legal counsel. Keith and his partner Gene Kimball had become the subject of a lawsuit by their former

partners in three or four real estate developments. The former partners of Keith and Gene felt they had been unfairly dealt with in the distribution of the profits from these developments.

My prior work experience had included accounting, auditing, and investigation relating to real estate development activity. At the time I received this assignment, I was somewhat new with this accounting firm and had most recently "retired" (at age thirty-four) after nearly five years as a special agent with the FBI.

My responsibility relating to Keith and Gene's lawsuit was to perform a reconstruction of the books of each of the subject developments, then determine, based on the underlying profit-sharing agreements, whether the plaintiffs in the case had been properly compensated consistent with the agreements. In the course of that assignment, I made detailed examinations of the underlying books and records of Keith's real estate developments. Consistent with my FBI training, I questioned the authenticity of much of what I examined. Eventually, I made calculations that revealed that Keith had overpaid the plaintiffs in the case by approximately $600,000. At the trial that followed, the judge agreed with my determinations and found in favor of Keith and Gene.

In the years that followed, I was on occasion called upon by Keith to perform similar analyses of the financial affairs of his business developments. Each time I found his books to be an accurate portrayal of the underlying transactions.

My training and experience has led me to maintain a high level of skepticism when I perform my examinations. Over the years, many of my examinations have revealed significant evidence of fraud. (On two occasions my examinations have even revealed that my own client was the perpetrator of the fraud!) My work with Keith has, on the other hand, been quite the opposite. I have always found his business dealings to have been conducted in an above-board fashion. Further, I have, as with the above cited first experience with Keith, found him to be generous with his means.

Alan concludes, "Over the past twenty plus years I have grown to appreciate some of the other good things that Keith has done. I learned of Keith's efforts at outlining the Book of Mormon. I subsequently made a similar effort, and, 200 pages later, discovered a greater appreciation for the truths of that book. I appreciate the great example Keith has been to me and will forever value his friendship."

After Keith's 1991 litigation nightmare, Alan Funk recommended in the most meritorious terms David L. Bird, an attorney practicing with McKay, Burton & Thurman. Prior to his meeting him and based on Alan's description of David's qualifications, Keith, accessing his acquaintance with Dr. Robert Whiteside's methodology as explained in his book *This Is Personology*, gave a detailed description of what he expected David to look like physically. When David walked into the reception area, he appeared just as Keith had described.

Keith, in a very elementary way using the general rules of personology and more specifically what Dr. Whiteside calls "face language," accurately calculates for example by the size of his lips a person's tendency towards brevity or verbosity, from the size of his eyes his tendency towards expressing or hiding emotion, and it goes on and on. According to the preface of Dr. Whiteside's October 1962 book, Pythagoras, the sixth century father of Western philosophy and science, was the first to apply the principles of personology when he selected his students by their appearance alone. As fantastic as the concept sounds, Keith who is always ready for a new adventure traveled to San Francisco to meet Dr. Whiteside.

Reading Dr. Whiteside's tracking of Keith's personality traits, his friends and even acquaintances, particularly those who were skeptical, would be compelled to admit the doctor is very precise. Keith, on the other hand, as would others with his makeup, takes issue with the accuracy of several of the lofty nouns and adjectives used. Nonetheless, amused and enthusiastic about his discovery, Keith told his friends and accompanied one of them, John Mackay, a prominent and successful Peninsula builder, on a visit to the doctor. "I told John about personology and how great it was. He wanted to go. Whiteside's office was on Geary Boulevard in San Francisco. We drove up together, and on the way up he said, 'Keith, I'd take it as a personal favor if you never tell anybody what I'm doing this morning.' I said, 'I'll never say a word about it.' Dr. Whiteside took him in and measured him. It takes a little time for him to study what he has, and so John came out and talked to me. He reminded me not to say a word. Then he went back in and met with Dr. Whiteside. He came out, and he was kind of pale. He said, 'You tell him anything about me?' I said, 'No, I don't know anything about you.' John said, 'He told me about everything in my life, what I like, what I don't like, everything.' So he told me, 'You can broadcast this thing if you want.'"

Without any such training, David Bird specified some of the traits in Keith that Dr. Whiteside had identified after meeting with him years before. "It has been my distinct pleasure to represent Keith Garner as his attorney since approximately 1993 in a wide variety of legal matters throughout the Western United States. My impressions of Keith from the first time we met, probably not different from anyone. Keith is charismatic, affable, amiable, optimistic, adventuresome, a great conversationalist and story teller. These characteristics coupled with Keith's industry and love of work have made him a business success and have enabled him to endure and surmount challenges both typical of the real estate development industry and, in some instances very unique to Keith Garner."

David echoes Mal's comment when he says, "I've certainly had as many interesting experiences or encounters representing Keith as I've had with any client. Probably more so."

He continues, "My one disappointment is that I didn't become acquainted with Keith earlier in his life and in his career. Nevertheless, Keith has remained actively engaged in a variety of businesses, at this point into his eighties.

In my representation of Keith, and as his friend, I've had the occasion to meet many of Keith's business associates including past and present bankers, accountants, partners, clients, customers, vendors and employees, each of whom, in various circumstances and occasions have expressed respect and admiration for Keith Garner, a respect and admiration I share."

Taking Alan Funk's recommendation to hire David Bird, Keith rates as one of his finest decisions. David's desire in his representation of Keith is to protect his peace. Misuraca's expressed desire was to "keep you [Keith] safe from tigers in the night." Arthur Nielsen's counsel to Keith during the time when tigers seemed to be loose not only at night but in the light of day was "Keith, if you see someone you know don't say hi; in fact, cross over to the other side of the street!"

Keith did not take Arthur's advice. With only the armor of a warm greeting, Keith never crossed the street to avoid anyone and never would.

One greeting Keith was known to use, even before hello, particularly with bankers financing his projects, duplicates the expression found in a letter his brother-in-law Gene Kimball received from one of his clients in which he wrote "There's corn in Egypt. Come pick up your check." Keith's inquiry, "Is there corn in Egypt?," is an allusion to the Biblical story of Joseph that has opened his conversations, not just with bankers, but in more general inquiries. Dispatched by their father Jacob, renamed Israel by the Lord, from famine-plagued Canaan to Egypt, Joseph's brothers, who had sold him to merchants going to Egypt, visited him without recognizing who he was. The key segment of this well-known story is the moment when Jacob tells his sons he has heard that there is corn in Egypt.

Even when Keith's things-to-do-today list written on a scrap of paper did not include financing, he could be heard asking the loan officer at Pacific Union Bank located on the first floor of 800 Oak Grove "Is there corn in Egypt?" before he ran up the stairs two steps at a time to his second floor office. For him the question turned into a statement, "There is corn in Egypt," which he jotted on notes sent with some of his gifts.

Keith explains his philosophical view of wealth by using a money to fertilizer comparison. "Money is like manure. When you pile it up, it stinks; when you spread it around, flowers grow, blossom, and fill the air with a sweet aroma." Keith happily spread both his counsel and cash around with an acute awareness that when money is involved, one may not end up in court, but it can sour relationships. H. Taylor Peery, Keith's friend, writes based on his own experiences, "You have got to make it possible for individuals as well as nations to work their way. You can't keep them happy or keep their self-respect if you give them a free ride, regardless of how luxurious you make the accommodations. At the end of the ride, they will resent you for not continuing the ride, or they will have forgotten how to get places on their own."

Elder Marion D. Hanks describes Keith's style of giving with these words, "But never was it a handout. It was a hand up, and that was typical of his whole life so far as I can tell."

The natural flow of Keith's life is fundamentally grounded in a steady stream of regular unheralded acts of giving. He avoids making a big splash in his selections. Uncomfortable talking about such matters, he does happily recall the results of one simple suggestion. "Eldon Bringhurst, a great guy, was a painter by profession, but he got tired of painting, so he opened a little delicatessen on Cambridge in Palo Alto. He and his wife were running it. I went in to see him one day and to buy some of the wonderful rice pudding his wife made. I said, 'Are you having a hard time, Eldon?' He said, 'Yes,' and I said, 'I've got a recommendation for you. I've got some extra chairs and tables, and I'll bring them down here. You get what you have, and you serve here. You've got enough room.' He became quite prosperous; the business went, his wife could cook, and well, I made a small contribution."

Perhaps Mrs. Bringhurst knew how fond Keith was of his mother's rice pudding, but she may not have known that, according to Keith, rice saved him in Asia and he's pretty sure rice is as close to Moses' manna from heaven as it is possible to get.

It seems Keith dispensed a little manna in the following tenderly shared story. Both Bishop Garner and Elder Hanks play significant roles; in fact, Dr. Leon R. Hartshorn proffers, "Bishop Garner and Elder Hanks were both there at the right time. It could not have been done without them. We are deeply appreciative."

Dr. Hartshorn tells the story, "I think it was probably the first Sunday we were in Palo Alto. At Church we visited awhile with Bishop Garner, and he said, 'Do you have enough money to see you through school?' I said, 'No, I don't.' He said, 'Let me know what you need. I've been helping four missionaries. One is coming home.' He said, 'I think you may be worth a missionary after you finish your education.' So he helped me. I got a check each month for one hundred dollars for three years; one hundred dollars was a lot more then than it is now."

Mrs. Hartshorn adds, "When we got through school, Leon said, 'Bishop Garner, I'm going to send you so much a month every month.' He said, 'No, you just help someone else.' And we've been able to do that."

Dr. Hartshorn continues, "We had a baby while we were there. Jeanne, our fourth child. There were complications, and we just did not have enough money.

Redwood City Hospital had an interesting policy; you don't take the baby until she's paid for. I don't know if they could have made it stick, but I didn't want to risk it. I sat down with him, explained my dilemma, and he helped us out and paid the additional expenses.

The years went by. Bishop Garner went on a mission. We came to Brigham Young University. I hadn't seen him for a long time. I was a member of the Young Adult Correlation Committee, and we were invited to a meeting in the Church Office Building. Also at that meeting were the Regional Representatives; Bishop Garner was one of them. We had a break in the meeting, and so I walked up and talked to him. I asked him what he'd been doing in Salt Lake. When I came home, I said to my wife Bea, 'Guess who I saw at the meeting.' She said, 'Who?' I said, 'Bishop Garner.' She asked about him, and then she said, 'Did you tell him how much we appreciate him?' I said, 'Yes.' She said, 'Well, what did you say?' I said, 'I didn't say anything.' She said, 'You just told me that you'd thanked him.' I said, 'I looked at his eyes, and he looked into mine, and he knew exactly how I felt.' I still become emotional because we couldn't have made it without him, and he just said, 'You help someone else.'"

Mrs. Hartshorn said, "One of Leon's assistant's wife had her first baby. She had tremendous complications, and they were going to have to leave school."

Dr. Hartshorn finishes their story. "They were very independent; they didn't want to take anything. I talked to the young man, and he said, 'I just can't do that.' I said, 'I want to bring my wife over and visit with you.' When we got there, I said, 'Bea, I'd like you to tell this young man our story.' She told how Bishop Garner helped us and did ask us to help somebody else. She said, 'This is our opportunity.' He said, 'Alright, under those circumstances I'll accept the help.' Each time we've helped, we just passed the same story along. I know for sure others have passed it on just as Bishop Garner wanted it to be."

Dr. Hartshorn further explains, "I got to Stanford on sheer desire I guess. After finishing my master's degree at BYU, I had a tremendous desire to go on to school. There was no money to do it, but I went up to the Church Office Building to talk to Elder Hanks. His secretary said, 'He's got a full schedule, but the person who's in there is about to leave, and I'll ask him if he would be able to see you.' She came back and said, 'He can see you for just a minute or two between appointments.' So I went in, and he said, 'I've got two minutes. Can I help you in two minutes?' I said, 'I finished my master's degree, and I'm really thinking about going for a doctor's degree. I don't know if I can do it; I don't know if I have the ability. I don't know where the money would come from, but I have strong feelings about it.' He said, 'Go get the degree, but go to a good school, and plow wide fields as you go. The Lord bless you. Good bye.' That's the reason I ended up going to Stanford rather than some place else.

As I continued my studies, I could see what Elder Hanks meant. There's a temptation on the part of graduate students to walk along a very narrow pathway, thinking only of themselves and their studies. He was telling me to plow and plant while I was going to school. I recalled that counsel, made every effort to do that, and had very interesting results from that time of planting. When I came home, I wrote Elder Hanks a letter thanking him. He wrote back and said, 'This is one of the more satisfying letters that I've ever received.' But then a little more counsel which I thought was very interesting. He said, 'Never get in a position where you can't pray like the sinner, O God help me.' That is the way he ended the letter. I had a doctorate from Stanford; why is he telling me that? Again it just turned out to be marvelous counsel because when the frustrations come and difficulties come as they do, always remember to pray humbly."

Dr. Hartshorn concludes, "Bishop Garner insisted that it be confidential. That's why I never used his name though he meant so much to me."

Quoting Matthew's "When thou doest alms, let not thy left hand know what thy right hand doeth: That thine alms may be in secret: and thy Father which seeth in secret himself shall reward thee openly," [16] Keith makes known his opposition to divulging gifts given in private. Nevertheless, here and in most of his gracious dealings, his generosity teaches lessons valuable to all. Now and then his desire to keep his identity undisclosed is not possible. Neither he nor his recipients publish his generous acts, but those who know Keith can identify his stamp in other people's lives. In this case, his and Dr. Hartshorn's wishes were preempted by Keith's perceptive missionary and Dr. Hartshorn's student.

David E. Poulsen, one of Keith's missionaries in Asia and later president and chief executive officer of American Express Centurion Bank, relates how he became aware of his mission president's assistance to Dr. Hartshorn. He, being under no compunction to keep Keith's action quiet, shares it openly. "When I was back from my mission and taking a religion class at BYU, the instructor was Leon Hartshorn. Near the end of the term, he was talking, not on the subject of the class, but about life's lessons. He told a story about when he went to graduate school at Stanford University. How in Church one day, he was sitting next to a gentlemen who just casually started talking. 'What are you doing?' 'Oh, you're here going to Stanford; that's very nice. What are you studying?' The man said, 'Stanford's an expensive school. How are you financing yourself?' He said, 'Well, I'm a little bit short. I've got a scholarship covering this much, I've got family funds for this, and on the balance I'm just really not sure what I'm going to do.' That was the extent of the conversation. Dr. Hartshorn said, 'This individual just went his own way.' At the first of the month for the next three years of his Ph.D. program, he received a check in the mail for the amount of his deficiency until he graduated. He said he would always be grateful for this building contractor, real estate developer in Menlo Park, who had so generously

---

[16] Matthew 6:3-4

and without any thought of reward assisted him in getting his education. So I went up after class. I said, 'Dr. Hartshorn, are you talking about Keith Garner?' He kind of got a little bit emotional and said, 'Yes, I was.' I said, 'I'm not surprised.'"

Because of the magnitude of others' donations, one cannot help noticing stadiums, hospitals, clinics, shelters, and more bearing the name of the donor. Keith's name is not to be found on any building, but as Elder Hanks notes, "When your association with Brother Garner is known, people approach you to tell about how Keith helped build their individual lives." He states, "There is no end to what Keith did, and there likely will never be."

One of the touchstone caveats Keith quotes to those seeking his advice is that "You cannot be of any service to anyone if you are bankrupt." And he adds, "Bankrupt in money, or wisdom, or good common sense."

He offers more counsel by referencing the Lord's admonition to Joseph Smith. [17] "The Lord told the American prophet Joseph Smith, 'I have lots of real estate so don't worry about it.'" After offering the statement, Keith will hastily add, "I don't know whether Joseph Smith said that or Keith Garner. Either way the principle is true. You don't want to covet land. You don't want to covet anything because it really isn't yours when you own it. You are just a tenant, a lessor, or more accurately a steward."

Based on that reality, he quotes Matthew:

> *Lay not up for yourselves treasures upon earth, where moth and rust doth corrupt, and where thieves break through and steal: But lay up for yourselves treasures in heaven, where neither moth nor rust doth corrupt, and where thieves do not break through nor steal: For where your treasure is, there will your heart be also.*" [18]

He smiles while emphasizing his point. "A rich man approached graduation day and told his wife he was going to take his considerable wealth with him when he died. To that end he stacked it up in the attic. He died. At the wake the wife remembered her husband's words and told the assembled mourners what he'd said. They all ran up to the attic, and there it was still sitting where he put it."

Before finishing the story, Keith parenthetically states, "This is the best part," and then proceeds. "One of his former business partners said, 'You know if he'd put it in the basement, it would be gone'."

Keith, emerging from Ann's Coffee Shop in Menlo Park after a delicious breakfast, saw a beautiful rainbow. Following its colorful curve to the rainbow's end, his eye was led to a Brink's armored truck parked outside the door of Wells Fargo

---

[17] Doctrine and Covenants 117:4-6

[18] Matthew 6:19-21

Elder Garner

Keith says "Hawaiians could really sing; they were born with great voices and with a guitar in their hands"

Keith directing traffic at his 11th Avenue enterprise

Keith at work and at play with Eugene L. Kimball

Keith surveying his Stoneridge development from atop a four-plex under construction

Keith and Arthur Nielsen in conference

Keith behind his desk at caretaker's home at Salt Lake Mausoleum

Keith riding in his favorite form of transportation

"Mr. Spindle Shanks" in Hawaii

Keith and Mitch Hunt in Mexico

The brass plate paid for with the cuff of his shirt

Keith in a sign of adoration at the Dome of the Rock

l to r Tom Ferguson, Keith Garner, and Bob Ord at the Museum of Antiquities in Tehran, Iran looking at the encased stone box containing golf plates; picture taken by Sid Badger

President Garner "hitchhiking" in Vietnam

Hong Kong-bound are President and Mrs. Keith E. Garner and their four children, Susan, 9; Lynne, 19; Gayle, 17; Keith Jr. 13

"President Garner, you are a great diplomat."--President Kimball
l to r: President Keith E. Garner, Sister Camilla Kimball, President Spencer W. Kimball

Bank. The security guard was busy unloading bags stuffed with money. Keith rushed across the street to the camera shop and hurriedly borrowed a camera so he could document this witnessed "pot of gold at the end of the rainbow." By the time he returned, he found the radiant proof dissipated in a cloudless sky. How fleeting to man is worldly wealth, but how lasting the parting counsel Keith gave to Stephen Richey, one of the missionaries with whom he would serve half a world away from California and who is now himself a successful insurance executive. It is instructive in explaining Keith's business success.

> I will never forget the last advice I received from President Garner. As a few companions and I were enroute home, we were all allowed to see some of the other parts of the Far East. President Garner was in Manila conducting a Zone Conference but insisted that we meet with him, though he was very busy with meeting plans and individual interviews with missionaries. When I was alone with him as a full time missionary for the last time, he warmly greeted me and immediately paid me a wonderful compliment. He always believed in me and assured me that I was one that had always remained constant and dependable. He then proceeded to counsel me about the affairs of men and the business of the 'world.' His final words were "Elder Richey, you know who you are, and you know how you stand with the Lord. That's all that matters. All the rest are just men." As he uttered this statement of 'just men,' referring to the great and powerful of the earth, he waved his arm dismissively and with singular impact communicated to me the utter truth of that observation. All of my business life and in all of my interpersonal relationships with my fellow man my greatest success has been in keeping that advise in proper perspective.

The key for Keith is to never let eternal perspectives evaporate into worldly nonsense, to never trade eternal rewards for worldly accolades. Simply stated by a partner in business and in Church work, "Keith believes in acting on Monday the same way he acts on Sunday."

Yes, Mr. Garner capitalized on a gold rush which took place in 1947 California, but his bank accounts, real estate deals, and land development projects pale in comparison to his far more valuable assets, holdings unaffected by markets, fluctuating interest rates, insecurities of the world, or storms of mortality. In no other way but through the gospel of Jesus Christ can one find the interest free loan, the ultimate insurance policy, the premier real estate deal, and the incomparable teaching contract.

As Mr. Garner, computing the value of his earthly estate, considers his last will and testament, he joyfully exclaims, "I leave a rich, golden legacy--my testimony of the Book of Mormon and an enthusiasm for building the Kingdom."

Chapter
S I X

The Minister of Menlo

And we talk of Christ, we rejoice in Christ we preach of Christ,
we prophesy of Christ, and we write according to our prophecies,
that our children may know to what source they may look
for a remission of their sins.
— II Nephi 25:26

California. Menlo Park. 1952. Just as Keith's ancestors had been in the right place, Sutter's Fort, at the right time, 1847, to participate in the discovery of gold, Keith had also found himself at a place and time where opportunities for economic success were at his fingertips. Yes, it was a golden era for material accumulation upon which he obviously capitalized, but more importantly it was a golden time of growth for the Church in northern California and for leadership roles which Keith readily accepted and magnified. For the next eleven years, Keith served as bishop of the newly formed Menlo Park Ward.

After a decade of proven professional success in construction, the occupational title of builder described a good part of Keith's situation well; however, based on the same decade plus one additional year of Bishop Garner's ministerial work and significant sway with his ward membership and beyond, Keith's career classification needs more specificity to accurately describe the field in which he spent the majority of his time. Builder, yes. Builder of men, absolutely.

Having returned home late after a long day selling insurance, Keith found the Palo Alto Stake President, David B. Haight, and his counselor, Sidney Badger, waiting

Palo Alto Stake High Council; picture taken November 1951; Front row: l to r--William A. Osmond, Elden Ashcroft, J.Winter Smith, LeRoi Cheney, Stanley S. Gibb, Gary Wilmarth; Back row: l to r--Ralph H. Martin, David B. Haight, Eugene Ludwigg, Roy Allen, Keith E. Garner, Vernon K. Beckstrand

for him. "What have I done now?" popped into his thoughts as he greeted his unexpected visitors. If he had asked the question, the answer surely would have been, "Nothing, quite the opposite," since the two men were there to extend a call to him to serve as bishop.

Keith's lifelong association with President Haight began several years before, shortly after the conclusion of World War II. Almost fifty years later, Elder Haight fondly recaptures those beginnings. "I first became acquainted with Keith when he and I were on the high council together. Keith was one of our leading preachers down in the San Francisco area because he was a returned missionary. In my youth I didn't go on a mission. Keith was smart enough to go out there. He was a lot smarter about the scriptures and the Church than I was. I was coming along in the side door." Keith, responding to Elder Haight's comment, quickly interrupted, "So modest." Elder Haight repeated himself, "Coming in the side door," and continued, "So we sat on the high council together in that little Palo Alto chapel. Remember Keith, they had that little alcove in the back of the chapel. The high council would sit back in there at stake conference. I would sit by Keith, and he had a Book of Mormon and his scriptures all marked up so anybody could find anything. Mine weren't marked up. They hadn't been used, but his were well-used and well-marked, and so he was my teacher. He'd kind of whisper in my ear, tell me what to mark, help me."

The Haights moved to Chicago for a short period, and Keith continued as a member of the high council in the Palo Alto Stake. It was not long after their return that Brother Haight became stake president. Elder Haight continues, "The time came they couldn't find anyone else to put in as stake president; they got down to me. They called me to be the stake president. We divided the Palo Alto Ward and created a new ward. Keith was one of the best men in the stake, a great leader, and so we called Keith to be the bishop of that new ward. We put the bishop's robe on him, and he was a great bishop. He had great activity; he expected a lot of the people, reactivated the inactive, and stirred up the ones that weren't doing very well. He really made things happen. Those were great days." Thus, an era still referred to by the participants as golden began.

On November 29, 1952, Elder Delbert L. Stapley, a member of the Quorum of the Twelve Apostles, set apart Keith Elliott Garner to preside over the Menlo Park Ward, Palo Alto Stake of California. Just as he had said twelve years earlier when called to the Hawaiian Mission, "It was a wonderful experience to be called, and I couldn't have found a better mission in all the world to go to than Hawaii," he now found a similar expression suitable. "It was a wonderful experience to be called, and I couldn't have found a better ward in all the Church in which to serve than Menlo Park."

While all Church assignments bring both great opportunities to serve and great challenges to master, Keith distinguishes the calling of bishop as the best job in the entire Church. The bishop is the presiding high priest. He is president of the priests' quorum and specifically responsible for the young men in his congregation. He is responsible for administering the ward welfare program and managing the ward finances.

Since the bishop's role is far from just administrative, the effective bishop takes a friendly, encouraging interest in each member of his ward, conscientiously showing genuine and informed concern for the happiness and well-being of his ward family. Likewise, every member knows the bishop, looks to him for leadership, and supports his calls to action. The bishop relies on a mutual trust established between him and his flock to gird this special relationship's underpinnings.

The bishop is a judge in Israel. He serves as a peacemaker. His ward thrives when ward members flourish in the assurance that the underlying principle guiding their bishop is always love, a love for the Master which assumes and requires love for all men.

The first time Keith physically viewed a congregation from a bishop's vantage point happened in his childhood. Young Keith's behavior during one Sunday School opening exercise supported the randomly applied maxim that the bishop's son or in this case nephew can be counted on to be the worst behaved child in the ward. "I was always a gabber, and I was sitting with my older sisters LaVon and Beatrice who I guess had been left with the charge to keep me quiet and to encourage me to behave.

Evidently I was making more commotion than I should have because the bishop, Horace Garner, my uncle, came down from the stand, took my hand, and led me back up. I had to sit on the stand next to him. I didn't mind it. What the heck; it's one way to get some fame and a comfortable seat. It really bothered my sisters. They were mortified; I'm not sure they ever got over it. I just remember going on the stand. That's one way to get on the stand. First time I'd ever been on the stand."

As Bishop Keith Garner for the first time looked over the Menlo Park Ward which numbered 534 members, he saw men, women, and children looking back at him with varying expectations. Among an entire congregation of celebrated citizens sat personable Claude Lindsay, the land developer who only weeks later elicited this compliment from the new bishop, "If I ever make as much gross as you make to pay tithing, I'll never complain"; his graceful wife Agnes, sister of television inventor Philo T. Farnsworth; soft spoken Robert Bowen, a prominent attorney and the brother of Apostle Albert R. Bowen; steady George Hughes Jr., a top accountant for Peat Marwick; artistic William Needham Lambert, attorney for Standard Oil; original William Osmond, an eminent salesman of industrial rubber products; his joyful wife Jennett; learned Sam Thurman, an assistant dean at Stanford University; and agreeable Joe Allen, executive secretary of Utah Construction. While this listing is woefully incomplete, almost without exception, Keith correctly saw seated before him talented, experienced, committed Latter-day Saints, who were too few in number and who would gladly answer calls to serve and work with him.

Never in his most fanciful moments had he imagined he would be marshalling this force for good as their bishop. He never dreamed he would be sitting in the seat he now occupied. Apparently some of the Menlo Park Ward members were as surprised as Keith to see him sitting there. Perhaps they had heard Keith's childhood story and thought President Haight rather than Keith's Uncle Horace was now marching Keith up to the stand. Keith's youth and exuberance troubled a few of the more successful, well-educated, older men and women. Keith quotes an unknown author's phrase, "The blunders of youth are preferable to the wisdom of old age." The sentiment applied here proved to be true. In fact, after a couple of years, Laura Lambourne, who had felt uneasy, even a little depressed, at Keith's being given this authority, came to Bishop Garner, confessed her doubts, and then said decidedly, "I was wrong; you are doing a wonderful job."

Another illuminating response to Keith's calling as bishop is offered by Angela Bowen. In 1952 she, then a teenager, had just moved with her parents from San Francisco where the Church social scene at that time held little promise compared to the Palo Alto Ward which offered the companionship of a group of bright, handsome young men and women. Shortly after this hopeful move, the Palo Alto Ward was divided by President Haight, her future father-in-law, and Angela was discouraged. Her parents, optimistic at the new change, encouraged her with superlatives such as "This will be the best ward in the Church." Angela gives credit to her parents'

Aaronic Priesthood Committee: l to r--Keith E. Garner, George Hughes, Sid Badger, Gary Wilmarth, and David B. Haight

positive role in helping her to become more optimistic. But the clincher to turn her head to more encouraging thoughts materialized when Bishop Garner and his counselors, Leon P. Hovik and Hugh S. West, visited every family in the ward, spreading the richness of an enthusiasm for those they had been called to serve and for the gospel message. Her eyes literally twinkle as she describes her memory of this young, handsome, energetic bishop and his two young, handsome, energetic counselors, dressed in dark suits sitting on the raised dais. She thought, "The ward division isn't going to be so bad!" And it wasn't. The only drawback, she reports, was that it took a little more effort to win the Haight boy's notice, an effort resulting in marriage and six children.

By all reports, Keith deserved the expressions of confidence from old and young. His praiseworthy job performance might well have been stimulated by his having had a prime reference point for self-evaluation. Bishop Claude Nalder exuded the gifts of the spirit which had blessed all those over whom he had ministered. Bishop Nalder was his bishop while he lived in the Hayes Ward, San Francisco Stake, prior to his first mission. Keith describes him in the most exalted of terms. "He was an ideal bishop. Being a master orator, everyone loved to listen to him speak. But I think the first thing that impressed me was he knew how to listen to others. He gave people the quality of his time. When he talked to you, that was it; he wasn't paying attention to anything or anyone else. Dr. Richard Moss quantified Bishop's Nalder's listening

Menlo Park Ward bishopric and former members of the bishopric from Dedication program.

Llewellyn Leigh
First Councilor
Sept. 11, 1960-June 30, 1963

Keith E. Garner
Bishop
Nov. 23, 1952-June 30, 1963

David S. Bacon
Second Councilor
Sept. 16, 1961-June 30, 1963

Hugh S.West
Nov. 23, 1952-Jan. 8, 1956

Leon P. Hovik
Nov. 23, 1952-Sept. 16, 1961

George D. Hughes
Jan. 8, 1956-Sept. 11, 1960

ear when he said, 'The greatest gift you can give another is the purity of your attention.'

Bishop Nalder was heavy set, friendly, and genuine. Having been in the stake for many years, he knew how to handle kids; he knew how to handle everybody. There were a lot of young people in the ward, and they loved him. He knew people and knew how to treat them. He was a mortician, and I think the great virtues he used in his profession extended over into his Church duties. In fact, I think they were simply a natural part of his metabolism.

He lived a couple of houses from the chapel on Hayes Street and was always available to any of us. In fact, I remember every once in a while after meeting we'd all go down to the ice cream parlor together and have root beer floats or milk shakes.

That was just part of the program.

Years later his lovely wife called me. She had been told of my public expressions of appreciation for Bishop Nalder's leadership and life. She called to thank me."

Bishop Garner declares, "Claude Nalder was the best bishop I ever knew."

Bishop Nalder joined President Cox as an early mentor and example of leadership and love. Keith admired these men, and more such devoted, multifaceted men would aid Keith in strapping on additional vestments of the armor of God, qualities he would need as he assumed this new role and others to come.

The Apostle Paul in I Timothy 3:1-7 outlines the attributes he feels necessary for a man to serve in the sacred calling of bishop. No man comes to this calling or perfectly performs to Paul's scriptural standard. Keith did not and is the first to so admit. In spite of his acknowledged deficiencies, it became clear throughout the years in which people called him Bishop Garner that he possessed many of these specified qualities to a degree rarely seen; he was "vigilant, sober, of good behavior, given to hospitality, and apt to teach."

This last trait the Apostle Paul names and the trait Keith's entire personality personifies, "apt to teach," served him well in fulfilling the bishop's role. Keith opines, "I guess we should be teaching the word all the time. The Lord says, 'Thou must open thy mouth at all times, declaring my gospel with the sound of rejoicing'."[19]

Without delay, Keith set out to know each member of the ward and to involve everyone. He made every effort to ensure enthusiastic participation in gospel activities through the energetic presentation of the gospel message. His disquiet was observable in his reaction to a lifeless presentation. His impatience with the half-hearted care of such priceless truths had surfaced years before. He, as a child, would opt to leave if classes were dull. "I'd just walk out, go out in the yard, find some other truant, and walk around the block. I figured the Sunday School teacher had the greatest thing in the world to teach. Every teacher ought to brighten it up and put some beautiful clothes on it. You know, don't make it boring by reading to the class out of the manual. So in this regard, I was famous when I was young."

Some of his administrative policies, all of which were ultimately tied to enhancing teaching proficiency, made him famous as bishop. The ward teaching or now perhaps more descriptively renamed home teaching program of the Church provides the natural avenue whereby a bishop can identify and address the needs of his ward members. Bishop Garner, enlightened by the senior president of the Council of Seventy, instituted a variation of the program which increased the percentage of visited members and therefore the efficacy and timeliness of the feedback. In recounting the genesis of this idea, Keith credits Elder Young. "Elder S. Dilworth Young came and met with me and my two counselors. He said that he'd tell us a great way to do ward

---

[19] Doctrine and Covenants 28:16

teaching which he had observed in one of the areas of the Church he had visited. The elements he outlined included dividing the ward into districts and calling a senior ward teacher for each district. The senior ward teacher is given no other calling in the ward; his only responsibility is to visit all the families in his unit, usually between ten and twelve, in their homes once a month.

We accepted the idea. In the case of the Menlo Park Ward, we created twelve units, called the same number of senior ward teachers, and assigned to each of these senior home teachers four or more Aaronic Priesthood boys to be junior companions. Since the senior home teacher visited three or four of his families in one night, it required several different outings to call on all the families in his district. On each outing he took a different boy with him."

Keith grasped the obvious advantages and elaborates, "We selected the best men to devote their Church service to this vital calling because the best teaching you can do is in the home. This way ward teaching isn't a shot in the dark. It isn't done at the eleventh hour. They know this is their full calling. While the senior ward teacher is doing his duty, he can teach his young companion how he should perform in his assignment; the boys are trained, and they know what they are doing. Once a month with my counselors, we'd meet with these twelve men, and they'd give a report on every family in the ward. We always knew what was going on. It wasn't fictitious nonsense; they'd actually visited with their assigned families. Then occasionally we would invite the Relief Society presidency, the Young Men's and Young Women's Mutual presidencies, the Primary presidency, and other leaders to join with the senior ward teachers. That way everyone was on the same page, serving in unison and with common goals. We introduced the program, and it was very efficacious for that particular time."

Bishop Garner went into action immediately and called Hyrum Crofts as the senior ward teacher for district one. Minutes for ward teacher report meetings steadily reflected, "Stake President very happy with results." Within a year, Bishop Garner reported in ward council meeting that the stake leaders had decided to adopt Menlo Park Ward's method of ward teaching for the stake. No wonder, since the Menlo Park Ward's statistics hit an unexaggerated ninety-five percent of ward families visited. No doubt while congratulating the men on the great job done, Bishop Garner would have wondered out loud, "What happened to the other five percent?"

Whether as bishop or in any other role, spiritual or temporal, one never found Keith stuck in a established rut. He quickly embraced new ideas just as he had in regard to ward teaching. This tendency surfaced early. At Sparks High School, he had participated in debate. To hear him tell it, he was not a very effective debater. He recalls that after giving his side's argument in support or in opposition to the resolution, if he heard a more convincing argument advanced by the opposing side, he would inwardly shrug and say, "I like that better." Of course, he had to continue the debate, but he did so with less conviction, his argument having been tempered by his notice that the other team had made a better case.

Some people found Keith's acceptance of new suggestions frustrating, and some even commented that the idea into which Keith breathed life was the one advanced by the last person to whom he spoke. Keith agrees that it did seem like someone was always coming up with a better idea than the last. Keith welcomed others input and made everyone feel like his idea was the best; thus, when Keith, after considering all the potential solutions, adopted what he considered the superior idea, his choice occasionally offended some who had been invited into the process. In actuality, these qualities of humility and willingness to learn gave Keith a wider selection of plausibly preferable choices.

Other aspects of Keith's tenure as bishop stand out. According to the minutes of ward council, correlation meetings, Priesthood meetings, and ward teaching report meetings, Bishop Garner counseled the Priesthood and ward leaders with words of encouragement and instruction. Almost without fail Bishop Garner opened these meetings by first acknowledging and then expressing his appreciation for the "work-horses of the ward and his happiness at seeing so many workers" and noted that "serving in the Church is the greatest leveler and stabilizer in our lives." He voiced his belief that "those who are laboring in Zion are happy people." He called on them to "give the same high performance to their Church assignments as they did in their Monday through Friday jobs." The message that Bishop Garner left with officers and teachers was to teach fundamental doctrines. In his sermons and lessons, he looked to fundamentals for his themes: "faith in the Lord Jesus Christ, repentance, baptism by immersion for the remission of sins, laying on of hands for the gift of the Holy Ghost," along with missionary work, Book of Mormon prophecies concerning the promised land of America, the Word of Wisdom, tithing, reverence, temple work, and family prayer.

He encouraged the brethren to honor their Priesthood. He instructed the young men of the Aaronic Priesthood in their duties as deacons, teachers, and priests. One minute book entry for a joint Aaronic Priesthood meeting reads, "Discussed and enlarged on the Atonement of Christ and the three kingdoms. The Bishop had a very good participation from the class and made the discussion very interesting." In teaching he took his own advice on dressing up the presentation.

When personnel problems arose, he discussed the importance of loving one another. He cautioned, "If hard feelings come, talk it out; give the other person the chance to correct it if he is at fault."

He highlighted humble, consecrated leadership. He warned, "We should set aside personal programs in favor of the Lord's program, thereby gaining the full confidence of our Father in Heaven. We have been called, and so we should not disqualify ourselves."

He talked about members' duties and privileges and reminded Priesthood members of their own responsibility to have two years food supply on hand or sufficient dollars to take care of those daily needs.

One of his easiest and happiest pronouncements transpired when he advised the brethren that he had received many requests for missionaries to visit homes in the ward.

Reminding each to be thankful for the blessings they all enjoyed, he added, "We all have so many." "Lack of gratitude," according to Brigham Young, "is the worst of sins," and not wishing to be found lacking, Keith internalized the axiom, stressed it then, as he does today, and often expressed that one of his blessings was working with the leaders and ward members.

Primarily he simply encouraged these ward leaders to live and teach the gospel, to help bring the Lord's children back to their Father. His counsel in these leadership settings can be summarized in one charge, "Live the gospel."

Another Menlo Park Ward practice probably had its origins while Keith still attended the Hayes Ward. "I was asked to be one of the speakers at sacrament meeting with Ira Somers. Isn't it funny I remember his name? He was the first speaker, and he took his time and part of my time. There wasn't very much time left. I got up and told them I enjoyed what Ira had said, but I couldn't develop my subject in the time left, so I would just bear my testimony, and we could have a short meeting. When I got through, the bishop got up and took twenty minutes, gave a great oration, and said at the conclusion 'Next Sunday we'll give the whole program to Keith.'" In ending the story, Keith reveals a slight embarrassment at his panache when he says, "I don't know if I was sick the next Sunday or not." He was not, and the minutes for the Hayes Ward sacrament meeting disclose that Keith Garner was the only speaker.

To solve this universal problem of a speaker losing track of time and finding himself inadvertently stepping on others' toes, Bishop Garner put a red light on the podium in the Menlo Park Ward. Prior to sacrament meeting he, like every other bishop, held a prayer meeting for all the participants. It was well-known in the ward that Bishop Garner had directed that the length of sacrament meeting should be held to an hour and that the speakers consider the interests of children. During prayer meeting when they had two speakers scheduled, Keith would ask them how they had divided the time. Usually they split the time equally. Approvingly Bishop Garner would say, "Great," and then would explain, "Now I want you to know there's a little red light on the rostrum, and when I turn the red light on, that means your time is up; the rest of the time belongs to the next speaker." To make the matter even plainer, he told them, "If you put your book over the red light and infringe on the time apportioned to the second speaker, I'll push a button, and you'll disappear." Once as Keith was telling this story, someone in the group, probably in jest, said that in his ward the bishop didn't have a trap door. His bishop invented an inclining pulpit, and as the speaker spoke beyond his allotted time, the pulpit gradually leaned forward. The next thing the speaker knew, he was horizontal with the floor. Bishop Garner never had a chance to implement that method, but he liked the idea since in that scenario there is no need for anyone to ask what happened to the speaker.

Bishop Garner regularly spoke to the Menlo Park congregation at least every three months as part of the monthly fast and testimony meeting. Fervently he would open testimony bearing with declarations like, "My testimony of the gospel is my whole life." Part of his testimony usually included the subject of gaining a testimony by studying the Book of Mormon. He always bore a convincing testimony of the truth of the work. The speakers and the listeners gained strength as audience members would rise to express their own witness of the gospel of Jesus Christ.

Without fail when Bishop Garner conducted, he included with the announcements his personalized thought for the day. These short speeches seemed to catch the imagination of his audience, and while the words may not be remembered, the fact that he never missed an opening to teach is not.

As indicated in the Menlo Park Ward minutes, Keith, throughout his term as bishop, spoke to his ward membership from the pulpit. The abundance of sermons he gave on vital gospel subjects precludes an exhaustive recounting. In one of his most effective sermons, Bishop Garner reviewed the life of the Prophet Joseph Smith from the time of his First Vision. He called on young men of the corresponding age seated in the audience to stand as he told about some of the important events that took place in the Prophet's life. Born December 23, 1805, Joseph's First Vision occurred in the spring of 1820 at the age of fourteen. The Book of Mormon prophet Moroni first visited the seventeen-year-old Joseph in September of 1823 and then every year for the next four years until twenty-two-year-old Joseph in 1827 was given the plates from which he would translate the Book of Mormon. In 1829 the New Testament prophet John the Baptist restored the Aaronic Priesthood to a now twenty-four year old Joseph Smith. Just a few months later, three of the Lord's apostles, Peter, James, and John, restored the Melchizedek Priesthood to him. In 1830 twenty-five-year-old Joseph Smith under the direction of Jesus Christ organized The Church of Jesus Christ of Latter-day Saints with an initial six members, ranging in age from twenty-one to thirty: Joseph Smith, Jr., Oliver Cowdrey, Hyrum Smith, Samuel Smith, David Whitmer, and David Whitmer, Jr. He concluded succinctly with, "Without a doubt Joseph Smith is a prophet of God." Looking at the young men fourteen to thirty years old called out of the audience and now standing next to Bishop Garner, one could only be impressed with this reservoir of Priesthood power.

The themes Bishop Garner wove through one inspiring address appeared in some form in every pronouncement he made. He stated without equivocation, "Our goal and destiny is eternal life. Jesus is our Savior. Repent always of human failure. Read and study the scriptures. Ponder them for wisdom and spiritual understanding. If you do, the mysteries will be unfolded. Joy and peace will be the reward." Concluding the meeting, the congregation sang the stirring hymn, *Onward Christian Soldiers*. Many left this sacrament meeting, after having partaken of the sacrament and renewed their baptismal covenants, with Keith's words reverberating in their minds and hearts, humming the melody of the closing hymn and more strongly committed to becoming indomitable soldiers in God's army.

Bishop Garner did not just preach from the pulpit. Like his father who in Keith's presence talked with sometimes captive candidates about gospel gems during train trips, Keith's teaching venues certainly were not confined to the chapel or the bishop's office. When teaching situations presented themselves, some under rather unique circumstances, Bishop Garner tried to be available and sensitive to the opening.

The results of one such episode still delight Keith. By way of background, a friend of Bishop Garner's, Leo Sant, had married a beautiful, charming, non-member, and they had made their home several miles beyond Bishop Garner's ward boundaries. Dutifully Leo would dress his young daughters in their Sunday best and bring them to the Menlo Park Ward. Keith bravely asserted, "Leo, we can't have this happen. I'll just go down and convert your wife. Then you can go to your own ward." Leo, knowing his wife's interest in the Church had been dulled by some unfortunate negative exposure, bluntly said, "Good luck!" Keith persisted and repeatedly drove down to their lovely home at 236 Angela Drive, Los Altos, an address he has not forgotten to this day. He taught her the gospel which she accepted wholeheartedly, and he exclaims, "She is a real believer!"

Another quite unusual teaching date arose. As part of a concerted effort to reactivate less active men, Bishop Garner had been calling one man in this group but had not been able to reach him by telephone and had received no return calls. This famous home builder with national awards lining his office shelves hit a patch of trouble, and because he was well-known, the newspapers picked up the story. Bishop Garner called his office and in a last attempt to get his attention left the word, "My councilors and I would like to meet with you." The bishop's statement must have motivated him because he started calling Keith. Keith says, "I thought he needed some time for reflection so I didn't respond. He finally got me either early in the morning or late at night." With his Church membership thought to be in jeopardy, all he said and all he needed to say was, "Before you take my name off the records of the Church, will you tell me what I'm going to lose?" Keith, pleased by his response, told him that he taught early morning seminary so he would meet him the next day after his class. This brilliant suppliant was waiting in the chapel for Bishop Garner the very next morning.

Bishop Garner's answer to that forthright question, "What am I going to lose?" was a simple restatement of what his seminary students repeatedly heard him refer to as "the big picture." "The Lord said, 'For what is a man profited, if he shall gain the whole world, and lose his own soul? or what shall a man give in exchange for his soul?'"[20] Keith opined, "You are very successful in your business life, and that's good, but by itself it is not enough to give you the blessings that God has in store. You have gained the whole world but neglected the program our Creator has given us for

---

[20] Matthew 16:26

gaining eternal life; for becoming like He is. It is self evident that all men waste time spent on things that do not go beyond the grave."

Confident when dealing with matters of such eternal seriousness, Bishop Garner in his characteristic straightforward manner declared, "You were created to be a god; if you don't qualify through the Atonement of Jesus Christ, then you will be subservient and in servitude. You will lose this greatest of all the gifts God has to offer."

Keith further explained, "The boy Joseph Smith had a question. In Joseph's First Vision, the Father and the Son by their very appearance answered it for him. They identified themselves to Joseph Smith so he would know who they were because on that truth everything else is built. If we accept through faith and study Joseph's account, we then know who God is. Number one in the order of the things in the world is to know the nature of God." Keith agreed with and quoted the celebrated English poet John Milton, author of *Paradise Lost*. "The end then of learning is to repair the ruins of our first parents by regaining to know God aright and out of that knowledge to love Him, to imitate Him, to be like Him."

Bishop Garner asked and answered, "Where does one go for a knowledge of God? We will go through the scriptures to clarify all these things that God teaches. The Lord says, 'For he that diligently seeketh shall find and the mysteries of God shall be unfolded unto them, by the power of the Holy Ghost.'"[21]

Keith finishes the story, "You don't pick up all these things at once; it's a process of learning. We met every week on Wednesday right after seminary and went through the scriptures together. He started coming to Church."

Keith and he found common ground on lesser issues. "I remember like me he hated Sunday School song practice. I agreed but told him that though minor it is a part of the program." His nickname Make A Million came to reflect not just a very successful business man but a man whose practical nature queried, "What am I going to lose?" In so doing, he reaped precious spiritual blessings as did his teacher. One aspect of his renewed activity touched both him and Keith; their friendship deepened as together they measured life by eternal precepts.

Another teaching time for Keith presented itself unexpectedly on a temple excursion to the Los Angeles Temple. Every few months the ward would travel by bus to attend an early morning session. Bishop Garner explains. "On one occasion I found myself at the gate of the temple without my recommend. In those days each temple had its own recommend; they were not interchangeable. Whether I didn't take my temple recommend or had the wrong one, the temple worker would not let me in. As their bishop, my signature was on everybody in our group's recommend who went through the temple that day." Keith asked the recommend checker, "Who do you think signed all these other temple recommends?" and then showed him his

----

[21] I Nephi 10:19

identification. The worker unmoved said, "Well, there's nobody to authorize your entrance." Keith summarizes the situation. "When I got through with the doorkeeper, I wasn't qualified to go in anyway." Initially he intended to wait for his group to complete their work, but since waiting held little appeal for him, he decided to take a cab to the airport and fly home. He ends the story with, "I preached the gospel message to the cab driver so the trip wouldn't be in vain."

Bishop Garner tells the following well-appreciated tale brought to the surface by his remembrance of his own preaching to this cab driver. "Itinerant preachers used to make the country circuit. They'd come into town and rent the largest hall available. One preacher entered the hall and found to his surprise only one in attendance. Of course, he had expected a full house. He made an announcement cancelling the meeting. The sole man in the audience called out, 'Are you a preacher of the gospel?' The preacher said, 'Yes.' 'Well, you're not very responsive to the needs of your parishioners. I'm a cattleman, and when I go out to feed my cattle, I feed them, one or a hundred.' The preacher said, 'If you feel that way about it, I'll deliver my sermon.' The minister went on and on for a long time. When he finally concluded, the cattleman said, 'I forgot to tell you; when I go out to feed my herd and only one or two cows show up, I don't drop the whole load.'" It's not clear whether the cabby thought Keith dropped the whole load. It is clear that Keith did always make a thought provoking impression.

Application of Paul's "apt to teach" also emerged in a rather extraordinary way for a bishop. Bishop Garner took upon himself the additional responsibility of teaching seminary. Like the bishop's seemingly full-time lay job, this too is an unpaid calling, at least in dollars. With the exception of a few regions in Utah and Idaho, Church seminary classes are taught early in the morning before public high school classes begin. The curriculum over four years consists of the standard works of the Church: Bible, Book of Mormon, Doctrine and Covenants and Church history, and Pearl of Great Price. The classes include youth of high school age. Bishop Garner, who was always an early riser, taught seminary two different intervals for a total of nine years. This required his having to arise, shampoo, shave, and dress in time to welcome on some days bright-eyed, inquisitive teenagers and on other days bleary-eyed, parent-prodded pupils. He loved teaching seminary and felt it helped him fulfill his charge to oversee the growth of the young men of his ward and by extension the growth of the young women.

Bishop Garner approached teaching seminary by utilizing all of his energetic flair. His classroom buzzed with learning and good humor. His students, in class and after class, witnessed his unforgettable application of many of the lessons he taught. To understand the excitement of a seminary class taught by Bishop Garner, one would have to be in attendance; yet through the eyes of many who were there, a vivid picture of him emerges.

At a recent gathering of some of his former seminary students, Ken Woolley, consequentially said, "I don't necessarily remember everything Bishop Garner said, but there was a spirit there that has always stayed with me."

Marcia Croft McLain echoed Ken's comment. "I remember the good feeling, not a specific lesson, other than he was always there for us, and the good feelings that resounded within that seminary program." One object lesson Bishop Garner brought to his seminary class she retells with clarity. "I do remember the bishop holding up his hand and saying, 'Now move your little finger,' and we would do that and he'd say, 'Isn't that a miracle that you can tell your finger to move, and it will move?' It gave me a profound reverence for our bodies. How magnificent the physical body is and what a wonder it is. I remember that very simple illustration as he stood in front of the seminary class on a number of occasions."

One of the women in the group remembers getting up at 6:00 a.m. to watch Bishop Garner draw circles on the blackboard representing the plan of salvation. She also joined almost without exception every other Garner seminary student in repeating Bishop Garner's advise to these young men and young women whose hormones were overtaking their heads. "Marry the right person, at the right time, in the right place, and the right place is the temple."

Another former seminary student recounts Bishop Garner's spontaneous, welcoming greeting to a student arriving a few minutes late. "He was teaching a Book of Mormon class and one of the young men in the class who had just got a nice all white nylon jacket wore it to seminary. As soon as this young man walked in with the jacket on Keith immediately said, 'Well, look who's here; it's the angel Moroni himself all dressed in white.' Given we were studying the Book of Mormon, and the angel Moroni, and the First Vision, it was humorous yet a perfect way to begin the class that day."

Although Bishop Garner earlier relinquished his pursuit of a law degree and later expressed sentiments on the subject which sounded similar to those spoken by Brigham Young, several of his former students became notable legal practitioners. Bishop Garner recently and figuratively stood before San Francisco Superior Court Judge Jerome T. Benson, to be judged as a bishop and seminary teacher and found himself deluged with praise. Judge Benson begins, "Keith was really a unique individual. He had the capacity through a terrific sense of humor and real, genuine interest in the high school kids, to break down those barriers that exist between young adults on the one hand and the adults on the other. Most school and church officials that youth see during their young lives are gray men in gray suits with gray ideas. He had terrific appeal for young people in the Church. I'm sixty-three years old and maybe I haven't seen as many bishops as a lot of other people, but I've never seen a man in or out of the Church that had that gift, to bring the young people into the orbit of the adult world. He really just had that touch and it's really unique."

Marcia also echoes Judge Benson's contemplations. "He had a great influence on the youth of the Church. He just knows how to touch people. I remember his laugh, a hearty, cute laugh, and the twinkle in his eye that we all just loved and gravitated to, and his acceptance of the youth. We not only had fun but we did learn about the gospel as well. I think I stood in awe of his being a bishop and getting up early and participating in the seminary program. Because of his good influence my testimony grew. There was no question I'd always be active in the Church, which I have been, and I can give credit to Bishop Garner for that."

Judge Benson, now teaching seminary himself, comments further on Bishop Garner's teaching style. "He didn't distinguish between students in his class who regularly came versus those that came part of the time or kids that were tardy--he treated everybody the same. He didn't treat it like a high-pressure academic class with rigorous grading. As far as how he treated people, he wasn't a disciplinarian type of a seminary teacher. He was a terrific teacher and we paid attention to everything he said."

Similar remarks of equally high regard offered by assistant United States attorney Richard Lambert bring blushes of embarrassment to Bishop Garner. Over lunch he recently visited with Keith about his affiliation with him as his bishop and his teacher. "In reminiscing about the ward, it seemed like a golden era upon which I look back with fondness. Menlo Park Ward was unusually fine across the board, a great environment. The members were men and women who were bright, educated, dedicated, successful in their own right, and fully committed to the gospel. You were kind of the exhibit of all of those qualities as the bishop. You had an enthusiasm and a love for the scriptures, a love for the gospel. You loved to teach. I learned from you in those early years that the gospel was something that was exciting. I think it is significant that you were not only willing to be bishop but also willing to be our seminary teacher. You know, most bishops don't have time to just be a teacher. You so loved the gospel that you were willing to be a teacher as well."

Bishop Garner calls teaching the noblest of professions but a profession not confined to the classroom. On many occasions and in many ways, Keith's seminary students saw him teach by example. Digging into his own abundant personal resources of commitment, capital, and compassion, he provided a framework upon which others could build.

Returning to Hawaii yearly for family vacations, Bishop Garner found others' version of relaxation, drinking up the sun on the warm Pacific beaches, dull, and would find a shady cool spot and immerse himself in the scriptures as he prepared lessons for the coming year's seminary classes. This dedication to being a good teacher, even on vacation, resounds in an additional recollection by Judge Benson. "He went on vacation once and came back to seminary and told us that he'd gone down to Mexico." His vacation destination was of interest to his students, but his rather unusual activity while on vacation proved more interesting. "His idea of a good time on vacation was to go to the mission home and help the missionaries preach the gospel. I assume he had a connection in the mission home down there or things must have been a little less formal then regarding the missionary program, because that's what he did while he was on his vacation."

Bishop Garner's generosity in dollars also drew unsolicited notice from his seminary students. "I think all of us remember his generosity and that he would use his personal resources. I think with the youth where he was so generous it did make an impression on how we spend our resources. He was very influential in building the youth's testimonies," states Marcia McLain.

The corrupting influence of a love of money seemed never to touch Keith. It freed him to be of service. Judge Benson submits, "Keith was an energetic man in business. He had a reputation for being financially successful, but he also was known to be generous with his money. He wasn't known as an economic snob. Some people in and out of the Church make a lot of money and then they change, but Keith always maintained a reputation that money wasn't his main goal in life."

His main goal in life usually took the form of desiring to assist as many as possible in living productive, gospel-centered lives. Continually involved in one or more land development projects, he often needed laborers and so extended summer work to his seminary students. Judge Benson continues, "Keith provided jobs for a lot of teenagers in the summer time. I worked for him on a few of his projects and he was generous to me regarding my hourly wage. I mean this was in the days when maybe seventy-five cents an hour or one dollar an hour was considered very good wages for a sixteen-year-old in the summer. I know my brother Earl worked for him for a couple of summers. Keith liked my brother and my brother really worked hard for Keith."

One never-to-be-forgotten task Keith gave Earl still induces smiles. "I remember one time my brother drove a big truckload of bathroom appliances, either from Las Vegas to the San Francisco Bay area or vise versa, on an emergency basis to make sure one of Keith's buildings got completed on time. Keith gave my brother a very generous bonus at the end of the summer because of my brother's hard work."

Whether Bishop Garner took twenty or thirty seminary pupils at year's end to a ritzy San Francisco restaurant or showed up at MIA on Tuesday night to take a group of young people to the soda fountain for refreshments and an informal chat or chaperoned and paid for the entire seminary class' trip to Disneyland, his motivation remained the same. He constantly focused on motivating gospel goal achievement. Such involved bishoping was reminiscent of Bishop Nalder's performance years before.

With undiminished amazement Judge Benson relates the following. "At the end of the seminary year he'd take all the class up to a swanky restaurant in San Francisco for dinner. We were typical suburban kids who mostly ate hamburgers. The fare in our homes and local restaurants was quality American food, but Keith would take us to these high-end, swanky, ritzy places in San Francisco. He'd come in with fifteen or twenty of us. We'd be handed these big elaborate menus and he'd say, 'Order anything on the menu.' So the kids would order the prime rib, the expensive steaks and lamb chops with what we thought were enormous prices; he'd say, 'It's all on me; eat up.' I remember the first time I was sitting next to him and when the bill came, I sort of saw what the bill was. I don't remember what it was but to me it was astronomical. This is a high-end very, very prestigious restaurant. I said to him, 'Holy cow, look at that bill,' and he said, 'Oh, don't think anything of it.' He reached into his pocket and pulled out a roll of hundred dollar bills and he just laid out a couple of hundred dollar bills on the table. Maybe there were twenty or thirty students there. He just paid it with hundred dollar bills. I mean we'd never seen a hundred dollar bill before. That dinner was something we looked forward to at the end of those seminary years."

With Keith it was never a one time big splash. His generosity in time and money consistently impacted his students and other ward members. Far more significant than the fancy dinners, Judge Benson recalls, "During the summer especially he'd just informally get everybody that showed up at mutual on Tuesday night and he'd take the young men and say, 'We're cutting classes short tonight. We'll all go out and have a soda together.' He'd take five or ten of us guys, and he'd do it with the gals too, to a soda fountain or somewhere like that and we'd have an informal social session with him. All the kids liked that because he was a very interesting and entertaining man."

Some of his nonsensical tales were told for pure pleasure. Animated by jestures, his telling of one roused repeated requests from young and old for its retelling. "This is the story of the Ickle Bickle Bird that lives on the highest limb of the highest tree of the highest mountain in the world. He comes down once a year in the springtime and slides down long blades of grass. As he slides down these blades of grass he utters the words, 'Ickle bickle, ickle bickle, ickle bickle.' Now that might not mean much to those who speak the languages of the humans, but in the language of the Ickle Bickle Bird it is 'Key-rye-mu-knee, what a sensation!'"

The Disneyland trips also scored very high on the youth's list of anticipated activities. Richard Lambert, referencing a particular Disneyland trip, continues his evaluation. This time he speaks to Keith of Bishop Garner's most generous gift, his compassion. "In connection with seminary was an incident which I think typifies your kind of approach to the youth. As I recall you were our seminary teacher my senior year of high school. I was not that faithful in attendance at seminary, and you had told the seminary class for those who made it through the year you were going to take them down to Disneyland. I remember towards the end of the year I, certainly by my attendance, had not qualified to go on that trip, but I recall you coming to me and saying, 'Dick, we'd like you to go. We'd like you to be part of the group; we'd like you to enjoy this outing.' I just had a great time. We had a wonderful outing."

"I remember," submits Marcia, "that wonderful challenge that if we didn't miss seminary he would take us down to Disneyland, which he did and we stayed at the Disneyland Hotel; it was righteous bribery for sure. We all participated and I think Richard's point is a good one. Maybe one or two of us either were late or didn't make the hundred percent but we were allowed to participate."

Richard continues, "It typified the principle of mercy and compassion. You had an interest in me that I really enjoyed. I loved you as a teacher. As I look back at the Menlo Park Ward, I had some good teachers, but I'd say you were the best. In fact, you set an example I've tried to follow."

As Mr. Lambert indicates, his story illustrates in a classic teaching moment Bishop Garner's application of compassion. Keith remembers, "I saw Dick and asked him if he were going to Disneyland. He told me he didn't qualify. I told him, 'Of course you qualify to go; what do you mean?'" As far as Keith is concerned, in mortality we all qualify for every opportunity to learn, grow, and become reacquainted with our divine nature and potential. He carries in his pocket an increasingly ragged, folded piece of paper upon which he has written the prophet Amulek's teaching, "For it is expedient that an atonement should be made; for according to the great plan of the Eternal God there must be an atonement made, or else all mankind must unavoidably perish; yea, all are hardened; yea, all are fallen and are lost, and must perish except it be through the atonement which it is expedient should be made."[22] Years after he noted this scripture, he ran across two corroborating statements. In Hugh Nibley's article, "The Last Days--Who Will Survive," Dr. Nibley capsulized the same message in one sentence. "The righteous are whoever are repenting, and the wicked whoever are not repenting." Avraham Gileadi adds, "Zion and Babylon possess strong spiritual overtones. They symbolize righteousness, which Isaiah defines as a disposition to repent, and wickedness, a disposition to oppress others, particularly the righteous. The one cannot flourish when the other rules."[23]

Two of Bishop Garner's favorite scriptures in concert define for him the gospel message. The first is the Lord's invitation found in Matthew 11:28-30. "Come unto me, all ye that labour and are heavy laden, and I will give you rest. Take my yoke upon you, and learn of me; for I am meek and lowly in heart: and ye shall find rest unto your souls. For my yoke is easy, and my burden is light."

The second is His promise found in Doctrine and Covenants 58:42. "Behold, he who has repenteth of his sins, the same is forgiven, and I, the Lord, remember them no more."

Imperfections permeate the mortal experience and are found without exception in leaders and followers, inside the Church and outside the Church. Because of this acknowledged reality, Bishop Garner gives no leeway to anyone who uses others' failings as an excuse for their own falling by the wayside or inactivity.

As a bishop and as a judge in Israel, Bishop Garner accepted wholeheartedly the Lord as the Keeper of the Gate and knew the role of the bishop encompassed striving mightily to open doors rather than close them. He always taught that all of

---

[22] Alma 34:9

[23] Avraham Gileadi, *The Book of Isaiah* (Salt Lake City: Deseret Book, 1998), 54.

us, without exception, are in desperate need of the atoning sacrifice of the Savior.

As with Jerry Benson, Richard Lambert, and Marcia Crofts, Bishop Garner's influence touched other young people in the ward. Stephen J. Swift relates, "When I was about sixteen Bishop Garner had a priesthood interview with me. I remember very distinctly and I've always remembered that during the course of the visit with me he paused and looked at me and then asked me, 'What suggestions do you have for running the ward?' That caught me by surprise and I said, 'He's asking me, a teenager. This is pretty amazing.' That just really meant a lot to me that he would care for my opinion. I remember how good that made me feel. I think I had a suggestion or two; I don't remember what they were. Maybe he sensed that I did. At any rate years later when I was bishop in McLean, Virginia, I remembered that interview with Bishop Garner, and so frequently I would ask the teenagers how we could improve the ward. They always seemed to appreciate, as I had, my asking. It was his example and my experience with Bishop Garner that caused me to provide that opportunity to the young people of my ward."

John Lindsay's mother, Agnes, who filled the role of Bishop Garner's last Relief Society president, graciously and gratefully writes, "The thing I remember most about Keith was his work with the young people of the ward. I give him credit for my son accepting a call to serve in Hong Kong. After my son John was called on a mission, Bishop Garner called me to his office and said it was time for me to serve the Lord as well, and asked me to be Relief Society president. This was a wonderful time in my life, and Bishop Garner was so supportive in all we attempted to do."

Agnes told Keith in referring to that beautiful garden spot where so many of these golden memories grew that upon her death if she woke up and found herself looking out her back window at her beautiful yard nestled in the trees of Atherton, she would know for sure she was in heaven.

Over his eleven years as bishop, Bishop Garner felt like he worked with six of the finest Relief Society presidents a bishop could ever find: Ruth Hales, Ruby Dobbins, Alicia Crofts, Ann Lund, Edith Mackay, and Agnes Lindsay. Bishop Garner rapidly and astutely realized, "If you want something done, you give the assignment to any of the women's organizations."

Recently Keith received a pat on the back from the two men who had "put the Bishop's robe on him." Sidney Badger lauded Keith with the lofty words, "Keith had a constancy of purpose, an inexhaustible energy used in his never-ending efforts to bring the good news of the gospel of Jesus Christ to all. He was the most diligent preacher of the scriptures I have ever known." Elder Haight agreed. "That's what I've always felt, and that's a nice compliment." Keith responding to such praise said, "I told Sid,' that's the nicest thing you could say. Now you can say anything else you want about my failures, but that covers it all.'"

Elder Haight as Keith's stake president had said something else, not quite as laudatory, to Keith on a couple of occasions. First, Keith heard that one of the better situated sisters in the ward had taken offense at a visit to her home by her visiting teachers. The rumor that got back to Keith was that these two sisters had gone to her home and she let them in reluctantly. She claimed that while she was out of the room they were going through her drawers. Keith recalls, "She felt they were not acting properly. When I heard about her complaint, I called her up and told her these women had left their children, their homes, and everything to come spend a little time with her. I told her it's the program of the Lord's church to do that. If she didn't want them to visit her, she should just let me know, and I'd take her name off the records, and they wouldn't bother her anymore. The next call I got was from David Haight, wondering if I were bringing people in or out of the Church."

Second, occasionally President Haight questioned Bishop Garner's use of the welfare funds of the Church. Once a month on fast Sunday, members refrain from eating two meals and give the money which would have been spent on those meals to the bishop. The fast offering is one means used to finance the welfare program, a program to help members who have fallen on hard times or who, for some reason, are unable to solve the problems life presents. In defining the Church welfare program the First Presidency wrote, "Our primary purpose was to set up, insofar as it might be possible, a system under which the curse of idleness would be done away with, the evils of a dole abolished, and independence, industry, thrift and self-respect to be once more established amongst our people. The aim of the Church is to help the people to help themselves. Work is to be re-enthroned as the ruling principle in the lives of our Church membership."[24] Bishop Garner understood and strongly advocated the underlying principle that when recipients work for what they are given it produces the ennobling benefit of helping them retain their dignity. Nevertheless, he also understood the reality of situations such as the single mother with five children who is unable to find enough energy or time in a day to both work and care for her family. He knew that however she had gotten there, she was there, and she needed help. Latter-day Saints in similar situations found Bishop Garner always ready to help. Known throughout his life for his personal generosity and while repeatedly counselled about the difference between wants and needs and the consequences of lavish handouts, Keith still erred, if it were an error, on the side of signing the check for those he saw in need. President Haight lightheartedly suggested he might have to confiscate Bishop Garner's checkbook to help him reign in his unbridled generosity.

Bishop Garner's generosity extended to his giving unselfishly of his time. Members of the ward, accustomed to his presence, counted on seeing Bishop Garner at every function. If he were absent, the question "Where's the bishop?" would always be asked. Everyone knew that wherever he appeared, things were happening. The

---

[24] *Conference Report* (Salt Lake City: The Church of Jesus Christ of Latter-day Saints, October 1936), 3.

answer to where is Bishop Garner might be that he is at the hospital visiting the sick, he is on an excursion to the Los Angeles Temple, he is in San Francisco speaking at the Hamilton Methodist Church or in Menlo Park at the First Congregational Church, he is taking his seminary students to Disneyland, he is addressing the ward in San Mateo or the youth of the San Francisco Stake, he is pounding nails at the new Menlo Park Chapel, or he is in Mexico looking for the sword of Laban.

Indeed, one of his favorite activities consisted of traveling to Mexico in pseudo-archeological pursuit of Book of Mormon civilizations. He tells of these adventures gleefully. "I went down to Mexico a number of times with Mitch Hunt." Gazing on a photo of the two of them in a primitive setting with a man holding a donkey in tow, Keith exclaims, "Mitch looks good. That's when we were young and carefree. We had a lot of fun on the trip because Mitch was a very colorful guy. There's nobody that had his zest for life and his ability to tell a great story. I take that back. The only one that ever equalled him was Julian Smith. When you got the two together, everybody else just faded away because they took middle stage." Pondering times past, Keith sighs, "Both of them are gone now. Gee whiz. Both went pretty early; Mitch in his fifties, and Julian in his sixties." As an aside Keith expands, "In fact, Julian passed away on April Fool's Day. He died in the hospital, and his wife, Rita, clinging to his gift for humor, nudged him and said, 'Now don't pull an April Fool's trick on me.'"

Engaging companions always complemented Keith's arresting excursions to Mexico and beyond. Mexico brims with archeological finds confirming the existence of major cities, relics which bespeak ancient cultures, and tantalizing digs which heighten hopes for new discoveries. The Teotihuacan Pyramids, in travel brochures referred to as City of the Gods, provided the magnificent backdrop for Keith and friends. Viewed from the Pyramid of the Moon, the eye can choose to rest upon the Plaza of the Moon, the Avenue of the Dead, or the Pyramid of the Sun (Quetzalcoatl). Walking through this monumental city, travelers feel the presence of the past thousand years of ceremony centered around natural cycles and expressed in astronomical and calendrical constructions.

Keith proceeds with his Mexican adventures, "One time we took Hayward Baker, one of our friends, and when we got down to the Teotihuacan Valley, we hired some Mexican laborers. Hayward started them digging around some of these pyramids in hopes of discovering ancient artifacts. They dug pretty deep. Undeterred, Hayward took out the geiger counter he had brought along as he followed them deeper and deeper into the earth. The geiger counter struck metal, and hearing its ringing, kidding, I yelled, 'Have you found Laban's sword?' It was exciting just to talk about the possibility."

Manifestly less committed than the others to unearthing the treasures of Mexico or perhaps just victimized by the blazing sun, Mitch and Keith left and went to Acapulco, checked into the hotel, and jumped into the pool. Later they rented a car and drove down the Pan American Highway to Guatemala, right into some kind of mini revolution. Luckily for them, they briskly boarded a plane and flew back to San Francisco, avoiding a possibly near fatal ordeal.

Another time Keith and Mitch, accompanied by Tom Ferguson, who had a friend in Mexico City with a plane, flew over the area surrounding Mexico City looking for the Hill Cumorah. Some supposedly credible source had theorized that the last great battles of the Nephites and Lamanites were fought in this general area. Keith shakes his head and expresses his doubts. "I don't think any of us considered it a serious venture, but it was an adventure. Mitch always remembered it well since his upset stomach gave him problems which made his taking the drapes off Tom's friend's plane windows necessary."

Back in Menlo Park, Bishop Garner developed and cultivated a good relationship with other churches in the area. This proved easy for him to do. No one could be offended by his unbridled enthusiasm for his own convictions. Whether you agreed with him, thought he'd lost his mind, or gradually warmed to his beliefs, the high value he placed on those beliefs and, no matter what anyone else thought, the fact that he knew they were true went unquestioned.

In explaining to members of the clergy or for that matter any non-member the position he held of bishop in the Mormon Church, he often had to start with the basic units of Church governance. He would give a cursory overview of general, stake, and ward units and the Priesthood, Relief Society, Young Men's Mutual Improvement Association, Young Women's Mutual Improvement Association, and Primary--organizations serving the men, women, young men, young women, and children of the Church.

Sometimes Keith felt like he needed a glossary of Mormonisms to hand out. Humorous misinterpretations generated many smiles. For instance, when Keith dressed in a business suit was introduced as bishop of Menlo Park, the curious onlookers wondered where the vestments of his office were. When told he presided over a "ward" in Menlo Park, some assumed he was the boss of the western equivalent of a Chicago political unit. Or when he told another associate he was going to conference at the "stake house," he assumed Keith was going to dinner with business colleagues and wished him good dining. Keith would be eating, but he would be spiritually fed.

Despite his sometimes misunderstood terminology, Keith enjoyed sharing Mormon practices and theology. Keith's time at the University of San Francisco had opened up Catholic theology and the goodness of the Catholic fathers to him. He narrates, "While attending USF, I became well acquainted with the Jesuit priests that were my instructors. I found they were high quality, dedicated, and learned. The Jesuit order is an order not so much of service but more of education. Father McLoin, one of the priests, was a historian, and I took a course in California history from him. We became well-acquainted. I was the only Mormon in the university, so he asked me to work with him on correcting the papers of the other students in the class and evaluating what they'd written, and I did that. I wasn't the top of the class, let me clue you, but I was atop of the spiritual order because I was a Mormon. He wanted to know more about us, and I wanted to know more about him, so we spent much time in each other's company. We talked about our theologies, and I took Catechism. One evening we were out on a hill looking over San Francisco, and he asked me to explain the Mormon concept of God. I told him our God is our Father in Heaven and we have a Mother in Heaven and we are the children of that marriage, that union. That was rather staggering to him. Finally, he said to me, 'I think you are attempting to diminish God in order to explain him.' I said, 'I'm not trying to explain him; I'm just telling you who he is. I don't know anything except that God is celestial and glorified and has all power on the earth and in heaven.' He said, 'That's interesting; you find great satisfaction in that type of a relationship.' I said, 'Well, I don't know any other way he would become our God. In teaching us how to pray, Jesus set the example we are to follow when he directs his prayer to "Our Father which art in Heaven." I understand who an earthly father is, and he's a heavenly father so that's the relationship.'"

His respect for these Catholic fathers also found expression in Menlo Park. "During the construction of the stake house, I was out in the back of the chapel on this pretty sizable lot where we were digging a trench for some reason. I climbed down a ladder into the depths of the hole to investigate a problem. From the bottom of the trench, I heard somebody yell 'Bishop, you are wanted.' I climbed up the ladder. As I neared the top, I looked up and saw a beautiful, shiny black car. The driver opened the door, and as the gentleman got out of the back seat, I saw the flowing black robes and red beading and recognized Monsignor Edward Kennedy, the Catholic priest in charge of the adjacent Catholic church. As I climbed out adorned in my work clothes, he said, 'Are you Bishop Garner?' and I said, inwardly smiling at our contrasting apparel, 'Yes, Monsignor, I am Bishop Garner.' After we had concluded our business, I suggested, 'Father, let's work together, or we're going to go down together.' He countered, 'Nah, let's work together and go up together.' I quickly said, 'That's a better approach.'"

Since Keith's true adventures and daily experiences were subject matter from which all who knew him or had heard of him could draw, apocryphal or exaggerated stories still unnecessarily embellished some of their conversations. Like all such tales, they were based on a smidgen of truth. One friend tells rightly, "As a bishop of a new ward, he was a man of action, heart always in the right place." But then this same friend crosses over into fiction. "Sometimes his followthrough and execution were a little awkward. One guy told me that one day he questioned the bishop's judgment because he got called to four different positions in one day." Bishop Garner's exuberance is legendary, but not quite that animated. Another friend remembers, "Keith never sits very long," which is a true understatement. To illustrate her point, JoAnne Rogers continues. "Keith used to drop by unannounced and out of nowhere, sit at the kitchen counter, and visit while I fixed meals for hungry teenagers, and then just as

*Bishop Dix M. Jones at the pulpit at the dedication of the Palo Alto Chapel; seated behind him: Bishop Keith E.
Garner; seated to the front left Hayward Baker; behind him from l to r--President Sidney Badger, President
David B. Haight, President Stephen L. Richards*

quickly vanish." Her embellishment comes when she refers to Keith as one of the
Three Nephites.

However overstated any description of Keith's role in erecting the Palo Alto
Stake Center/Menlo Park Chapel may sound, one would be hard pressed to find
anyone who was involved in the effort who would disagree. While resident bishops
fill similar roles in the building of chapels worldwide, the Menlo Park chapel
singularly stands on its own merits in the annals of Church construction. Bishop
Garner's shepherding to completion the Palo Alto Stake Center/Menlo Park Chapel
is still recognized as one of his great achievements. More than one long-time resident
of Menlo Park proffers, "I never walk into that beautiful building without thinking of
Keith Garner."

When the Palo Alto Ward was divided in 1952 and Keith became Bishop
Garner, the reorganization took place in the chapel at 771 Addison Avenue, Palo Alto,
according to the *Palo Alto Times* of November 24, 1952. The article further informed
its readers that this site "is being enlarged and renovated and will be the meeting place
for both wards." On December 13, 1954, President Stephen L. Richards of the First
Presidency presided and offered the dedicatory prayer for the Palo Alto Ward/Menlo
Park Ward Chapel located at 950 Guinda Street, Palo Alto, an address change made
necessary by the expansion. President Haight, Bishop Dix M. Jones, and Bishop

Garner offered remarks. Even then Keith saw that Church growth would overtake this splendid new building's capacity. His instincts proved right, and he moved forward, later receiving kudos for his farsightedness.

In the *Menlo Park, California Recorder and Gazette* of Thursday, September 2, 1954, the headline read, "Latterday Group Seeks Property." The copy read, "Menlo Park Ward of Church of the Latterday Saints is currently negotiating to purchase the six acre Harking property in the area surrounded by Altschul and Harkins Avenues, Alameda de las Pulgas and Sharon Roads, it was learned yesterday. The property on which is situated the Harkins family's twelve room home, built in 1887, is currently the residence of Miss Katherine Harkins. If the purchase goes through the site will become the location of a church for the Menlo Park congregation, which is headed by Keith Garner, Bishop, who resides at 1555 Bay Laurel Drive." This was the first step towards the acquisition of the property on which the Menlo Park Ward meeting house would finally stand.

A year and six months later Arnold Fluckiger, the ward clerk, on the June 1956 quarterly report typed, "Sale of 5.6 acres to Domar Land Company for gross sale of $84,000. In September of '54 the Church purchased the property for the ward. On February 3, 1956, the Church and the ward purchased 3.1 acres on the corner of Valparaiso and Arbor Road in Menlo Park for $90,000. The Church allowed the $25,000 profit from the sale of the Alameda property to be applied to the sale of the new property. The ward paid $15,000. The balance was loaned to the ward on a six month note. A home exists which is suitable for a temporary meeting house."

Multitudinous tasks leading up to the groundbreaking ceremonies came to fruition. The Menlo Park Ward burned the mortgage taken out to finance the ward's contribution towards the purchase of the Valparaiso property at the ward's New Year's Eve party. The Church General Authorities and stake officers selected the Menlo Park property to be the stake center. Members of the Menlo Park Ward voted unanimously to support the chapel's erection. Bids went out. With a variance secured, architectural renderings and plans were approved by Salt Lake and by the city building department.

Eldon Bringhurst writes, "June 14, 1959. Groundbreaking ceremonies at 1:30 p.m. with Stake President David B. Haight presiding and Bishop Keith E. Garner conducting. Palo Alto bishops and high councilmen were in attendance. One hundred in attendance; earth turned by ten men.

Bishop Garner related some of the details relative to our purchasing the property at 1105 Valparaiso Avenue in Menlo Park after selling the property originally purchased for a meeting house on Alameda de las Pulgas. He expressed his appreciation for the Church. He introduced John Reed who will supervise the construction of the building.

President Haight said this is a glorious occasion to start our new stake house, and it will be a beautiful building when it is completed.

In preparing this report for the stake historical records, I would like to praise

Menlo Park Ward Chapel ground breaking on June 14, 1959: Notice who is leaning on his shovel thinking, "Other than this being a wonderful beginning, what good is this going to do?"

our wonderful bishop, Keith E. Garner, for his love for the people of Menlo Park and for his untiring efforts to make the Menlo Park Ward a really nice place to attend Church, and for his devotion to his family and friends--also the amount of effort and push he has exerted in getting this new building started. He may neglect his work, but never his Church duties."

Over the next several building months, the old Wreden mansion, located on the site, was retrofitted to accommodate the needs of the ward until the new building could be occupied.

Elder David B. Haight describes Keith's role in this momentous building project. "When we built the stake house, we had to have somebody in charge. Someone has to make the decisions; otherwise, you get in trouble, and so Keith was what we refer to as the resident bishop. It was a big building with lots of problems and challenges, but Keith did a marvelous job. It was finished within eleven months, and he was the pusher to bring that about.

It was the most expensive chapel that we ever built because up to that time the stakes and wards were raising half the money; I believe it was half the money. Now that money comes from Salt Lake, but back in those days, we raised half the money to buy the land; we raised half the money to pay for the building. We had all of the wards raise some of the money which they did, but Keith carried the load on it. I think we came in close to budget. Keith was riding herd on that."

Keith accepts that praise reluctantly and points out Wesley T. Benson's contribution. "Wes was the chairman of the finance committee and later project clerk. I knew he'd raise the money, and he did." Fund raisers including paper drives, ward dinners, reunions, Relief Society bazaars, matching fund patrons, honey and wheat sales, and meetings where invited guests spoke were organized to supplement the building fund for which members had already been assessed and contributed.

Whether for a fund-raising event or as a musical gift to the community, Alexander Schreiner, the Mormon Tabernacle organist, was invited prior to the dedication to play the newly arrived seventeen rank organ made in Germany, which had cost $20,000 and had been called the finest on the Peninsula. Keith reminisces, "I don't recall what the specific occasion was, but I do remember that in a prayer meeting attended by Lund Johnson, a member of the stake presidency, and myself prior to Brother Schreiner's performance, we outlined the program. Alexander Schreiner's only comment regarding the opening prayer was 'Don't you have anyone talk to the Lord about having my fingers hit the right keys because I can assure you my fingers will hit the right keys.' President Johnson and I kind of winked at each other and grinned because Alexander Schreiner rightly carried the confidence, idiosyncracies, and bearing of the master organist which he was."

Elder Haight rightly notes that the Menlo Park Ward building came in close to budget and that it was completed in eleven months, the first meeting being held on May 15, 1960. Two components made that happen. Keith was a successful builder and could call on subcontractors with whom he had worked. Art Whitely, Keith's superintendent, worked with John Reed, the Church's superintendent, and they were able to use to great advantage the generous volunteer laborers. In fact, on one Saturday fifty-five men showed up, and most nights after work, a good number of volunteers were on the job. Bishop Garner exclaims, "We had terrific participation!" and further explains, "Wherever in the course of construction we could do it ourselves, we did. We put the plywood on the roof, and that roof went on forever. We helped with some of the framing, siding, sheet rock, and flooring. We carried equipment and pounded nails."

One night after the volunteers had completed the attachment of the underlament making the roof ready for its covering, Keith received word that he should expect the delivery of the slate roofing the next morning. Keith relates how his concern about the delivery unfortunately proved correct. "In the morning I woke up and thought, 'You know, when they deliver that today, I hope they deliver it on the Arbor Street side because if they go to the other side, they are going to get stuck.' Sure enough while I was having breakfast, I got a call saying that this big truck loaded with all our slate tiles was stuck in the mud. The weather was turning bad, and I didn't want the rain to come before we got it on. Here we were rushing to get the roof on, and they were stuck. I went over and kind of shook my head. My counselor Llew Leigh had just arrived, and I said to him, 'You know, I just can't understand why he

Church building superintendent John Reed and Bishop Garner working on chapel

would do that.' He made a statement I have recalled over the years when I've found myself perplexed by witless behavior, 'Keith, he isn't president of City Bank.'"

Some volunteers now and then provided needed comic relief. Giggling throughout, Keith tells the story of one inactive member's consternation at the loss of his hammer. "I'd get all the inactive members out and put them to work. They didn't mind working on the chapel just so as long as they didn't have to go to Church. That was their contribution, and it was a great one. I was working next to one inactive fellow who said that he'd misplaced his hammer. What he really said was 'Some SOB took my hammer.' Then he had everyone laughing so hard their eyes were watering when without thinking he blurted out, 'Bishop, do you have it?' Smiling and barely able to retain my composure, I answered, 'No, I don't have it.' Well, we got him out to help; it was really funny."

Keith could not have been close by, let alone in charge, without innovations being part of the mix. He had carpeting laid not just down the chapel aisles but under the pews, in the classrooms, even in the closets. This prevented the noise made from children dropping toys or adults dropping song books, purses, and shoes on the floor from resounding throughout the building and disturbing the reverent atmosphere. Because Bishop Garner chose not to use the standard materials of linoleum and tile, the caretaker wasn't always on his knees trying to erase heel marks.

In another innovative move, he had installed a first-class sound and lighting system which gave all the ward's and stake's would-be thespians the tools to make the

Mutual Improvement Association's road shows performed in that building seem like Broadway productions.

Innovators are men of vision, and looking at this or to any other era in his life, there is no question Bishop Garner qualified as a man of vision. Fortunately in this supervised position, he reaped all the blessings of having an overseer, President Haight, who embraced the same vision. He needed this support. Someone from Church headquarters showed up on-site and challenged one of Bishop Garner's decisions. Keith, annoyed with both his dictatorial demeanor and a perceived overstepping of authority, simply asked him, "To whom do I report?" or in other words, who is my boss? He answered, "Your stake president." Keith responded confidently, "Then you get on the phone and talk to President Haight." Keith closes this incident with, "President Haight backed me up one hundred percent; he was always there for me; he gave me his almost unconditional support."

Elder Haight returns the compliment. "Well, swell, when somebody's a good manager and doing it right, you always support them. You stop supporting somebody when you have to because he's a crook or dishonest and the job is failing, but that was just the opposite with Keith. You knew what he was saying would happen. It would be accomplished, and he'd make it work."

President Haight had his own clash with the bureaucracy in Salt Lake. It is a story he tells with relish. "We had an interesting incident on that building when they were going to put in the landscaping. Somebody came with the landscaping plan, and it called for taking down some old oak trees that were out in front, and I think also a redwood tree. I don't know what Keith had told them, but by the time I heard about it, I said, 'You can't take those trees out because they were there when the Mexican Army came up from Monterey when this was part of Mexico. They came up to try to discover the San Francisco Bay, and that Mexican Army decided to divide into two groups: one to go up the Peninsula to determine its size. This would have been back in 1847, '48, '49. When the army divided, they agreed to meet at the Palo Alto. Now in Spanish that means tall tree." Pointing to the tree symbol on a plaque the City of Palo Alto gave to him commemorating his having been the mayor of Palo Alto, Elder Haight continued, "So Palo Alto means tall tree. There was one of those trees over on this property that Keith helped negotiate to buy on Valparaiso. So the landscape people said we'd have to take that tree out to put parking in. I said, 'You can't take that tree out. That's a historical tree.' They said, 'No, no, no, no, you have to take 'em out because Salt Lake said so.' I said, 'Who in Salt Lake said so?' and they said, 'Well, President McKay is President of the Church.' I said, 'If President McKay writes us a letter and tells us to take those trees out, we'll take them out, but if it's somebody else, we won't take them out.' He said, 'You're defying the leadership of the Church.' I said, 'No, I'm not. I'm only defying the landscape people.' So they sent out another plan. They'd changed it a little, but the trees were still gone. I said, 'You can't do that. We won't allow you to do that. We're not going to spoil the beauty of this lot. We want to preserve it.'

A short time later Henry Moyle came down. He was a member of the First Presidency of the Church, and he came down for a meeting with Consolidated Freightways up in Menlo Park. He would often come by and see us. I'd pick him up from his meeting, and he'd have dinner with Ruby and me, and then I'd take him to the airport. On one of those visits, I said, 'Let me take you over and show you our new stake house.' We went in the back door over by the back parking lot, in through the amusement hall, and out the front door. We were standing out in front, and those beautiful trees were out there. President Moyle said, 'My those are beautiful trees.' I said, 'President Moyle, they are beautiful trees, but I'm about to be excommunicated from the Church.' He said, 'You are?' I said, 'Well, your building department back there said that those trees have to go.' He said, 'Oh, don't do that. President McKay's always teaching us to hold on to all the things that are beautiful, hold on to the trees. We can build around them but we don't take them out.' I said, 'Well you'll be coming down here putting in a new stake president because they're after me.' He said, 'I'll send Irv Nelson down here. He does the landscaping for the temples.'

In a couple of days, Irv Nelson was at the airport in San Francisco, and he said President Moyle had called, told him to get down here, and that I'd tell him what to do. I said, 'Oh, I don't know what to tell you to do.' I took him out to Stanford to see the landscaping and went around to see some of the new buildings, some of the new shrubbery that had been put in so he'd get a flavor of California and not just snowy Salt Lake. He went back and drew up the general plan that was finally put in down there. We kept the trees." Keith happily adds, "The trees are still there."

Bishop Garner also called on Sister Lucille Olpin for help in this phase. "I had Sister Olpin help with the landscape design. She was terrific. Her husband's brother, Ray, was president of the University of Utah. He could have had her teach a course. She did a great job for us. She'd pick and place the plants, and we would plant them."

Elder Haight tells the story he told Keith at the time which foreshadowed another lesson on authority Keith would later be taught. "When I told President Moyle that I was about to lose my membership, he took his finger and put it right on my collar bone, right there, and said, 'You're the president of this stake; we put you in there. If you see something is being done that you don't agree with, you don't think it would fit in to what we're trying to do, you stop it.' He beat me right on that collar bone, and I remembered it."

On February 25, 1962, the Palo Alto Stake Center and Menlo Park Ward Chapel were dedicated. The dedication was quite an event and caught the notice of California and Utah newspaper reporters. Keith circled one of these newspaper stories and wrote, "Not every day a Garner makes the front page." The $600,000, 26,000 square foot basalite brick building's facilities are variously described in newspaper articles written at the time. These descriptions admiringly point out the numerous amenities including stake president's office, high council room, two bishop's

President Moyle speaking at dedication of Palo Alto Stake Center and Menlo Park Chapel on February 25, 1962

offices, two ward clerk's offices, a stake clerk's office, a senior chapel seating 365 which can be expanded to 2300, double windowed quiet rooms on each side, a spacious Junior Sunday School chapel with small-sized pews and a rostrum to fit the five-year old, upholstered pews in both chapels, thick carpets throughout, baptismal font, Relief Society room, large kitchen complete with dishwasher and cabinets on rollers for easier serving, two library rooms, Aaronic Priesthood room, large recreation hall featuring a full-size high school basketball court and a stage equipped with a professional theatrical lighting system, stuccoed interior with light colored wood trim and furnishings, twenty-six classroom areas, men's and women's locker rooms and showers, floodlit large inner patio and outer patio surrounded by planter boxes, automatic sprinkler system, and off-the-street parking for two hundred automobiles.

President Henry D. Moyle, First Counselor in the First Presidency, gave the dedicatory address and prayer. "The chapel construction establishes a record for 'completing a project of such magnitude' in eleven months," President Moyle said. He described the location as "'Garden of Eden' beauty which should inspire the viewer to draw nearer to God."

Elder Haight, at the time of this interview, had served twenty-four years as a member of the Quorum of the Twelve, and with a undiminished pride perhaps said it best, "It's one of the most beautiful Church settings. It's on a beautiful street in Menlo Park, and when people drive by there, they see beautifully landscaped one of, if not the most beautiful chapel in the Church."

At the bottom of the dedication program, the tribute reads, "This beautiful chapel being dedicated today fits comfortably into its peaceful setting among the oaks. It reflects the quiet dignity and strength of The Church of Jesus Christ of Latter-day Saints, the faith and loyalty of the many Church members who made it possible, and the courage, sacrifice and devotion of Bishop Garner and the other stake and ward leaders who provided the inspiration to pursue this noble effort to its conclusion."

Elder Haight concludes, "Keith was the action man, and he was the man behind that beautiful building and a lot of the growth that we had. And so we developed, we improved our image down there, we had good buildings, and they looked well, and on the foundation we laid, the Church now has fifteen stakes in what was

"Will you please sign my program?"
l to r:Wendell Mendenhall, President Henry D. Moyle, Bishop Keith E. Garner, and President David B. Haight

the old Palo Alto Stake." "Brother," Keith observes, "It's hard to believe that happened in one man's lifetime. Yours and mine."

The maintenance of the completed building drew the bishop's attention. Bishop Garner was a true disciple when it came to personally following the adage, "Cleanliness is next to godliness." His appreciation for a job well-done laid the predicate for the following story. Brother Tidwell was employed as the custodian and took care of the chapel. When Bishop Garner would inspect it, he would always say, "Brother Tidwell, you do beautiful work, and you're going to make the kingdom!" After he became really active and involved and learned that there are three kingdoms of differing glory when Bishop Garner complimented him in the same manner, he asked, "Bishop, which one of these kingdoms am I going to make?"

While Keith never had neglected his advocacy of the principle of cleanliness, his endorsement intensified with the new building in use. Bishop Garner, walking through the chapel, heard voices coming from the other side of the closed anodized aluminum folding doors dividing the chapel from the amusement hall. Apparently a young lad with a pencil in hand was running along side the partition doors causing quite a racket and a need for janitorial service to remove the graphite markings. Unaware of Bishop Garner's close proximity, a voice firmly cautioned, "If Bishop Garner catches him, he'll really get a scolding." Another voice, the boy's mother, retorted, "I'm so tired of hearing about Bishop Garner." Keith grinned and said almost out loud, "I'm tired of hearing about Bishop Garner too!" After serving eleven years as the first and only bishop of the Menlo Park Ward, Keith went to Dick Sonne, the stake president, and said "It's time for a change!"

Wonderful changes had already come. The Los Angeles Temple graced the southern California city and the Oakland Temple cornerstone had just been laid. General conference broadcasts from Salt Lake City were televised locally. The Church was flourishing in the area.

In Bishop Garner's first address as bishop, he had said, "I am sure I will enjoy the work, and I desire to see the growth and development of the new Menlo Park Ward." He had enjoyed the work, and his desires had been realized.

More changes came. On January 27, 1963, a little less than a year after President Moyle dedicated the Palo Alto Stake Center/Menlo Park Ward, President Haight had been released and called to preside over the Scottish Mission. On June 30, 1963, five months later, Bishop Garner was released. Bishop Garner had for the past eleven years basked in President Haight's qualities of leadership, specifically his delegation to capable individuals of vital assignments followed by his loyal support. With both men's releases, the formality of Bishop Garner looking to President Haight as his file leader and President Haight standing behind Bishop Garner's decisions had ended. Nonetheless, Keith was about to experience the same kind of opportunities and loyalty from two other formidable Church servants, Elder Gordon B. Hinckley and Elder Marion D. Hanks. Like President Haight, neither of them ever clipped his wings, but rather let him soar in his new Church assignment. Another leadership calling which tapped his missionary zeal and expanded his already exercised talents lay only a short eighteen months away.

Yet as full of revelations as his bishop duties had been and as full of wonder as his new Church calling would be, a spiritual mother lode sighting had appeared on Keith's eastern horizon; a pure gold memory had already been made. Keith, responding to the thought provoking, even perplexing question, "What experience do you treasure most?" relates how privileged he felt to have held in his hands perhaps the most thrilling physical evidence pointing towards the reality of the Book of Mormon.'

Chapter
SEVEN

We Beheld the Gold Plates

Darius conquered his known world, but himself was conquered;
Alexander looted the treasures of Darius, but unbeknownst
to him left behind priceless gold plates.
– Keith E. Garner

In the spring of 1961, Bishop Garner, Thomas Stuart Ferguson, Sidney Badger, and Robert Ord traveled to the Middle East. Tom Ferguson, president of the New World Archeological Foundation and author of *One Fold and One Shepherd*, a book examining the ancestry of ancient populations in Central America and Mexico, had never been to the land from which Book of Mormon civilizations--Nephites, Jaredites, and Mulekites--originated. Ferguson's thesis found in his 1958 book is clearly captured in the following excerpt:

> *Jesus declared there were other sheep of the fold of Israel in addition*
> *to those in Palestine. Further, He made it clear that He planned*
> *to visit them. They were in a part of the world far removed from*
> *the Mediterranean region. Certain of the ancient inhabitants of*
> *Middle America claimed to be a branch of Israel. There is much*
> *evidence which corroborates their claims. The earliest documentary*
> *material from the natives and from the first European visitors*
> *sustains this position. Hundreds of cultural elements were common*
> *to ancient Bible lands and Middle America, supporting cultural*

transfers from the Near East to Mexico and Central America.
Middle America--where the ancient inhabitants claimed to be of
Israel--is the logical place to look for evidence of a possible appearance
of Jesus far beyond the borders of the Bible world. [25]

Bishop Garner became aware of Tom Ferguson's work and also of his proximity since he lived just across the San Francisco Bay in Orinda, and so he invited Tom to speak to members of the Menlo Park Ward about his fascinating archeological research. Additionally motivated by his appreciation for Tom's exploration, Keith felt Tom's deep interest and scholarship gave him the credentials of one who must see pertinent sites in the Middle East firsthand. Therefore, Bishop Garner organized a journey to visit Biblical lands and invited not only Tom but two of his friends, Sid Badger and Bob Ord, to accompany them.

Years before, Keith had become acquainted with Sid through Church service; Keith served on the Palo Alto high council, and Sid served in the Palo Alto Stake presidency. In fact, Sid had been the one who encouraged him to move from San Mateo to "God's country," Menlo Park, California. When the Garners took up residence in their Menlo Park home on Bay Laurel Drive, their neighbors were the Badgers, who lived just down the block.

Bob Ord completed the foursome. Bob had graduated from Brigham Young University and had come to Palo Alto to pursue a master's degree at Stanford University. Keith had made his acquaintance in Church circles and had given him a job as a rough carpenter, a job which Bob eventually turned into his own construction company.

Tom stood 6'1", a lean 180 pounds, with wire rimmed professorial glasses, dark hair, Iranianesque build. He was an independent thinker and an attorney by training. Sid stood 6', 195 pounds, good-looking, Romanesque, a fluent speaker, persuasive, polished, always making a great first impression. He was an accountant by training. Bob stood 5'9", 170 pounds, muscular, baby-faced, fair complexion, calm, constant, and was a history teacher by training, although a builder by profession. Their appearances, their interests, their past experiences, and their personalities were dissimilar; however, they shared in common their proclivity for seeking truth and their comradeship. This disparate combination of travelers promised an adventure in the making.

The itinerary, carefully planned with the consideration in mind that no one was allowed to enter any Arabian country from Israel, took the travelers first to the exotic, mysterious cities of Tehran, Shiraz, Cairo, Beirut, then to the modern city of

---

[25] Thomas Stuart Ferguson, *One Fold and One Shepherd* (San Francisco: Books of California, 1958), 381.

Tel Aviv, and finally to the eternal city of Jerusalem.

In Lebanon they walked into the tragic repercussions of the Israeli-Palestinian conflict already over eighty years old, a refugee camp holding roughly one hundred thousand men, women, and children "groveling in the dirt." It is estimated that by 1950 over one million exiles lived in United Nations supported refugee camps in Gaza, the West Bank, Jordan, and Lebanon. Some commentators claimed the camps provided a political tool used like a picture postcard to advance the dire need for a Palestinian state. It saddened these four men and roused conversations among them filled with musings about why the living areas were left in such distasteful conditions, why they were not given jobs, and why they were held in sympathetic countries without hope. They joined a host of other peace loving individuals in their desire to see an amelioration, portending a resolution, to the conflict so starkly before them. Such relief did not happen in 1961, and the underlying struggle still eludes settlement. Nevertheless, it did open their eyes to the reality of the enigmatic Middle East. Keith later learned that histories outlining the Israeli-Palestinian conflict included a notation naming two military groups: Menachem Begin's Irgun Zvai Leumi and Yitzhak Shamir's Lehi or Stern Gang. The title's use of the name Lehi jumped off the page; Keith had been unaware of the Book of Mormon prophet's name appearing with such prominence within the framework of the 1944-47 Jewish fight to expel the British protectorate and claim Palestine as their homeland.

On the Mount of Olives stands l to r: Robert M. Ord, Keith E. Garner, Sidney Badger, Thomas Stuart Ferguson

In Egypt, Keith, Tom, Sid, and Bob got lost in a world dated in millenniums as they gazed on the great pyramids at Luxor, anciently known as the city of Thebes and marvelled at the lost technology which had created these colossal monuments. They visited the Valley of the Kings and saw tombs of Pharaohs hewn out of the massive limestone cliffs, thought to be easier to conceal and less accessible to tomb robbers. They climbed atop camels that kneeled, then rose to their full height, and with a jaunt more jarring than a horse, moved across the desert terrain.

The seriousness and retrospection of the trip was balanced with amusements and, of course, included some harmless teasing. At a tent city outside Cairo, the four were seated with two other men who were also intent upon absorbing the Eastern entertainment culture, complete with belly dancers and sheiks' bazaars. Keith, the prankster, after becoming acquainted with these men, enlisted their help and clandestinely poured part of one of their glasses of bourbon into Ferguson's half consumed Coca Cola. Keith raised his Coke and toasted "Bottoms Up!" Tom tasted his drink and in one gulp emptied it. Putting the empty glass down matter-of-factly while smacking his lips, Tom exclaimed, "The Lord knows I didn't ask for it."

Sid gleefully reports that Tom was not the only recipient of a joke. Keith was on the other end of the prank when an ingredient in his salad was identified to him by his companions as grapes. In truth, the delicacy he relished eating was fish eyes. Keith, after hearing the punch line to the joke, ever so much more carefully consumed the indigenous foods served to him; in fact, according to Sid, he never ate a full meal until they returned to Rome.

Exotic foods certainly gave rise not only to pranks but also to new tastes. In a barber shop in Cairo, they watched Tom drink from a demitasse in which a spoon stood straight up anchored by the thickness of the beverage and wondered if Tom would drink the spoon as well as the "liquid" refreshment.

After the unfamiliar foods of Iran and Egypt, the four prepared to enjoy a delicious meal of fresh fish in Beirut. Unfortunately, each one had without the knowledge of the others taken more than an adequate amount of over-the-counter medicine to relieve the discomfort he was experiencing. Thus the savored meal was intermittently eaten between hurriedly taken and repeated trips to the restroom.

Shopping in these foreign lands also provided interesting anecdotes. On one of the bustling streets of Tehran, Keith walked into a jewelry emporium. The young proprietor took his ring size as he showed him an array of jewels among which was an uncommonly beautiful onyx stone. Keith apologetically told him he was in a hurry; his flight was scheduled to leave at a quickly approaching hour. To Keith's surprise, when the four arrived at the airport, this determined merchant was already there waiting. He had fashioned a ring especially for him, using a polished star sapphire, the very stone Keith had admired. The stone and the craftsmanship sparkled from the eighteen carat gold setting. Keith recalls, "It was magnificent. I thought anybody who would go to the airport to sell it--great! Anyone who could perform like that should be rewarded. Anyone who had enough English to understand what I was talking about deserved some consideration. I think it was under fifty dollars, and so I bought it."

Another purchase also made in Tehran surprised Keith's banker at home. Even in 1961 when credit cards were not a universal necessity and when pin numbers and bank account numbers didn't trump a personal signature, Keith's form of payment caused the bank establishment a little perplexity in its practical yet atypical application.

Persian vendors were selling large brass plates adorned around the circumference with hand carvings depicting the guards at Persepolis. Keith wanted one, but he didn't have any money with him, not even a check. However, he was wearing a white shirt. He impulsively tore his cuff off, wrote out a check on the spotless white surface, and gave it to the seller with the following instructions. "When it clears my bank, ship the plate to me." He left after giving the vendor his address. Several weeks later and a short time after his arrival home, a large package appeared at his home in Menlo Park from Persia via San Francisco. Unblemished, the disc's arrival brought numerous reactions of amazement at its intricate workmanship as well as amusement at its procurement.

Experiences full of spiritual import enhanced the fun-loving explorers' excursion, especially in Israel. They looked on Jerusalem from the Mount of Olives where the Savior had commanded his Apostles "Go ye into all the world and preach the gospel to every creature."[26] They drank in the sacred atmosphere of the Garden Tomb replete with blooming spring flowers and fragrances. They visited Jacob's well where the Savior promised the woman, "Whosoever drinketh of this water shall thirst again; But whosoever drinketh of the water that I shall give him shall never thirst...."[27] They climbed down the dank, narrow stairs to the tomb of Lazarus. They knelt humbly in the Garden of Gethsemene among two thousand year old olive trees, witnesses to the Son's atoning sacrifice. They visited ornate churches built over designated sites of important events in Christ's worldly ministry. They crowded through the cramped, aroma-laden streets of Old Jerusalem lined with eclectic merchants selling religious replicas made of olive wood, Oriental spices, and live chickens ready for the butcher's blade.

The Jerusalem Times dated Tuesday, April 11, 1961, Jerusalem-Jordan gives their visit a framework. Reading the headlines FIRST SOVIET MAN LAUNCHED INTO SPACE, W. GERMAN ATTITUDE TOWARDS EICHMANN, BRITISH PLANS FOR PROMPT CEASE-FIRE IN LAOS, REDS ACCEPT ANGLO-AMERICAN A-TEST BAN PROPOSALS is a reminder of how different yet how much the same the world is forty years later. An article headlined PLUNDER IN THE HOLY LAND begins

---

[26] Mark 16:15

[27] John 4:13-14

Keith in Luxor

with "We lost everything," say Palestine refugees--"and time will bring acceptance of Israel's gun-point thievery." Another front page story titled ROYAL AUDIENCES announces "His Majesty King Hussein received in audience at the Royal Hashemite court yesterday afternoon Mr. Samir Rifai', president of the senate, Mr. William Maccomber, U.S. Ambassador to Jordan, Mr. Abdul Rahman Aqqoun representative of the Algerian provisional government in Jordan."

At this time the only point of passage between the Old City or East Jerusalem and the New City or West Jerusalem was through the Mandelbaum Gate located in New Jerusalem. After the 1948 War of Independence in which West Jerusalem became the capital of the state of Israel, the Old City returned to the control of Jordan. Having to pass through the gate only accentuated the palpable distrust that various descendants of Abraham felt toward each other regarding long-standing claims to the same land made by differing branches of the family. If the four had come six years later after the 1967 war in which Israel recaptured the Old City, they would have found the separating wall torn down. Though perpetually strained relations between Moslems, Christians, and Jews would still have been in evidence, they would have found a notably different and freer access to three of the most revered places on earth at the Temple Mount. The four found their way through the Mandelbaum Gate and absorbed the mystique of monuments to the accomplishments of men in service to Allah, Jesus, and Jehovah. Keith viewed the Dome of the Rock with profound admiration for the technical skill, the artistic gifts, and the reverence for Allah which was unmistakably manifested in this structure. The Dome built in 691 C.E. by the Caliph Abd al-Malik surrounds a rock from which tradition says the Prophet Muhammad ascended to heaven during his Night Journey. Jews call this rock the Foundation Stone, representing the place where the world was created as well as the place upon which Father Abraham willingly bound his son Isaac in preparation for sacrifice. [28] For Jews and Christians, it is also the site of Solomon's Temple, and according to Christian prophecy found in Isaiah 2, it is the place where a new temple will be built to welcome the Savior at his Second Coming. On a later visit to this site, Keith, even more expressive in his veneration, raised his arms above his head and lowered them in a gesture of profound respect.

The Church of the Holy Sepulcher produced a more sterile reaction for Keith. Prompted by distressing reports Constantine the Great's mother had received of the dire neglect of hallowed places associated with the life and death of Jesus, Queen Helena visited Jerusalem (Aelia Capitolina) in 326 A.D. She identified the site upon which the Church of the Holy Sepulcher now stands as Golgotha and the nearby tomb of the Resurrection. Perhaps the state of disrepair in 1961, as a prospective restoration was still in the excavating and planning stage, or perhaps the ornateness, the suffocating atmosphere of crowds in a small space, the darkness of the enclosed courtyard, or perhaps all of these contributed to Keith's disappointment in this memorial to the greatest event in human history.

The stone wall, called the Western Wall in acknowledgement of its designation as the remains of the original western wall of King Solomon's temple destroyed in 70 A.D., embodies Jewish hopes of a promised homeland governed by a king/prophet as great and revered as King David and King Solomon. It is also called the Wailing Wall where verbalized prayers ascend heavenward and written prayers on slips of paper are inserted between cracks in the wall in solemn belief that these supplications will be answered. The Temple Mount, the site of King Solomon's ancient temple, the Dome of the Rock and the Al-Aqsa Mosque, and also the location many believe of a new temple to be built some time in the future, can be clearly viewed from the Mount of Olives. In 1961 Orthodox Jews longed to perform their sacred rituals within sight of the temple wall, a privilege they would not freely experience until after the 1967 War.

The four travelers found the sacred sites reverenced by three major religions in the divided city of Jerusalem architecturally impressive, historically significant, and spiritually uplifting. Nonetheless, the highlight of this adventure in the Middle East occurred earlier. The four truth seekers had flown from Tehran to Shiraz and driven the short thirty miles northeast to the ceremonial capital Persepolis, where Darius I,

---

[28] Genesis 22

Xerxes, and Artaxerxes ruled concurrent with Book of Mormon happenings.

Since this site, believed to have been occupied only on great occasions of national importance, held such preeminence in the Persian Empire, it seems appropriate that it was in this area where significant ancient writings manifest themselves to pursuers of ancient worlds. The Iranian Travel Internet site teaches, "Persepolis was used as a setting for an invocation by the whole nation, led by the divinely invested King, by the grace of the Great God Ahura-Mazda, overcame all enemies and established a world empire which was planned to bring peace, order and prosperity into a chaotic world. Darius declared, 'I am one who loves righteousness and hates iniquity…It is not my will that the strong should oppress the weak…God's plan for the earth is not turmoil but peace, prosperity and good government.' And for a while this part of the world enjoyed such." These words of Darius could have been spoken by the Book of Mormon prophet Lehi, who left Jerusalem in 600 B.C.

The showplace of Darius's vast Achaemenian Empire is believed to have been constructed beginning in 516 B.C.; unfortunately, its majestic audience halls and residential palaces were burned and looted by the conqueror Alexander the Great in 330 B.C. Plutarch, an ancient historian, asserts that it took 20,000 mules and 5,000 camels to carry away the booty Alexander had acquired by ravaging the empire he had conquered at Persepolis. [29]

Notwithstanding, Keith was about to discover that Alexander had not found and removed all the Achaemenian kings' treasures. He and his friends climbed the one hundred six stairs to the Terrace and walked among the ruins of Persepolis. They looked upward at eagle, bull, and lion capitals. They observed relief sculptures in stone depicting the kings, their households, their chariots, their military, their servants. They took note of the cuneiform inscriptions. While they gazed on the sixty foot high columns of King Darius' Audience Hall (Apadana), a caretaker told the interested visitors of the discovery in 1931-34 of two gold plates and two silver plates in each of the four cornerstones. These treasures excavated from the very foundation walls of the Audience Hall, he informed them, were housed in the Persian Museum of Antiquities in Tehran. The four set off to see this marvelous discovery as if trekking to the Hill Cumorah in upstate New York, the site where gold plates were buried anciently and later in 1827 entrusted for translation to the young man Joseph Smith. With great anticipation they cancelled their planned journey to Baghdad, changed their itinerary, boarded an Iranian plane flown by an American pilot, and returned to Tehran, arriving at the Museum of Antiquities just before closing.

The director of the Persian Museum of Antiquities, Dr. Argudonni, impressed with Tom's credentials as the president of the New World Archeological Foundation

---

[29] Erich F. Schmidt, *Persepolis I: Structures, Reliefs, Inscriptions*. OIP LXVIII (Chicago: University of Chicago Press, 1953), 63.

and seeing their uncloaked enthusiasm for the tablets of Darius which had been described to them in Persepolis, unlocked the glass display case, removed the ancient records, and allowed them to hold and photograph this unanticipated evidence of the veracity of the Book of Mormon. The Venetian style blinds on the windows diffused the setting sun as pictures recorded a find more precious than gold.

As Keith held in his very own hands an engraved plate of gold excavated from the foundation walls of the palace of King Darius, he recalled his youthful missionary answer to the question always posed, "Where are these gold plates?" He was not holding Moroni's gold plates, but he was holding a plate of gold--a plate made by Darius, a contemporary of the Book of Mormon prophet Nephi, to preserve his most important events and message, a plate not even imagined in Joseph Smith's time and whose purported existence skeptics pointed to as alarming proof of the fantasy of Smith's account.

Perhaps their unabashed excitement was a two-edged sword, or perhaps the director's pending appointment hastened their departure, but suddenly guards armed with uzzis appeared, the plates were taken elsewhere, and they were told the museum was closing. Not knowing the reason for the atmospheric change from friendly to hostile and being concerned that their prize pictures might be confiscated, Keith, unnoticed, slipped the film from the camera to Sid and Bob who immediately left the museum while he and Tom stayed behind saying their thank-yous and goodbyes.

Outside they successfully hailed a taxicab. The director appeared, and Keith, noticing that he was also attempting to procure a cab, offered their awaiting taxi to him. Grateful for the kindness, he invited them to return in the morning for a leisurely tour of other more recently discovered treasures, including two gold tablets found at Hamadan, Persia. The next morning Keith and Tom, after having drawn straws to determine who would accept the director's invitation and who would proceed to the airport to check in and hold the plane, hailed a taxi, the typical Mercedes Benz cab used in that part of the world. Looking at his watch, Keith instructed the driver to hurry. Perhaps not realizing this taxi driver needed no such direction, Keith and Tom grabbed the door handles as the taxi flew down the street, the sidewalk, and then crashed into another vehicle. Keith, knowing they could be tied up for hours, handed the driver a ten dollar bill, and he and Tom ran the remaining blocks to the museum. Arriving breathless and feeling the time constraints of their plane's imminent departure, the two explorers excitedly greeted their host. Keith and Tom were told that what they were about to be shown was not for public viewing, pending the Shah's dedication of the exhibit. They followed the director to a locked upper room where he revealed a marvelous collection of ancient gold artifacts, including two gold tablets covered with cuneiform script. These two gold plates, thinner and smaller than the plate Keith had held the day before, were similar in size and weight to those described by Joseph Smith. The entire collection dazzled the two, not only with its physical brilliance, but also with its brilliant ability to substantiate the use of gold for historical recording as Joseph had witnessed.

Tom, armed with all the information and pictures necessary to write an article, "Gold Plates and the Book of Mormon," published the next spring in the *Improvement Era*, [30] and Keith, possessing the precious photograph of him holding a gold plate which later appeared inside the English and Chinese Church tract, "Gold Plates Used Anciently," felt full of fervor.

Following this spectacular visit, the two rushed to the airport only to find the departure of their Afghan Air flight delayed. The airport was bare with no shops or distractions, so Keith pulled out an old paperback novel. He would read one page, tear it out, and pass it on to Tom; Tom would read the page and pass it on to Sid. Sid would read the page and pass it on to Bob, who, after reading it, would deposit the page in the nearest trash can. They read the whole novel, and in this interesting manner spent the entire day awaiting the plane's takeoff. One could hardly imagine a more stark contrast than this mundane wait for a very late plane in the austere Tehran Airport compared with the phenomenal sight of glittering gold treasures in the Museum of Antiquities. Unimagined by him then, making his way through airports across the globe onto occasionally late planes would become almost commonplace for Keith.

---

[30] Thomas Stuart Ferguson, "Gold Plates and the Book of Mormon," *Improvement Era*, April 1962, 232-233, 270-271.

Chapter
EIGHT

Other Sheep, Not of This Fold

No ray of sunlight is ever lost but the green which it awakens into existence needs time to sprout. And it is not always granted to the sower to see the harvest. All work that is worth anything is done in faith.
— Albert Schweitzer

Beneath a surgical table in a makeshift hospital in Vietnam crouched Elder Gordon B. Hinckley, Elder Marion D. Hanks, and President Keith E. Garner. Each one's eyes darted anxiously to confirm the safety of his two companions. The faithful act that had led Keith to these surroundings steadied the natural impulse to reconsider the decision in light of his failure to factor in, let alone envision, these present ominous conditions in which he now found himself. If he had known, it would have made no difference. He had already reviewed other pressing considerations which had been brought to his attention before accepting this call.

A few months before, an overflow crowd, many who were business contacts of President Garner, had gathered at the Palo Alto Stake Center/Menlo Park Chapel for a specially arranged Missionary Fireside prior to his leaving to serve as president of the Southern Far East Mission. Bishop Mitchell W. Hunt, Keith's successor, addressed the assembled well-wishers, "The other day I met on the street an executive from one of the large construction companies in the Bay area. He was shaking his head and said, 'I just heard that Mr. Garner is leaving his business, has sold his home, and is going to of all places Hong Kong. Whatever possessed that man?"

Bishop Hunt continued, "I realized then the thoughts that must be going

through countless minds. Here is a strange situation to the mind of the modern businessman. Why would a man leave his prospering business when he's just reaching his
prime? Why did he sell his lovely home, take his children out of these tremendous
schools here in the states to go to a land of complete foreigners in which he will live
for three years, completely apart from his loved ones? Leave a widowed mother of
more than fourscore years in age and leave other dear ones here behind, choice
friends, leave all this to go to an unknown?"

    Bishop Hunt spoke for many. These questions sparked conversations among
Keith's business associates up and down the peninsula, most of whom found untan-
gling such a peculiar decision challenging. Some in his circle of contacts, especially
those who were sufficiently informed to evaluate the cost of what they referenced as
his "sacrifice," had found Keith's answer to these questions simply inexplicable. These
were questions, particularly the timing of the call, about which Bishop Hunt, Keith's
business associate, a man who knew and wholeheartedly embraced the answer, had
considered with Keith earlier.

*353rd Quorum of Seventy, Palo Alto Stake; l to r: Clark Hamblin, Myron Brown, George Felsch, Keith Garner,
Charles Wall, Lloyd Johnson, Eldon Bringhurst*

    The disadvantages of accepting such an assignment clearly appeared to out-
weigh the advantages; that is until the bounty inherent in his accepting the call is put
on the scale. In truth, the answer to these practical questions seems to make sense
only when couched in spiritual terms and understanding. Judged in any other way, his

leaving appears imprudent, as it does in varying degrees for all of the other hundreds of men and women called by a prophet to serve without monetary remuneration in world-wide mission fields.

Almost a quarter of a century earlier, he had met the same expressions of bewilderment at his choice to leave gainful employment and schooling to serve a mission in Hawaii. Once again, when appraising his acceptance of this second mission call in the light of spiritual measures and practical considerations, he demonstrated that he preferred, as he always had, "the Lord's pay for the Lord's work."

A widely acknowledged astute businessman, Keith, in his farewell closing remarks, rehearsed the unchallenged blessings available to a servant whose assignment consists of helping to expand the Lord's kingdom on earth. "After the impact of this call came, to leave our home, not our home so much, because we can leave our home and material things; they don't count much, but we hate to leave our family and our friends. After we received this call, one scripture found in the New Testament kept going through my mind. The New Testament was the text for the seminary class I taught. So having become a little better acquainted with the Savior's life and teachings and being bound as we are to accept calls, not forcibly nor by coercion, we wonder how others act under similar circumstances.

I read in the New Testament in John. The Savior had told his disciples that he was the Son of God and the Redeemer of the world. John states, 'From that time many of his disciples went back and walked no more with him. Then Jesus turned to his twelve and said, "Will ye also go away?" Simon Peter acting as the spokesman, as he was, said, "Lord, to whom shall we go? thou hast the words of eternal life. And we believe and are sure that thou art that Christ, the Son of the living God."' [31]

That's the way we are when we receive these calls in the Church, which we believe is the Church of Jesus Christ. Where do we run? We can't hide behind no, or I want to stay home, or I don't want to leave. The only answer we can give is, as Peter said, 'Lord, to whom shall we go? thou hast the words of eternal life.'

I know 'the Lord moves in mysterious ways; his wonders to perform.' I know we all have our callings in life, and we're prepared for them in a series of events. Two years ago we were constructing an apartment house in Salt Lake. As it was completed, a young law student at the University of Utah called me and asked if he could manage the apartment."

Having determined that this young man was the father of a six-month-old baby and having had much experience with apartment managers who had children, Keith turned him down with the suggestion that he contact other apartment-house owners.

"Two days later I received a call from my sister who lives in Syracuse, and she said, 'Keith, I don't like to interfere in your business, but I felt impressed to drive up

---

[31] John 6:65-69

to your apartment building, a drive I only take once in awhile. When I got there, I found a young man. He said he'd been watching this building go up and needed the job as manager to fund his schooling. He'd fasted and prayed about it, and I feel impressed to tell you to hire him.' I said, 'Well, I'll hire him then if you feel that I should.' I gave him the job. I became acquainted with him over these last two years. Every time I saw him in Salt Lake, it wasn't very often, he said, 'You know, of all the men I know, you should be a mission president, Bishop.' I said, 'Well, if the Lord wants me as a mission president, I'll get the call.' Well, when Brother Hinckley came down to our stake conference, he told me that he wasn't initially assigned to the Palo Alto conference. There was a sudden change, and that on the street just as he was getting on the plane, he ran into this same brother who expressed an interest in his travel plans. 'Brother Hinckley, where are you going?' Brother Hinckley said, 'I'm going to Palo Alto for a conference.' He said, 'Well, be sure you tell Keith Garner hello for me, and Brother Hinckley, if you are looking for a good mission president, you pick Keith Garner.'"

Coincidence? Providence? Keith described his feelings. "I don't know where it originated, but we accepted the call. I think of the first time I was called on a mission as a young man. I was going to school at night and working as a messenger boy in the daytime. When I received the call, those I ran messages for at the bank, some of whom later became very fine friends of mine, told me don't leave your school and an excellent future in this bank to do that. You think about it seriously. I told them I'd already thought about it seriously, and I had no answer to give but yes, and I went on the mission. I've often thought since then what would have happened to Keith Garner had I refused that call. Years later when I needed help financially, Ed O'Brien, whom I'd known at the bank, remembered me when I was nineteen years of age. When I went to him in need of money, he remembered that I took this call, and I really think he authorized the loan because of what had happened those many years ago. He's been in my corner ever since." With distinct good humor in his voice, Keith quipped, "Many people think I'm able to borrow so much money because the Mormon Church guarantees my loans."

Resolutely he continued, "This Church has brought me my awareness. When we say, 'Seek ye first the kingdom of God and his righteousness and all these things shall be added,' we know that's true. If we form a partnership with the Lord early in life and make a real effort to keep the commandments, the Lord will bless us in everything we pursue. Jacob in the Book of Mormon says in the promise that he gives to us, and these are real promises because these come from the Creator of the World to his prophets, that after we have obtained a hope in Christ, if we seek riches, for instance, he said, I will give them to you only to the extent that you help your brethren, that you make your brethren rich like unto yourself, that you impart your substance to the poor, and that you take care of the widows and the needy. You think of all the promises that have been given to us. As I've mentioned many times, meaningful fulfillment is only found in keeping the commandments, loving the Lord, and gaining a true friendship with Him where we can pray to Him and have confidence that He hears and answers our prayers."

In the audience that evening in the middle section sat President and Sister Claude B. Peterson. In the same section near the front sat Willie Ward and Andy Anderson. Keith, honored by their attendance, singled out from the pulpit the four of them for expressions of thankfulness. These twosomes were disparate in their appearances, their check books, their life choices, but alike in their love and respect for the man seated in the place of honor that evening. Keith, so naturally and seemingly without any effort, brought together, formed alliances, and developed bonds of inclusion with people reflecting the entire kaleidoscope of human experience.

Claude Peterson, an admired leader, had been Keith's stake president and, according to Keith, gave him after he returned from his Hawaiian mission, his first real opportunity at Church service. He called him as one of the seven presidents of the 353rd Quorum of Seventy, a missionary stewardship and a fulfilling opportunity to serve, for which Keith at this meeting expressed eternal gratitude.

Willie and Andy had worked for him a number of years, proving to be diligent construction laborers. Not members of the Church, they occupied seats front and center to show Keith their support and gratitude. Throughout his life he developed an affinity for men who pounded nails. His interaction with them often introduced him to environments with which he personally was unfamiliar. One such experience he tells about occurred during the construction of The Glass Slipper Motel in Palo Alto. As was his habit, Keith drove by the job, and on one particular day didn't see Andy. A few days later Andy still remained absent. On the third try, Keith saw him, stopped, and said, "Andy, I've missed seeing you." Andy said, "I've been in the hospital; I was shot." Surprised by his answer and very concerned, Keith asked, "How did that happen?" He revealed he'd been gambling, one of the other players had pulled out a pistol, and shot him. Keith strongly suggested the obvious, "Andy, it isn't wise for you to gamble." Quite unexpectedly Andy replied, "I don't know about that, but I'm not going to cheat anymore!"

Even before he boarded the plane taking him to Hong Kong, an awareness of his good work, this time related to the work these and other men had done in constructing the chapel in which they were seated, preceded him. One of the farewell speakers, President David Bacon, a councilor to Stake President Richard B. Sonne and previously one of Keith's counselors in the bishopric, made the audience aware of this fact when he recalled one incident indicative of the smallness of the world. Apparently stimulated by his destination, the magnificent Palo Alto Stake Center, Elder Hinckley casually conversing with President Bacon, who had been assigned to pick him up at the airport, said that on a recent trip to the Far East he had met, quite fortuitously with the owner of a piece of land the Church wished to procure for a chapel in that part of the world. The man made known to Elder Hinckley that he was acquainted with the Mormons. In fact, he owned a home in Atherton, California, where he spent a month or two every year. He told of his driving by the Valparaiso construction site many times and of his positive impressions of the structure and of the work of the Mormon people. He ended Elder Hinckley's visit with the declaration, "I will make my property available to you."

The following concluding statement of President Bacon's speech was echoed by the listeners, "Now, brothers and sisters, all of us here tonight know that if any one man was responsible for the erection of this building it was Bishop Garner, now President Garner. I tell you this incident to indicate his influence is not just local; it's been world-wide. His influence will be ever wider in the years ahead."

Missionaries, who had returned from Asia and who had offered to carry President Garner's bags in order to return to their beloved field of labor, concluded the meeting by singing in Chinese the moving hymn *God Be With You Till We Meet Again*. With this good wish sending them on their way, the Garners left to fulfill this assignment. Throughout the next three years as missionaries completed their full-time calling to serve the Lord in the Southern Far East Mission and left for home, President Garner lifted his warm tenor voice with other missionaries and members in this same poignant supplication. Sung in any language, English, Cantonese, Mandarin, in any situation, the words of this familiar hymn always fill the room with heartfelt sentiments of partings, many of which center on times spent encircled in missionary service.

The evening of August 13, 1965, President Garner and his family landed at Kaitak Airport. When the door of the plane opened, they descended into a hot and humid world--actually a new, unknown realm alive with promise and full of what were to be wonderful experiences which would turn the Asian heat into warm memories.

Retiring President Jay A. Quealy, Jr. met them at the airport with gracious and kind words of welcome. Only a few days later President Garner, after having been introduced to Hong Kong Mission leaders and other key personnel including the Church attorney, banker, and architect, drove President Quealy to the airport in a newly acquired Plymouth station wagon for his departure to the United States. The Plymouth was at that time one of the largest cars in Hong Kong, and for the next three years, Keith's fondness, if he ever had such an emotion for this form of transportation, plummeted, especially when looking for that nonexistent large parking space.

Parking spaces, streets, sidewalks, apartments, all seemed to shrink in size to accommodate the approximately four and a half million inhabitants who made Hong Kong, a city with the highest density of human beings in the world and about the size of San Francisco, their home. Keith laughed, "And to think I used to complain about the traffic jams on Bayshore Freeway!"

Those were the only aspects of Hong Kong that were shrinking. If, for no other reason, the huge population and extensive geography of the Southern Far East

Mission made it unique among seventy-six missions operating across the globe in 1965. Elder Marion D. Hanks states it most succinctly, "The mission field in which Keith served as mission president literally included over half the world's population." In addition to Hong Kong, the boundaries of the Southern Far East Mission, an area in various stages of missionary work, enveloped all of Asia except Japan and Korea where mission presidents Adney Y. Komatsu and Spencer J. Palmer served respectively.

As President Garner assumed his duties, two hundred and sixty missionaries served in one of three places--Hong Kong, Taiwan, or the Philippines. In several of the other countries, President Garner found one member or a family; in others, small enclaves of LDS men and women living and working. Some of these enclaves were large enough for organized groups to be formed, but still lacked the personnel and resources to sustain full time missionaries. In areas ruled by governments and ideologies forbidding or restricting religious expression, Keith found closed borders. In war-ravaged Vietnam, he found, though no officially called full-time missionaries, over five thousand LDS servicemen, who by their lives and examples performed powerful missionary mentoring.

A Pan American world map with the boundaries of the Southern Far East Mission clearly drawn hung on the wall just behind President Garner's desk. Gazing at the map, a missionary assigned to Hong Kong and caught in a confluence of circumstances experienced one of those breakthrough moments of enlightenment. Finding himself at the mission home with a companion too ill to tract, he began inventing ways to fill his time. In the mission office and with President Garner visiting missionaries under his stewardship in other lands, the elder struck up a conversation with other elders there in the mission office. Out of a swirl of topics their discussion focused on President Garner's whereabouts. What part of the mission field was he visiting? Before either the children's geography game, *Where In The World Is Carmen Sandiego?* or the morning show feature "Where in the world is Matt Lauer?" used the phrase, missionaries were asking "Where in the world is President Garner?" The answer to that question led these missionaries to examine in detail the world map. They conjectured that President Garner's responsibilities included one-quarter of the world landmass and at least one-half of the world population. They noted that within these boundaries lived peoples of distinct nationalities, languages, cultures, religions, and customs. On an intellectual level, each of these missionaries knew the boundary lines of the Southern Far East Mission before this exercise, but this half-hour of calculation cemented an already heightened respect for the man running the mission and focused their thoughts on their privilege to serve with him in such a golden field of labor.

President Garner, of course, also knew the boundaries, but he really never took time, or more accurately, had time to stop and allow himself to absorb the vastness of its reaches. Years later after this assignment had ended and when frequent flyer miles rewarded travelers, then perhaps the wish flashed through his mind, "If only

those miles had been offered sooner, I would have flown free for the rest of my life."
Of course, his frequent flyer miles would have been redeemable only on the airlines
he flew throughout Asia: Air Vietnam, Philippine Air, Quantas Airways, Singapore
Airlines, Cathay Pacific Airways. He would not have wished to redeem any miles,
free or not, on the airplanes he flew in Vietnam: C130s, DC3s, C-47 "goonie birds,"
choppers, or gun ships.

As of December 2002 within the borders of one mission field, the 1965
Southern Far East Mission, twenty-two mission presidents serve; three serve on
Taiwan, thirteen in the Philippines, one in Singapore, one in Thailand, one in
Cambodia, one in Indonesia, one in India, and one in China Hong Kong; these num-
bers will surely increase as the gospel message fills the earth.

The momentous growth of the Church in Asia over the last thirty-five years is
reflected in the number of stakes which have been organized: five stakes in Hong
Kong, seven stakes in Taiwan, and eighty-one stakes in the Philippines. However,
before membership in The Church of Jesus Christ of Latter-day Saints matured to
facilitate the organization of stakes in almost every part of the globe, many a mission
president's role also included duties which normally stake presidents and ward bishops
handle. The day Keith assumed his duties in 1965, the organization of the first stake in
the Philippines was still another eight years away and stakes in Hong Kong and Taiwan
still another ten years in the future. Therefore, President Garner's responsibilities
included not only the principal duty of every mission president which was
the care, motivation, and instruction, in his case over his three year presidency,
of approximately five hundred full-time missionaries serving in Hong Kong, Taiwan,
and the Philippines, and later in Thailand and Singapore, but also the ecclesiastical
care of all members of the Church residing in the mission boundaries, including those
in East Pakistan, India, Thailand, Kuala Lumpur, Malaysia, Singapore, Indonesia, Laos,
and beyond.

These dual duties were outlined by the First Presidency when they extended
the call to Keith to preside over the Southern Far East Mission. In the May 25, 1965,
letter signed by David O. McKay, Hugh B. Brown, and N. Eldon Tanner, they wrote:

> This assignment will bring to you the full responsibility
> for the supervision and conduct of the mission, to direct all of
> its affairs in keeping with the instructions of the First
> Presidency. The corps of missionaries assigned to your mission
> to labor under your presidency will be reliant upon you for
> assignments to duty, and for guidance and stimulation to put
> forth their best effort.
>
> In a measure they are entrusted to your custody. They
> will need and deserve your understanding and sympathetic
> counsel. To be close to them is an essential element in your

leadership.

The membership of the Church and its establishments
in the mission will be under your presidency. The Saints will
likewise need your guidance and counsel, and the branches
and other organizations will be officered and maintained
under your direction. You are empowered by virtue of the
priesthood you hold and this appointment to exercise righteous judgment and set in order the work of the Church
within your jurisdiction.

Truly, in Southeast Asia the buck stopped at President Garner's desk.

His inspired delegation facilitated his ability to function so successfully in such
an overwhelmingly responsible position. As is customary, President Garner called
missionaries to serve in the mission home as assistants to the president. APs met with
zone leaders who supervised three to four district leaders who worked with four to
ten missionaries. Other missionaries served for varying time periods as mission secretaries, "commissarians," financial clerks, and traveling elders. Because of the wide
expanse of this particular mission field, President Garner found it necessary and effec-
tual to place assistants to the president in the Philippines and in Taiwan. To some, his
trust of nineteen to twenty-one year old young men to carry out important
Priesthood leadership roles in places far from his on-the-spot supervision may seem
baffling. To Keith, such mandated trust is the byproduct of faith in the Lord's promise
to magnify the talents of those who accept callings to serve. Keith's delegation,
labelled baffling or faithful, worked. Elder Hanks describes it this way. "He was sending out missionaries to direct the work in each place, and choosing through much
obvious inspiration the ones who should be there, who could be trusted in terms of
their personal fidelity and their ability to be minor league mission presidents at that
point. They still had responsibility to President Garner but they had the responsibility
and opportunity to lead, and they became leaders and they were outstanding ones."

Recently President Garner, exchanging recollections with one of the missionaries who served with him, commented, "We say B.C. and A.D. to specify the era
before and after the birth of Christ. Similarly a missionary can always tell you when
he entered the mission field and when he left for home. Those are the really important time frames in a missionary's life." The missionary responded, "When people say,
'Where did you grow up?' I say, 'I grew up in Hong Kong.'" Keith agreed and
remarked that he grew up in Hawaii.

Just as Keith grew up under the tutelage of his Hawaiian mission president,
Roscoe Cox, many of Keith's missionaries would look back and "garner-ize" their own

future service as mission presidents. [32] J. Kent Larkin in an August 1, 2002, letter from Taiwan, which he signs, "Sincerely a Fellow Mission President," writes:

> ...as I turn fifty-eight next year, I find myself reviewing my past--and whatever is good in my life has Garner footsteps all over it. You have had a big impact on my life...Forty years later returning back as the Mission President for the Taiwan Taichung Mission I find myself Garner-izing my missionaries. It seems only natural that you are a part of my greatest church calling. You had a way of making me feel and perform above average. Upon reflection the Garner footprints are very evident in how I run the mission. Do any of these leadership principles look familiar?
>
> 1. Always build the missionary.
>
> 2. Answer missionary correspondence in writing, complimenting the missionary. (I still have my Garner letters.)
>
> 3. Meet with missionaries as often as you can and sometimes go out with them for dinner--at their favorite spots.
>
> 4. Those who do the Lord's work will get the Lord's pay.
>
> 5. Write to the parents once in a while.
>
> 6. Stay in touch with the missionaries as best you can even after their missions.
>
> 7. Expect the best--missionaries will rarely disappoint you.

Stephen L. Richey identifies perhaps the most motivational tool President Garner dispensed to his missionaries which often resulted in the unearthing of talents these young men had not yet discovered. His August 2, 1966, personal journal entry states, "I rather enjoy a job where you have authority to do as you feel it should be done. President Garner is a great advocate of a person being *free*. That being, free to do the work without worry or strife--whether it be from an outside source or due to your own weaknesses. So often he let's us go ahead on things pretty much up to our own discretion. I don't imagine that I will probably ever hold a job again as long as I live where I can be so completely free. Working for the Lord as a missionary makes for pretty desirable 'employment.'"

Even though there were no full-time missionaries called in South Vietnam but

---

[32] Recently one of President Garner's missionaries brought to my attention that at least twenty of the approximately five hundred missionaries who served in the Southern Far East Mission under Keith's presidency had or now serve as mission presidents, a very high percentage indeed.

still responsible for the members there, mostly servicemen, President Garner, full of the same spirit, chose leaders to administer the Church programs in this war-torn country. At the October 1965 General Conference of the Church when President Joseph Fielding Smith and Thorpe B. Isaacson were sustained as counselors in the First Presidency bringing the number of counselors to President David O. McKay to four instead of two, Keith took note and duplicated what he thought was "the new program and a good model to follow." In a letter to Elder Hinckley dated June 3, 1966, Keith delineated the rather interesting organizational move he had made in South Vietnam.

> For four days last week I had a great time in Saigon. As I mentioned in a previous letter, Brother James Duncan will be returning to Sacramento the third of June, so the Lord sent some wonderfully qualified brethren just in the right time to take over our zone leadership.
> Last Sunday morning, May twenty-ninth, we reorganized the Zone Presidency and put Brother Allen C. Rozsa in as President with Harvey Dean Brown, Charles B. Sturgell, Robert James Lewis and LaVoi B. Davis as counsellors and with Claude Roy Egbert as clerk...."

In a letter dated June 21, 1966, Elder Hinckley replied:

> I have read with great interest your letter of June 3 concerning the reorganization of the work in South Vietnam. The only question I have is on the counselors in the zone presidency. Do we understand correctly that you put four counselors in?
> I recognize that there is some precedence for this in the First Presidency, but the Brethren have felt that we should have only two counselors in the presidencies in the stakes and missions.

President Garner's response was two fold. First, he said, "I need six or seven counselors out here!" Then Keith rectified the situation by releasing the extra counselors with the words, "As you were."

The vitality obviously needed to fulfill this assignment makes one wonder if first on the list of necessary qualifications the brethren perceived in Keith was energy! Elder David B. Haight recounts Elder Hinckley telling the story of his noticing that Keith had holes in his shoes. "Keith was running so fast to get the job done and to help others that he didn't have time to go find a shoe shop and get his own shoes fixed. The Democrats used to play up what a great man Adlai Stevenson was when they were running him for President of the United States because he had holes in his shoes. President Hinckley would tell about President Garner. He had holes in his shoes, and over there in the Far East, he was a greater man than Adlai Stevenson." As Elder Haight phrases it, "Elder Hinckley came back singing the song and saying the praises of President Keith Garner, president of the Southern Far East Mission."

In fact, several of Elder Hinckley's associates recall Elder Hinckley's returning from his tours of the Southern Far East Mission full of praise for this young mission president. President Spencer W. Kimball wrote Keith after his four day stay in Hong Kong in February of 1968, "President, I can appreciate now what Brother Hinckley has been saying about you and the Southern Far East. I commend you for doing a wonderful service. You are a great diplomat."

Diplomatic does not describe his reaction to his first tour of the Hong Kong Zone. Elder Jim Derrick writes, "One of the first things that President and Sister Garner did upon arriving in Hong Kong was to tour the missionaries' flats. Apparently they were shocked at our living conditions, which we had learned to ignore. President Garner commanded that all of our three legged furniture be thrown out."

Elder Stephen L. Richey went into more detail when he wrote in his missionary journal for October 14, 1965.

> "President Garner has started a campaign to clean up the missionary living quarters in Hong Kong. He says after having visited all the apartments he was literally astonished at what poor conditions the elders are living under. He feels that it is the major factor in the illness constantly present in this zone-- (I've never mentioned anything before, but there's always somebody with skin diseases, boils, athletes foot, etc. piles, yellow jaundice, worms, well you name it.) In fact, ever since I've been in Hong Kong, there has been lots of these things existing. Pres. Garner says 'Cleanliness is next to Godliness,' and his wife says she doesn't see how the Spirit of the Lord could dwell in a dirty house. Well, this evidently isn't all the elders' fault. It seems the general living quarters and facilities are also not too great. Pres. Garner remarked that soon after his arrival and upon touring the apts, he felt self-conscious returning to the luxury of the mission home's air conditioning and everything else, so he says if he doesn't do another thing he's going to have the elders living in quarters that are at least fit for habitation. He claims he hasn't sat down in one of the apts. yet. Well, he came out to Unlong yesterday and said the Unlong apt should be bombed. He's for throwing away all the

furniture, buying new, remodeling all the inside and out, and
installing an air conditioner. He wants to move us out for a
couple of weeks and move in workmen to fumigate, lye and
Lysol the place down, sand down the walls, put a ceiling in it.
(Now it's like a big shed.) We live with everything. Since
being in Unlong, I've killed bats almost every other night,
thrown out frogs, lizards, snails, rats, cockroaches, millions of
ants, birds and bird nests, stray cats, spiders and salamanders--
besides that we kill a few snakes, poisonous and non, every
once in awhile. Well, Bro. Teeples, the builder on the church,
said 'Pres. Garner, you'll spoil them. They won't want to leave
their apartments' Pres. Garner said, 'They know who they're
working for. That's all they need to know.'"

Elder Jerry James summarizes, "When President Garner arrived there, the
missionaries were living in really terrible, deplorable conditions. It was pretty dis-
gusting. I remember the first apartments we were in before President Garner upgraded them had huge cockroaches, three and four inches long, and rats. We'd come home
at night, turn on the light, and have kind of hand-to-hand combat to take the apartment back from the cockroaches. We'd lay in bed at night, look out across at the high-
rise next to us, and watch the rats racing up and down the walls. That was quite
entertaining. And then we'd have the mold during the rainy season. The mold would
grow on your scriptures; it was just so moist, hot."

President Garner certainly did not mind the missionaries working hard, but
he found their living quarters unacceptable. He uttered what he thought was the
indisputable, "Missionaries have got to have a decent place to sleep and eat, and then
they can take any type of challenge that comes. I told them they are sons and
daughters of God, and let's live like it."

President Garner saw to it that air conditioning, access to hot water, refriger-
ators, and other standard amenity upgrades brightened these living spaces. This effort
may not have made the *Church News*, but it clearly made the missionaries' list of most
appreciated accomplishments.

"One of the great things, one of the blessings that President Garner bestowed
on the missionaries was he upgraded the living conditions for all of the apartments,
one at a time throughout the whole mission. He helped to teach the missionaries how
to live better. I think it really helped morale and helped the work go forward. By the
end of my mission, we all had hot water. We all had air conditioning. That really was
one of the great legacies of President Garner," states Elder James.

Elder Derrick agrees, "Within just a few months, our flats were upgraded to
'that which dignified our callings as servants of the Lord.'" This witnessed action and
attitude is referenced by a number of missionary recipients as it is passed on to others.

Elder Derrick continues, "Over the years I have often used this quote to teach neatness and cleanliness to those with whom I have had some influence."

And how were the Garners living? Keith says without hesitation, "In the mission home, we lived like kings and queens."

The mission home at No. 2 Cornwall Road, Kowloon-Tong, Kowloon, Hong Kong, while exuding the lifestyle of the early British colonizers, functioned as the mission president's home and the offices and seat of Church governance in the Southern Far East. It was a welcoming hostelry for missionaries waiting their first assignments throughout Southeast Asia and the Philippines. The gated, landscaped mansion, reminiscent of the architecture of the Old South with its four stories, tile roof, stuccoed walls, and pillars supporting a portico seemed set apart from the hurried, crowded world outside.

Alan Hess, a former Southern Far East missionary, who lived in the mission home for six months while serving as financial secretary, today opens the doors and graciously gives a guided tour through the old mission home as he remembers it during President Garner's sojourn. Even after all these years, he recalls the layout of the home primarily because it housed so many memories and warm feelings.

As he in his mind's eye walks up Cornwall Road, Alan points out that the setting for the mission home is unlike the more usual vertically rising, stacked architecture of Hong Kong; it is one of the few areas in the whole colony where two-story

Mission Home of the Southern Far East Mission located in Kowloon Tong, Hong Kong

structures are the norm. Located in a fashionable residential area and, like its neighbors, enclosed behind a wall, it functioned as a protected compound. He draws attention to the glistening from the broken glass stuck into the four or five inch rounded
cement cap atop the outside wall. Built in the Chinese way to prevent thieves or others from climbing over it, the wall is divided by two gates facing Cornwall Street.

As Alan describes entering through the right gate and making his way up the
drive bordered on one side by a manicured grassy area, it is easy to imagine following
in the footsteps of hundreds of young men and women who actually walked through
those gates. One of those women, Sister Erlyn Gould Madsen, comments, "There was
a gardener named Ah Chow who kept the place beautiful with flowers all the time.
He would rake the lawn areas over and over. Not even a fallen leaf would be found on
the pathways. When General Authorities came, which was very often, President
Garner would have the pathways in the mission compound lined with potted daisies.
It was beautiful. He used to take this sweet man to meet the guests, and they would
all praise his efforts. President Garner never took him for granted, and he lived for
President Garner's praise."

Following Elder Hess as he imagines himself entering the large, open,
comfortable living room, complete with a baby grand piano, where President Garner
assembled his family, mission staff, and other missionaries for regular gospel study
sessions and where the whole Hong Kong Zone met for testimony meetings, one can
feel the familiar spirit of certainty in the mission of Jesus Christ and the Book of
Mormon of which Keith still teaches and testifies. One imagines the mission home
being full of music with Sister Garner raising her voice in song, a voice President
Garner calls the most beautiful woman's voice he has ever heard, and their children
playing the piano. One hears hundreds of missionary voices singing President
Garner's favorite hymn and what some missionaries labelled the mission theme song,
Precious Savior; Dear Redeemer.

Elder Hess says, "One of the great memories I have is of the wonderful
testimony meetings we had there with all the Hong Kong missionaries. There were
about a hundred. When we'd have a General Authority or some other special circumstance, we'd all gather. Those meetings would last all day, literally eight or nine hours,
everybody sitting on the sofas or on the floor. Those were powerful experiences that
we shared."

Franklin L. West, another missionary, echoes this view as he writes to
President Garner many years later. "I have such positive memories of meeting together
every Monday night in the mission home, sharing our thoughts with one another and
bearing testimonies.... Once the meetings were finished, it was always such a shock
to go out into the world because you had been able to create a spiritual haven for all
of us, which gave us an opportunity to have some respite from the daily travail of
tracting and being rejected. It made us all renew our commitment to go out and give
it our best for another week."

Another former missionary, Lee H. Van Dam, adds, "As I think about the influence that President Garner had on me while serving in the Southern Far East Mission, I believe that some of my best memories have to do with the daily gospel study he conducted for his family and for those of us who served in the mission office. Each day that President Garner was in town, he would gather us together before dinner in the beautiful living room of the mission home at #2 Cornwall Street and lead us in a gospel study. President Garner deeply loved the Book of Mormon, and that book was normally our topic. He knew it backwards and forwards and was an expert at teaching from it. He had great insight into the meanings of the scriptures and how they could help us in our missionary work and how they could be part of our daily lives. I loved those gospel studies. They gave me a deeper love of the scriptures, and I

"Four Counselors," front row, l to r: Harvey Dean Brown, Allen C. Rozsa, Charles B. Sturgill; back row, l to r: Claude Roy Egbert, LaVoi B. Davis, Robert James Lewis

always appreciated President Garner for sharing his knowledge of the scriptures with us."

President Garner was not just content to know the scriptures "backwards and forwards" himself. He wanted his missionaries to possess the same wealth of knowledge. Elder Richey writes on October 8, 1965, "This morning we went to the mission home, our district and another, held a gospel study with Pres. Garner--very, very good. His advice was that we diligently study the Book of Mormon--use it for our text while we're on our mission--learn it backwards and forwards--he said it has the answers and solutions to every problem life can bring, and I'm sure it does…Pres. Garner feels that it is the answer to unifying the saints here in Hong Kong. By the way, the first copies of the Book of Mormon in Chinese are to come out this December."

He was not content to merely admonish the missionaries to study the Book of Mormon. He called them together often, set the example, and gave the assignment. "President Garner was actually quite a scriptorian. He really knew and loved his scriptures. Obviously only to emphasize his point, he used to tell us that if he and his family were in a boat and it was sinking, he would grab his scriptures first (ho, ho), and he ALWAYS had mission home scripture study time each day. Often twice. We would go around the room, and each read a verse, and he would ask us what we were learning (often nothing), and then he would explain to us what we had just read, and it would be like there had been a whole continent there which none of the rest of us had even noticed," remembers Sister Gould.

Addressing the same subject and expanding on one Book of Mormon assignment President Garner gave, George E. Brown, Jr. asserts, "President Garner was interesting. He would have informal answer periods where the missionaries could ask questions. He was really a scriptorian because when he answered the question he would take people to the scriptures and say, 'This is what I think and I base it on this,' and he would turn to it.

It was about that time that he said, 'I want all of you missionaries to outline the Book of Mormon. What I want you to do is read it chapter by chapter. I want you to tell me the things you find where you learn something significant. I want you to send it to me once a week.' He didn't just want us to say, 'chapter one, verse one says, and two says.' He didn't want that; he wanted us to read it and tell him when we learned something significant from it.

I was thinking, 'Wow, he's really serious. We've really got to do this. We've got to send it in.' We started to outline the Book of Mormon. We'd send him a weekly summary. He'd make comments and return our outline to us. I really learned about the scriptures that way. It is one thing to read them; it is another thing to write down what you have learned. In fact, I've gone back occasionally to my old missionary Book of Mormon. It takes me to those times when I was sitting down writing that outline, and I'd think this is important, and I'd write a couple of words up at the top of my scriptures."

In an aside, Elder Hess, who presently is bishop of the Thai-Lao Ward reveals, "I tell my children I was a missionary so long ago we didn't even wear name tags. They say 'How did they know you were missionaries?' I say, 'President Garner said to carry your scriptures.'" His missionaries not only carried their scriptures, but if they followed their mission president's counsel, they knew what was in them.

Elder Marvin Brinkerhoff adds, "The best counsel President Garner ever gave me was to read the Book of Mormon daily, and the relationship I had with President Garner has given me the confidence and faith to apply the scriptures to solve the daily challenges of life." This good counsel is still a regular part of many a 1965-1968 Southern Far East missionary's life, even now when mission experiences have turned into stories they tell their children and grandchildren.

Recommencing the tour one listens to Elder Hess's direction to glance to the right into a lovely guest bedroom. A long list of notables might have signed the guest registry if such a book had existed including Elder and Sister Gordon B. Hinckley; Elder and Sister Marion D. Hanks; President Hugh B. Brown; Rotary International President Elder Richard L. Evans; Presiding Bishop Victor L. Brown; Elder J. Thomas Fyans; Church legal counsel Wilford R. Kirton; Young Women's Mutual Improvement Association general president Florence S. Jacobsen; Primary general president LaVern W. Parmley and her husband Thomas, professor of physics at the Univeristy of Utah; Church building committee members Emil Fetzer and Mark Garff; Brigham Young University professors and authors Dr. Richard P. Gunn and Dr. W. Cleon Skousen; golf pro Billy Casper and his wife Shirley; sports editor at the *Deseret News* Hack Miller; and Pan American pilots Leo Sant and Wilford Salter. Parents of missionaries and others who just dropped by to say "hello" also stayed in this lovely room during their visits.

Continuing on Elder Hess' tour, all the way back to the left there is a beautiful dining room adjoining the kitchen. It takes little effort to visualize the acts of service performed here that inspired the following February 2, 1968, letter signed "The Mission Home Staff."

> Dear President Garner,
>
> This afternoon as you were waiting the table, these few verses in Matthew kept running through my mind:
> Matthew 20:26-28
> *...but whosoever will be great among you, let him be your minister; And whosoever will be chief among you, let him be your servant. Even as the Son of Man came not to be ministered unto, but to minister, and to give his life a ransom for many.*
>
> We will be praying for you, and for Sister Garner, for your success and safety, until your return.

In the mission home, the cooks, Ah-Seem, Ah-Fook, and Ah-Mui worked hard. Erlyn Gould Madsen describes them. "Ah-Seem was the head cook. She had floated down the river from Red China with a ball under her shirt for a flotation device. She cooked by smell, not wanting to taste our food. She did a very special pseudo-Chinese meal which she would bring out when we had American guests so they could think they were eating Chinese; it would be delicious. Most Americans wouldn't like real Chinese food was Sister Garner's thought."

Ah-Fook and Ah-Mui were contrasts. Ah-Fook was more distant as she inter-

President Ng Kat Hing

acted with the missionaries, and Ah-Mui was chubby and fun. Sister Gould especially relished the special consideration all three cooks gave to the sister missionaries. "They always had cookies in a big cookie jar which we sisters would snack on at night because Sister Garner wouldn't let the sisters have dessert at mealtimes. The cooks always made sure we sisters knew the cookies were there when they were just baked." President Garner relished their contribution as well. Erlyn suggests that Keith and the cooks had a mutually beneficial and happy relationship. "President Garner liked the place to look spotless. I know he unselfishly spent thousands and thousands of his own dollars to pay all these people because the allowance given by SLC for the various missions is very small for such an undertaking. I'm sure that President Garner paid them well. He was VERY generous with everyone. He was very considerate of them at all times and praised them continuously. They were very well-cared for indeed. He knew how to appreciate talent, and theirs was an enormous contribution to all that was going on." President Garner says he was so delighted with their work that if it had been possible he would have taken all three of them to America with him.

Elder Hess reiterates a sentiment he shares with other missionaries, "I have never in my life lived better than I lived in the mission home. Those three women who cooked prepared fabulous food."

Perhaps a longing for their cooking led Elder Hess to a rather disconcerting decision. "One of the funny things after going to Thailand and being there a little while, I had written home in a letter, just joking of course, being stupid and young, I said, 'It's so hot here I just can't keep any weight on, and I'm down to ninety pounds,' thinking nobody would believe such a ridiculous thing. I'd forgotten all about it when one night at our home in Bangkok I got a phone call. President Garner was on the phone; the connection was very bad. I knew it was him, but I couldn't hear what he was saying. Finally I made out after a couple of attempts he was saying, 'Elder Hess, how much do you weigh?' I immediately knew how much trouble I was in. He had

Invoice for Chinese translation of the Book of Mormon

gotten a cable, I think, from Salt Lake City, wanting to know if Elder Hess was dying because my mother had believed the ninety pounds. What was worse I discovered that the entire ward was fasting for me. They were sending money so I could buy food, including Carol, my girlfriend who became my wife, sending me her last dollars, so I wouldn't starve to death. So I had some serious, serious repair work to do. I had to get letters off immediately, but it created quite a stir."

One cannot help smiling at his youthful indiscretion as Elder Hess' tour moves straight ahead to some locking doors which when open reveal another smaller, very pleasant bedroom big enough for two or three people, with an adjoining bathroom and an entry room. Elder Hess indicates that missionary accommodations included this bedroom and also most of the rooms on the second floor. From the second floor, missionaries could look down upon what used to be the swimming pool. It had been drained and converted into a commissary. Elders, sliding back the cast iron pool cover which acted as a roof and climbing down the stairs, were met by the musty smell of stored books and pamphlets. Alan indicates, "That's where the commissarian worked, kind of like a subterranean creature."

Above the Garner family quarters, Ng Kat Hing, a sweet, converted Latter-day Saint who always made himself available to advance the work in his homeland and who later became the first president of the Hong Kong Temple, poured over stacks of conference talks, doctrinal pamphlets, and lesson manuals in a never-ending effort to make these words available to the Asian people in their own language. This translation office, a smaller area because of the shape of the roof, with two desks, phones, and office equipment, encapsulated the difficulty to be conquered in sharing the message of salvation.

Only taking into account the major languages spoken within the boundaries of the Southern Far East Mission, a missionary arriving in Hong Kong could find himself assigned to areas where the people spoke Cantonese, Mandarin, and the Filipino dialects of Cebuano and Tagalog. The MTC, Missionary Training Center, or even its predecessor the LTM, Language Training Mission, which would offer missionaries linguistic tutorials in almost any language spoken, belonged to the future. Most of President Garner's missionaries spent only a preparatory week in Salt Lake City, much like the week Keith had enjoyed in 1939 before leaving for the Hawaiian Mission. During the years 1965-1968, some missionaries sent to foreign countries attended the LTM, located in Provo, Utah, on the Brigham Young University campus, but only three languages were taught there: French, German, and Spanish. The missionaries sent to the Southern Far East Mission during Keith's time and before, as well as most of the mission presidents, arrived speaking English and, except for a few words they may have picked up on their own, nothing else. Keith enlisted elders as tutors to school him in the languages but realized early that his stewardship required so much travel to a number of countries each speaking a different language that his best instruction came when he was in the field attempting to talk with the people.

George Brown, whose assignments over two and one-half years required him to speak Cantonese, Mandarin, and Thai, embraced President Garner's counsel, perhaps out of necessity, in regard to the mastery of the language. "President Garner was focused. His job was to proclaim the gospel and to get the missionaries to proclaim the gospel. He told us to do our proselyting, work sixty hours a week, study the language, and it would come to us; the Lord would make up the difference. Some people thought we should spend more time studying the language. President Garner said, 'No. Don't think you can put your book under your pillow and get it through osmosis; it isn't going to work that way. You have to study, but you spend your sixty hours a week working, and the language will come; you do the Lord's work, and the language will come.'"

President Garner often found himself in Hong Kong in the morning saying, "Good morning, zou2 san4" (早晨) in Cantonese, in Taiwan in the afternoon having crossed the Formosa Straits saying, "Good Afternoon, wu2 an1" (午安) in Mandarin, and in the Philippines the next day asking, "How are you doing?" in English.

On President Garner's watch, one pivotal first happened. On December 20, 1965, the first 3000 copies of the Book of Mormon published in Chinese were delivered to him. Before his arrival the translation, much of it performed by members on Taiwan, and other preparatory work was in the concluding phase. Three months after his arrival, he was privileged to hold the results of those labors in his hands. Missionaries recall with their own exhilaration clearly evident President Garner's opening the boxes and handling these first editions. One can sense the tender, excited feelings that must have filled the room.

The first edition of the Book of Mormon, translated by the Prophet Joseph from gold plates, was published in 1830 in Palmyra, New York. In Hong Kong in 1965, this sentinel book could now be read in the native language of a people located a continent and an ocean away from the book's origin. President Garner's love for the Prophet Joseph and his love for the Book of Mormon combined in this landmark event as he knew immediately the impact these translated five hundred and twenty two pages would have on sharing the gospel message with millions of Chinese people.

In a letter to President Garner dated January 20, 1966, Elder Hinckley writes, "I should have acknowledged your letter of December 20 before this. Needless to say, I share with you the great enthusiasm over publication of the Book of Mormon in the Chinese language.

I gave President McKay one of the books you sent. As you may know, he dedicated the Chinese realm for the preaching of the gospel in 1921. Tears came to his eyes as he handled this book and expressed his deep appreciation for all who have had to do with this translation and publication."

In a subsequent letter dated February 14, 1966, Elder Hinckley further writes, "I was both surprised and pleased to learn that the first edition of the Book of Mormon in Chinese is already gone. I suppose that inevitably some mistakes have come to light, and you indicated that President Hu is correcting these.

You say that a new edition is now on the press. I have just had a phone call from Brother Coleman Madsen of Florida who has been in touch with The Honorable L.K. Kung of Taiwan who spends much of his time in Washington. He is Chinese and a brother of Madam Chiang Kai Shek. He has expressed an interest in getting a copy of the Book of Mormon in Chinese for himself and also one for his sister."

President Garner promptly made additional bound copies available for Elder Hinckley to distribute.

From the translation room, it is possible to walk to a small adjoining area on the tile roof, an inspiring place to contemplate the enormity of having the ability to give a copy of the Book of Mormon in Chinese to interested investigators. Elder Hess felt this top-of-the-roof hide-away was a great area, especially in the evening, to ponder.

President Garner found another secluded spot just a short distance from the mission home where he could walk into a completely different world. He called it Shangri-la because it was quiet, peaceful, subdued, and so different from the congested, busy world which surrounded it. When he looked down into the adjacent valley, he viewed what seemed to be the backdrop for an earlier era, yet undisturbed by British colonization. He watched Chinese farmers watering their crops with the tools of labor of centuries past. Attached to each end of a long pole carried over their shoulders hung a bucket containing water or other nutrients used in the care of their crop, usually rice. Alone, away from the noise of life, President Garner felt an atmosphere of solitude in which the whisperings of the spirit could more easily be heard.

Refreshed and replenished, he would leave this world of seclusion and step back into the world of action as he walked back to the mission home. As Elder Hess describes a second building on the mission home grounds, one visualizes President Garner opening the entrance gate on his left and walking to the front door of an approximately fifty to sixty foot long, slender building. This building originally intended for cars had been converted to mission offices. One can picture him entering, waving his greetings to staff in the reception area, their responding with warm salutations, his proceeding down the long walkway with his buoyant, brisk gait, glancing through the windows on his right at the mission home, passing the financial secretary's office, moving through the staff area, and finally climbing up a couple of steps to a small office.

In the staff area, *The Orientor Gazette of the Southern Far East Mission* came to life. With the mission spread far and wide, this publication helped to keep the missionaries united, informed, encouraged, and recognized for their good work. President Garner directed this effort in his normal way. He gave "full range of power over the project" and then fully supported the effort by making available the tools necessary for success. Sister Gould experienced this both as mission historian and as editor-in-chief of *The Orientor*. She indicates, "I would write up the historical reports. President Garner would look them over and say, 'Is this what you want above your signature?' I would say yes and marvel that he trusted me and didn't correct or criticize what I did." She says of her work on *The Orientor*, "I had fun working my amateurish pages out with a real publisher."

Commonly contained in an issue were a letter from President Garner, birthdays for the month, new arrivals, departures, personnel changes, and articles of instruction, invitation, interest, and inspiration. The September 1966 issue sent to President McKay produced a November 30, 1966, letter of commendation from his secretary, Clare Middlemiss:

> Congratulations upon the excellence of your September 1966 issue of "The Orientor," a publication of the Southern Far East Mission.
>
> I have shown this issue to President McKay, and he commends you and your associates upon the quality of your mission publication. He thanks you and deeply appreciates the article honoring him on his Ninety-third Birthday Anniversary.
>
> The President also sends his commendation and greetings to the missionaries for the dedicated service they are rendering in the Southern Far East Mission, and wants each of them to know that he is praying each day that the Lord will bless and inspire them in their missionary efforts.
>
> As I wish to preserve this special number in President McKay's scrapbook, I am wondering if you would please send me three additional copies of the September 1966 issue.

Typical of the articles that appeared is one taken from this same issue entitled "Be Ye Doers" (An Interview with President Garner).

> Generally speaking one that comes into the Mission field isn't here because he suddenly decided to accept a Mission call. Quite the contrary, it has been planned for, for many years, as one great experience to which we looked forward. I'm sure that if you would search your own hearts, you'd find that a Mission has always been a part of your plan. Now that you are here, be a first class missionary. You are working for the Lord and you will receive the Lord's pay in direct proportion to the way you serve.
>
> District leaders, Travelers and a Mission President are here to guide, direct and persuade. But in reality, your employer is the **Holy One of Israel**. You talk to Him many times during the day and He speaks to you through the spirit and the scrip-

tures. Be responsive to both and your Mission will blossom into a beautiful and never-ending dream of accomplishment.

Think of your two and a half year mission in the following terms: You will be here 21,900 hours, 7,300 of which will be used sleeping, 675 of which will be used in "Take-Five Days" (President Garner's version of D [Diversion] Day or P [Preparation] Day), and 1,825 of which will be used at meals. This leaves 12,100 hours for study, prayer and work.

Think of your life without a Mission.

Where could you possibly gain this enviable time for discovering theological truths and serving your Heavenly Father without conflicting interests? You're literally leap years ahead of those that aren't able or who fail to fulfill this opportunity. And what you gain in wisdom, judgement, self-confidence and applied sociology will remain with you forever.

I have observed that those who lead effectively in the Lord's work, love the people. We are whole heartedly involved in a labor of love and if we genuinely demonstrate this quality of character our leadership will be fruitful and rewarding, for the people will respond with *love*, more activity and greater desire to live righteously. You who love have set the proper example in leadership. Wherever you find a good Branch or District, you will find at its head **men who love the Lord and the people**.

The best text for learning how to become an effective teacher of the gospel is found in Alma 17:2, 3, 4. I'd recommended that every missionary commit these to memory and recite them to himself every morning as a reminder of what can happen to him.

'Now these sons of Mosiah.....had waxed strong in the knowledge of the truth; for they were men of a sound understanding and they had searched the scriptures diligently, that they might know the word of God. But this is not all; they had given themselves to much prayer, and fasting; therefore they had the spirit of revelation, and when they taught, they taught with power and authority of God.'

From his windowed office, furnished with a Chinese desk, chairs, a wall size Pan American map, a reproduction of the Harry Anderson painting of Jesus ordaining the Twelve, Asian memorabilia and accoutrements, President Garner attended to his duties when he was in Hong Kong and prepared for his travels elsewhere. When he traveled to Taiwan, the Philippines, and other far-flung destinations within the mission, he found other suitable settings from which to conduct his charge.

President Garner interviewed as often as possible the three hundred missionaries under his direction. This exercise exposed his philosophy of leadership and enveloped him in the triumphs, the struggles, and the lapses of the mission experience.

His missionaries best identify the qualities they found in their mission president that made him such an exceptional leader. One of President Garner's first interviews brought this response as recorded in Stephen L. Richey's August 27, 1965, journal entry, "In my first interview with Pres. Garner, he told me to put my health number one in priority. He said if I have to miss a meeting to get in by 10:30--miss it. Wow!! What a tremendous man! I've only actually talked to him once, but I already have a great love and respect for him." Another elder, Douglas McOmber, writes about the things President Garner stressed. "Focus on the things that matter most. Never stop reading the Book of Mormon." In addition, Elder McOmber found his mission president to be kind, concerned, loving, and exacting. He also mentioned his impatience with laziness or an unwillingness to try. Most of all, Douglas points to President Garner's commitment to the truth.

Missionary George Brown reports, "The thing I remember about President Garner when I first met him in Hong Kong and received my assignment to Taiwan was he had a very piercing gaze, and it was like he was just looking right through me. I got this impression about him that he was a person who knew what he was doing and was in a hurry to get it done. He'd interview us on a regular basis. He was not harsh in his interviews, but he'd get after you if there was a problem. He didn't mince words with you.

He was sort of your father away from home. He always understood. He seemed to have this perception of what your needs were. If you had a concern, you didn't usually have to bring it up because he was asking you questions that brought it out. I know after his many interviews he was skilled in dealing with things, but I think in a large part it was the Spirit guiding him in the things that he was doing. President Garner was so different. If you had a problem, you wanted to deal with him. He had such a huge area to cover, but somehow he left you with the impression that if there was a problem he'd be johnny-on-the-spot; he'd be there. As I look back, if you just factor in the missionaries that needed assistance, I think what a big challenge for him. He really had to be perceptive and listen to the Spirit. He took care of us; he didn't waste time on things, got to it, done with it, moved on. You felt like 'Hey, that's over. Let's forget it, put it in the past, and let's move on.'"

This quality is part of President Garner's nature, and it has not diminished but rather has spanned the years since it motivated his missionaries. Today with an allusion to daylight savings time he will say, "I would rather spring forward than fall back."

George concludes, "There was always that positive incentive to move forward."

These young Mormon missionaries under President Garner's direction were truly getting on with the work! The article written by a staff reporter in the *Hong Kong Standard* for Monday, April 17, 1967, headlined "Young Mormons peddle faith from door-to-door" from under a picture: Mr. Kent Whiteley, assistant to the mission president, is seen with Mr. L Van Dam, a young missionary.--Standard photo, reads:

> Missionaries of today, apart from being well-versed in their religion, must also be top-calibre door-to-door salesmen, facing hazards similar to those confronting any salesman, the uncertainty before a knock, a hostile reception or indifferent audience. The only difference is that the missionaries do not work for self-profit. Such a breed are the Mormons and 80 of them, between the ages of 19 and 25, roam the streets of Hongkong, going from door to door, asking for a chance to be listened to.
>
> Clean-cut and neatly-dressed, they are hardly distinguishable from the ordinary tourist in the street.
>
> But beneath the youthful appearance lies the determination of a person who takes upon himself, voluntarily, an almost herculean task.
>
> The dedication of these young men can be gauged from the number of steps they mount daily and their will to go on after having countless doors slammed in their faces.
>
> Most of them are Americans in an alien country and often plunged into situations where the language poses a considerable obstacle to their work, but they have nevertheless achieved some success.
>
> According to Mr. Kent Whiteley, assistant to the mission president, they have managed to win over 4,000 converts during the past ten years.
>
> "This number represents a great portion of the people we have managed to convert in Southeast Asia," he said.
>
> He also described the Chinese as a race who take religion lightly, but added that there are some in their church who are devout Mormons and who take an active interest in their work.
>
> About the reception they receive during their work, he said: "On the whole the people are very hospitable, but then there are some who aren't."
>
> Volunteers, they are specially selected by their headquarters in Salt Lake City, Utah, and serve 2 1/2 years before returning to the US.

> They take their work seriously, spending most of their
> time in resettlement estates and often visiting the New
> Territories to spread the Gospel.
> In a way these young men portray the responsibility the
> youth of today must bear in helping his less fortunate neigh-
> bour and the unflagging enthusiasm with which to carry it.

President Garner created an atmosphere where his admonishment "Be Ye Doers" opened his door to missionary suggestions, to enlargement of talents, and to innovative ideas for presenting the gospel. His encouragement to exceed basic standards of excellence allowed his missionaries' ideas to find fruition. His enthusiastic approval, "Let's give it a try!" prompted novel ideas for capturing the notice of potential investigators. Consequentially, one elder unrolled a screen in the plaza of a resettlement area on which he projected the Church-produced films and film strips, attracting the attention and questions of those passing by. Other elders organized basketball leagues which turned some of the sports-minded into gospel-interested participants. Another group of elders formed a missionary double quartet, entered a contest that was broadcast on nationwide television in Taiwan, and won first prize.

A door which President Garner opened for a sister missionary serving in the mission home in Hong Kong proved quite spectacular for her. Because he had assigned her to the mission home staff, he became acquainted with Sister Erlyn Gould's proficiency in playing the violin. Almost every Sunday he gave her the opportunity to play a violin solo at various branches accompanied on the piano by different elders. She tells the rest, "One day President Garner suggested that I tryout for the symphony as a way of reaching different levels of people in missionary work. So I tried out and was placed third stand on the outside or fifth chair. Pretty great. And in fact, we did teach some discussions to various of the other instrumentalists, getting the farthest with one flutist. Also later in my mission while walking along the road with my companion, I was spotted a few times by people who had seen me play in the symphony, and conversations about the Church resulted…It was really a thrill playing with the Hong Kong Symphony. Their new concert hall on the water of the Hong Kong side was so gorgeous. I made a contribution and could play all the music with ease without much practice, so I could still do the missionary work during the day."

President Garner and these young men and women were building on the work of those who had come before, and their contributions were significant. In the *Church News*, week ending January 20, 1968, an article "THE GOSPEL IN CHINA" by George L. Scott, scores the past and the present efforts and accomplishments and the future promise.

> It has been 114 years since the first Mormon missionaries
> began preaching the Gospel to Chinese people in Hong Kong.
> Persecutions and language barriers have caused delays in pre-

senting the restored Church of Jesus Christ of Latter-day Saints to the millions of people in the Orient but the work continues to progress.

One of the crowning events was the dedication of the Un Long Chapel in Hong Kong in 1967 by President Hugh B. Brown of the First Presidency. He was accompanied by Elder Gordon B. Hinckley of the Council of the Twelve. They also went to Taipei in Taiwan where a congregation of 460 met for a district conference in the new district center chapel.

The first two missionaries arrived in Hong Kong in 1853. Their stay was brief due to hardships involved and opposition by the Chinese.

Nothing further was done officially until 1921 when President David O. McKay, then an Apostle, dedicated the vast nation of China for the preaching of the Gospel.

The Chinese Mission was born on the 19th of July, 1949. Elders Matthew Cowley, Hilton A. Robertson and Henry W. Aki with their wives were chosen by the First Presidency to begin the work in China. They first attempted to set up headquarters in Canton but because of adverse conditions they returned to Hong Kong and established the mission office.

Elder Cowley described the ceremony performed in establishing the work in China. He said: "…We went up on what is known as the 'Peak', the highest eminence overlooking the beautiful city of Hong Kong and onto the mainland of China and there we officially opened the mission by a brief service, each of us praying in turn. I will never forget the prayer of Brother Henry Aki, who, as he stood there facing his homeland with its four hundred and sixty-five million inhabitants, poured out his soul to God that he might be the means of bringing salvation to his kindred people. What great odds, one man holding the Priesthood of God among four hundred and sixty-five million of his race. I was never so impressed with the preciousness of the priesthood of God as I was when this dear Chinese brother, who felt the burden that was upon him implored God to bring salvation to his people."

The first two missionaries, according to a report published in the "Voice of the Saints," Southern Far East Mission, were H. Grant Heaton and William K. Paalani. They arrived Feb. 25, 1950, and within a year, eight missionaries were in Hong Kong and two baptismal services held. Church membership rose to 17.

More difficulties arose and because of civil strife, President McKay instructed the mission staff to evacuate to the Hawaiian Islands. From there, they were later transferred to Chinatown in San Francisco.

The mission was re-established in 1955 under a new name when President and Mrs. Joseph Fielding Smith went to Japan and divided the Japanese Mission into the Northern Far East Mission and the Southern Far East Mission. Once more eight missionaries entered Hong Kong and on August 23 began the work among the Chinese.

By 1957 there were four branches of the Church in Hong Kong known as the Kowloon City, Happy Valley, Sham Shui Po, and Tsim Sha Tsui branches.

Mission affairs were turned over to Pres. Robert S. Taylor on Sept 15, 1959, and when Pres. J. A. Quealy took over on Sept 15, 1962, there were 12 branches established.

Local members were given added responsibility in staffing the branches. Toward the end of 1964, the Hong Kong District was organized with Loh Ying Hwa as the district president. The new presidency conducted the March 1965 quarterly conference.

Pres. Keith E. Garner arrived to take over the Southern Far East Mission on Aug 13, 1965. Progressive work continued with auxiliaries organized in the growing branches. The Hong Kong District was divided into the Hong Kong District and Kowloon District in October, 1965. C. I. Chan became the first local member to preside over the new Hong Kong District in 1966.

One of the most important events in the mission was the translation and publishing of the Book of Mormon in Chinese. It became available to Chinese members in December, 1965, and has led to the growth in membership.

Dedication of the Un Long Chapel marks another important historical event in the progress of the Church in China.

Chapel building continues to go forward.

In addition to the newly dedicated Taipei Chapel in the East Coast District of Formosa, construction work is going forward on another beautiful chapel for the Kao Hsiung Branch in the South Taiwan District.

Membership is steadily increasing in Taiwan (Formosa) as

well as Hong Kong. On the island of Taiwan, where some four
million Chinese have established the Republic of China away
from the Communist-controlled Chinese mainland, the Church
now has 16 branches and nearly 2,000 members.

This remarkable growth has been established since 1956
when the first missionaries were sent to Taiwan, more familiarly
known as Formosa.

Building missionaries were sent to Taiwan to help the
local members build their new chapels.

Elder Hinckley was deeply impressed with the cooperation, love and respect that has grown up among the missionaries and Chinese members on Taiwan. He quoted one Chinese
woman as saying, "We love the missionaries because they love
us and treat us as equals."

Young Chinese members have served full-time missions
among their own people. More of the members are anxious to
prepare for similar calls of responsibility as missionaries and
officers in their branches.

Elder Hinckley sees a great work growing among the
Chinese people of East Asia and declares the future of the
church in this area is "unlimited."

"Those Gregory Peck and Clark Gable movies skip some of the Hong Kong
story," President Garner told interviewer Richard Harris upon his return to Menlo
Park. Yes, he found Hong Kong intriguingly unique, a place where the flavors, the
smells, the sights remain with a person a very long time. Hong Kong was a combination of staid British presence and Chinese cultural mystique, Christmas celebrations
eclipsed by Chinese New Year, the Star Ferry met by scores of rickshaws, and cruise
liners sharing the famous Repulse Bay and Deep Water harbor with squatter huts and
fishing boats.   President Garner moves back to Hong Kong in his thoughts as he tells
about the rows of store fronts, each exuding a different smell as the gates were rolled
up and doors were opened to the street. Samtani, the tailor's shop, displayed wools,
silks, and other quality materials being busily stitched to custom fitted suits; the
leather shop stocked gloves, shoes, suitcases, portfolios; the little book shops sold, in
addition to books, stationary, pens, ink, pencils; electronic shops offered cameras to
calculators; the jewelry shop owned by Sheldon Poon, a Church member, marketed
watches, rings, necklaces, earrings, tie clips, and every stone imaginable; and the
fruit, vegetable, spice, and bread stands emitted familiar and exotic aromas. Keith
enjoyed the bustle of capitalism in action and found all of the smells inviting; none of
them seemed repugnant to him.

However, the direction on signs, "Please do not spit," did cause him and the missionaries some apprehension and revulsion, and the signs were not Hollywood props. Jerry James, remembering one of the more unpleasant aspects of his mission experience, explains, "The Chinese are famous for spitting big mucous wads. Sometimes when tracting in the slums of Hong Kong, you'd be walking, and you'd feel something on your head." And that wasn't all. "People lived in these high-rise buildings everywhere and would just throw garbage over the railing. If you were there at the wrong time you might get it." When he went tracting with the elders, President Garner discovered from personal experience the garbage deposited on the stairways and thrown over the railings. His comment is that "Every mission has its blessings and curses."

Those curses included, according to President Garner, "the monsoons that dump sixty inches of rain between May and August and the heat made more uncomfortable by the high humidity."

Interestingly enough, Hong Kong in the summer of 1967 suffered a severe man-made drought. Mainland China withheld water from British leased Hong Kong. The water for the entire colony ran for only four hours once every four days. Luckily, the mission home's large galvanized tank on the roof when filled contained a sufficient amount of water for showers for a few days. Missionaries not living in the mission home resorted to filling garbage cans with water and using that supply for the next four days, which in the hot and humid weather meant only being able to sponge off using one cereal bowl of water.

Despite these environmental challenges for the mission president, his family, and the missionaries, the Church grew. A picture of the new Un Long chapel appeared in the *Church News*.

The property was purchased in 1965, one mile east of Un Long, and under direction of work missionaries and with cooperation of both missionaries and members, the chapel was completed in early 1966.

When President Garner thought of the comparable ease with which the Menlo Park Ward chapel had been completed, he must

HONG KONG

First Chinese Chapel

This beautiful chapel was dedicated on April 16 by President Hugh B. Brown of the First Presidency. The chapel is at Un Long in the Hong Kong zone and is the first to be dedicated on the mainland of ancient China.

have marvelled at the primitive methods available to Brother Teeples, the Church building superintendent for the Un Long chapel. Elders who worked on the building recall vividly, perhaps revisiting memories of their sore backs, the single drum con-crete mixer pouring concrete into the one available wheelbarrow. The volunteers would then push it up the platform and dump its load, thus creating footings, a foun-dation, and walls. Their determination, perseverance, and hard work paid off. The chapel was a welcomed advancement.

Prior to the completion of this chapel, "chapel" in Hong Kong meant the top floor of various apartment buildings used as meeting places for the Tsim Sha Tsui Branch-Kowloon City Branch, Sham Shui Po Branch-Lai Chi Kok Branch, and Causeway Bay Branch-North Point Branch. A rented apartment provided space for the Fan-Ling Branch. The crown of the buildings was Kam Tong Hall, which the Church purchased for use as the district center for the Hong Kong District and the West Point Branch. This hall described by one missionary was a gorgeous, multilayered building with twists and turns, chapel rooms, a baptismal font, and elders' quarters.

President Garner saw not only the dedication of the new chapel on Mainland China, but he had also already witnessed in 1966 the dedication of a chapel on Taiwan. An article in the *Church News*, week ending November 12, 1966, announced this premier event.

CHAPELS GROW AROUND WORLD

...Dedication of the Taipei chapel climaxed three years of praying, planning, fund-raising and construction of this historic "first" for the Church in China. It serves as a house of worship for over 900 members in two branches and is district center for eight more branches with a total of almost 2,000 members.

Before Elder Hinckley spoke and dedicated the chapel, other speakers included Mission President Keith E, Garner, his counselor President Hu Wei, North Taiwan District Pres. Liang Jen Sheng, and West Taipei Branch Pres. Shen Hsueh Lun.

More than 500 members and friends attended the dedica-tion, including some noted non-member Chinese government officials and diplomats.

Many of those who came from the mainland as well as local people have accepted the gospel. There are now 3000 members in 16 branch organizations on the island, located from Ping Tung in the south to Kelung seaport in the north.

Four branches are located in the capital of Taipei in addi-tion to an active American servicemen's group...

Members on Taiwan now have the Book of Mormon translated in Chinese through the efforts of President Hu Wei I and Larry Browning. The Doctrine and Covenants and Pearl of Great Price are in the hands of translators now and should be

completed in 1967 under the direction of former Branch Pres.
Che Tsai Tien.

President Garner's comment on this occasion was shorter. "The Taipei Chapel
in Taiwan was dedicated on October sixteenth by Brother Hinckley. The dedicatory
service was inspiring, and the prayer was comforting and reassuring to the Saints in
that wonderful land."

The new chapel in Taipei had nearly all the accoutrements of chapels in the
United States, including hot water heaters, showers, and a gymnasium. The elders on
their take-five days enjoyed playing pick up games of basketball and relaxing in the
newly available luxury.

This same chapel serves as the backdrop for the following story told by
George Brown. "At one all-island conference held at the Taipei chapel, the heat was
out. Everyone was wearing his coat because it was the middle of winter. We were in
the chapel, and President Garner got up and said, 'It's cold in here. I want you to
crowd together and fill up this first half of the chapel.' It basically was a full chapel of
missionaries that he put in the first half of the pews. It made a big difference. This
one sister missionary, Sister Horne, stood up and said, 'This reminds me of that
famous scripture, "Many are cold but few are frozen."'

Her play on the words 'Many are called but few are chosen,' brought down
the house. President Garner started laughing. Everyone was laughing, but President
Garner, it just really hit him; we almost had to pick him up and carry him out of the
aisle. She said it so seriously, completely deadpan."

President Garner had an excellent sense of humor. He would not only laugh
heartily at other people's jokes, but he would tell jokes and entertain the missionaries.
Wilford W. Kirton, Jr. acknowledges the benefit of Keith's sense of humor in the following written note. "It was a very rich experience to be able to spend several days
with President Garner. This opportunity of getting to know better one of the choice
servants of the Lord was a great experience for me. President Garner's great sense
of humor with the challenging responsibility of his office was stimulating and refresh-
ing. His great ability to deal with people successfully is a mark of leadership and capa-
bility."

Marcia Smith Merrill recognized these same qualities which brought out these
same feelings almost without exception among his missionaries. "It didn't take long to
be mightily influenced by President Garner's personality. As soon as I arrived in Hong
Kong I realized I was being interviewed by a man of deep insight and commitment to
his calling. But I also sensed a man with a keen and sharp sense of humor and a sincere delight in the human experience."

He had much to delight him in his present associations, some of which took
him back to his first mission in Hawaii. Mary Ann Soong writes in 2001, "We first
met Keith Garner when he served as a missionary on the island of Kauai, also known

as the Garden Island. He was very friendly to everyone, and it was so easy to talk
with him. All the members in the Kapa'a Branch loved Elder Garner, and often the
elderly members would refer to him as 'keiki o ka aina' (child of the land). He
learned to speak Hawaiian from Louise P. Sheldon, a refined and educated lady of pure
Hawaiian descent and someone who was like a mother to me. I believe he still
remembers the language.

My husband, Kai On Soong, and I were privileged to again be associated with
President Garner when we served as missionaries in Hong Kong from April 1966 to
October 1968. It was a happy reunion for us. I think of President Garner as one who
has an understanding heart. In one of our weekly morning meetings, he reminded us
about the instruction given earlier--keeping one arm's length distance between ourselves and the opposite sex while conversing. I was fifty-five years old at that time,
and because I continued to hug 'my boys' (the young elders), I wasn't strictly abiding
by that rule. It was brought to President Garner's attention, and his response was,
'It's all right for Sister Soong to hug anyone because that's the way the Hawaiians do
it.' To me that was a reaffirmation of his understanding and kind heart. That made me
love him even more, and to us he was the best mission president ever!"

Karl H. Wheatley also writes about President Garner's innate qualities that
endeared him to many. "I was still a relatively young elder when he came to the
Southern Far East Mission as our new president. I immediately became fond of him.
He was a loving, understanding, and concerned president--more like a father to us all.
He was always happy, and the spirit of the Lord seemed to radiate from his being. I
think we all loved being around him. He always inspired confidence and a desire to
do the work.

I didn't have the blessing of working with him daily, but we looked forward to
his visits in our apartment. He was unpretentious with us, and we always felt that we
could share with him our inner thoughts and concerns. We were motivated by his
enthusiasm for the work, his strong testimony rather than statistics and competition.
His advice to me at the conclusion of my mission has remained with me and has been
a guiding strength to my own life. All six of our children have served missions partly
due to the rewarding missionary experiences that I enjoyed in Hong Kong."

Edwin K. Andrus concurs. In a very recent chance meeting, Ed and his wife,
who were at Costco picking up supplies for the Olympus High School's fortieth class
reunion, ran into Keith unexpectedly. During their conversation Ed said, "I remember
standing in front of the mission home just before I got in the car waiting to take me to
the airport for my flight home. I have never forgotten your parting counsel. You told
me three things. First, do everything in the name of Christ. Two, let your mother
choose your wife or at least approve of your decision; she knows you better than anyone
else in the world. Third, when you are asked to serve in the church...say yes."

Another of his elders Ronald Lam told him, "I wanted to share one experience that I had with you that was most memorable. Prior to receiving my call on my

mission my father did not want me to go on a mission. He was not a member of the Church. We had a lot of contention in our home then, so I was anxious to go on a mission. When I received my call my father was quite pleased that I had an assignment to go to Hong Kong. I left on my mission not really having a father. I was quite disappointed; I lacked having a father image in my life. I can't remember if I had talked to you privately about that or not but in my heart I always felt that you were the first person that I identified with as my father. I had learned a lot from following your example and having you as my mission president. It made a big difference in my life and in fact, while I was serving there in Hong Kong there was a turning point in my life where I realized that I needed to correct my relationship with my own father, which I did years later. Today my father and I are the best of friends and there's a lot of love and affection between us. I owe a lot of that to the first experience that I had in having you as my father figure so I want to thank you again, Brother Garner, for all that you did for me in my personal life as I was growing up as a young missionary and trying to find myself."

All mission presidents enjoy the privilege and heavy responsibility of influencing for good these young men and women under their stewardship. Some of their decisions for their futures are made under the tutelage of their mission's "father figure," or as his missionaries additionally titled him "a real friend of the missionaries." While it is impossible to include all President Garner's missionary's narratives or even find each one almost forty years later, President Garner is blessed to see some of his missionaries frequently. Five of these, among many others, trace to their formative years in the mission field interests sparked there. Newell K. Johnson, a partner at the accounting firm of Hansen, Barnett, and Maxwell, who served as mission financial clerk, prepares his taxes. Jerry W. James, an entrepreneurial attorney, who is always engaged in the "good work," spends an hour a week with him discussing the Book of Mormon. John J. McSweeney, Director of Development and Construction, Flying J Inc. or as he prefers a poor immigrant worker from Australia, greets him as they meet at the Salt Lake Temple for an early morning session. William J. Christiansen, a physics and geology teacher in the Salt Lake City School District, who on a six week teaching program introduced his son to China, and Donald P. Brown, Director of Asia Marketing at Evans & Sutherland, who spends more time in Asia than America, visit with him occasionally over lunch.

Sitting across a dinner table seems to invite openness, or at the very least the possibility of more casual, wide-ranging conversations, even if the place is of four-star elegance. One of President Garner's favorite restaurants, and for that matter also Elder Hanks', was the old British Peninsula Hotel in Kowloon which serves a smashing smorgasbord. Elder Brown writes, "Whenever President Garner would come to the island depending on the time frames, he'd take the missionaries out to eat. We missionaries would say, 'Great, President Garner's coming so he'll take us some place to eat. We'll get something really good.' And he always did. I remember I had a dinner with him once in the Peninsula Hotel in Hong Kong. It was so enjoyable to sit down with him in a less formal setting than when he'd interview you. The Peninsula Hotel was so spectacular anyway."

In a December 6, 1966, entry, Elder Richey further identifies the desired result of these invitations. "Speaking of President Garner, the other day he took me and Elder Jenson aside and told us to meet him at the Peninsula Hotel tomorrow for a fabulous steak dinner. I'm so happy that I've been able to establish a good name and friendship with President Garner. He talks to us two like missionary companions--like the poem I like so well about true friends that can say anything knowing that a faithful friend will take what is worthwhile and with the breath of kindness blow the rest away. Really a close bond, I've certainly learned and grown to love and respect him."

Keith's prized practice of feeding and counseling missionaries continues to this day. Three decades later and thousands of miles from Hong Kong he still savors, as he did then, the company of these young men and women on the Lord's errand and as often as possible invites them to join him for lunch or dinner. In a note to Keith from Elder Mike Blackmore, serving in the Utah Salt Lake City Mission, written January 8, 2003, he expresses these sentiments before being transferred out of the area in which Keith resides. "I just wanted to say thank you for all the help you have given me. First, for these great dinners, and secondly, for the great thoughts and conversations we had...."

This much appreciated recent note mirrors similar experiences of President Garner's Southern Far East missionaries. Not even trying to crush the spontaneous smile, Keith says, "Appreciation for food always comes first," and then he repeats the statement reportedly uttered by Ghandi, "When I meet the Lord we will dine first, and talk during and after."

Sister Marcia Smith Merrill says, "President Garner was a most generous man. There were times when he would treat the mission home staff to a movie or dinner, and we even had mission-wide (Hong Kong wide, that is) outings which I believe were at his personal expense. And these were just the obvious generosities. Knowing him, there were probably many private generous moments with his missionaries--generous with regard to money, time, and prayer."

Hong Kong events mentioned in missionary reminiscences range from taking a hydrofoil to Macau, the Portuguese protectorate off the Chinese coast, to Hong Kong Zone tournaments at a local Kowloon bowling alley.

Though the movies' depictions of Hong Kong may not have been entirely accurate, President Garner did occasionally take the missionaries to a movie or two. In fact, he recently saw one of the lady missionaries who served in Hong Kong. The first remark she made to him was, "You know, President, I'll never forget that Monday we went and saw *A Man For All Seasons*." This conversation took place forty years later.

President Garner describes the circumstances. "I'd read Sir Thomas More's story, and when it came out in movie form, I felt it was as good as any sacrament meeting I'd ever attended; it taught the fundamentals of life. There are some great lines in it."

Some of his favorites occur when Thomas More advises Richard, whom More identifies as "a young friend from Cambridge who wants what they all want, a position," "Why not be a teacher, you'd be a fine teacher, perhaps a great one." Aspiring Richard asks, "If I was, who would know it?" Sir Thomas answers, "You, your pupils, your friends, God, not a bad public that…Be a teacher." Keith comments, "The recommendation that he be a teacher, which I think is the greatest of all professions, fell on deaf ears. The movie was full of important decisions that people have to make in life."

The classic lines he enjoys most come at the end as Sir Thomas More is being tried for treason. After Richard falsifies his testimony to condemn Sir Thomas to death, More compassionately states, "I'm sorrier for your perjury than my peril." He states, "There is one question I'd like to ask the witness." Gazing on the medallion hanging around Richard's neck, he asks, "May I see it?" He identifies it. "That's a chain of office you are wearing. The red dragon." More, wanting a clarification regarding why Richard is wearing it, inquires, "What's this?" Cromwell speaks, "Sir Richard is appointed attorney general for Wales." Paul Scofield portraying More utters some of the most profound lines in cinema, based on the scripture in Matthew 16:26. "For Wales? Why Richard, it profits a man nothing to give his soul for the whole world, but for Wales!"

President Garner would think of those words on applicable occasions, but in May 1966, brought on by some unusual circumstances, he, out of necessity, had to deal with worldly concerns trying to impede his work for the Lord in Hong Kong. He felt he had left for this mission having taken care of all business concerns; however, less than a year after his arrival in Hong Kong, Keith, with Elder Hinckley's permission, flew back to the States to attend to a serious matter that had arisen.

The blessing given him when he was set apart to serve included this language. "We bless you for your willingness to set aside the world and to give your total consecration for this period, for which you are called." It further read, "We bless you … and your interests here and all that pertains to you…." The proof of this pronouncement became apparent as recorded in Keith's May 21, 1966, letter to President Hinckley:

> Dear Brother Hinckley:
> If you have a few minutes, I'd like to relate a personal experience which I consider a most remarkable answer to prayer. Last June, after accepting the call to preside over the Southern Far East Mission, I borrowed several thousand dollars on deeds of trust and left the cash with Gene Kimball, (my brother-in-law, and the person I chose to take over my business in my absence), to pay all the subcontractors on the remaining

construction still in progress.

During the intervening months and principally because of
the Viet Nam War's effect on our economy, he was $125,000
short at the completion of the jobs. In fact, upon my arrival
home, May fourth, I learned that several of the subs had served
notice that they would file liens if they were not paid by the
fifteenth of May.

Gene, being aware of the problem in March, had
contacted a doctor who had had a keen interest in purchasing
two of my buildings. However, in April, he had cooled off
and decided against the purchase. I suggested that he call the
doctor again and tell him I was in town and try to arrange
another meeting to discuss the sale and purchase. So, that
afternoon, May fourth, Gene called, but the doctor told him
he definitely wasn't interested and that nothing would be
gained by getting together.

If you remember, I came to Salt Lake Thursday and
returned to San Francisco early Friday. All Friday and Saturday
morning I searched for prospective buyers. I promised Gene I
would not return to Hong Kong until I could put $125,000 in
his hands, and I had promised you that I would return to the
mission field Sunday morning.

We are in a tight money market, and I knew my only
solution would be to sell something that would generate the
needed cash. I have done a lot of buying and selling during the
past years, and regardless of the size of the sale, few sales produce that much cash since I usually took a large second mortgage with forty or fifty thousand in cash. Knowing this reality,
I took my problem to the Lord and received the sure conviction that I would be able to take that Sunday plane and that I
would be able to leave Gene the money.

Saturday afternoon, having spent two days in a futile
search for a purchaser, I decided to contact the doctor personally. Gene had serious doubts as he recalled the doctor had
expressed such a negative reaction on Wednesday. I called
the doctor's office, however, and learned that he had gone
to Los Angeles for the week-end and wouldn't return until
Sunday evening.

I asked the nurse for his address or telephone in Los
Angeles, and since she didn't know me, she refused. After
some urgent conversation with her, she gave me the doctor's

son's telephone number. I called him and explained that I was here from Hong Kong and it was urgent that I talk to his father. So, he gave me the telephone number.

At four o'clock I reached him and found that because he suddenly wasn't feeling well, he intended to fly back to San Francisco within the hour. This unexpected circumstance provided an opportunity I needed, and I asked if I might pick him and his wife up at the airport. When we met him, we learned that because of his hurried departure from Southern California, his baggage had been detained and wouldn't arrive for an hour. This delay afforded one precious hour which was another fortunate opportunity for me. Gene, the doctor and his wife, and I sat in Gene's car and reopened the discussion of the proposed purchase. Within the hour, he decided to buy one of the buildings giving me a check for $10,000 and assurance that the remaining $110,000 would be paid Friday, May the thirteenth.

I took the plane Sunday morning rejoicing and with the full assurance that the Lord had indeed answered my prayer of need.

Yesterday, May seventeenth, I learned that the sale had gone through escrow.

With the Lord's help, Keith had accomplished what appeared to be impossible. Having spent only four days away, one in Salt Lake and a weekend in Menlo Park, he had concluded his business, left worldly concerns resolved, and returned to his missionary work in Hong Kong, his enthusiasm and energy for the work, not only in tact, but heightened by this special experience. That fact was evident in his P.S. "We are leaving now for the North Taipei Conference and Missionary Workshop. Next weekend I will be in Saigon setting apart a new zone President as President James Duncan is returning to the States, and the following week, we will hold the Luzon District Conference and Missionary Workshop in Manila. All is well in the Southern Far East."

The bas-relief world maps on the sides of the twenty-six story Church Office Building in Salt Lake City illustrate the scripture found in Doctrine and Covenants 133:37. "And this gospel shall be preached unto every nation, and kindred, and tongue, and people." Though the maps gracing the Church Office Building were still in the future, President Garner, having returned from Salt Lake via Menlo Park, could not help feeling those same feelings that the gospel of Jesus Christ is a message for all the world. In fact, he had already written of them in the mission newsletter *The Orientor* in March of 1966.

We feel that progress is being made and that the future
is bright in these far away lands for the gospel. As I look down
into these Chinese faces at the Conferences and hear them
sing "We Thank Thee, O God, for a Prophet," there is just
something which affects my normal metabolism, and I say in
my heart: "Surely God has made of one blood all the nations
of man."

One never-to-be-forgotten trip to the Asian people of the world happened in
October of 1966. Elder Gordon B. Hinckley, supervisor over Asia, and his associate,
Elder Marion D. Hanks of the Seventy, joined President Garner for a visit to many
parts of the Southern Far East Mission. President Garner refers to this month as
"a glorious month." They visited Taiwan, the Philippines, Hong Kong, Vietnam,
Thailand, and Singapore together, and Elder Hinckley and President Garner concluded their travels in India.

President Garner addressed his missionaries, "My dear companions, these
weeks traveling with and observing an Apostle of the Lord strengthened my testimony

*Elder Marion D. Hanks, Elder Gordon B. Hinckley and President Keith E. Garner begin their
travels-- "A Never-to-be-forgotten Trip" October 1966*

in the truth of the declaration--that the true Church of Jesus Christ is built upon the foundation of apostles and of prophets!"

Elder Hinckley and Elder Hanks, these two General Authorities, assisted by President Garner were performing the same mission as the ancient workers in the Kingdom in the meridian of time. Elder Hanks quite seriously likened President Garner's role to that of the Apostle Paul.

A no more appropriate appellation could be ascribed to Paul and his journeys throughout the Middle East than missionary. Likewise, President Garner also was breaking new ground in the spread of the gospel throughout Asia. These missionary efforts would ripple throughout the whole world as converts spread "the news" within their own spheres of influence.

Within Keith's sphere of stewardship, full-time missionaries would be transferred to Thailand and Singapore, and the Philippines would no longer be included in the Southern Far East Mission, but would become a mission of its own. Elder Hanks most graciously expresses what many had observed. "It took me about thirty minutes to begin to really appreciate the ability of this little dynamo who moved swiftly, ran up stairs. He was wise and gentle and not arrogant. You knew and trusted the man. He'd been preceded by some good people, but things as they have a habit to do when this man is assigned responsibility for them began to liven up, and perk up, and function up, not because he put on a demonstration for anybody about his particular excellence, he just was, a very modest and very mild young man of great ability. I've never known, and I can say this having traversed the whole earth available at my period of time, of a mission president who was more loved by his missionaries and greater than Keith."

Elder Hanks continues, "Keith's whole mission was geared to build up development, not consciously. He wasn't trying to establish an empire or divide things himself. It just worked that way. When he sent missionaries into the Philippines, they happened to be the missionaries who just did such a great job that they could be recommended and their area with them for divestiture from Southeast Asia."

The work to open Thailand to missionaries began early in President Garner's tenure. In a letter to his sister Loma and her husband Joe, dated March 27, 1966, written on stationary from the Rama Hotel, Bangkok, Keith says, "We are in Thailand this week. It's a wonderful land full of the ancient and new. The U.S. influence is tremendous. Big, beautiful divided highways and trillions of crazy reckless drivers-- just like Mexico City, Tehran, and San Francisco!

We had a great Sunday. Some fifty-two came out to the Bangkok Group. I set a Brother (Lieutenant Colonel) J. Sterling Merrill apart as Thailand district president with two counselors. He is a solid citizen of the Kingdom and will help organize new groups throughout this tremendously large land."

Much preparatory work was now being done, and some gallant and dedicated efforts had predated President Garner's stewardship in Thailand.

President Brigham Young called thirteen elders to serve
missions in southern Asia, including four to serve in Siam.
The thirteen elders boarded the ship *Monsoon* at San Francisco
in early 1853 and arrived in Calcutta, India, on 26 April 1853.
There two of the four elders called to Siam were reassigned.
The remaining two, Elder Elam Luddington and Elder Levi
Savage, tried to reach Siam, via Rangoon, Burma, but their
ship sprang a leak and they had to return to Calcutta. Once
repaired, the ship headed again to Burma and arrived in
Rangoon on 10 August 1853. According to their report, the
missionaries felt penniless and alone; strangers in a foreign
land, nothing but war and bloodshed.

Only Elder Luddington went on to Siam, his companion
being too ill to continue. He arrived on 6 April 1854, nearly
a year after he left America. Three days after the ship landed,
Elder Luddington baptized James Trail, the ship's captain, and
Trail's wife. They would be his only baptisms during the four
months and five days he lived in Bangkok. Stoned twice and
poisoned once, Elder Luddington remained persistent and
faithful. He worked among the Europeans because he could
not speak the language of the country.

In a letter to Church leaders dated 1 June 1854, a lonely
and discouraged Elder Luddington wrote: "I am situated in
a insalubrious clime, among a few friends and surrounded by
many foes…I visited one of their festivals a few days ago.
I was cautioned to go armed…It was picturesque, fire works,
Burmese dancing, masks and Indian paintings, in true Asiatic
style…I have delivered one lecture every Sabbath since my
arrival in Bangkok; some eight or ten Europeans generally
attend. I am trying to learn the native language…I will keep
digging till you all say enough, and then if you see fit to call me
home I shall be truly in heaven and happy in the extreme; or if
you say "Spend your days," it shall be even so; not my will, but
my Heavenly Father's be done.

Shortly thereafter, Elder Luddington was called home.
On his return ocean voyage, he experienced a typhoon, a
mutiny, a ship's fire, and a famine. Having survived these
and many other dangers during his mission of more than two
years, he finally reached San Francisco safely on 27 June 1853.
Though his mission was among the most distant and challenging

of the early Church, he obediently fulfilled it with courage and faith.

It would be nearly a century after Elder Luddington's mission before The Church of Jesus Christ of Latter-day Saints would again have a presence in Thailand. During the 1950's and early 1960's Latter-day families in Bangkok were authorized to hold services. As the Vietnam War intensified and Latter-day Saint servicemen longed to worship together, groups were started at some bases of the United States Air Force, such as those at Udorn, Ubon, Thakli, and Korat. [33]

As President Garner's preparatory labors continued, he found himself in Thailand with Elder Hinckley and Elder Hanks. On one occasion these three men handled a rather perplexing situation dealing with the Word of Wisdom. Of course, without good health, one is stymied in his ability to perform energetic service and muted in his rejoicing in the gifts of an invigorated body. President Garner explains his understanding of the Word of Wisdom: "I think the whole nub of the dissertation by Joseph Smith on the Word of Wisdom deals with wheat for man. I think that's all you have to know, and then to avoid coffee, tea, tobacco, alcohol, and moderation in the eating of meat. In fact, the Lord says that we should avoid meat. If we do eat it, we eat it in times of famine and cold. Vegetables and fruits should be the main diet of man if he wants to retain good health in his lifetime."

However, in this situation, an explanation of the 89th section of the Doctrine and Covenants was not what was needed. As Keith tells it, "Elder Hinckley received some kind of a lead on a piece of property where we could build a chapel, and so we went to discuss the property with the family that owned it. It was a wealthy Chinese family. The woman greeted us at the door, very hospitable, and we went in and had a chair. When she came out, she said, 'Would you like a cup of tea?' We said, 'No, thanks very much; we are only going to be here a moment.' Our answer seemed to bother her a little bit, and she came back and said, 'Would you like a cup of coffee?' We said, 'No, thanks very much.' The third time she came, and she said, 'Would you like a Coca-Cola?' I said, 'Yes, we'd like a Coca-Cola.' She was gratified that she'd finally pushed the right button, and she brought us out three Cokes. We all thanked her. I don't know to this day whether any of us drank the offered beverage or not, but I do know all three of us were gracious in our acceptance that day."

President Garner continues, "That's the story we find with Theodore White, *Time* magazine's correspondent in China. He had cultivated a friendship with Chou-

---

[33] Joan Porter Ford and LaRene Porter Gaunt, "The Gospel Dawning in Thailand," *Ensign*, September 1995, 48.

en-li, and so out of this fondness for White, Chou threw a dinner party for him at Chungking's best restaurant, the Juan Sun Yuan. Right at the height of the party feast with the music playing, the trumpets bellowing the main course's arrival, the Chinese chefs brought in a stuffed pig, beautifully decorated in the Chinese way, but unmistakably a pig. At that moment Chou-en-li realized that White, a staunch Jew, didn't eat pork. In order to relieve the anxiety of his guest, Chou declared, 'Teddy, this is China. Look again, it looks to you like a pig. But in China, this is not a pig--this is a duck.' Chou-en-li, Theodore White, and the whole table laughed, and the evening was saved. [34]

It requires wisdom and judgment, but sometimes the occasion supersedes the tradition and the prohibition."

During this trip, Siam, the country in which Elder Luddington had faced enormous odds to plant missionary seeds with what he must have felt was little or no success, would be dedicated for the preaching of the gospel by one of the Lord's latter-day Apostles.

President Garner in March of 1966, as he had already informed his sister, had organized the Thailand District, primarily to serve the American servicemen stationed there. These men were sent there to protect the Thai homeland from the Communist threat in Southeast Asia. Interestingly, Thailand, or in the Thai language, Muang Thai, means Land of the Free. *Free*, a term President Garner cherishes, was prominently embodied in the name given to Siam in 1939, a country that according to President Garner grew the most luscious bananas and pineapples in the world, better even than Hawaii, and whose women were the most beautiful in the world. The Priesthood keys were about to be turned in behalf of the peoples of this lovely land.

The March 1968 issue of the Southern Far East Mission publication, *The Orientor*, reprised the event.

> Elder Hinckley, with President Marion D. Hanks of the First Council of Seventy and President Keith E. Garner of the Southern Far East Mission, held meetings the previous three days with members of the Church in Thailand. At 6:30 a.m. on the morning of November 2, 1966, they, with a small group, met in a quiet area of Lumpini Park in the heart of Bangkok and held a brief service. The opening prayer was offered by President Hanks. Elder Hinckley offered the following prayer of dedication after speaking briefly, and the closing prayer was offered by President Keith E. Garner.

> *Our Father and God, we come unto Thee in the name of Thy Son, Jesus*

---

[34] Theodore H. White, *In Search of History* (New York: Harper & Row, 1978), 119-120.

*Christ, with grateful hearts this beautiful morning. We are thankful,
Father, for the purpose for which we are met, to turn the key to the
preaching of the gospel in this ancient land of Thailand. Our hearts
are full of gratitude unto Thee for the gift of Thy Son, the Lord Jesus
Christ, and for the gift of His life which has made possible eternal life
for all who will hearken unto His teachings. We thank Thee, Father, for
His atonement, everlasting in its consequences. We thank Thee for the
light of the gospel restored in this dispensation of time, for Thy coming,
and the coming of Thy Son to the boy Joseph Smith, and for Thy declaration unto him. We thank Thee for the coming of heavenly messengers
thereafter with a bestowal of keys and authority, bringing to pass a
restoration of all of previous dispensations for the blessing of Thy children throughout the earth. We thank Thee, Father, for faithful servants,
missionaries who in times past gathered our forbearers from among the
nations of the earth and for the glorious blessings of the gospel which
have come to us because of their faith. We thank Thee for those who are
abroad in the earth today preaching the restored gospel. We pray Thy
blessings upon them wherever they may be that their labors may be
fruitful and that their joy may be great.*

*This morning we are particularly grateful for those of Thy Church
who have come to this land in the service of the United States
and who, while so serving, have gathered together frequently to bear
testimony one to another and to increase their faith in Thee. As they
have worshipped Thee, there has come into their hearts a desire to share
that which they have with others. We thank Thee for their
great desire that this land be opened to missionary endeavor.*

*And now, our Father, in the authority of the Holy Priesthood, even that
authority of the Holy Apostleship in us vested, we dedicate
and consecrate this land of Thailand, this ancient Kingdom of Siam, to
the preaching of the everlasting gospel, even the
Restored Gospel of the Lord Jesus Christ.*

*We pray that Thy spirit may rest upon this land and this nation.
Soften the hearts of the people that they may listen with
understanding and accept the truth. Bless those who shall teach
Thy gospel, the missionaries who will be sent here--bless them with
Thy holy spirit and love for the people among whom they labor.
Loosen their tongues that they shall speak the language of the people
and bless them that they shall be effective in proclaiming Thy word;*

*and may there be many, Father, yea, thousands and tens of thousands
who will hearken to their message. Open the way before Thy servants
that the blessings of Thy work and Thy word may come to the people of
this land, that they may draw near unto Thee, and that there may be
fulfilled here the revealed purposes for which Thy gospel has been
restored in this dispensation; namely, that every man might speak to
the name of God, the Lord, even the Savior of the world; that faith also
might increase in the earth; that Thine everlasting covenant might be
established; and that the fullness of Thy gospel might be
proclaimed by the weak and the simple unto the ends of the world
and before kings and rulers, that they might come to understanding.*

*Father in Heaven, pour out Thy spirit upon this land. Soften the
hearts of the people. Take from them the elements of cruelty and
meanness which have troubled so many in the past. Increase their love
one for another and may the bonds of brotherhood and affection
be strengthened among them. May they grow in leadership in Thy
kingdom as they partake of the blessings of Thy glorious truth.*

*Holy Father, we pray that Thou wilt bless those who govern
this nation that they may be men of judgment and understanding, of
goodness and virtue, that the lives of the citizens of the land may be
blessed. Touch the hearts of these rulers that they may be kindly to
Thy servants, that the way may be opened without difficulty, that Thy
servants may travel here in the coming years to preach Thy word and
find a friendly reception, not only at the hands of the people but at the
hands of those who stand in positions of government. Open
the way, Father, that properties may be found, that houses of worship
may be established, that Thy word may be taught, and
instruction given to all who will hear.*

*Now, Holy Father, as we gather this morning, we sustain before Thee
Thy anointed servant, the prophet of this day, under whose authority
we exercise the keys of the Apostleship in dedicating this land. We pray
likewise for all who stand in positions of responsibility in Thy kingdom
wherever they may be. And we invoke upon this land and this nation
the blessings of peace and pray that Thou wilt overrule throughout the
realm of Southeast Asia, that some honorable solution may be found to
the terrible conflict which is presently bringing so much suffering and
oppression to the peoples of this part of the earth.*

*Holy Father, we acknowledge before Thee our love for Thee and our love
for Thy Son. We acknowledge Thee as the God of the Heavens, the
Creator and Ruler of the Universe, our Father. We acknowledge before
Thee Thy beloved Son as our Savior and Redeemer and express unto
Thee and unto Him our love for Him. Accept our gratitude, accept of
this dedication, accept of our faith, we ask as we rededicate ourselves to
Thy holy service and invoke Thy blessing upon that which we here do
and upon those who shall follow us in Thy ministry, in the
name of Thy Son, Jesus Christ, Amen.* [35]

BANGKOK

Missionaries In Thailand

Six full-time missionaries from Hong Kong and Formosa in the
Southern Far East Mission are now laboring in Thailand with
headquarters at Bangkok. Elder Gordon B. Hinckley of the Council of the Twelve dedicated the land for the preaching of the
Gospel last fall. Missionaries are front, l. to r., Craig Christensen,
Larry White, and Peter Basker; back are Alan Hess, Carl Hanson, and Robert Winegar.

Missionaries in Thailand from Church News

---

[35] *The Orientor Gazette of the Southern Far East Mission*, III:3, March 1968, 6-9.

The Orientor story continues.

It was hoped that after such an auspicious beginning, missionaries could immediately be sent into Thailand to begin the work of preaching the gospel among the Thai people. However, the realization of this hope was slow in coming. The Church was not officially recognized by the Thai government until November 1, 1967, almost a year after the land had been dedicated. Then, in late January, 1968, word was received from Elder Gordon B. Hinckley that authorization had been given by the First Presidency and the Council of the Twelve Apostles to open Thailand to the missionary work. Immediately after this notification had been received Elder Alan Hess from the Hongkong Zone, and Elders Craig Christensen, Larry White, Peter Basker, Carl Hanson, and Robert Winegar of the Taiwan Zone were called to be the first missionaries into Thailand. These six Elders were brought to the Mission Home for a week of orientation and instruction in the Thai language.

On February 2, 1968, these six missionaries arrived in Bangkok, with President and Sister Garner. The following Sunday morning at the Thailand District Conference, they were introduced to the Saints, who received them with much enthusiasm. The waiting was ended, and the gospel is going forth among the Thai nation. [36]

Immediately after Elder Hinckley dedicated the land, President Garner went into action, selecting elders to be sent to Thailand as soon as possible. Six elders were chosen and began some preparatory training. Over a year later, when President Garner received word to proceed, the original six were in the last phase of their two and one-half year terms. Therefore, he decided it was the better part of wisdom to send six elders whose time in the mission field extended further into the future.

Two of the six pioneer elders selected, as well as one sent later to replace one of the original six, offer some insights into the beginnings of work in Thailand. Elder Alan Hess, the only elder then working in the Hong Kong Zone, recalls, "January of '68 I was selected to go to Thailand. An amazing shock that began a tremendous adventure in my life.

During the week five elders from Taiwan came in, and I lived with them at Kam Tong Hall. During that week we had some Thai books that we made an attempt

---

[36] *The Orientor Gazette of the Southern Far East Mission*, III:3, March 1968, 4-5.

Elder Gordon B. Hinckley, President Hugh B. Brown, President Keith E. Garner

*"Visitors from Salt Lake"--l to r, Bishop Victor L. Brown, President
Keith E. Garner, and Elder J. Thomas Fyans*

Ah-Fook, Ah-Seem, Ah-Mui, Ah-Chow

Sisters Marcia Smith and Erlyn Gould

Keith in Hong Kong in 1988

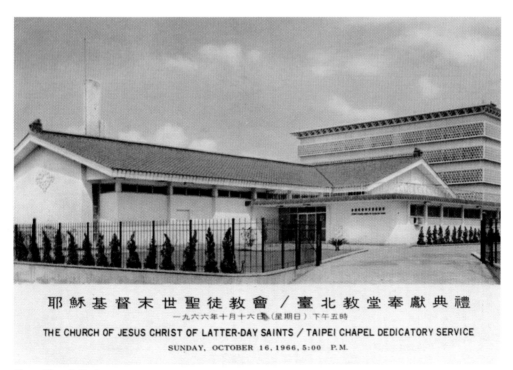

耶穌基督末世聖徒教會／臺北教堂奉獻典禮

一九六六年十月十六日（星期日）下午五時

THE CHURCH OF JESUS CHRIST OF LATTER-DAY SAINTS / TAIPEI CHAPEL DEDICATORY SERVICE

SUNDAY, OCTOBER 16, 1966, 5:00 P.M.

Taipei Chapel--Dedication program

At ninety-two Sister Soong is still hugging 'her boys.' Here 'one of her boys,' President Garner is eighty-three.
Sister Mary Ann Soong and President Garner at missionary luncheon at Golden Phoenix Restaurant in
Salt Lake City

Elder Gordon B. Hinckley, Elder Marion D. Hanks, and President Keith E. Garner in Thailand -- "we will dine first
and talk during and after"

ASIAN WeekEnd

TELS: Editorial 763353, Advtg. 228822

30 CENTS.

MOB CHASES 2 MORMONS

TWO AMERICAN missionaries escaped a severe beating when they fled from screaming young rioters in a housing estate at the top of Taishing Street in Wongtaisin yesterday.

They are Joel Richards (20) and Denis Barlow (19) members of the Mormon Sect.

Denis was hit on the arm by one of the young demonstrators armed with a lump of wood.

Both ran to the protection of a nearby squad of riot police who later made a baton charge on the building.

Joel said: "we went there today to hold a church meeting.

"We were there all day yesterday and had no trouble with the people.

"But as soon as we walked into the estates building today a group of boys on the third floor started yelling and screaming.

"One Chinese youth told us in broken English to leave quickly.

"We did just as about 10 screaming youths

● Turn to Page 23

One of many meetings with LDS military personnel

Elder Marion D. Hanks and President Keith E. Garner on the "Here After 727"

Elder Hinckley

Elder Hanks

President Garner

President Garner made fifteen trips to Vietnam

to study, but we were gone in about ten days. President Garner and Sister Garner accompanied us to Bangkok."

Before he left Thailand, President Garner made arrangements for living quarters with a rather peculiar man who became the six elders' landlord. President Garner paid for a whole year with his personal check. This generous gesture gave the landlord cause to confront the elders coming and going from their rented home, that is until President Garner's check cleared his bank. Apparently after that, he was less interested in talking with them.

Another obstacle which President Garner investigated and addressed dealt with the missionaries' status in the country. Because missionaries had to enter Thailand as tourists, they were compelled to renew their tourist visa every two weeks. They were permitted to do this in Thailand for up to two months; however, after two months the missionaries were required to leave the country. President Garner discovered a workable solution. He had the missionaries make the short trip to the neighboring country of Laos, an adventure in and of itself, get their passports stamped, and then return to Thailand.

Determined to provide these young men with every advantage in their efforts to communicate the message, President Garner also contacted the American University Alumni Association Language Center in Bangkok and arranged for their training in the Thai language. Peter W. Basker, another one of the first six missionaries President Garner took into Thailand, writes, "When we first went to Thailand, we had no scriptures outside of the Bible, no tracts, nothing to have potential members read. President Garner started to ask around for ways to have the Book of Mormon translated as he knew that it would really help the Thai people to know God."

Peter adds in sincere tones, "I admired him as a great leader and the right man at the right time for the huge mission he presided over. He loved the people." He finishes with a rather comical digression, "He told us quite a lot, 'Elders, there are only two things that could get me to Asia--a gun and God.' He really has a wonderful sense of humor."

Elder George Brown ended up in Thailand only four months after the initial vanguard of elders entered the country. He'd recently been transferred to Hong Kong after having served a year in Taiwan. George reports, "I went to the mission home to see President Garner, and he said, 'How's your Cantonese?' I told him that I'd taught four of the six missionary discussions, but I could teach all six. I'm good to go as far as Cantonese; I thought he was talking about being a senior companion since all these new elders were coming. He said, 'This past spring we opened up Singapore and we opened up Thailand. In Singapore they speak Mandarin, Cantonese, and English. You really fit the bill for that because you speak Mandarin, and you've worked with Cantonese now for five and a half months, and your companion tells me you speak quite well.' He told me to go get a visa and shots and to let him know when I was ready. I called and told President Garner, 'It's all done.' He said that he'd talk to me at the mission home.

Every Monday night we went to the mission home, and I figured he was going to tell me when I was going to Singapore. When I got to the mission home, I saw Elder Hanson back from Thailand; I'd known him in Taiwan. He was limping and had come back to Hong Kong for some special treatment on his foot.

President Garner said, 'Tonight we're going to hear from Elder Hanson, and he's going to tell you about Thailand.' In the course of the conversation, Elder Hanson said, 'Thai is a little different than Mandarin.' I raised my hand and asked, 'Does it have any tones in it?' He answered, 'It has five tones.' I just waved my hand and dismissively said, 'Well, you can have it then because Mandarin had four tones and Cantonese had seven.' He started to laugh. After this meeting in which Elder Hanson painted an intriguing picture of Thailand and portrayed it in a very positive way, I went up to him. 'What in the world were you laughing about?' and he said, 'You're going to Thailand; go talk to President Garner.' President Garner said, 'Yes, but I want to talk to you about it tomorrow.'"

The next day President Garner visited with Elder Brown about his feelings regarding this new challenge. He stated, "'This will be your third language,' and then asked, 'Can you handle that, Elder?' 'Of course.' What could I say to a man who had that much commitment to his calling and that much faith in me? He explored it with me further. 'This is going to be a challenge for you; this is going to be your third language. It isn't going to be Mandarin or Cantonese, but there are some similarities. You'll be back being a junior companion again. Will that bother you?' That sobered me up a little bit, but I said, 'I'll just do my best at it.' He said, 'Okay, you'll be all right.'"

Because Elder Brown suggested it would be easier for him to collect his own plane ticket at the airport, a rather exciting unfolding of his trip to Thailand took place before he ever left the ground. Perhaps this was one of the experiences that caused Elder Brown to say, "You could count on President Garner. I always felt safe and confident when he was around that everything was okay."

"I got on the airplane, looked up, and here comes President Garner walking down the aisle. He said 'Elder, do you know where you're going?' I said, 'Thailand.' 'When you get to Thailand where are you going to go after that? The missionaries won't be there to meet you because the airport is a long way from Bangkok. It's out in the hinterlands, and it's too far for them to do that. Here, I'm going to give you instructions on how to get there.' I'm sitting there ready to go, wondering how President Garner got on the plane without a ticket, and thinking 'Thank goodness he is concerned about me.'

I would have been lost. The International Airport is way out in the country-side. It's a twenty minute taxi ride into town. But here he was to save me. He said, 'Go to the Hotel Rex. There's a street that comes directly in from the north into the Hotel Rex, and you go up that street. Tell one of those fellows who drives the three wheel carts to take you to the Americans' house, and they'll take you up there.' I said, 'You've had to do that?' He said, 'I told them to take me to the Americans' house, and fortunately it was the missionaries.'"

Larry R. White, another of the first six missionaries, on March 11, 1994, then serving as Thailand Mission president, wrote to President Garner:

> As I enter the final turn of this three-year marathon race, you have been on my mind as I think of the great influence you had on me as a young missionary. Some elders hang onto my words. I was like that, and fortunately, because of you, I had some awfully good words to grab onto.
>
> I was talking about you to another one of your former elders who happened to pass through Bangkok this past Sunday, and we both marvelled after all these years how we could still remember your talks, your advice, and your instruction. My letter to the missionaries before they go home quotes the same scripture you quoted to us in the telegram you sent to Bangkok before you went home.
>
> The number of missionaries in Thailand starting with the little group of six you sent, has risen and fallen over the years due to problems with the Thai government, but presently we have 120 missionaries. We have four districts, twenty-four branches, and almost 7,000 members…As you can see, the little seed you planted here so many years ago has flourished. As the Prophet Joseph Smith foretold, no one would be able to stay this work…
>
> My affection, admiration, and respect for you grows with each passing year…As I said earlier, you have been in my thoughts lately. I wanted to write and report again as I did weekly long years ago."

And in a poignant P.S., "I just received word that I will be accompanying the missionaries into Cambodia on March 23. Following in your footsteps so to speak."

Others had noticed his footprints as they toured the world. Elder Neal A. Maxwell in a note of appreciation dated August 25, 1999, succinctly expresses what really matters, "Most of all, Keith, thank you for all that you have done to build the Kingdom and leave your footprints in so many places. I am grateful to have you as an everlasting friend."

President Garner's pioneering footsteps found in Thailand would also be found in Singapore. This clean, industrious, regimented, now independent state welcomed President Garner and four of his missionaries only a month after he and six of his missionaries had entered Thailand.

This story is also told in *The Orientor*.

Opening of Singapore in March 1968

An unpretentious Royal vessel anchored off the Malay Peninsula in 1819, and there, just one year before Joseph Smith's first vision, Sir Thomas Raffles claimed the Island of Singapore for the British Crown.

When Joseph Smith went to the Hill Cumorah in 1824, the Island of Singapore and the Malay States became an independent Crown Colony.

The principal British defended harbor in the Far East, Singapore fell to the Japanese in February, 1942; one of the last Japanese strongholds to be recaptured by the Allies, in September, 1945. In 1946, Singapore was constituted as a separate Crown colony.

Just ten years ago, 1958, Britain granted Singapore her

Missionaries in Singapore--l to r: President Keith E. Garner, Kim A. Shipley, Joel Richards, Melvin D. Schurtz, and R. Todd Bake

independence.

March 19th, 1968, President Keith E. Garner, Elders Kim A. Shipley, Joel Richards, Melvin D. Shurtz, and R. Todd Bake arrived in Singapore, the first Mormon missionaries. There were no rocks thrown, no insults, no mobs. Time…and history have changed all that.

Their entry, as ambassadors of the Lord and as emissaries of real Peace, embodies centuries of preparation, and many, many lives.

May God bless them! [37]

In the flurry of establishing missionary activity in Singapore, President Garner may have taken a moment to remember that Singapore was the spot where in World War II the Japanese had attacked in an unexpected way, thus cancelling his, Lieutenant Garner's, plans to protect the West Coast from the comfort of the Mark Hopkins Hotel.

World War II memories hidden in some recess of President Garner's mind also resurfaced, if only for brief moments, as after twenty years he stepped on Filipino soil once again. He found that some things had not changed much and would not for years to come. It appeared to Keith that jeeps were the only transportation available in the Philippines. "When I went back there as a mission president, we were still running around in those jeeps we left behind in '45. The Filipinos got them fixed up and decorated. They were very appealing." If he had had the time, and he manifestly did not, since he never even visited the site of his former accommodations on the Pasig River, he would have loved to have seen the customized jeep he'd driven around Manila.

President Garner had returned, but not just like MacArthur. He had traded in his Army attire and rifle for a white shirt, dress slacks, tie, and the powerful ammunition contained in the Book of Mormon. Poised at the podium, President Garner delivered his invited remarks, followed by Elder Gordon B. Hinckley's Dedication Address and Prayer. Gathered on October 23, 1966, at the dedication of the first LDS chapel in the Philippines, the Luzon District Chapel in Makati, the members of the Church in the Philippines were celebrating a great milestone.

On the inside cover of the dedication program was printed a compilation of the progress being made in the Philippines entitled, "A Brief History of the Church in the Philippines." President Garner read with interest the first paragraph.

The first recorded history of the Church of Jesus Christ in the Philippines began with liberation of the country from the

---

[37] *The Orientor Gazette of the Southern Far East Mission*, III:4, April 1968, 10-11.

Japanese occupation by the American landings on the island of
Leyte on 20 October 1944 and culminating in the fall of
Manila on the island of Luzon on February 1945. Along with
the [other] American G.I.'s came the Latter-Day Saint service-
man anxious to get things settled so he could start holding his
Church meetings even in small groups....

He noted that the program mentioned early meetings held at the residence of
Sister Maxine Grimm, at the Normal School, and at American bases at Clark Field,
Sangley Point, and Subic Bay.

He read further.

In August 1955 the Luzon Servicemen's District became
part of the newly organized Southern Far East Mission with
headquarters in Hongkong, and on the 21st of the same
month, President Joseph Fielding Smith dedicated the land for
the preaching of the Gospel at Clark Air Force Base....

Six years after President Joseph Fielding Smith dedicated
the Islands for the preaching of the Gospel, a small L.D.S.
Group led by Elder Gordon B. Hinckley of the Council of the
Twelve gathered at the hallowed grounds of the American
Battle Memorial Cemetery at Fort Wm. McKinley on the early
morning of 28 May 1961 to officially start the missionary work
in the Philippines. Among those present on this historical
meeting besides Elder Gordon B. Hinckley were Sis. Maxine
Grimm, Pres. Robert S, Taylor of the Southern Far East
Mission, Bro. Donald G. Bowen, Bro. Theon Laney, and Bro.
David Lagman, the first Filipino to be ordained an Elder in the
Philippines. A week later or on 5 June 1961, the first four
missionaries, namely, Elders Ray Goodson, Harry Murray,
Kent Lowe, and Nestor Ledesma arrived in Manila as pioneers
in a new field. The number of missionaries gradually increased
with the original four in 1961 to...sixty-one as of October 1966.

Convert baptisms and total membership in the Church
has likewise grown tremendously with about a hundred in
1961 to...about 1,800 as of October 1966. It is safe to assume
that before the years' end the Luzon District will reach a level
of about two thousand members or a growth rate of about
75% annually for the last five years. The harvest is truly great
with but few laborers in the field.....

...On 6 September 1964 at the afternoon session of the

Picture appearing in The Philippines Herald of Friday, April 14, 1967, "Here for One-Day Visit"
Hugh B. Brown (third from left), president and first counsellor to the first Presidency of the Church of Jesus Christ of
Latter-Day Saints (Mormon), and Gordon B. Hinckley (at Brown's left), elder member of the Council of Twelve
Apostles, arrived yesterday for a one-day visit here. They were met at the Manila International Airport by Keith E.
Garner, president of the Southern Far East Mission, and Elder Ivan Teuscher, and a large group of local members of
the Church. A reception was tendered in the visitors' honor at Buendia Chapel last night.

12th Luzon District Conference, ground breaking ceremonies
were held at Buendia St. Makati with E.M. Grimm turning
the first shovel of dirt to signal the start of construction on
the Chapel with Lester Tracy as supervisor and builder.

As of the present writing (23 October 1966) when
the first L.D.S. Chapel in the Philippines is to be dedicated
by Elder Gordon B. Hinckley of the Quorum of the Twelve
Apostles, the Luzon District has grown to nine (9) independent
branches and one mission dependent group. The total distribution of membership in the district is as follows:

Name of Branch	Year established as independent	Membership
Baguio	1966	63
Caloocan	1966	104
Clark	1953	138
Cavite	1963	124
Manila	1963	712
Quezon City	1961	420
San Fernando	1964	99
Subic	1965	38
Tarlac	1953	45
Dagupan (dependent)	1966	52
	TOTAL	1795

Significant dates and statistics on the First L.D.S. Chapel to be built in the Philippines are the following:

Land area..................................5,000 square meters
Date land purchased ....February, 1964
Ground broken ....6 September 1964
Work started ....28 September 1964
Inspection/completion certificate.............28 June 1966
Total man-hours of construction ....63,000 man-hours
Total donated man-hours ....28,300 man-hours
Building floor area ....15,300 square feet

No wonder upon his return to Hong Kong and just a few months later, President Garner wrote, "Five years ago in 1961 when the missionaries were first sent into the Philippines to supplement the servicemen's groups, the Church was just beginning. Today, with twelve branches and an average of fifty-five missionaries, the Philippines is our most productive area."

While President Garner and Elder Hinckley were visiting the saints in the Philippines, Elder Hinckley practiced a principle often cited by President Garner. Keith explains, "While traveling with Elder Hinckley, if any of the members asked questions of him, he, on a number of occasions, said, 'President Garner will answer that for you.' So I would answer it. One time we were sitting next to each other, and the sister on my right leaned over me to get the ear of Elder Hinckley. He did not hear her question, and so I did as he instructed me in similar circumstances. On the side I said, 'They asked you the question, and then you referred it to me.' He said, 'Well, I'm a general authority; you're the specific authority, so you answer the question because you're president of this mission.' He taught a great principle about leadership and delegation that day."

President Hinckley, even in those early days when success was small but steady, always exuded a firm belief that the growth in the Philippines would become a great chapter in Church history, one of the big success stories of the Church, and it has. There are 496,062 members as of December 31, 2002.

Elder Maun T. Petersen, assistant to the president, Southern Far East Mission-Philippine Mission wrote the following letter full of historical data to Henry A. Smith the editor of the *Church News*:

> Dear Brother Smith:
> President Keith E. Garner of the Southern Far East Mission, acting by authority of the First Presidency and under the direction of Elder Gordon B. Hinckley, formally created the Philippine Mission with Paul S. Rose as the new president in a conference of the Luzon District August 20, 1967. The conference was held in the new Buendia Chapel, the first built by the Church in the Philippines with 1100 saints in attendance. The new mission covers the area of the Republic of the Philippines and includes 1 district, 14 branches, 3 groups and has 90 missionaries laboring there.
>
> The Philippines was dedicated for missionary work in 1955 by President Joseph Fielding Smith at Clark Field, a United States Air Force Base. In 1961 Elder Gordon B. Hinckley commenced the work and four missionaries were sent to the land. Impressive statistics show that the Lord certainly has touched the hearts of the Filipino people. Beginning in 1961 with 100 converts, today the Church has 2000 members with a projected growth of 3000 by the end of the year and 6000 by 1970. President Rose begins his work in the only Christian nation in Asia with opportunities for great expansion, as the work has been carried to only twelve cities in the country.
>
> We know that the above information will be of great interest to the members of the Church throughout the world.

The growth and strength of the Filipino membership demanded a mission president's undivided attention, and by 2002 it demanded the undivided attention of thirteen mission presidents. The divestiture of the Philippines from the Southern Far East Mission would appear to have lightened President Garner's load, and in some ways, it had. However, Keith had his hands full in Hong Kong.

Hong Kong made up of Hong Kong Island, Kowloon, and the New Territories is, as President Garner told an interviewer, "not much more than a dot on the map--a

NO TWO WIVES, SAYS HK MORMON CHIEF

MORMONS are not nudists, polygamists, nor do they wear special long underwear, or do "most of the things they're accused of."

These "popular misconceptions" were strongly denied yesterday by Mr Keith E. Garner, the new leader of Hongkong's band of Mormons.

Mr Garner is just starting his three-year term as President of the Southern Far East Mission of the Church of Jesus Christ of Latter-day Saints, the official title of the Mormon sect.

As president of the Kowloon-Tong mission, Mr Garner presides over 7,400 followers in Hongkong, Macau, the Philippines, Taiwan and other parts of South-East Asia.

'Strong action'

Anyone with a tendency to taking more than one spouse will get little sympathy from the new Mormon president.

"The church takes strong action against anyone taking more than one wife or one husband," he said.

"We banned polygamy back in 1890."

some, Mr Garner looks more like a businessman than a cleric.

In fact he is supported by their own savings.

The Mormon church, itself seems to have no lack of funds.

"Every Mormon is expected to donate 10 per cent of his yearly earnings to the church," Mr Garner said.

This money goes to building about one new chapel a day every year.

It also builds universities and helps "members only" when they are in need of help.

Mr Garner spoke of a young Chinese

He was a bishop in his church for 11 years, and is now a member of the Palo Alto Stake High Council.

At the same time, Mr Garner has managed to be a successful land developer and home builder.

He described this as his 'life's work'—of course on the temporal side of things.

It is probably just as well for the Mormon sect its new Southern Far East President has been so materially successful.

He receives no salary. Not do any other Mormon church officials.

Savings

Several of the Mormon "church elders" — the most popular age is from 19 to 25 — are

supported by their cripple, from West Point, who is being treated in America, completely free of charge.

Mr Garner pointed out this was the exception not the rule.

He said: "It's more than the old maxim of God helps those who help themselves — everyone must help each other."

He said Chinese were excellent potential converts.

"Almost 100 per cent of the Hongkong diocese is Chinese." And about 1,500 new converts are added each year.

● MR and Mrs Keith E. Garner

President Garner's first interview after arriving in Hong Kong

tiny island and peninsula occupied by British troops in 1842 under a treaty with
China. In 1898 Britain obtained a lease for 99 years. But China, now Communist,
is getting anxious to regain the territory. And so terrorist activities are common.
And there are the problems that are associated with gambling, narcotics, prostitution--
even bigamy and polygamy. Refugees from China overrun the shanty towns, and sam-
pans clog the harbor."

Knowing the hazards lurking on the streets of Hong Kong, President Garner
must have shuddered, even knowing it was completely false when a newspaper story
announced, "Mission Head Denies Elder Missing," HONG KONG (UPI).

> Keith E. Garner, president of the Southern Far East
> Mission of the Church of Jesus Christ of Latter-day Saints,
> denies the rumor that a Mormon missionary is missing in
> Hong Kong. Expressing surprise at the reports, Garner said,
> "This is the first time I have heard of it, and I can tell you that
> it is absolutely not true."
>
> "The mission has 240 missionaries in three countries and
> every one has been at his post," he said. "Certainly I should be
> the first one to know if any of them was missing, particularly
> those in Hong Kong."
>
> Hong Kong police also said they had no reports of a miss-
> ing Mormon missionary.

Only a couple of days after President Garner reached China, an elder showing
him a newspaper article which he had translated teased, "We've been looking for you."
An article in Chinese appeared in the *Kung Sheung Yat Po* (a Hong Kong daily newspaper) on August 10th headlined "New Mormon Leader in Hong Kong." President
Garner arrived on August 13, 1965. The elder had added this notation, "This article
appeared three days too early because of simple misunderstanding or desire to be first
to break the news."

President Garner could have only wished all the newspaper coverage was as
inaccurate or mistaken as missing elders and arrivals three days before they happened.
It would not be.

In May of 1967, the Communist or Red Brigade tried to subvert the British
government forces that administered the territory of Hong Kong. Sister Gould
remarks, "When the Cultural Revolution began in Red China...the barbed wire went
up in Hong Kong. The tanks disrupted everything." Missionaries were not exempt,
as an article that appeared in the *Asian WeekEnd*, Hongkong, Sunday, May 14, 1967,
Vol. 1, No. 69 informed its readers.

"Mob Chases 2 Mormons"

Two American missionaries escape a severe beating when they flew from screaming young rioters in a housing estate at the top of Taishing Street in Wongtaisin yesterday. They are Joel Richards (20) and Denis Barlow (19) members of the Mormon Sect.

Denis was hit on the arm by one of the young demonstrators armed with a lump of wood.

Both ran to the protection of a nearby squad of riot police who later made a baton charge on the building.

Joel said, "We went there today to hold a church meeting.

"We were there all day yesterday and had no trouble with the people.

But as soon as we walked into the estates building today, a group of boys on the third floor started yelling and screaming.

"One Chinese youth told us in broken English to leave quickly.

"We did just as about 10 screaming youths came out of the building screaming at the top of their voices."

The Mormons said they started to run as the youths came at them.

Joel said: 'I pushed one aside as he tried to attack me and then ran as fast as I could.

"Another struck Denis on the arm with a large piece of wood."

Both said more demonstrators swarmed out of the buildings as they ran past, but they reached the safety of the police.

Previously the demonstrators led by a youth in a black shirt and a handkerchief tied around his face like a mask, threw rocks, bottles, and pieces of furniture at the riot police.

They tipped garbage out of the windows and tins of night soil.

The situation became precarious and prompted a July 12, 1967, letter from Elder Marion D. Hanks.

I have been thinking about you and worrying about you a bit. Gordon Hinckley came in yesterday and discussed his conversation with you and the tentative decisions made to begin changing things there. I told him that I had thought of calling him that morning with the same suggestions.

Please do not confuse faith with foolishness. [38] If you are invited to move your family out, do it at once.

President Garner did not waste any time implementing the measures suggested by Elder Hinckley to secure the safety of his missionaries. One of his elders, Craig Morrison, wrote in the July 1967 newsletter for the Japan Mission an article entitled "The Lord's Work in Hong Kong."

It is a blessing and a challenge to be a missionary. We have the choice opportunity to declare God's work in a relatively short time. It never ceases to amaze me just how little time we have. This fact was impressed on my mind as we left Hong Kong.

Each mission, because of conditions and leadership, is run differently throughout the world. The Hong Kong method of proselyting consisted mainly of door-to-door tracting in eight to twenty story buildings, getting referrals from members, and looking like the Lord's messengers on the street.

When the riots began three months ago, we, being foreigners, saw our work's effectiveness decrease a bit, but nevertheless, we were still able to proselyte. At one time because of safety precautions, we were asked to stay in our apartments for two or three days, but were able to begin our work again by using wisdom in where we went and how we acted. About a month ago, because the riots were getting worse day to day, President Garner felt the necessity of calling President Hinckley to inform him of the situation. The matter was taken before the brethren of the Church, and it was determined to decrease the number of missionaries in Hong Kong. We were quite surprised when we heard some missionaries were going to leave the Hong Kong area. Because Taiwan and the Philippine Islands were about filled to capacity, it necessitated the Elders leaving Hong Kong to leave the Southern Far East Mission. Originally, there were about ninety Elders in Hong Kong. After much prayer, the President sent twenty missionaries to Taiwan and the Philippines, ten came to Japan, and thirty went to the Canadian or States' missions. Thirty missionaries remained in Hong Kong (14 are local missionaries) to continue

---

[38] Emphasis added.

the proselyting work and to help the Church continue to grow.

> We felt it a great blessing to have served in Hong Kong;
> to have seen what miracles the Lord performed in preserving
> the lives of the missionaries; and to have had our eyes opened
> to the greatness of our holy callings from God. A district
> leader and companion were returning to their apartment late
> one night from a baptism. They met a group of young people
> on their way that started to jeer and threaten them. The group
> of forty decided to use their bottles and boards to beat up the
> two missionaries. Just as they were about to hit them, a
> youngster in the back hurried to the front and said, "Don't hit
> them, they're ministers, they're Mormons." With no questions
> asked, the crowd immediately dispersed. Many Elders have
> similar stories of the protection given them by the Lord....

President Garner never forced compliance. When one elder expressed his dissatisfaction with his decision to move him by saying, "I was called to Hong Kong. I want to stay," President Garner's response was just as definitive. "Go unpack your bags."

Elder Gordon F. Esplin writes, "One interesting experience we shared was a missionary leadership meeting where Jerry James played a tape recording of numerous bomb blasts that occurred outside the missionary apartment in Tsun Wan during the riots that occurred in Hong Kong during the Red Guard movement."

Latent fears among the missionaries rightfully escalated. Elder Alan Hess explains, "The summer of 1967 there was turmoil and civil disturbance with the riots in Hong Kong. There was so much going on that we were wondering about things like what if the Chinese army comes across the border? How do we get out of this?'"

Missionaries serving on Taiwan also faced unsettled threats from mainland China. Once comrades in arms, Chiang-ki-Shek and Mao-Tse-Tung had come to a serious and bloody parting of the ways. Mao's one China policy spelled out his desired future for Chiang's remaining stronghold on the island of Taiwan (Formosa). Even American backing of Taiwan did not allay the normal apprehensions felt by those serving on the disputed island. There was the possibility Chinese troops might try to reclaim Formosa.

Aware of the dangers, President Garner's coded cryptogram communicated to the missionaries throughout the island what they were to do. "Ship books" meant they should immediately get to Taipei for evacuation off the island. "Pack books" was the equivalent of a fire drill: there is no present danger; this is a test run.

Chapter
N I N E

'Till the Conflict is O'er

"President Garner visited Vietnam on many occasions. He did a marvelous and remarkable work. To me it is a miraculous thing that he did not lose his life somewhere in that hot and deadly land. The foundation which he laid will yet be built upon."
— President Gordon B. Hinckley

There were no test runs for President Garner when visiting Vietnam, a country for which he, as president of the Southern Far East Mission, had responsibility. Latter-day Saints fighting the undeclared war to which their country had committed them needed succor and support, and there was no responsibility President Garner felt more keenly. "It was the traveling to Vietnam and meeting with the soldier/members there," Sister Smith says, "that affected him in a different way than meeting with the members in non-war torn areas."

A month before President Garner stepped on Asian soil, President Lyndon B. Johnson committed 180,000 American troops to Vietnam. The predicate for United States involvement in Southeast Asia, particularly Vietnam, began as early as 1949, and when Keith arrived, an American presence had already spanned the presidencies of Truman, Eisenhower, Kennedy, and now Johnson. In 1950 Truman, alarmed by the 1949 Communist takeover of China and the possibility of Communist infiltration into Southeast Asian countries, sent to the French, along with armaments and monetary aid, thirty-five "advisors." Despite these reinforcements the French, though still in power throughout French Indochina including Cambodia, Laos, and Vietnam, had

been significantly weakened by the Viet Minh, a resistance group led by a hard core
Communist Vietnam nationalist named Ho Chi Minh.

In 1954, the French pulled out of Vietnam, and the country was temporarily
divided along the 17th parallel by the Geneva Agreements: North Vietnam under Ho
Chi Minh and South Vietnam under anti-communist Catholic Ngo Dinh Diem.
Nonetheless, two of the nine conferees, the United States and the French, backed
South Vietnam and refused to sign fearing such an agreement would hand the country
to the Communists and doom democratic desires.

In November of 1961, President John F. Kennedy sent U.S. soldiers into
South Vietnam to act as "combat advisors." Ever so slowly, U.S. involvement escalated, and when an American destroyer stationed off the coast of North Vietnam was
attacked by North Vietnamese ships, President Johnson in August of 1964 ordered the
bombing of North Vietnam naval bases in retaliation. Shortly thereafter, Congress
passed the Gulf of Tonkin resolution, giving the President power to take all necessary
steps, including the use of armed force in order to defend South Vietnam. The United
States was committed.

The Vietnam War, still to this day shrouded in controversy, would give rise to
a decade of protests on college campuses, to debates ad nauseam over the reasons for
U.S. participation, to the 1969 news reports of the My Lai Massacre, to the publication of the "Pentagon Papers," to the Westmoreland/Wallace court battle, and to
Defense Secretary Robert McNamara's mea culpa. Keith would be home before the
peace agreement was signed, the War Powers Act written into law, the capture of
Saigon by the Communists, and the U.S. evacuation of its last personnel in April
1975.

But in November 1965, war was ravaging the beautiful country of Vietnam as
President Garner flew into Saigon for the first time. His thoughts rested on the hero-
ism of men caught in the horrors of war. His musings roused memories of radio
reports he listened to on Kauai days after Pearl Harbor, telling of men trapped in sinking ships and tapping on the side walls with drowning hopes of rescue. He thought of
watching young infantry boys he had trained mustered out of Camps Maxey, Gruber,
and Rucker for overseas assignments to fight the Germans and Japanese during World
War II. He thought of George P. Hughes, one of five men who had served as his
counselor in the Menlo Park Ward bishopric and a veteran of the First World War,
telling his stories about trench warfare. Keith remembers. "In one story he described
having heard a GI's screams for help coming from in front of the trench where he lay
wounded. George said that he stood up in the trench and held both of his hands up in
a brave attempt to signal the enemy to stop firing. He captivated many of us when he
said that the gunfire ceased. He went over, picked up the suffering man, carried him
back to the trench, waved thanks, and then the firing started again. I can see George
doing that because he was a courageous, compassionate man. I appreciated those
qualities in him in our Church service together." These memories were summoned

because Church service now placed Keith right in the center of the Vietnam War, along with approximately five thousand Latter-day Saint GIs.

In a letter to his fellow missionaries dated July 16, 1966, Keith writes:

> Dear Companions,
>
> This past month has been a very special time for me. Working with you young men and women under any circumstances would be enjoyable. But our common cause unites us in the bonds of love, and we strive more diligently each day to be "one," and thus our joy is exquisite. Last week I had the privilege of visiting some of our soldier missionaries throughout Viet Nam. While in Da Nang, (a northern city of that war torn land), I witnessed the baptism of two young Marines who had been taught the gospel by their buddies. The setting for the baptism was a beach of the South China Sea just outside of the city.
>
> It was a beautiful Sabbath Day. The selected place for the sacred ordinance was equally impressive with its soft sandy beach and clear, inviting water. The sky was a deep blue with large white fleeting clouds. The whole scene carried my thoughts back in memories of lovely places in Hawaii.
>
> About fifteen young servicemen with rifles slung over their shoulders attended the pre-baptism service. As I glanced around I noticed sentries on duty, sand bagged gun emplacements with ominous weapons of war, barbed wire entanglements stretching high and far. Overhead the screaming of jets and the persistent noise of helicopters interrupted the stillness of the day. As our little group sang the songs of Zion, I noticed our four young brethren--soldiers for God and Country dressed in white with bright eyes and happy faces. The lurid contrast of God's creation and His beautiful plan of life with man's folly was present that day.
>
> During the course of the meeting, I asked the two young soldier applicants, "Tell me, why are you here being baptized today?" In essence, they both said: "My friend taught me by example. I liked what I saw in his life, so I changed my ways to be more like him. I enjoyed what I felt. I became free! Although in the military service and at war, I am free!"
>
> I'm certain they felt free from the addiction of tobacco and liquor. Clean thoughts and righteous living were their covenant and promise.

On my return to Hong Kong, I thought how can this choice experience help and bless my missionary companions. Many of us celebrate July as Freedom month. We are physically free! Brave men of years past and of today have and are fighting to keep us free.

However, you and I during this 'dedicated time' of our lives should fight to keep ourselves and all hearers of our message really free morally and spiritually.

Knowing the truth in and of itself does not guarantee these freedoms, for the devils know and fear! We must be obedient to truth. Then and only then will we understand and appreciate the true significance of being free.

Sincerely your brother,
Keith E. Garner
Mission President [39]

Richard Harris in his article for the Menlo Park Ward Message quotes Keith: "'The LDS soldier,' Bishop Garner says, 'is a light to the Gentiles. If there is one LDS in a company or a platoon, he becomes a light to all the others. They soon come to know that he's LDS.' And so the LDS soldier continues to be a missionary."

Though no full-time missionaries under his supervision would visit Vietnam during this critical time, the impact of President Garner's missives and personal conversations with the servicemen was incalculable. Robert G. Mouritsen expresses the sentiment of many.

Your impact upon my life and upon the lives of the hundreds of young men and women who served under your presidency has been profound. It is my belief that those who serve in the office of Mission President today really have no idea-- you presided over a mission that stretched for thousands of miles, that encompassed numerous nations, cultures, and peoples, during a time when young men were profoundly apprehensive about the future, when the Communist threat was very real throughout the region, and in fact a major war raged right in the very heart of your assigned mission area. It was my privilege to serve as your secretary for eight months of that time, and I know and vividly recall my feelings of the sense of the enormous, the overwhelming responsibility that rested

---

[39] *The Orientor Gazette of the Southern Far East Mission*, I:5, July 1966, 1-2.

upon you. I remember the expressions of tenderness and care
that washed over your countenance as you talked of the servicemen in Vietnam and Thailand and the Philippines, and in
the Navy, of your feelings of deep yearning to be with them, to
seek to serve them, to lift them up, and to teach and comfort
them. I remember the anxiousness in your face as you talked
about them and dictated letters to them and to their parents.
I remember that you said to me, on more than one occasion as
I tried to organize your files and assist you in the mission
office, that you really wanted to be in Vietnam, that Vietnam
was where you were really needed.

The repercussions of the war in Vietnam touched life at the mission home in
Hong Kong. Greeting newly arrived elders and sisters was one duty to which
President Garner looked forward as he anticipated their enthusiasm and innocence.
Occasionally when he was traveling, this assignment fell to the assistant to the president. One incident reported to him upon his return to Hong Kong and remembered
by Jerry James concerned the arrival of an expected elder from a little island in Fiji.
As instructed, the elder gave the mission home address, #2 Cornwall Road, to a cab
driver at the airport. Several factors played into an embarrassing misunderstanding
for this young elder. First, those were the days of "rest and recuperation soldiers" who
came in from Vietnam. Second, the elder didn't speak any Chinese, and the cabby
didn't speak any English, and third, there are two Cornwall Streets in Hong Kong;
"one was in the remote, luxurious area where the mission home was located, and the
other was in the very center of the red light district." Jerry explains, "When a single
boy like that showed up at the airport, the taxi driver headed for one of many of these
fancy hotels. The mission home had been trying to track him down. All of sudden
there was a call on his phone. He was the happiest boy because it was the assistant to
the president calling from downstairs. They'd tracked him down and got there just in
the nick of time I think."

President Garner not only welcomed new missionaries but hundreds of servicemen in Hong Kong for R & R who turned up at the mission home. Sister Gould
says with some astonishment, "When they came to the mission home, which was really something of a chore to locate, the commissarian at their request would take them
down to the converted swimming pool so they could buy books to take back to their
ship with them. The mission home was a safe haven for many a distressed young LDS
serviceman suffering the indignities of brutish fellow soldiers during wartime, and
President Garner always had time for them."

For him these were exciting days to be alive. Vietnam was alive with beauty.
The men in whose company he visited this land were alive with compassion, bravery,
and testimony. The LDS servicemen with whom he had the privilege of meeting were

DANANG AIR BASE BILLETING

NO. **2133**   DATE

RECEIPT

REC'D FR: GARNER $ .50

Fifty   Cents

FOR 1 but 3 bed 13

FROM 9 NOV 65   TO 9 NOV 65

C.Q. SIGNATURE: Toal

"50 cent bed charge at Danang"

alive with loyalty, gratitude, and dedication. However, death was ever present.

Keith tells of the first of fifteen trips he made into Vietnam while mission president. "The first time I went our boys were under mortar attack. That was my introduction. And then I went up to Da Nang, and they were under attack. They charged me fifty cents to sleep." He still has the receipt. What concerned and frankly irritated Keith, a World War II veteran and a graduate of Fort Benning Infantry School with an expert rifleman's crest, was "They wouldn't even give me a rifle!" He still considered himself in his prime at forty-six, but to the eighteen year old issuing the rifles, he was too old!

Colonel LaVoi B. Davis, the vice-commander and a first rate Latter-day Saint, probably would have issued the rifle, for he makes this evaluation about President Garner's, Elder Hinckley's, and Elder Hanks' presence "in country." "It was a very dangerous mission they were on. I guess they didn't think much about it. We were paid in the military to risk our lives, and after we'd done it for three or four wars, it was no big thing. The president and those with him didn't consider that they were in much danger, especially when compared to what the men in uniform were doing. They were just really glad to see the service personnel."

The reality of war every once in a while intruded on the peace of a sacrament meeting. Colonel Davis explains, "I remember one time we had a meeting set up for this one regiment. We got up there, had the opening song, a prayer, and the sacrament. About that time the sirens started to wail. All the men raced to get their gear. The choppers came in, and there we were left standing, watching all of our congregation disappear down toward the battle zone.

Most of the time they were able to talk to the service personnel, get their names, and the addresses of their families. The personnel could ask any questions of the president, or Elder Hinckley, or Elder Hanks, or whoever might be accompanying President Garner. They really did take care of these men. The men felt so much better that they were there to just talk to them, encourage them, and tell them to keep living the principles of the gospel. The men really did appreciate them coming down when they didn't have to be in the war zone, didn't have to come."

President Garner discounts Colonel Davis' evaluation by saying, "We wanted to come. You always go where the need is the greatest."

On one occasion Colonel Davis made his quarters available to President Garner and to Elder Hanks and witnessed their devotion in action. "One morning I came in at about three o'clock in the morning after all the men had landed safely. President Garner's and Elder Hanks' rooms were lighted up. I could hear President Hanks dictating letters to the parents of men he'd met during the day and see Keith writing letters longhand to the parents of those he had met. I thought it was absolutely fabulous. I saw their dedication. They'd fly and hold meetings during the day and then spend the night writing the letters, and getting the data out to the parents, letting them know they'd seen their sons, and then get up the next morning and do the same thing."

One of Keith's most cherished letters, certainly because of its author, but also because of its subject matter, came from President David O. McKay:

> We have received this day a copy of a letter which you sent to the parents of J. Richard Willey, who is one of our LDS servicemen in Da Nang.
>
> It pleased me to know that you are keeping in close touch with our servicemen, and I want to commend and congratulate you for the wonderful service you are rendering these boys who are so far away from home and subject to hardships and temptations.
>
> The parents who sent me a copy of your letter were very grateful for the interest that you had shown in their son. This spirit of interest and brotherhood will have an everlasting effect upon both the parents and boys.

A previous short note had come from Bishop Victor L. Brown who wrote: "I thought you would be interested to know that during my visit to the Grantsville Stake Conference yesterday, I called on Louis Bowring and Cardell Gull to bear their testimonies. It was a real inspiration to have these brethren, who have spent so much time in South Vietnam, speak to the membership of the stake. Brother Bowring in particular has great affection for you and is aware of your contribution to the servicemen in Vietnam."

One time the schedule President Garner kept became so jammed with meetings that it led to a rather harrowing experience on the flight back to Saigon. Keith recalls, "Two or three of us left Tan San Nhut Air Base and flew up to Da Nang. (Da Nang was up in the northeast section of the country on the shoreline and just south of

Camaroon Bay, the big supply base.) On the way back to Saigon, the pilot became lost. Tan San Nhut was blacked out, and the pilot overflew the airport. I've forgotten all the details, but I do remember thinking, 'Here I am in the same situation I'd been in when I was in the military and a couple of my friends and I flew from Manila to Yokohama.' The only differences, it occurred to me, were I was over Vietnam, and the war had not ended. I didn't dare mention that I'd already promised the Lord back in the Second World War that if He let me get out of that one I'd never get in an airplane again. My gosh, here I was in the same position.

I said, 'Look, if we're lost,' and Major Rozsa, the pilot who flew me all over Vietnam for eleven months out of the thirty-six that I was there, said, 'I'm sorry; we're lost.' I recommended, 'Well, we'd better go into Cambodia then. We've got an alliance there.' He looked at me as if to say, 'Are you kidding?' and said, 'We'll get shot down if we go into Cambodia. We've got to find Tan San Nhut!' I said, 'I'm on a mission; I've got two more years here, so let's not terminate them now.'

We were supposed to have left Da Nang sooner, but we had all these meetings, and I'd overextended my commitments, so we got back later than we were expected.

Evidently somebody, maybe Colonel Davis, who had the power to turn on every light on the air base, saw us coming, or heard us, and they turned the lights on the airstrip, just that long," Keith says snapping his fingers, "and we were able to land. That was the only time I was really stretched out a little bit. I know we were doing a lot of praying up there."

These pilots, Major Rozsa and others, who, when they were available, made it more convenient for President Garner and others to tend to their duties in Vietnam, were highly skilled. Some could land their aircraft "on a quarter and give you change." Other personnel were lucky. Major Rozsa had alluded to one such incident when President Garner inquired of him regarding why he didn't request the tower at Tan San Nhut to turn on the lights. He said, "I'm afraid if I do they'll get a missile." Every Mormon on the base had heard the story of Chaplain Farrell Smith's brush with death.

Elder Hanks repeated it. "We were using a newly constructed non-denominational chapel; it wasn't at Bien Hoa, but it was not too far from there. Because there wasn't anywhere else for him to stay, Chaplain Smith was lying on a cot in the foyer of the chapel when a Fansong missile entered the building. He, at that moment, somehow had the intuition and inspiration to get up on his hands and knees. That thing went under him, took his skin off his middle, went right through the chapel, blew it up, and it burned down. This kind of thing was not unusual, although it sounds like it." Keith comments, "He was such a nice guy. He was always there when the soldiers needed his help."

In his Asian assignment, Elder Hanks visited President Garner at least three times. In telling one experience he and Keith shared, Elder Hanks begins, "Maybe one little incident would suffice to reflect many," and continues, "As we wanted to go north to Da Nang where the major fighting was in Vietnam, we usually left from the headquarter's city, now called Ho Chi Minh. A number of times we had to fly all night, and go back, and start over because the fighting would be encroaching the territory where we had meant to land. A number of those countries were inflamed, if not by actual warfare, by the addendum to warfare where there was hatred and international involvement and so forth. One time in Vietnam, we went to the office of the airlines that flew to all destinations, except those that were going on a route to the United States. You could fly in and out of Saigon, no trouble, but you couldn't fly from Saigon any place inside that country on any big commercial airplane. You went in goonie birds, old DC 3's turned into transport with their two small engines with all the seating taken out of the airplane, except bulkheads along the side; they were just long benches. We went in to get a passageway up north into Da Nang where we had a lot of men. They were all under fire, many getting killed, and all of them in trouble. We were anxious not to miss an appointment, and so we asked them to sell us tickets to Da Nang. They said, 'Well, you can't go in there.' I said, 'Why not?' 'It's all under fire all the time.' I said, 'We're aware of that, but we haven't been hit yet. We want to go.' He said, 'Look, I won't kid you; you might go, but you'll never get out of there. Every seat into the indefinite future is sold out. The government takes so many, and the few people who are free from governmental restraint or constraint have a very hard time getting a seat. If you're not there representing an arm of the United States government or the Vietnamese government, you can't go very far.' I said, 'They must have something coming out of Da Nang.' He said, 'Yes, they'll go as far as Dalat, the university city. They're still maintaining a presence, and if you get there, you're worse off because there's a big line up of people, professors and others in there teaching, awaiting a way to get out, so you may never come back.' I said, 'Well, you have to understand one thing about us, sir. We have to go. We don't have to come back. We'll get back but our men are up there waiting for us and expect us to come, and we want to go.' So they sold us the tickets. We got on.

We held our meetings there at Da Nang. Keith Garner, always hovering in the background, arranging everything, had his district presidency and others all prepared. Then the big wheels from Salt Lake would roll in, take the center stage, and try to tell what little we knew, and hold the meetings. He was always called on and always did well, but never presumed, and never really insisted, or really wanted to take much part at that point. 'You are the visiting fireman; come in, and put out the blaze, or throw some incendiaries in the air.'"

Elder Hanks continued, "When our meetings were over, Keith and I got on a flight to Dalat. We were in two seats adjacent to each other alongside the bulkhead. We were both soaking, all either of us had on was a short sleeve white shirt, a tie, and britches, and our shoes which were wet. It was not pleasant.

We were sitting there when the plane landed, and President Garner started to get up. I pulled him quickly back by the britches to the bill and said, 'Sit down, and shut up, and don't look up, and when they come aboard with their tickets, continue to look downward as if you belong here. Dalat was where our seats ended, and we'd already been told, 'You'll never get out of there until this war's over.'

Aboard the aircraft came two men with tickets in their hands. Interestingly, they had short sleeved white shirts with a little sign on them. They were not missionaries. One was Ray Hillam, professor at Brigham Young University, who became a lifelong, wonderfully respected friend. He'd been teaching at the university. Here they came and headed right toward our seats. They stood in front of us, and we were both looking at our feet by executive order. I looked up and recognized Ray Hillam. I said, 'Brother Hillam, you are outnumbered and outauthoritied here. If you ever want to get to Saigon, quickly sort out your priorities, and decide whether you two, (the other was a handsome, young American overseas worker), feel you can assimilate the honor of sitting with the two of us in these two seats already occupied. If so sit down, keep still, and look at your feet as we are. If they come, just outstare them because we're all going to ride back together in peace toward safety,' and we did."

Dr. Ray C. Hillam, in a January 4, 2002, letter to Keith, put a slightly different spin on the same story. "In May I shared some bucket seats with you and Elder Hanks on a C 130 from Dalat to Saigon. It was a missed opportunity to demonstrate my 'power.' You were 'Hitch-hiking,' and the plane was overloaded. When I started to board the plane, I was told there were no seats. Since I had priority status (Ph.D's had Colonel status), I assumed someone would be 'bumped.' Imagine, me bumping a general authority and a mission president. I had no idea that two 'men of the cloth' were vulnerable. The airman told me he would make room. Finally, he pointed to a bucket seat across from you. It was a shock to see you, but an unexpected pleasure to squeeze into a seat next to you and enjoy your company. However, a worse thing than being stranded in Dalat could have happened to you. Dalat may be the end of the world, but it was a beautiful and peaceful retreat for French colonials. You could have stayed at the Dalat Palace Hotel on the lake. The French colonials hunted tigers. You could have hunted VC."

Dr. Hillam's delightful telling of his "power" points out the unique and touching respect with which Priesthood authority is honored. While laying the background for an example of the respect felt among the LDS servicemen for each other's Priesthood, Elder Hanks attests, "While I went back a few times, a time or two or three, I don't even know, but Keith went in regularly, visited them regularly on his own."

In fact, when Dr. Hillam uses the term "hitchhiking," he literally describes Keith's usual transportation method when trying to get around Vietnam. He would fly into Saigon and then board any plane he could dash down.

Elder Hanks proceeds, "Keith took with him some civilians who were part of his district presidency and others, but the whole place was organized in every sector,

Sector One, Sector Two, Sector Three with a full Mormon load leadership."

This organizing made the following event, duplicated all over Vietnam, possible. Elder Hanks explains, "We saw remarkable things, like a group of men getting ready to fly to the north, some of whom would not come back. They'd all be there in uniform ready to fly, and we'd hold a meeting at Nha Trang or Saigon or some place else. This particular time on top of a hotel, the men had formed a kind of human wall to allocate a space where we could have settings apart and so forth. You'd see three men, not high ranking men, captains and majors, who were pilots, standing around a chair. They were the district presidency setting apart a colonel as a district missionary. Very humble sweet men, the leadership there selected, would be setting this man apart, who was their military superior and their Priesthood follower. And they all would be weeping. For some it would be the last time they would see each other. Many times I saw that and shed a tear."

The reality of war hits squarely when attached to an organizational memo. On stationary titled "From the Desk of Eugene P. Till," Brother Till hurriedly dashed off the following note:

Eugene P. Till memo front and back

8-30

President Garner,
Additions and corrections have been made to the attached.
P.S. Bro. Hess was shot down in Vietnam on 24 Aug 67. On 25
Aug he talked to another pilot on his survival radio and told
him that he is ok and is presently hiding out in the jungle. He
feels that he will probably be captured soon, but at least he is
alive. We will be changing the Group Presidency as soon as we
know for sure that he has been captured.

Colonel LaVoi B. Davis marvels at how much dedicated LDS servicemen accomplished in Church callings when he exclaims, "We were in war. We had to run the war!"

Fortunately, President Garner's optimistic self never faltered. He enjoyed, perhaps more than under normal circumstances, the humorous moments. And there were some of those.

Elder Hanks tells of one such time, remembering it with glee. "Keith and I were waiting to get an airplane from Saigon to Hong Kong once when a big, lovely fellow with a colonel's insignia on his Air Force uniform came and stood by us. We had a couple of porcelain elephants. The Vietnamese were clever workers with their hands, and they made beautiful things. These were small display porcelain elephants we had bought while we were in the country. Here came this wonderful man with his command posture, and he was just on his way back to his wife and family after a long tour in Vietnam. I said to him, 'President Meacham, they won't let us carry these aboard. We're just civilians. That give you any idea of how you could be helpful?' He said, 'Oh no, oh no. I can't sit with one of those things on my lap.' I said 'Well, you'll figure out a way. Just hold your shoulder boards forward.' And that's how they got here to the United States. We had dear friends, and, as far as I know, we didn't impose upon anybody, but we gave people an opportunity to be gracious on a few occasions like that."

Each of these days of travel pulsated with exceptional experiences. Who else and where else, except Keith Garner in the Southern Far East Mission, could anyone have found himself an integral part of such an exciting time doing such important work? His October 1966 tour of the mission with Elder Gordon B. Hinckley and Elder Marion D. Hanks placed him on center stage surrounded by significant Church historical events.

Keith's oft-quoted sentiment of Charles Dickens may apply. Though the remembered details may vary slightly, the impact of what these men witnessed and felt was the same and was seared into their souls forever.

President Garner wrote, "President Allen C. Rozsa, an Air Force major and President of the Vietnam Zone, piloted the aircraft which took Apostle Hinckley,

President Hanks, and me from group to group to visit the servicemen throughout the nation. The visiting of the Vietnam groups was indeed better than ever. Eighty were in attendance in Da Nang, one hundred forty-eight were present in Nha Trang, and two hundred four were present in Saigon. Attendance has always been high, but it was especially good this trip.

Apostle Hinckley gave many inspiring talks one of which began, 'I could weep as I look into your faces. Not that I feel sorry for you, because I don't! You aren't without opportunity. I have a perfect faith that an honorable solution will come to this part of the world.'

He admonished them to increase their knowledge, magnify their Priesthood, and to strengthen their personal discipline. He told them that they could not draw too near to God and that they could not read the Book of Mormon too much. They were also taught that they should extend themselves to teach the gospel to their fellow soldiers. Finally, Elder Hinckley reminded them that out of all the trials, turmoil, and disappointments that seem to come into lives at times, growth and progress is made and a foundation of this Church is established in strength and power.

President Hanks also gave sound and welcome counsel: 'We take ourselves with us wherever we go. God has entrusted me to myself. I am an agent.' He spoke of the wrong attitude held by many people: 'Oh God, make me a better man, but not now.' He warned all to be willing to enjoy what the gospel has to offer. We can only be blessed in proportion to that which we are prepared to receive. (D & C 88:32)"[40]

Brother Hanks recalls the same trip. "Major Rozsa was flying the plane when one of the engines quit. There were only two. The plane took a decided slant, but we were assured that one engine could carry that small airplane. We were loaded though, the whole middle of it with equipment and food stuffs being flown up north, and all of us were sitting around the sides. Elder Hinckley was on one side, and President Garner near him, and I was on the other side of the plane. We landed safely at the air base at Da Nang.

A colonel at the air field was out to meet us. When this little gooney bird landed, he said, 'Who's Elder Hanks?' I said, 'I am.' He said, 'Do you remember General Spencer?' I said, 'Yes, I used to help him across the street to kindergarten.' He said, 'Well, I was his wing man in World War II, and he has called and said you Church leaders were coming and asked us to take good care of you. I'm happy to do that; it'll be an honor. Your places are all established, but he said that set of black helicopters that landed just ahead of you is going to attract my attention because that's the Chief of Naval Operations and the Commanding General of all American Air Forces in this place, and we need to pay attention to him if we want to keep our place in the Army.'

---

[40] *The Orientor Gazette of the Southern Far East Mission*, I:9, November 1966, 17-20, 23.

Anyway, we went out into the field, and Elder Hinckley said, 'They must have flown up the same corridor we did.' This Colonel asked, 'What corridor was that, Mr. Hinckley? You've been over enemy territory every inch of the way. He's the Chief of Naval Operations so they do have quite an escort.'

On that one visit, we were out in the boonies in an old abandoned hospital when the airplanes were flying over, and the flares were up. They were lighting up those fields, so they could see when the Viet Cong came out of the bushes twenty-four hours a day. At that moment small arms fire and machine guns were heard, and we discovered that all three of us were quickly under the table for a little protection. We all crawled under there and prayed and waited. Experiences in Vietnam, while I wouldn't magnify them or exaggerate them, were always tremendously sobering."

An event just as sobering, but in a wonderful way, happened when they returned to Saigon. At the first meeting in Saigon, Elder Hinckley told those present, among whom were Colonel Davis and Dr. Hillam, that he'd been authorized by the Brethren, if he felt so inclined, to dedicate the land of Vietnam for missionary work. Some must have thought there was no way this could ever happen because of the hatred that then consumed the Vietnamese people.

Another man they met at the meeting in Saigon was Sam Soloman. Elder Hanks recounts the circumstances. "A huge Samoan came. He was a first sergeant, the highest qualified enlisted man, a big, bronze, beautiful guy, been a bishop a couple of times. He could have picked me up off the ground with one hand or his little finger. I wrote his wife the next day and said, 'You'll be pleased to know, Sister Soloman,' (then living in Orem, Utah, waiting with the children for him to come home), 'we had a wonderful visit with Sam last night. We were so proud of him.'"

Elder Hinckley and Elder Hanks unfailingly relayed news home from the personnel they met to anxious families. Elder Hanks explains, "I dictated into a tape recorder, and then our Mormon leaders would get the tapes and send them out in the package that was authorized to go out. They'd get to my secretary Phyllis Peterson as quickly as they could get across the ocean and those two continents, and she would begin typing. She'd type through the night until she had a letter to every parent or wife and child just saying, 'We saw your fine husband in a great meeting today, heard him bear his testimony, or weep while others did, and it was a great meeting.'"

Elder Hanks reports, "That letter to Sam's wife was apparently received almost immediately because three days later she wrote back, and said, 'Thank you, Brother Hanks, Sam was so delighted to see you and Elder Hinckley and the mission president. He's had a pretty rugged war. We're glad to hear about him. I'm sorry to tell you that three days after your letter arrived the word came that on his second load that morning he had carried two men, a wounded man under each arm, when machine guns cut him in two.'" Elder Hinckley received the same sweet appreciative letter bearing the same news with this concluding paragraph.

His loss is deeply felt as I don't believe any man could be a more devoted husband and father than he was. But the reassurance that the gospel of Jesus Christ gives and the knowledge that we will be together eternally gives me great peace and the courage to go on. Sam had such a strong testimony of the truthfulness of the gospel and felt such a strong missionary calling that I felt from the time I received the news of his passing that he was needed to teach the gospel in the spirit world. [41]

After the first meeting held in Saigon, everyone went up to the top of the Caravelle Hotel. "As part of this service held in the roof garden room of the Caravelle Hotel in the heart of Saigon, a dedicatory prayer was offered by Elder Gordon B. Hinckley, Sunday, October 30, 1966. Because of war conditions it was deemed inadvisable to hold the service in a park and infeasible to seek a hill on the outskirts of the city. The roof of the hotel was accordingly chosen.

Elder Hinckley, with President Marion D. Hanks of the First Counsel of Seventy and President Keith E. Garner of the Southern Far East Mission, conducted district conferences in Da Nang, Nha Trang, and Saigon on Saturday and Sunday, October 29 and 30, and this dedicatory prayer was offered at the conclusion of the conference held in Saigon which was attended by 205 members of the Church.

> *O God, our Eternal Father, with humble hearts we meet before Thee this day in this land of South Vietnam, a land which presently is torn by war, destruction, and dissension. We meet in the name of Thy Son, the Lord Jesus Christ, the Prince of Peace, to invoke Thy special blessing. We are grateful, Father, for the land of America, from which most of us have come, and for the cause of human liberty which was established there under a constitution written by those whom Thou raised up unto this very purpose. We are grateful for the restoration of the gospel of the Lord Jesus Christ in that land, and for its spread from there to many other lands and to many other places.*
>
> *We have seen in other parts of Asia the manner in which Thou hast turned the hand and the work of the adversary to the good and the blessing of many of Thy children. And now we call upon Thee at this time that Thou wilt similarly pour out Thy spirit upon this land. We plead with Thee, our Father and our God, that Thou wilt touch the hearts of the leaders of those people who war one against another with a spirit of understanding, a recognition of the fact that all men are*

---

[41] Gordon B. Hinckley, "Asian Diary" (speech given at Brigham Young University Devotional in Provo, Utah on 10 January 1967).

sons of Thine and therefore brothers, and implant in each a desire to labor for a settlement of the great conflict which rages over this land, a settlement which will be honorable and one which will promote the cause of liberty and justice and which will guarantee the agency of those who love freedom. Overrule, Father, that those who would stifle agency and liberty may be stopped in their evil designs, that righteousness may reign, and that those who live in this beautiful land may be free to follow honorable pursuits without trouble, without hindrance, without injury, and without compulsion.

Holy Father, many good men holding Thy Priesthood have come to this land incident to the war. While here they have sought to establish Thy divine work in this part of the world. They have shared the gospel of Thy Son with their associates, their fellow Americans and with the Vietnamese people. With gratitude we have witnessed the baptism of a number of these people. And so we feel it expedient at this time, under the authority given us by Thy Prophet, him whom Thou hast anointed and appointed to stand at the head of Thy work in this day, to dedicate this land, and invoke Thy blessings upon it.

We accordingly come before Thee in the exercise of the Holy Priesthood, and in the authority of the Holy Apostleship in us vested, we dedicate and consecrate this land of South Vietnam for the preaching of the Gospel of the Lord Jesus Christ as restored through the Prophet Joseph Smith. May there from this time forward, Father, come upon this land an added measure of Thy holy spirit to touch the hearts of the people and rulers thereof. May they open their hearts to the teaching of the truth and be receptive to the gospel of Thy Son. May those who have these blessings feel a new urge in their hearts to share with others the great gifts and powers and authority which are theirs, which have come from Thee, that many may be the partakers of these choice gifts.

Father, again we pray for the land that peace may be established, that righteousness may prevail, that this nation may take its place among the peoples of the earth as a freedom-loving nation established on principles of divine liberty, that Thy children may grow in righteousness, in goodness, and in harmonious relationships one with another. Prosper the works of those who seek to serve Thee. Hasten the day when the noise of battle may cease and there may grow again a love and understanding and appreciation one for another among the citizens of this part of the earth.

Open the way for the coming of missionaries and make their labors fruitful of great and everlasting good in the lives of the people.

To this end we seek Thy blessing this holy day as we bow before Thee
and acknowledge with thankful hearts Thy goodness unto us. As we
thus dedicate this land and this nation for the preaching of Thy word,
we rededicate ourselves to Thy service, all of which we do in the name
of our Redeemer, the Lord Jesus Christ. Amen." [42]

The work moved forward, and President Garner so reported in a
December 13, 1967, letter home.

> Yesterday morning we put President Hanks on
> Northwestern for Tokyo. He spent ten days with us visiting
> several areas of the mission. We held a district conference in
> Hong Kong, interviews, instructions, and conference on
> Formosa with the saints and eighty-five missionaries, and six
> days in Vietnam. Prior to our arrival there, we received official
> recognition from Washington, so for the first time since I've
> been here, and visited there, the red carpet was out, and the
> VIP treatment was gratefully appreciated.
>
> We estimate that there are 6,000 LDS servicemen in
> Vietnam. During the six days we met and talked to some
> 1,200. In addition to our own brethren, we were met and
> kindly treated by the chief chaplains and commanding generals.
>
> Finally on our last day, General Westmoreland extended
> an invitation to come and visit him. We were advised that he
> would grant fifteen minutes or less to us. Well, we discovered
> a wonderful thing. The higher we ascended in the command
> circle, the more cordial and gracious the reception and treat-
> ment. All were complimentary and solicitous, but General
> Westmoreland was the peer of gentility. Imagine his greetings,
> "It was kind of you to take the time from your busy schedule
> to come by and see me." One half hour later we took the first
> gesture to terminate a fascinating thirty minutes. He is opti-
> mistic about the outcome of the war, as are we, and spoke
> highly of the LDS soldiers. He said he has never known of a bad
> LDS serviceman. It was good and comforting to be reassured
> that our military leadership is of the highest moral quality.
>
> The chief of chaplains in each corps command was kind,

---

[42] Preamble and Dedicatory Prayer offered by Elder Gordon B. Hinckley in Saigon,
Vietnam, 30 October 1966 in Keith E. Garner's possession.

interested, and anxious to be of service. They spoke highly of
our four LDS chaplains and were especially pleased to note
that they are equally interested in all servicemen under their
responsibility whether Mormon, Catholic, or Protestant. They
were all surprised to learn that we had three large district
organizations with sixty groups, one branch, all functioning
with dedicated lay leadership.

I've toured Vietnam many times during these last few
years, but this was significantly more productive in that we
were able to see so many servicemen all over the land. They
came from the Delta area to Can Tho and Saigon, Nha Trang in
the Central District and Da Nang in the North. Many came
out of the "bush," M16 slung over their shoulders, or just completing sixty-one flights over the target with thirty-nine left
before rotation date.

The realism of the war is everywhere. The moral decay of
our troops is alarming. I'm hesitant to quote statistics of the
number that contract V.D. Sensuality and carnality is running
rampant. Few escape the hands of the servants of Satan that do
uphold his work. Even our boys hardly escape and then only
through sheer moral courage. Abuse, invitation, and ridicule
are present with them always.

It was a joy to be the companion of President Hanks
again. He is a great soul. Full of love and charity for all
mankind. It's rough to have to speak three and four times daily
over a ten-day period, especially with the master of speech as
your companion, but somehow the Lord assists and the right
things are said because the situation and circumstances merit
intervention and inspiration.

It's amazing how physically exhausted you become,
especially when you're unable to sleep at nights due to many
unheard of obstacles and problems; But still because of the
nature of the work, there is a spiritual renewal of your body,
and it doesn't matter, nor does it impede the progress or
quality of your contribution to the work.

In each area we held testimony meetings so that 150 servicemen had an opportunity to talk. We heard such expressions as, "I'm glad I'm here doing this work so the missionaries
can be out doing the Lord's work,"--"I'm fighting a hard fight,
but my life can stand inspection."

This has been a rich and glorious time in our lives. We

wish that all our dear friends - all - could have the opportunity and privilege. This assignment in particular has been a joy. So varied, exciting, isolated, rugged, full of millions of humanity with their myriad of traditions, customs, religions and superstitions. War and poverty - language barriers that harass and immobilize the transmitting of thoughts and stifle the communication of ideals, even simple messages of life.

Our time is rapidly coming to a close. It's been choice. Life is rich indeed when you have for sure friendships, but equally important, "good memories."

Certainly President Garner overjoyed at his mission experience still felt some comraderie with the elder who very shortly would be going home, mission completed, and who rose to his feet at a testimony meeting in the mission home and in his exuberance regretted that he was leaving so soon when he had many interested con-

Standing (l to r) by DC3 "Gooney Bird": Larry Atkinson, Lawrence Jenkins, Robert J. Lewis, Pres. Keith E. Garner, Southern Far East Mission; Elder Gordon B. Hinckley, Council of the Twelve; Major Allen C. Rozsa, Pres. Viet Nam Zone of Church; Elder Marion D. Hanks, First Council of the Seventy; Ray Cox, Capt Herman Twede, Theodore Okiishi

tacts and was better qualified to preach than he'd ever been. He declared, "I wish I had another six months." At the conclusion of his remarks, President Garner said, "Elder, you have six more months." Quite startled, the elder didn't seem to know how to respond. The next day he visited President Garner, telling him that all the arrangements had been made for his departure, that his parents would be picking him up, and that he wondered if President Garner had the authority to extend his mission. President Garner smiled having made his point and told him he would be leaving on schedule.

President Garner's days in the mission field were winding down too. He had only a few months left, and because of the events in Vietnam, he also felt some frustration. After the visit he made in December of 1967, the Tet offensive in January of 1968 made it impossible for him to visit Vietnam as planned. His regularly scheduled visits were cancelled. Keith noted the reasons, "War intensified-no commercial flights, North Vietnam Conference-had to forget about Vietnam conference in Da Nang, couldn't get there, Central Vietnam Conference-unable to attend because of hostilities, red tape, transportation."

Finally, on May 11, 1968, his forty-ninth birthday, he visited Vietnam again. He describes his feeling in a letter to his mother dated May 11-13, Saigon, Vietnam.

> Dearest Mother:
>
> It is a beautiful Monday morning in Saigon. We held a great conference yesterday with all the troopers in the Southern area of Vietnam that could make it. Most of them were young boys with peach fuzz on their cheeks and right out of the battle. As I write this letter in the chaplain's office here on the Tan San Nhut Air Base, I can hear the explosion of 500 lb bombs being dropped in Cholon (Chinese Area) Saigon and on the fringes of the air strips. Omar Green, one of our brethren, is in charge of the mortuary here, and he told me he handles some 200 bodies every day. So the war is real-and has been for the last three years that I have travelled into this beautiful land.
>
> I had a chance to talk to Gene on the phone a few days ago, and he told me that you celebrated your 86th birthday with confidence that you would make it to 100. Wouldn't that be wonderful--congratulations and love to you from all of us. The Lord has been good to you because you live without malice. You are also a peacemaker-and the peace makers for "they shall be called the children of God." Well, you are full of wonderful virtues too many to enumerate--suffice it to say that all respect and love you.

Last week Brother Hinckley called and suggested that I
not come to Vietnam because of the serious nature of the war
in and around Saigon. I told him that I had requested that all
the district presidents and all the chaplains serving in this land
meet me in Saigon on Mother's Day, May 12, and it was
imperative that I be in attendance. So when I arrived, sure
enough all had made the journey from the far north to the
south to attend the leadership meeting and Southern District
Conference. It is interesting to note that during the time I
have been here the Tan San Nhut Air Base has not been
attacked or mortared. One of the good LDS chaplains, Farrell
Smith, who incidentally was wounded about two months ago
by a 122 rocket that struck the new chapel here and completely destroyed it, suggested that I stay around so the VC will
desist and let the war subside until something tolerable is
worked out in the peace offensive in Paris. I reassured him
that it was a mere co-incidence.

The night before the conference the VC destroyed one of
the bridges coming into Saigon from Long Binh and Bien Hoa
so about 100 of our men were unable to come to the conference.

In a handwritten postscript he concludes, "I was interrupted and was taken out to
catch my plane back to Hong Kong. In flight now and in two hours will be back
home. Love, Keith."

His June 20 diary entry reads: "Conference Da Nang Sat & Sun--trying to
decide whether to go." While on the phone with Elder Hinckley, and almost as an
after-thought, President Garner spoke to him about going into Vietnam again. "It was
June of '68, and I was going home in August. I said, 'You know, Elder Hinckley, I've
always read about the guy who went ten times, and the last time he got shot. I think I
won't go.'" Keith reports Elder Hinckley replied, "Well, President, you're the specific
authority; you do what you want to do." "I no sooner hung up than I got a cablegram
from Vietnam. They were having this big conference. Could I come? I got on Air
Vietnam with all the ducks and goats and flew down there. I was there three days at
Da Nang. They gave me a great big plaque."

The cherished plaque given to Keith and embellished with the insignias of I
Corp and Air Ground Team III Marine Amphibious Force, hanging in his office today,
reads:

Presented to
KEITH E. GARNER
President of the Southern Far East Mission
Church of Jesus Christ of Latter-day Saints

in appreciation for
strengthening the L.D.S. Servicemen in VietNam
Northern (I Corps) District Conference
21, 22, and 23 June 1968
China Beach, Danang, VietNam

President Garner says with that faraway look in his eyes, "It was a wonderful experience."

As he thinks about it today, he marvels at Elder's Hinckley's having recommended him for such splendid yet challenging experiences. President Garner writes, "Having worked under his supervision in many parts of the world over many years, I want to convey the truth that President Hinckley, now President of The Church of Jesus Christ of Latter-day Saints, is a giant in the Kingdom because he is dedicated to the work, he's a doer of the word, and he is wise. He loves the English language and uses it so effectively in his teachings and instructions. I watched him interview hundreds of missionaries and servicemen, always communicating the simple message that they are the chosen children of God. His greatest compliment to them was the 'purity of his attention.' It is our blessing to have both Brigham Young and Joseph Smith as our prophet and leader today, for President Hinckley emanates in his life and doing both of these great prophets."

Elder Hanks after reading Keith's words describing President Hinckley commented, "He's stated it just as it should be."

Thirty-four years later, Elder, now President, Gordon B. Hinckley summarizes this foundational three year planting in the Southern Far East vineyard.

I first met Keith when I attended the Palo Alto Stake Conference many years ago. I did not know him. I think he was then serving on the high council. Between meetings he came up to me and handed me a substantial check as a contribution to the missionary fund of the Church. I engaged him in conversation and learned something about him. I also talked with David B. Haight, who had been president of the stake where Keith had been a bishop, concerning him.

I discovered that he was well off and that he could probably serve as a mission president. At the time we were under considerable pressure to find a president for Hong Kong. His family consisted of his wife, Marilyn, and four young children.

When I returned home I told the Brethren that I thought Keith would make an excellent mission president.

The Brethren considered the recommendation and issued a call.

He readily responded, and the family moved to Hong Kong where he succeeded President Jay Quealy.

He proved to be a wonderful leader. He was young and energetic. He loved people and mixed with them easily. He had excellent rapport with the missionaries.

The mission then included Hong Kong, Taiwan, the Philippines, and South Vietnam. We had no missionaries in Vietnam. The war was then raging and we had many members of the Church heavily involved in it.

There were no stakes in any of this area at that time. However, there were many branches, as well as a servicemen's district in South Vietnam.

President Garner was constantly traveling to cover all of this territory. He was a well-read scriptorian, having developed a thorough knowledge of the scriptures as a missionary and as a seminary teacher. In meetings with the missionaries he would lead them through the scriptures, finding extremely meaningful matters in verses that most of us overlooked. The missionaries loved him as their leader.

At that time I had responsibility for the work in Asia, along with Elder Marion D. Hanks of the Seventy. We would visit him about three times a year. In my interviews with the missionaries, I never found any who complained about their president, but very many who praised him and were grateful for his leadership.

It was during this tenure that we made an historic visit to Vietnam. Major (later Colonel) Allen Rozsa was the Church district president. He, too, was a very able and dedicated man. He was with the U.S. Air Force.

President Garner, Elder Hanks, and I arrived at Tan San Nhut Air Base in October 1966.

Brother Rozsa gave us a paper to sign. I asked what it was. He said that it relieved the United Sates Government from any responsibility for whatever might happen to us.

We boarded a "gooney bird," a two-prop aircraft. It had bench seats along the side. I looked to the rear at the restroom door which had painted on it, "The Guts Airline. God will understand."

The door of the plane was still open when we took off,

*"Our family of missionaries
are the elite of this generation."*
– President Keith E. Garner

*Pictured are three zones: Hong Kong October 1966, Taiwan
September 1965, and the Philippines December 10, 1966.
They are representative of the five hundred missionaries who served
in the Southern Far East Mission during the months of August 1965
to August 1968 and called Keith Garner president.*

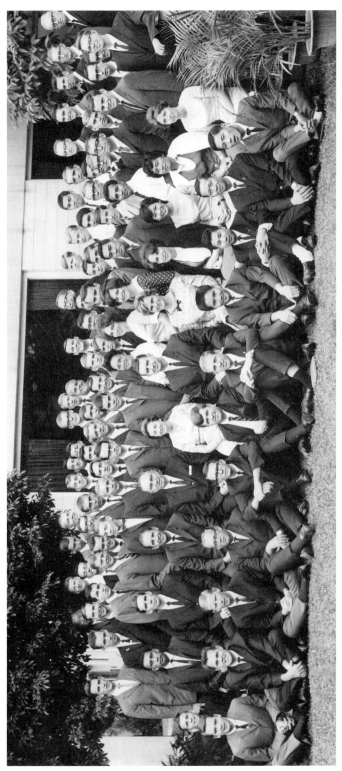

Hong Kong Zone, October 1966:

l to r: Front row: David L. Lowe, Scott M. Nelson, Richard Chatelain, Raymond Jennings, Richard F. Luke, Stephen Petersen, Clyde L. Harvey, Charles W. H. Goo, Wan, L. K. Yu, C.W. Shum, H. J. Second row: Gary B. Gedge, Paumea H. McKay, Kraig K. Jenson, President Keith E. Garner, Elder Gordon B. Hinckley, Sister Marjorie Hinckley, President Marion D. Hanks, Sister Maxine Hanks, Linda L. Carlson, Chung, M. C., Alberta N. Au, Rosalie Powell. Third row: Ross O. D. Hannant, Richard E. Widdison, William J. Christiansen, Douglas R. Livingston, Jerry W. James, J. Marvin Graff, LeRoy E. Whitehead, Lee H. Van Dam, Mary Ann Soong, Marcia L. Smith, Erlyn S. Gould, Kenneth Ching, Keith E. Garner II, Shiu Narayan, Bryce V. Redd, John J. McSweeney, Barry M. Hancock. Fourth row: Douglas R. Buck, Ernest V. Cluff, Hal H. Jones, George M. Yeiter, Kent W. Davis, Stephen L. Richey, Roger Peel, Greg F. Schenk, Clinton M. Merrell, Dale W. Cameron, Steven Egbert, Vernon S. Eggen, Douglas A. McOmber, E. Winston Elton, O. Kent Whiteley, Joel T. Richards, Charles W. Goff, Richard M. Moon, Gordon F. Esplin, Richard G. Stevens, Richard G. Berryessa, Kim A. Shipley, Daniel C. Cummings. Fifth row: Kai On Soong, John K. Sadler, Franklin L. Jones, Myron D. Hammond, Alan H. Hess, Michael J. Pratt, F. Anthony Whitehorn, Van Symons, Steven Johnson, Roger H. Neslen, Stephen K. Norris, Gerald R. Earl, Gary K. Nielsen, Robert A. Jenson, Walter J. Henry, Gary G. Kau, M. Wayne Wilhelm, Bradley W. Steuart, Donald R. Hinton, Leslie M. Jacobs, Barry L. Nielson, Theodore C. Anderson

Taiwan Zone All-Island Missionary Conference, September 1965:
From left to right: Front row: Lloyd A. Wienig, Richard J. Belliston, Robert Morris, Donald P. Brown, Frederick W. Martin, Andries Hazenbroek, Edward R. Kunkel, John S. Lineback, Phil L. Frandsen, Max J. Reeder, Steven R. Hendryx, Patrick A. Dooley, Ronald L. Alberts Jr., Anthony W. Ferguson, David B. Miner, Melvin M. Kalama Jr. Second row: Gordon D. Jones, Kaye Woodward, Mei H. Kuo, Jean A. Taylor, Shen, Frances Kamauoha, Liu, Lien Yao, Ch'en Yen Tzu, Joyce M. Lundell, Alice Chadwick, Gloria I. Richman, Jacquelin M. Herman, LaMai N. Hooper, Lucy P. Leonard, President Keith E. Garner. Third row: Duane C. Hatch, Terrel M. Hill, Larry Waltz, Stanley B. Smith, John E. Larson, Reginald L. Tenney, Virgil W. Mickelsen, James K. Larkin, David E. Shaffer, Charles D. Freeman, Clinton L. Murdock, Patrick H. Price II, Richard J. Latham, David J. Terry, Melvin P. Thatcher, David E. Poulsen Jr., Raymond K. Felsted, Kent D. Watson, Steven W. Durrant, Ted A. Telford, Marc W. Mortensen, Douglas R. Payne, Carl Elderidge Jr. Fourth row: Allen Getz, Jay M. Graff, Kenneth S. Isom, Harvey G. Horner, Alan M. Rich, Henry H. Kaoha, Kenneth J. Allen, Karl Koerner, Jon M. Hess, L. Dennis Hancey, David G. Higginson, Mark T. Sampson, Dan F. Nelson, Joseph G. Stringham, Sherman G. Sorensen, Doyle Brown. Back: Daniel H. Crook, Blaine R. Hanson, Sherman C. Miller, Nathan W. Johnson. Not Present: Gerald L. Skaggs, Ronald L. Urry, Michael Hill

Philippine Zone Conference, December 10, 1966:
From l to r: First row: James Ackroyd, Jimmie Hales, Richard Mabey, Alan Petrich, Ron Jones, John Perriton, Kenneth Fairbanks, Kent McDonald, Rudy Raralio, Lloyd Philips, Julian Rasmussen, Walter Marlowe, Alan Hassel, L. Carl Hanson, Richard Thorsen, Michael Merrihew. Second row: Duayne Davis, Robert Davis, Don Hess, Elwood Wall, David Chase, President Keith Garner, Hazel Huntington, Clifford Huntington, Ria Anderson, Margaret Peters, Rufelia Salangad, Virginia Calica, Ivy Johnson, Pamela James, Allen Geslison. Third row: Michael Taylor, David Mattson, Dennis Singh, Dale Duke, Lee Fielding, Don Al Asay, Tom Pearce, Gary Gedge, Daniel Cummings, Lewis Groberg, Anthony Amata, Dale Pratt, Mitchell Hunt III, Ruthard Mannus, Samuel Bodily, Moises Mabunga, Richard Mouritsen, Rodolfo Santos, Errol Brown, James Gibson, Mark Elggren, D. Jack Brimhall. Fourth row: Roger Holt, Kenneth Handley, Douglas Harmston, Lorenzo Bott, James Jacob, Paul Boyden, Jay Crandel, Lanney Larsen, Donald Hadden, James Stoddard, J. Paul Wright, Larry Perkins, Maun Petersen, Clyde Oliphant, Richard Lambert, James Kearl, Ross Hannant, Richard Free

and when I asked the pilot why, he said, "It's too damn hot to close it."

We flew north in the direction of Da Nang. The left engine began to sputter, and I asked Major Rozsa if we were flying up a good safe corridor. He responded that we were safe as long as we kept above the reach of the enemy fire.

When we approached Da Nang, a navy admiral in a helicopter came in just ahead of us. Major Rozsa said, "If we are going to get hit, this is where it will happen as we lower our elevation."

The admiral had gunners pointing their weapons from the helicopter. He got in alright, and we followed him in.

Having landed safely, we were loaded into an old ambulance and taken to a quonset hut meeting hall. It was filled with our members. They had parked their rifles on the rear benches and were sitting quietly in the hall as we entered. They had gathered from areas of intense military activity. They had known the smell of cordite and had heard the cries of the wounded and dying.

We held a meeting, a wonderful meeting. We had the sacrament and it was a great blessing. We bore testimony to one another. We observed the death of two of our members the week before. It was a hallowed experience.

The Jewish group were to have their meeting this Saturday evening. We went out under the eaves to a chow line and had ham sandwiches. When the Jewish brethren came along, they noticed our large number and their few. They graciously told us to go back and use the hall, that their small number would gather somewhere else. We thanked them and did so.

Following the meeting we were taken in the ambulance to an uncompleted field hospital. It had been made in the states in sections and was being bolted together. It was made for air conditioning, but this was not operating. We had 55 gallon drums filled with water since the plumbing was not yet ready.

We went to bed between clean sheets in a hot room. Through the night every few minutes the sound of an aircraft would be heard from overhead. It was going north to strafe bomb the enemy. We wondered if the pilot would return.

The next morning we boarded our aircraft and flew to Nha Trang where there was a great gathering of our brethren.

We had the sacrament, sang together, and bore testimony to one another. We then said goodbye and flew back to Saigon.

We were staying at the Caravelle Hotel in Saigon. We wished to dedicate South Vietnam for the preaching of the gospel. We did not know of a safe place, a mountain or a park or anything of the kind, where we might do this. We determined to do it on the roof of the Caravelle Hotel.

A large group of servicemen gathered there. I should judge there were about 200.

Elder Hanks offered the opening prayer and President Garner the closing prayer.

I offered a dedicatory prayer. In that prayer I prayed for the day when we would be able to preach the gospel in the nation of Vietnam.

That day has not yet come, but I am absolutely confident that it will come.

The servicemen taught many of the Vietnamese and quite a number were baptized. The Book of Mormon was translated. A small chapel was built. The final chapter on our work of South Vietnam was not written when the United States left there in 1975.

President Garner visited Vietnam on many occasions. He did a marvelous and remarkable work. To me it is a miraculous thing that he did not lose his life somewhere in that hot and deadly land. The foundation which he laid will yet be built upon.

On another occasion President Garner, Elder Hanks, and I went to India to see about opening the work there. I had been there previously. Paul Thirithuvodoss, a native Indian living in Coimbatore, had been baptized and was pleading that the work be opened.

We first flew to Calcutta. We thought we had hotel reservations, but discovered that through an oversight on the part of Pan Am we did not have reservations. It was only through the ingenuity of President Garner that we were provided with a special apartment reserved for the rajah. Keith just stood at the counter and stared at the clerk until he finally admitted the rajah's apartment was vacant. Ever since that night I have had a tremendous respect for the capacity of Keith Garner to accomplish what seemed impossible.

On one occasion when I went to Hong Kong, I stayed at

the mission home. President Garner invited me to take a short walk with him. We walked along Cornwall Road and then down into a little park that I did not know existed. Evidently it was not known to too many others. It was quiet and vacant. There we sat in the shade of a bridge while he told me that it was to this place that he came to read the scriptures, to ponder his problems, and to seek the help and direction of the Lord in his work.

I count among the great and fruitful experiences of my life those days when I was with Keith Garner while he presided over the Southern Far East Mission of the Church. His energy was boundless. His devotion to his missionaries was total. His love for his brethren and sisters in the Church, regardless of where they might be in that vast and interesting part of the world, was absolute.

The seeds President Garner had inherited, overseen, planted, nurtured, watched grow, and even blossom, included the first district established in Hong Kong in 1965, the Book of Mormon printed in Chinese, the first meetinghouse in Hong Kong completed in 1966, the Philippine Mission created in 1967; Thailand and Singapore opened to missionary work in 1968, and Vietnam dedicated for the preaching of the gospel.

After three years, President Garner, his assignment concluding, wrote, "Our family of missionaries are the elite of this generation. We will miss the celestial atmosphere of our mission home. The world of 'love' that we have traveled in for many months has been productive and rewarding."

His missionaries were truly special, and they thought the same of their mission president. One speaks for many. Elder Richey drafted this tribute: "President Garner was the first true leader and friend outside of my own father in my early manhood. He was a man without guile, indeed, a prince of a man. He was possessed of a simple yet powerful and great faith. He believed in people and trusted them. I would no more have violated that trust and love than cut off my own hand. He led by example and pure love. He never intimidated or threatened anyone. Yet, he was absolutely governed by principle and would not compromise what was right. A champion of free agency, he placed great trust in others and inspired them to heights of achievement that they, alone, would never have dared to seek. He esteemed his missionaries as his friends, companions and constantly showed his love for them in both action and deed. He could not, and would not, set himself above others. His love for the Lord, the scriptures (especially the Book of Mormon) was compelling and inspired many to improve their relationship with the Lord and their gospel scholarship."

Elder Hanks wrote movingly in a June 13, 1968, letter signed "Very Sincerely":

> At the conclusion of your outstanding service in the leadership of the Southern Far East Mission, I wish to offer this official expression of appreciation and affection. It has been my blessing to serve with you for the three years of your missionary assignment, acting as executive administrator of the Oriental missions, and I am extremely grateful for that wonderful privilege.
>
> In the various areas under your supervision, with your missionaries, in the branches, in the military field, in your lovely home in Hong Kong--in all these places I have enjoyed memorable and marvelous experiences which have blessed my life and which I shall always remember.
>
> No mission president in my knowledge or experience has done more to lift and strengthen and energize young missionaries to action and to spiritual vigor than President Keith E. Garner has done. It must be said in honesty that man for man your missionaries have been spiritually motivated and strengthened in a measure many others have not. Good and wonderful men and women work in all the areas, and each has something special to offer, but the missionaries who have labored under your direction have been especially blessed in what I consider the most significant elements of a participating and contributing life, and you have every reason to rejoice and thank the Lord that you have been thus able to inspire them.
>
> Your home has been blessed with a sweet and wonderful spirit. No hostess could be more gracious or considerate or skilled in the choice art of making people feel at home and tending to their needs and being withal a gracious and good friend in the process. Sister Garner has left a mark of tremendous meaning in the lives of many young men whose own homes will be different for their experience with her.
>
> I cannot speak of our experiences in Vietnam and Thailand without the lump and the tear. Thank the Lord for those sweet and wonderful days and for the comfort and spiritual strength we were blessed to be able to share with them. I count our times together as sweet examples of true companionship and true friendship.
>
> Your family has sustained you and been wonderfully effec-

tive in their own contributions. Certainly there are no sweeter
or finer or better children in this world, and again you should
be grateful and feel a sweet sense of satisfaction.

Your personal kindness to Maxine and me, your generosity and thoughtfulness and tenderness and confidence, the
things we've shared and the things we have felt with you are all
precious and will be remembered with joy forever.

You leave the mission having contributed meaningfully.
You will be released in a few days, and another will take your
place in Hong Kong. Be sobered and lifted by the knowledge
that no one will ever take your place in the hearts of your missionaries who will always love you and respond to you and
refer to you as their mission president and mission mother.

God bless you always.

As President Garner read President Hinckley's synopsis, reviewed Elder
Hanks' letter and Elder Richey's tribute, he shook his head noticeably moved and said,
"No one could improve on those obituaries!" He was assured that he was not close to
needing such a document of his life. In fact, Elder Hanks had already pronounced that
"You would hardly notice he's age eighty, unless you knew him when he was dashing
all over the universe practically."

When President Garner was set apart June 30, 1965, by President N. Eldon
Tanner, a counselor in the First Presidency, and Elder Spencer W. Kimball, Elder
Kimball being the voice prayed, "We bless you, our dear brother, that new powers
may come to you, that you may be far bigger than you have ever been, and that you
may rise to great heights as you take leadership of the missionaries and the saints and
the nonmembers…We send you forth with the blessings of the Lord, for the Lord has
been kind to you to give you this calling, and *He will be watching over you with great
interest.*"[43]

President Garner had felt the renewal of his body and the enlargement of his
soul as the promises of this sacred blessing washed over him. Throughout these three
years, he had enjoyed the companionship and support of men of faith and testimony
who watched him with great interest, and nobody could deny that Keith's service as
president of the Southern Far East Mission had been interesting.

Having filled out the "Report of Change of Mission President and Transfer of
Mission Accounts and Records" and having met with incoming president, W. Brent
Hardy, President Garner headed for the airport.

Missionaries joked that he needed a porter to carry his passport for him. The
passport looked like an epoch novel, page after page added bearing the immigration,

---

[43] Emphasis added.

visa, admitted, departed stamps of countries with exotic, foreign names that had become familiar to him over the past thirty-six months. With his stamped passport in hand, he boarded his flight for home. As he took off from Kaitak, he might have been thinking about that first dinner meeting in Salt Lake City with Elder Hinckley and Elder Hanks that had brought him here or of the first time he had landed in Hong Kong and discovered airplanes on their approach at certain times flew lower than buildings, exposing their passengers to people eating rice in their apartments. Or more likely in his most usual mood, he was not looking back but looking forward and thinking "What can I do now to move the work along?"

Nevertheless, as he took off, the plane would have banked to the right away from the ocean, allowing President Garner a last distant glimpse of #2 Cornwall Road, the beautiful old mansion in Kowloon-Tong and the future site of the magnificent Hong Kong Temple.

C h a p t e r

T   E   N

On the Lord's Errand

"If you miss the joy, you miss it all."

Amicable controversy flourishes between Bishop Garner's ward members and President Garner's missionaries over which period of time should be designated the "golden age," since both his eleven years as bishop in California and his three years as mission president in Southeast Asia spanned momentous periods of growth, expansion, and change.

When Keith returned in 1968 from Asia, the world he had left had a few new wrinkles or at least to him the wrinkles seemed more obvious. Stepping once again into the seminary classroom, he was thrust into the decade of the sixties, with all its rebellion, assertiveness, marginalization, and disrespect for anyone over thirty. Keith reports, "I was used to rapt attention from my missionaries. When I got back into that classroom, students had their own program. It was to continuously chatter on the events of the world. I warned them a few times. If I am boring you, don't talk, just leave. I'll get the picture, and you won't insult me."

Keith remembers, "They didn't pay any attention. I took it for a couple of days. Then the third or fourth day the class started, and we went into the same program again. Just a few; it wasn't the masses, but a few in the back; they're always in the back row. I closed my scriptures, opened my briefcase, put my scriptures inside, and walked to the door.

I said, 'Goodbye, kids. I'm sure you'll have a new seminary teacher, but it won't be Keith Garner. It's been nice discovering a new generation. It would be well if you talked to your older brothers and sisters and find out what it's all about. See you again, bye bye.'

I had my car parked right by the door. I got in and drove away.

I got a letter in the mail a few days later. It was addressed to 'Mr. Seminary Man, 955 Westridge Dr., Portola Valley, Calif.' I went back as a result of the letter."

The younger sister of Ken Woolley, one of those older brothers to whom Keith had referred, wrote the letter.

> Dear President Garner,
>
> I just thought I [would] send a short note to thank you for sticking it out this far in our seminary class. CONGRADULATION!!!
>
> You know what? In the last ten year[s], there must have [been] at least twenty-five members of this ward who dismissed our class as a bunch of no-good, unspiritual kids who don't deserve the opportunity to come to church. As I reflect, I can see them all standing at the front of the room saying the same old thing-"I just can't handle you; maybe someone else will be able to. I'm sorry." It was no fun going home after those kind of speeches and thinking that somebody just can't handle ME. And I can tell you, it was awfully hard to pray to God when I had just been told that day that our class wasn't ready for studying the gospel.
>
> The new teachers have always come in saying- "Well, I have heard you're a rough group and I am going to tackle you." But, somehow, in all their running after us, they always would lose us along the way, and they were gone in two months.
>
> What I am trying to say is that the *message of the gospel* is the only "tackler," and what we have always needed is a messenger to give it to us. And *this* is the reason why I think that you have an advantage over all those others..... you come to us as a messenger and not as a tackler. And it is that message that we need....as much as the seminary class of 1960 or '61 or '62 and as much as any missionary in Hong Kong (or where-ever). Please keep on saying, "This is the most important thing that could happen to you today." And please keep smiling at us when you come in each day. And please keep giving us that message. And, for goodness sake, please don't give it up! I WANT YOU TO STAY!
>
> Sincerely, Ginger!

P.S. Did you hear that Brig wants to go on a mission after high school?

When he returned he found them to be "very devoted, no whispering." He always assured them "If I bore you, leave. I would leave because the message is too exciting."

Barely home from Asia but endowed with an enthusiasm for the message of the gospel of Jesus Christ which had immediately taken him back into the seminary classroom, Keith received another call from the First Presidency, David O. McKay, Hugh B. Brown, and N. Eldon Tanner. This time he was asked to serve as a Regional Representative of the Quorum of the Twelve. Dated August 8, 1968, the letter reads:

> Dear Brother Garner:
>
> With the ever increasing growth of the Church there becomes evident a greater need to train our stake and ward leaders in the programs of the Church that they in turn might train the membership in their responsibilities before the Lord.
>
> To assist in accomplishing this we are calling you to serve as a Regional Representative of the Twelve to work with the leadership of certain stakes. You have been recommended by the Twelve to serve in this important capacity. We earnestly hope that you are in a position to respond to this call.
>
> Those so called will be expected to give Church service time only, as do bishops and stake presidents. However, it will be necessary that they be released from other Church administrative responsibilities. Furthermore, it is anticipated that there will be a rotation of these assignments from time to time with no fixed term of service.
>
> We repose in you our confidence and extend our appreciation for your devoted service in the cause of the Master.

Keith had been forewarned.

At the request of Ernest L. Wilkinson, president of Brigham Young University, Keith traveled with him to Texas to look at one of his real estate ventures. From the notes Keith made, this trip's itinerary had no leisure moments scheduled. In fact, Keith says that President Wilkinson ran faster than he did himself. Quite a statement. Many of those who knew them assert that physically they are comparable, and both were always running ahead of the ceaseless expansions on which they were forever working. In fact, remembering Elder Hinckley's characterization of him as a person who ran so fast he had holes in his shoes, Keith's comment in this situation was "Having holes in your shoes is better than having holes in the seat of your pants from sitting down wondering what's happening." President Wilkinson found a kindred spirit in President Garner and asked him to join the Brigham Young University staff as the head of Industrial Development. Advised by Elder Hinckley that another Church calling was imminent, Keith declined this very interesting offer.

The office of Regional Representative came with clear duties. While Keith was still serving in Hong Kong, the first sixty-nine Regional Representatives of the Twelve were called on September 29, 1967. This calling was designated as "a new administrative position." As President McKay had written to Keith when he was called a year later, the creation of this new leadership position had been made necessary by the growth of the Church and the necessity to train leaders in their duties.

As a Regional Representative, his region, the Oakland-Walnut Creek Region, was comprised of nine stakes made up of stake presidents B. Darrell Call, Napa Stake; Weston L. Roe, Marin Stake; Joseph R. Hilton, Walnut Creek Stake; Ted E. Madsen, Concord Stake; Sidney B. Henderson, Santa Rosa Stake; Sterling Nicolaysen, Fremont Stake; D. Ross McClellan, Hayward Stake; Elmo R. Smith, Oakland-Berkeley Stake; and A. Gifford Jackson, San Leandro Stake.

While administrative in nature, he approached this assignment the same way he had approached his seminary teaching assignment. Whether training the youth, his missionaries, or now mature, experienced stake presidents, Keith felt keeping one's eyes firmly fixed on the goal, eternal life for each of God's children, was the secret to success. He knew programs were only as good as the leaders' administration, and reminding them to never lose sight of the individual's salvation seemed uppermost in his mind.

Speaking at the San Leandro Stake Conference was the first of many assignments, most characterized by speeches given to wide ranging groups with considerable numbers such as at stake conferences, regional leadership meetings with stake presidencies, senior Aaronic Priesthood meetings, scout seminars, gospel doctrine classes, firesides, chapel dedications, youth conferences, seminary graduations, Relief Society socials, and genealogical workshops.

At the October 3, 1968, Seminar for Regional Representatives, the first Keith attended, Elder Harold B. Lee introduced him to the group, and he also announced that Brother Garner would be one of four Regional Representatives to pilot a new Church program. The pilot program to be started in northern California focused on the growing contingent of LDS servicemen who were going to war in Vietnam. The brethren were desirous that the LDS serviceman receive the same support and recognition that his missionary counterpart received rather than, as Brother Lee described it, "slip out unnoticed and unheralded into a strange world of military discipline." A two day seminar similar to the weeklong seminar for outgoing missionaries would be made available to these young men in northern California. Elder Lee announced, "We propose that these meetings be held in the Institute building and under the supervision of the Regional Representatives of the Twelve, Elder David B. Haight, Elder Keith

Garner, Elder Raymond Barnes, and Elder Clifton D. Boyack. We would like to begin this first seminar on a trial basis under the leadership of these competent Regional Representatives, Keith Garner, who is keenly conscious of the needs of our military men, having just come from the battle area of Vietnam.

We would then, from the experience of this first seminar, plan to reach out to other areas conveniently located in an effort to give similar attention to all outgoing servicemen."

Before leaving for California and having been made chairman of the servicemen's committee, he and the three other Regional Representative committee desig-

Official Photo 7th National Jamboree Farragat State Park, Idaho 1969--l to r Carlos Smith, M. D. Hanks, Folkman Brown, Keith Garner

nates met with Elders Lee, Hinckley, and Peterson, and chaplains Kearsley, Wood, and
Newby. Three months later the featured guests at the LDS Servicemen's Pre-Service
Orientation, which included dinner and speeches, were Elders Gordon B. Hinckley,
Mark E. Peterson, and Boyd K. Packer. Sixteen young men were in attendance.

Many of Keith's Saturdays and/or Sundays over the next four years were
spent at the Oakland Interstake Center attending these servicemen orientations.
Unlike his World War II days where he had only heard stories of battles in the
European and Asian theaters before the troops he trained were called up, he knew
firsthand the horrors these peachy cheeked boys would confront in Vietnam. He also
knew how very much the companionship of other LDS boys and the occasional visit of
LDS authorities meant to the LDS soldiers throughout Vietnam. Elder Lee had mentioned Keith's qualifications for this assignment. His experiences certainly prepared
him to contribute greatly to this important effort. Thankfully the necessity for this
effort would disappear in 1975 when the Vietnam War ended.

The address Elder Lee gave entitled "Special Challenges Facing The Church In
Our Time," Keith called masterful. Elder Lee began, "In the last two seminars we have
stressed two themes--the need for the Church to become more effective organization-
ally in order to cope with the challenges of growth on a world-wide basis, and the
need for all leaders in the Church, to 'know' our people in order to bring Church
programs to bear on their lives more effectively," or as stated later in this same talk,
"...so that members can better realize that the goals of the Church are tied to happiness both here and hereafter."

Elder Garner's own assessment and priorities based on his experiences as
bishop and mission president might have been expressed in substantially the same
words. He underlined on his copy of Elder Lee's speech some thoughts which he
shared with the members in the Oakland-Walnut Creek Region. "The Gospel con-
tains the answer to every human problem, but we must bring those answers to bear on
the problems of individual members more than is now the case, so that our
members can witness for themselves that the principles of the Gospel really work
in meeting the challenges of life.

The Gospel is not a collection of abstractions; the Church is more than a
system of reports and meetings; it is the Gospel in action!" Keith agreed.

"If, for instance, one truly believes in eternity and in a personal resurrection,
this should raise the quality of his life. Merely giving mental assent to the teachings of
the Church without a corresponding change in our lives is a ritual, but it is not real
religion! One may be skilled and smooth in reciting the teachings of the Church, but
unless these teachings make him gradually more Christ-like, his knowledge and articu-
lation are of little value. President David O. McKay has said something which should
live forever: 'What a person thinks of Christ will largely determine what he is.'"

Keith reciting silently Paul's words, "And now abideth faith, hope, charity,
these three; but the greatest of these is charity,"[44] thought "Charity, 'the pure love of

Christ,'[45] first, last, and always."

Elder Lee continued, "Realizing, as we must, our individual tasks in this great mission He has shared with us, should not give us a sense of false pride, but a keen sense of responsibility for our individual leadership tasks. We have been called to difficult tasks in a difficult age, but this could be for each of us a time of high adventure, of great learning, of great inner satisfaction. For the converging challenges posed by war, urbanization, dilution of doctrine, and domestic decay surely provide for us the modern equivalent of crossing the plains, enduring misunderstanding, establishing a Kingdom throughout the world in the midst of adversity."

Put in this position and schooled at the Regional Representative semi-annual seminars, which provided training that Keith referred to as "exceptional, tiring but inspiring," he definitely felt the weight of the responsibility. He had heard the words Elder Lee spoke, "We for our part must do better and be more effective communicators--communicators with conviction--if we are to offset and to match the challenges of urbanization and communication. Can we improve the quality of family life, and our Church classrooms so that the precious minutes there spent can offset the deluge of other influences? Somehow the word of the Lord must be heard above and through the din, and you are among the voices that must be so raised!"

Regional Representative Garner attended a stake Aaronic Priesthood banquet for the young men and their mothers. In a journal note, Keith wrote, "I spoke--It was fair. I struggle too much for *words*." A younger friend of his, Bruce Haight, enunciated the basis for such an evaluation. "Keith thinks fast, walks fast, moves fast, always." Slow is not in Keith's vocabulary, and so this self-appraisal came from a man of pronounced impatience, especially with himself. It is highly suspect that his estimation of this speech is accurate, and Elder Lee disagreed with the premise. At the April 1969 regional meetings in Salt Lake City, Brother Lee was heard telling Keith in conversation how much he appreciated his companionship at the Oakland Conference and that his morning stake conference address was "a classic." Hearing such a critique, some in attendance asked Keith if he had a copy of his "classic" speech. In his usual, sincerely modest way, he deflected and down-played Elder Lee's words of praise with "Imagine anybody giving me such a wonderful compliment." While with him at another stake conference, Elder Lee had counseled him as he had many others who felt keenly their inadequacies, "If you are seeking perfection before you preach, you will never preach." Of course, he continued to preach.

As part of his assignment, he frequently and effectively introduced programs initiated by the general officers of the Church to the stake presidents in his region, including the new Aaronic Priesthood MIA program, the new teacher training program,

---

[44] I Corinthians 13:13

[45] Moroni 7:47

and the new bishop's orientation.

He enjoyed many one-on-one exchanges when he accompanied General Authorities to stake conferences. On one memorable weekend, he assisted Elder LeGrand Richards in selecting and setting apart a new stake presidency in the Fremont Stake.

He attended the National Scout Jamboree at Farragut State Park in Idaho with Elder Marion D. Hanks, Bishop Robert L. Simpson, Carlos Smith, Folkman Brown, 28,300 scouts, and 6,700 staff.

As varied and pleasant as these general assignments were, Keith, having ascertained the complexities facing the stake leaders with whom he worked and readied by his own experiences, knew confronting and solving these challenges happened best within the boundaries of stake and ward memberships. Only the other eight stake presidents in Keith's region would know as much about his impact on helping leadership to meet those needs as President Sidney B. Henderson.

In a recent telephone conversation, President Henderson shared his thoughts. "Regional Representatives of the Twelve at that time were like the Area Authority

Mission Representatives of the Twelve and First Council of the Seventy, October 5, 1972;
Elder Garner first row, center

Seventies now. They had line authority, presided over the stakes in matters of building approvals, division of wards, really any matter except Church courts.

As a stake president, I worked under several Regional Representatives, and then I was made a Regional Representative of the Twelve myself. When I became a Regional Representative, I tried, I didn't match him, but I tried to be like him.

There were a couple of times when I was in a jam with some buildings; he was so practical. In my stake we built eleven buildings. I remember one time he called me and said, 'Come on down here; you've got to see this building.' I can remember he steered me away from a contractor that the neighboring stake hired. It was just a disaster, and he kept me away from that.

He had a very special effect on me with regard to the Book of Mormon. I can remember the meetings we held. We didn't get into a lot of details about running a stake. He often times would just get into the scriptures. He'd say things like, 'Can you imagine how Moroni (or he would name another person in the Book of Mormon), can you imagine his feelings at the time and under those circumstances?'

It was never a meeting where he said, 'Well, you should do better than this or that or the other.' I just always felt good coming away from him after our meetings, or the couple of stake conferences in Santa Rosa in which as the presiding authority he spoke, or his dedication of the Sebastapol Ward building. He also had the stake presidents in his home, and we just had a glorious time.

Keith really had a strong impact on me. He is a real representative of the Lord and was fearless and capable in teaching. He took a personal interest in me, and we became very close friends. Keith's friendship is everlasting.

The other Regional Representatives I had, well, he was not like other people; he was just different."

He vocalized these feelings throughout the ensuing years. Elder Hanks heard these same thoughts on several different occasions when he would run into President Henderson in Provo, Utah. Elder Hanks recounts, "President Henderson told me, 'I was just a dentist and a stake president surviving until Brother Garner became our Regional Representative at which time my whole ministry changed and the emphasis went to the individual. A dentist can't put new fillings in half a dozen people's teeth all at the same time; it is one-on-one, and you care about them. Brother Garner just changed our whole attitude.'"

President Henderson agreed with President Joseph Fielding Smith who had told Keith, "You are no stuffed shirt."

Elder Hanks further quotes President Henderson. "Brother Garner taught all the time in the way he approached things. He made it plain to us that we were the leaders in our stakes, and he didn't intend to ever let that be misunderstood. He simply wished to help strengthen our hands so we could strengthen our stakes. After we got to know him a little while, we knew exactly what to do. Teach the people. Stand and use these great examples out of the books, which will help the people sustain us, because that's what we needed."

President Henderson and others attested that Keith's recurrent message whenever he had the opportunity in conversation or from the pulpit was his personal testimony of the reality of the Book of Mormon as a second witness for Christ. A 1992 cover letter addressed, "Greetings to my family and my friends" could have been a copy of his message to the stake presidents over which he presided or to the mission presidents he supervised. It reads:

> While sitting in a fireside group with LaVon's friends in San Francisco in 1938, fifty-four years ago, I resolved to study the Book of Mormon to determine in my own mind and heart whether it was just another book or a revelation from God.
>
> I want you to know that was the wisest decision of my whole life for I received a firm conviction in my heart that the Book of Mormon is truly a new witness to us and all mankind that Jesus is the Christ, the Redeemer of the World.
>
> Follow me for a few paragraphs as I attempt to introduce Moroni, a man and a prophet who deposited records from whence this Book of Mormon was translated.
>
> The book contains the special testimony of Moroni, his personal visit with Jesus. In these words he tells us:
>
> > *...I have seen Jesus, and that he hath talked with me*
> > *face to face, and that he told me in plain humility,*
> > *even as a man telleth another in mine own*
> > *language, concerning these things.* [46]
>
> Moroni recounts for us the death by the sword of his father Mormon, and the utter destruction of his people in fratricidal war, his wanderings for thirty-six years alone, the sole survivor of his people, for the "safety of mine own life" because of his unwillingness to deny the Christ, and his laboring to engrave his own account on plates while he continued the translating, organizing and editing of the writings of other prophets--work Mormon had begun and which would eventually bear his father's name: the Book of Mormon.
>
> Concluding his reflective account of his life Moroni's farewell message is powerful, urges action, and is a benediction of belief. "And now, I would commend you to seek this Jesus

---

[46] Ether 12:39

of whom the prophets and apostles have written, that the grace of God the Father, and also the Lord Jesus Christ, and the Holy Ghost, which beareth record of them, may be and abide in you forever."[47]

Moroni died about 421 A.D.. Some 1,400 years later in 1827, as miraculous and marvelous as it seems, Moroni appeared to Joseph Smith not far from the boy's home in Palmyra, New York at the Hill Cumorah; this is where Moroni at the close of his mortal life had buried plates of gold. He entrusted Joseph with these sacred records.

What a book! What a message!

We have the book before our eyes. We can know of its divinity and rejoice in its message.

Keith has the ability to empathize with the life stories of these ancient people. They seem to come alive for him. He visualizes their day-to-day lives, thus feeling a human connection. For Keith, these prophets, and for that matter, scoundrels of the Book of Mormon were not one dimensional; they were living, breathing, mortal men.

He pictures in detailed ways Moroni's struggle with loneliness; his fight for survival; his battle with his surroundings; wild animals, mosquitoes, drenching rains, the blazing sun; his need for food, clothing, and shelter; and his dealing with all this while he was compiling records left with him by his father Mormon and writing his own words on plates of gold. Keith states, "How indescribably difficult those thirty-six years Moroni spent alone must have been," and then rejoices that out of Moroni's necessity, having suffered so much the Lord came to him. He envisions him sitting on rock outcroppings talking with his Savior and friend "face to face."

Only weeks before her death, Elaine Cannon, who was Keith's friend and whose husband Jim served with Keith in the Hawaiian Mission, remarked to many, "I've studied the Book of Mormon all my life, and because of the last months of thought provoking conversation with Keith, I know how to read it."

Bound with Keith's letter are the testimonies of Jesus Christ born by thirteen prophets as recorded in the Book of Mormon.

Lehi	Alma, the younger	Samuel, the Lamanite
Nephi	Aaron	Mormon
Jacob	Amulek	Moroni
King Benjamin	Alma	
Abinadi	Helaman	

---

[47] Ether 12:41

Centrally included is the Savior's own witness of his divine mission.

On October 5, 1972, his assignment was changed to Mission Representative of the Council of the Twelve and of the First Council of the Seventy. A *Church News* article titled "Keeping Pace With The Growth, 29 Mission Representatives Expand Proselyting Program" Week Ending July 1, 1972, explains:

> To meet the pressing demands of a fast growing world-wide church membership, a new and revolutionary supervisory organization was introduced June 29 by the First Presidency.
>
> President N. Eldon Tanner, second counselor to President Joseph Fielding Smith, detailed the new program at a seminar for newly called mission presidents and then at a special press conference at the Church Office Building.
>
> Growth in the church necessitating the expanded supervisory organization was shown graphically at the press conference on a world map revealing that:
>
> World membership has increased 94 percent in the past 12 years (1960-72) to the total of 3,090,953.
>
> Growth rate for the same period within the U.S. has been 50 percent to a total of 2,133,758.
>
> Growth outside of the U.S. is up 250 percent for the 12-year period.
>
> South America is setting the pace for rapid growth with a 1100 percent increase in the past 12 years, followed by Central America with 948 percent, and Asia with 751 percent.
>
> With the church's almost doubling its size since 1960, the First Presidency emphasized the necessity of keeping pace with supervision and training for leaders, members and proselyting missionaries and providing for an accelerated growth in the years ahead.
>
> The newly introduced supervisory program has three parts:
>
> 1 - Giving to the First Council of Seventy expanded responsibilities for missionary work in both the 581 stakes and 101 missions of the world.
>
> 2 - The appointment of 29 experienced leaders from various parts of the church to serve in a new assignment as mission representatives of the Council of the Twelve and First Council of Seventy. These men will serve under direction of the First Council in consultation with the Missionary Executive Committee of the Twelve, in giving special help to both stake

and full-time missions in proselyting.

3 - The calling of 35 new Regional Representatives of the Twelve, expansion of their supervisory assignments to include training among the mission districts like that now given in the stakes. This will bring the total number of regional representatives to 108. The stakes and mission districts they will give supervisory leadership are divided into more than 240 regions.

In announcing the new organization, the First Presidency also explained that the present program wherein members of the Council of the Twelve and others of the General Authorities have supervised specific areas of world missions will be discontinued as of July 1.

An organizational chart of the new supervisory program relating to the missions, affecting full-time missionaries and part-time stake and district missionaries, shows that the Council of the Twelve continues as the Missionary Committee of the church under the First Presidency.

Three members of the Twelve, Acting President Spencer W. Kimball, and Elders Gordon B. Hinckley and Thomas S. Monson, will continue to serve as the Missionary Executive Committee.

Under their supervision the First Council of Seventy will give leadership to missionary proselyting throughout the world…

At the seminar it was explained that under the new arrangement, training for proselyting, church-wide, will come under mission representatives whereas instruction for member work will come under the Regional Representatives…

The newly called Mission Representatives, their biographies and pictures, and the missions assigned to them follow: Paul C. Andrus, Robert B. Arnold, James P. Christensen, David G. Clark, Gene Raymond Cook, Stephen R. Covey, Stewart A. Durrant, Keith E. Garner…He will supervise the Hong Kong, Philippine and Southeast Asia missions; Orville C. Gunther, Clifton Ivan Johnson, William N. Jones, Walter H. Kindt, Allen E. Litster, Edward Yukio Okazaki, Herschel N. Pedersen, Don H. Rasmussen, J. Murray Rawson, Phillip G. Redd, Sidney F. Sager, R. Wayne Shute, Milton E. Smith, Asael T. Sorensen, Thomas R. Stone, Gerald R. Ursenbach, Clark M. Wood.

So after four years of Church assignments within the confines of northern

California, Keith's new calling meant overseas travel to countries almost duplicative of his 1965 Southern Far East mission field. Over the next two years, he made seven trips to Asia, averaging two and a half weeks each. He visited the familiar cities of Hong Kong, Bangkok, Singapore, and Manila. He made Djakarta, Bandung, Madras, Cebu City, Mindanao, Davao, Coimbutore, Semarang--cities he had visited much less frequently if at all as mission president--normal stops on his mission representative itinerary.

He relived having been asked in 1966 about the expansion of missionary work into Indonesia and counseling against it. Unable to cover his incredulity, he tells how not long after his release missionaries were in Indonesia, and now so was he.

His 1972 assignment brought him back to the Philippines too. While mission president he had been instrumental in the creation of the first mission in the Philippines, a mission which was split off the Southern Far East Mission. While he was a Mission Representative with oversight over the Philippines, the Philippines Mission was divided into the Philippines Manilla Mission and the Philippines Cebu City Mission.

Despite the late planes; the long sometimes hazardous car rides; the hotels without lights, hot water, or air conditioning; the miserable beds; the oppressive heat; the time changes; the rats in restaurants and hotel rooms, Keith wrote happily of his experiences. "Had good attendance, wonderful meetings in humble circumstances making the spirit available and abundant." He even resourcefully overcame one of the problems, exhaustion, when he slept comfortably stretched out on three seats in one row on a Philippines Airlines flight.

Men like Presidents Miller F. Shurtleff, Carl D. Jones, William S. Bradshaw, Paul D. Morris, Malan R. Jackson, Dewitt C. Smith, G. Carlos Smith and Raymond L. Goodson would have been surprised to know that the vibrant and animated leader who heartened each mission president with whom he spoke had during this time written, "Really am down--almost feel lost because of my failures." This entry had been brought on by a sore back which kept him in bed all day. Nonetheless, he prepared a speech for a regional meeting titled, "Leadership, A Must Have," under which he listed 1. Desire, 2. Commitment, 3. Worthiness, 4. Discernment, and 5. Skill plus personality training and talents.

Keith's head was never really turned by the adulation given to Church leaders. He never forgot being dropped off at one of the international airports with much fanfare, people carrying his bags and seeing to his every need. After the entourage left, his flight was cancelled until the next morning, and he spent a long night alone in the airport writing a report on his meetings to Elder Hinckley.

With all its challenges, Keith's new assignment combined his teaching skills and love of missionary work. Having a firm basis upon which to draw as he counselled mission presidents, he identified the key to the successful missionary when he told the following story. "When I was mission president, a Polynesian elder came into my office in Hong Kong. He brought this older fellow with him. The elder didn't have the language. I said, 'How can I help you?' He said, 'I've been talking to him, and he wants to talk to you about the Church. He wants to join it.' I said, 'Well, let's chat. Get an elder who can speak Cantonese.' When an elder who could act as a translator arrived, I said to the Chinese gentleman, 'Why do you want to join the Church?' He pointed to the Hawaiian elder and said, 'I want to be just like this man. He's full of love and compassion. If this Church produces this kind of man, I want to belong.'"

Keith's point was exactly the same as the one Elder Lee had made in the first Regional Representative meeting he attended. President Lee had quoted Dr. Elliott Landau, a Jewish convert, "I joined this Church because my heart told me things that my mind did not know."

The wise old Chinese gentleman had noticed in President Garner's young elder's easygoing, charitable, humble soul traits Keith had seen in the Polynesian elders serving throughout the Southern Far East Mission. Charlie W. H. Goo, who later became president of the Hong Kong Mission, reflected on the buoyant spirit President Garner brought to his missionaries, in this case those of Polynesian heritage when he told him, "One thing I really appreciated was your coming to our little farewell in Salt Lake City. I still remember one of your comments. You said that you really loved the Hawaiian elders. One observation you had was that they sure didn't make it to meetings on time, but when they arrived they made things happen. In a way that was a compliment to us missionaries from Hawaii who made things happen. At least we tried to do that."

In helping to train the mission presidents on how to help their missionaries, Keith emphasized the same priorities he had while he was mission president. In a telephone conversation, David Poulsen capsulized President Garner's methodology. "President Garner created a superb focus that was felt but unspoken. These days I think there's an emphasis on getting out and baptizing, getting the numbers up. While that is important, President Garner always seemed to have highest in his priority list the development of the missionaries, giving them experiences that would build their testimonies and giving them leadership experiences. So when they went back home to wherever that was in the world, they would have had a very good developmental experience, stronger faith, better testimony while in the process they served the investigators and saints in Taiwan. He seemed to have a really keen interest in making sure the missionaries had appropriate assignments that would develop them. I think that was felt by a lot of missionaries."

His assignment as Mission Representative in the same area in which he had presided as mission president provided new and gratifying experiences. For example Keith wrote in a September 5, 1973, letter from the Hotel Siam Inter-Continental, "We held our Thailand regional meeting yesterday at 5 p.m. There are still more American members than Thai, and the majority are military. When I spoke to them, two recognized me and told of our meetings in 1966. One came to the Church after the conference to tell me of his advancement in the Priesthood, temple marriage, and of my recommendation to him personally to read this book. I extended the Book of Mormon to him and said, 'This is the book; it will change your life for the good.' He said, 'I took your counsel and can tell you that my life is richer and improved. I came to the Church to thank you.' He also spoke of Elder Hinckley and Elder Hanks in glowing terms of spirituality while visiting military personnel during those crucial war years of '65, '66, '67 and '68."

Keith's interest when he revisited the Philippines took him straightway to the Makati Chapel. While he was mission president, construction of this first chapel in the Philippines was underway. A superintendent from Utah was in charge. "I told the superintendent that because of the termite problem in the Philippines, the wood glu-lams they were using wouldn't last very long. They would provide a real feast for the termites, and the roof would come tumbling down. He told me, 'You take care of the mission, President, and I'll take care of the construction.' When I went back as a Mission Representative in 1973, the first thing I wanted to look at was the Makati Chapel."

Keith recounts with an I-told-him-so tone in his voice, "As I suspected, they were taking out the remains of the glulams. The branch president told me the only thing holding that roof up was the prayers of the Filipino saints."

Another amusing incident which occurred during Keith's Mission Representative days is told by David Poulsen. "Long after our mission, I was living in the Southern Philippines as a business man working in international banking. President Garner by this time was a Regional Representative over Taiwan, Hong Kong, the Philippines. Every few months he would make a trip back to Asia to work on leadership development. This would have been in maybe 1973 or early '74. He came to the Philippines. I was a member of the Cebu Country Club, and they had a nice little dining facility. I think it was a Saturday evening leadership conference we'd had. Afterwards we took everyone over to the country club for dinner. We arranged for a private room with a nice big long table. There must have been thirty or so Church leaders. The waiters were going around the room taking orders for drinks. The members were ordering lemonade, 7-Up, and water. The setting was very pleas-ant, and the leaders were enjoying themselves. There was a lot of pleasant chitchat going on around the table. The waiter got to President Garner, and he said, 'I'll have a Coke, please.' The room went dead silent, and every eyeball swung around and looked at President Garner. He, in a very matter-of-fact fashion, said, 'Oh, whenever I travel to foreign countries like this, I always drink Coke. I don't want to get sick, and you know nothing can live in Coke.' He broke the ice, and the crowd cracked up laughing."

It is true that Keith emphasized in his actions, including not drinking the water in most foreign countries in which he traveled, a regimen of physical fitness thereby insuring to the extent possible the health and energy necessary to do his work well without any time-outs for sickness. For years that regimen has included eating cracked wheat for breakfast and meat sparingly, running up stairs two at a time, and swimming when possible. Perhaps his physical routine landed him a seat on the Deseret Gym's Board of Directors along with Elder Hanks and Elaine Cannon before the gymnasium was torn down to make room for the new Conference Center. He was not responsible for the gym's demise, but exercise purely for the sake of exercising is quite unimpressive to him. In fact, when people choose to run only for exercise, he thinks they could get the same benefits if they used the energy spent on their run doing something he would judge more productive. Whether this is sound medical advice may be in dispute, but the fact that it works for him is not. He often quotes one of his friends who when asked how he exercises states, "I speak at the funerals of joggers." The listener sometimes responds, "You are a rare bird, and so is your friend."

Whether President Henderson's estimable observation, "Keith is just different," or the nickname he hears most often, "rare bird," suits him best, he truly is one of a kind! Without any pretense of false humility when this is pointed out to him, he'll furrow his brow in disbelief and with his piercing blue eyes question the sincerity behind the statement with an emphatic "Who me?" It can be concluded that he is a man who on most occasions sees himself and his accomplishments as generated from his responding to the open doors of his history, by seizing the moment, by doing what any person of faith could choose to do in that situation, by getting up each morning and putting one foot in front of the other, by going to bed each night determined to do better upon arising. All actions he considers the norm, certainly not a gold standard for duplication.

His enthusiastic, directed, practical devotion in moving the work forward to bless the growing membership of the Church in individual and customized ways amplified his work as a Regional Representative and Mission Representative. Keith was one of a small number of men who would ever serve in these offices since both were discontinued when the First Council of the Seventy became the First Quorum of the Seventy. On October 21, 1974, as part of accepting a new Church assignment, and before the eventual dissolution of these callings, he received his release from this chapter of his life.

> Elder Keith E. Garner
> 1330 University Drive
> Menlo Park, California 94025
>
> Dear Brother Garner:
>   In view of your new call to serve as the director of the
> Salt Lake Visitors Center Mission, we hereby extend to you an
> honorable release as a Regional Representative of the Twelve

effective January 1, 1975. At the same time, we express our sincere appreciation for the able and dedicated service you rendered in your capacity as a Regional Representative of the Twelve.

Through your long experience in Church service you have learned of the great blessing of having devoted and reliable co-workers to share the burdens and responsibilities entrusted to your care. With this insight you can better appreciate the good feelings which we and the Quorum of the Twelve have toward you for the selfless way in which you have served, thereby easing our load and helping to advance the Lord's work...

Faithfully your brethren,
Spencer W. Kimball, N Eldon Tanner,
Marion G. Romney, The First Presidency

Chapter
ELEVEN

With a Hand to the Square

"The gospel picks out all the big souls out of all creation."
— Hyrum Smith
Times & Seasons, 1 Aug 1844

Just like Keith, calls to service from the First Presidency were not unfamiliar to his ancestors. Tales of the Garner clan embody the exhilaration and bustle of Joseph Smith's Nauvoo; the trials and deprivation of the Mormon pioneer trek from Illinois to the Great Salt Lake Valley; the cold, loneliness of Winter Quarters; the patriotism and resourcefulness of the Mormon Battalion; the discovery of gold at Sutter's Fort; the anticipated invasion of Johnston's Army; and the settling of the West.

The earliest Garner convert to The Church of Jesus Christ of Latter-day Saints was Keith's great, great grandfather David Garner, who was born in 1768 in Fayetteville, Cumberland, North Carolina, to Phillip and Elizabeth Winkler Garner, the fifth child of nine. He died September 3, 1872, in Iowa at the grand old age of 104. Interestingly, Garners farmed the verdant grounds of North Carolina at least a decade before the American Revolution commenced.

His son Phillip Garner was born 11 October 1808, in Rowen County, North Carolina. He was the second child of eleven children born to David and Jane Stephens Garner. Phillip's mother Jane's cousin was Alexander Stephens, vice-president of the Confederacy. Jane died while on a visit to her son John in California in 1868. She, like her husband, lived a long, productive life and died at the age of ninety-six.

Three of David and Jane's sons, Keith's great grandfather Phillip and Phillip's two younger brothers David and William, were members of the Mormon Battalion. David settled in Ogden and raised a large and faithful posterity. William returned to Pottawattamie County. In recognition of his agricultural and entrepreneurial contributions to the community, Garner Township was named after him. He and his father are buried in Garner Cemetery near Council Bluffs.

Another brother, John, did not serve in the Battalion; nonetheless, he ended up in California and was one of the earliest settlers of San Bernardino. The significance of his contributions to his community can be better estimated when one notes that Garner Grove, the city he lived in most of his life, was named for him.

Phillip settled in Ogden, and the Garner Farm encompassed most of today's downtown Ogden. He is credited with bringing the first alfalfa seed from California to Weber County. Of note, one of his descendants Kent Garner, a seminary teacher now living in Texas, has in his possession Phillip's Mormon Battalion sword.

Phillip's son and Keith's grandfather, Frederick Garner, was born 13 October 1837 near Lima, Hancock, Illinois, the fifth child of twelve born to Phillip and Mary Hedrick Garner. Phillip and Mary received their endowments on February 6, 1846, in the Nauvoo Temple, along with some of the last saints to be so privileged. They, no doubt, were among those who road down Parley Street (the Street of Tears), crossed the Mississippi River in sub-zero temperatures during February 1846, and looked back with longing at the once enterprising City of Nauvoo.

At the young age of thirteen, Frederick walked, sometimes barefoot, across the plains to the Salt Lake Valley. Because he was handy with a bow and arrow, he made friends with the Indians and learned their language. When Johnston's Army was sent to "Utah," Frederick was left on detail to set the torch to the houses in case the army advanced.

He was a snare drummer in B.D. Sprague's Martial Band, the band that met Brigham Young on his visits to Ogden and the band Brigham Young called his favorite. He helped build the Weber Canal and the first road through Ogden Canyon. He was a school trustee and road supervisor. He was gifted as a fluent speaker, a good singer, a proficient step dancer, and was an active member of the debating club. He was well-known for his kindness and help to the sick.

Frederick's son and Keith's father, Benjamin Franklin Garner, was born 26 March 1881 in Ogden, Utah, the ninth child of ten born to Frederick and Ann Horrocks Garner.

Ben's son Keith Elliott Garner was born 11 May 1919 in Sugar City, Madison, Idaho, the sixth child of seven born to Benjamin Franklin and Mary Selina Carr Garner.

Applicable to all generations of Garners, it has been strikingly observed, "We can easily follow the trails of the Garner family by the green spots they have left behind them; at every place they have set their feet a bunch of grass has grown."[48]

From Church history's Nauvoo Period, 1839-1846, Garners emerged and made their mark on the kingdom's progression. In the 1930s, Keith's indefatigable missionary spirit surfaced, and he carried on the family tradition as he continues to make his own meaningful mark. In a speech based on the Parable of the Sower found in Matthew given to Temple Square tour guides, President Garner found his ancestors' stories illustrative.

He speaks.

> I would like to begin by telling something of my own heritage. In the early 1830s, a sixty-four year old man sold his plantation in western North Carolina and along with several of his children, some of whom were married, started West.
>
> They were active members of the Church in Nauvoo, married for time and eternity in the Nauvoo Temple, did ordinance work for their dead ancestors, suffered the persecutions others suffered during the ten year period 1836-1846, and with others were driven from their homes in that February winter to seek refuge 'westward.' Some Garners were in the congregation when the call came from the government for soldiers to make up that group which came to be known as the Mormon Battalion, and at least three of the brothers enlisted for that service, leaving their wives and children camped in tents on the banks of the river.
>
> Somewhere early in March, one of the brothers fell down a steep embankment, broke several ribs, and was returned home. The others continued that trek and were mustered out in southern California.
>
> Desiring to return to their families, they made their way northward to Sutter's Fort where they were employed for a time and were party to the discovery of gold. By the time they had made their way to the Great Salt Lake Valley, the main body of saints had arrived.
>
> Brigham Young's diary for March 1848 records that Wm. Garner and others had left Salt Lake to join their families in Winter Quarters and had 'carried many letters with them.'
>
> Upon arriving in Council Bluffs, the Garners purchased

---

[48] Solomon C. Stephens, "History of the Garner Family" (sermon given at funeral service of Frederick Garner on 4 May 1920), copy in possession of Keith E. Garner.

8,000 acres of good land by means of the gold they had acquired in California, thinking, apparently, that they had arrived at a place where they could settle down and spend the rest of their lives in peace.

When the call came for those saints to join the rest in the valley of the Great Salt Lake at least two of the brothers and the father said, 'No.' They remained in the Council Bluffs area on their fertile lands. Along with others they joined with the Reorganites, were honorable and respected citizens of their community, well-to-do farmers and stockmen, active in the local Masonic movement, and died outside the Church.

Others of the family accepted the call and moved West to the Salt Lake Valley. Not long after another call came for the saints to go to California with the Charles C. Rich company to acquire land from the Mexicans inhabiting certain regions of southern California. In that company were at least two Garner brothers, who had already been in that California region as members of the Mormon Battalion.

The land was acquired, and the Mormons were settled down when a call came to return to the Salt Lake because the United States Army was approaching the city from the East.

One Garner brother, John, said, 'No.' He remained in that California land, became a wealthy landowner and stock raiser, one of the first commissioners of what is now San Bernardino County, left the Church, became one of the most respected men in the Reorganite movement in southern California, active in the community as evidenced by the fact that the county history records that some of the most memorable Fourths of July ever held were held in 'Garner Grove--made complete by the firing of his canon,' and upon his death, Joseph Smith III, son of the Prophet, traveled to California and preached a memorial service, extolling the virtues of the man, John Garner. John is buried in San Bernardino County and incidentally, so is his mother who traveled from Council Bluffs, down the Mississippi River, through the Panama Canal, up to Los Angeles, thence to San Bernardino, all of this after her 96th year accompanied by her seventy-year-old son, George.

George left California and returned to Iowa by wagon on his 72nd birthday.

The Garners who returned to Salt Lake were subsequently

called, again, to leave and settle in the Idaho country where they were hardworking people, honored and respected in their community, relatively poor--but faithful to the Church. It is through that branch of the family that I descend.

Now, why all of this? Two points. First, through our missionary endeavors, the gospel message gathers 'all sort of fish.' Some remain faithful, some 'get off' somewhere along the way and leave, preferring other pathways. But the Parable of the Gospel Net is realized or fulfilled.

Secondly, and to me more important for today's message, is the concept that there seems to be in some people a greater affinity for the gospel message when they hear it.

President Stephen L. Richards said: 'I don't know that I understand it, but I have thought that the significance of the 'blood of Israel' is that there is in that great blood strain, because of the blessings and promises of the Lord, a susceptibility to the Holy Spirit that does not run in other strains...I believe that testimony is inheritable, and that the tendency to faith may descend from father to son.'

This seems to be true in my own Garner family. I think it would be true in other families through the history of the Church.

My own father passed away while I was still a young man serving in a faraway mission field, leaving me with not much other than a good family and his devotion to the Church.

My message comes down to something like this. As we do our work on Temple Square, we meet people from all over the world and from all walks of life. Sometimes rather fantastic experiences take place, but above and beyond that is our hope that with the first convert we touch, we may be triggering a whole nation eventually of faithful fellow members of the ever increasing Kingdom of God and helping to bring to pass the purpose of the Book of Mormon in bringing souls unto Christ.

Keith's ancestors' faith promoting stories pass on a priceless inheritance, the riches of testimony.

Like Keith, his ancestors were also land developers. Both discovered gold in northern California, his ancestors in 1847 and Keith in 1947. Both helped build prosperous communities, his ancestors in Nauvoo, Illinois, and Keith in Menlo Park, California. They both referred to these respective cities as the Garden of Eden. They

Father: Frederick Garner, Mother: Ann Horrocks Garner, Children: Ann Elizabeth Garner, Frederick William Garner, James Nathan Garner, Alice Mozelle Garner, Horace Eugene Garner, Burk Leroy Garner, Benjamin Franklin Garner, Alpha Garner

both responded to Church governance, his ancestors following Brigham Young on the trek West, and Keith accepting a call from the First Presidency to preside over Temple Square. They both ended up in Utah, his ancestors in Ogden, and Keith in Salt Lake City. They both brought skills which enhanced their new homes, his ancestors farming and brass bands, and Keith stucco and red tile roofs. Nonetheless, they both left their beloved communities with heavy hearts.

While casually thumbing through a special 2002 edition of *Forbes Magazine* touting the 400 richest people in America, Keith rested his eyes on pictures of several men who were reported to be worth a billion dollars. For a moment he remembered his association with them and his 1965 call to the Southern Far East Mission and his 1974 call to Temple Square which surely interrupted his own accumulation of excessive wealth.

That same week an old friend, a Palo Alto broker, sent him a real estate mailer listing under the category Local Real Estate Update, "the top selling home in Menlo Park, Bay Laurel Drive at $4,500,000." He had written on it, "How bad it is! Garners old home. Thought you would be interested in seeing this." "Unbelievable," Keith exclaimed. "I bought that lot for $5000 and built the house with a couple of carpenters."

President Garner's short-lived reaction to the pile of money he had left on the table to accept Church callings requiring him to move thousands of miles away was overcome by his far more moving remembrance of holding gold plates in Tehran and his understanding of what those gold plates represented to him. Yes, acceptance of calls may or may not have lessened his bank account, but he is quick to affirm that the riches he gained from being "actively engaged" in the Lord's service are immeasurable.

His Temple Square call extended in an October 18, 1974, letter addressed to Elder Keith E. Garner, 1330 University Drive, Menlo Park, California 94025 from The First Presidency, Spencer W. Kimball, N. Eldon Tanner, and Marion G. Romney, reads:

> Dear Brother Garner:
>
> This letter will confirm your recent telephone conversations with President Marion D. Romney.
>
> We hereby extend to you a formal call to serve as the Director of the Visitors' Center on Temple Square in Salt Lake City, replacing Brother T. C. Jacobsen. This call will become effective when you are able to take over the duties from Brother Jacobsen and will extend for an indefinite period of time.
>
> Since this call will occupy all of your Church-service time, we are concurrently extending to you an honorable release as a Regional Representative of the Twelve which is enclosed.
>
> As the Director, you will be responsible for supervising all of the activities of the Visitors' Center, including the periodic tours conducted each day, the exhibits, and the films shown in the theaters located in the Center. We expect that you will want to have one or two associate directors to assist you. After you have had time to become acquainted with your duties and to give consideration to those whom you would like to have assist you, we shall appreciate your recommendations about an associate director or directors.
>
> As soon as it is convenient, we suggest that you contact Elders Mark E. Petersen and Gordon B. Hinckley, who are the advisors to the Public Communications Department of the Church, who will brief you about the details of your duties and about the relationship of the Visitors' Center to both the Department of Public Communications and the Missionary Executive Committee. In this respect, Elder Hinckley also serves as a member of the Missionary Executive Committee.

As you undertake these new and important duties, we
assume that you will bear in mind that the Visitors' Center
provides one of the finest missionary opportunities available in
the Church. We hope that in the discharge of your duties this
thought will be uppermost in your mind, and that you will
prayerfully consider effective and appropriate ways in which
the principles of the Gospel can best be taught to the thousands of nonmembers who come to Temple Square each year.

With this call, we extend our love and best wishes and a
prayer for your success.

Keith received a general, though not specific, heads up just as he had before
his call to be a Regional Representative. In Salt Lake City for General Conference, he
had dined at the Hinckleys. In the course of the conversation, Keith records, "Elder
Hinckley told me they had a special calling for me and asked when we would be moving to SLC." After President Romney's call the next Friday, Keith journaled, "Eight-
thirty a.m. President Marion Romney called me to take three year President of
Temple Square Mission. I called Elder Hinckley. Marilynn and I talked to him and
Marjorie. That was the call he was referring to on Sunday night. I called Elder
Hanks. He said it was great."

Immediately after the call had been extended, Elder Hinckley sent a hand-
written note attached to the "Accumulative Report of Visitors' Centers" for January 1,
1974, through August 1974, directing Keith to page two on which he'd circled the statistic showing in excess of one million non-member visitors to Temple Square. The
number seems to verify Elder Hinckley's missive, "Keith, you may wish to look at this
report. It emphasizes the magnitude of the missionary opportunity on Temple Square
– the greatest in the world."

In 1974, regardless of the advantages or disadvantages of remaining in northern California, Keith accepted Brigham Young's "This is the place" declaration as now
applicable to him. Even though his Utah friends were officed across the street from
Temple Square at the Church Administration Building, and he himself had generated a
significant reputation through his service in Hawaii, the Southern Far East, and northern California, he was largely unknown in his new surroundings; therefore, taking his
place in Salt Lake City came with daunting but expected challenges.

During his days as president of the Southern Far East Mission, President
Garner had a stamp imprinted with the initials B M T, standing for "Before My Time."
When missionaries sent their new mission president transmittals for his authorizing
signature fashioned after the instructions of the previous mission president or asserted
that Keith's instructions were not in compliance with the way it was done by the previous president, he would use this hand stamp or its equivalent oral stamp. At Temple
Square after President Jacobsen's long tenure, Keith found the same naturally arising

Keith E. Garner, left newly-called director of Temple Square, chats about duties with
T.C. Jacobsen, released.

tendency in some personnel and volunteers who clung tightly to the way it had been done in the past. By some he was viewed as an interloper; after all, why had the Brethren mined the Church in California to find a new director of Temple Square when they had many desirable local choices among the volunteer guides who led weekly Temple Square tours and who were prominent citizens and fully credentialed churchmen? Keith wondered himself!

In the *Church News*, week ending December 7, 1974, announcing his release and President Garner's call, Brother Jacobsen is quoted as saying, "I feel this has been the greatest period of my life." The article goes on to say, "On his plans Brother Garner said it is too early to define 'what my plans for Temple Square are.' But, he said, he is there to see that the wishes of 'the Brethren and the committee are carried out.'"

He added, "From what I can see everything is in excellent condition, from the physical properties and grounds to the quality of the guides and hosts in the center."

These stated opinions were based on information he gathered first-hand. After his call, but prior to his assuming his duties, he moved to Salt Lake City, initially staying at Little America Hotel. This arrangement for a couple of months allowed him to supervise the building of his family's new home in Ensign Downs. It also gave him the opportunity to visit Temple Square unidentified and unannounced. He made these visits quite often.

Keith viewed laudatorily what must have seemed to him like the "Fraternal Order of Temple Square Guides." As he assumed his responsibilities and became better acquainted with these two hundred and sixty men, he found them to be quality men of substance, prominence, and position. They felt deeply, and rightly so, the honor of serving in such a rich, vital calling.

The guides were joined by equally credentialed Church employees, Kay Garff, Diane Dunford, and Geraldine Clark who worked as supervisors on Temple Square. Among other Church assignments Sister Garff had served on the general board of the Relief Society, Sister Dunford sang in the Tabernacle Choir, and Sister Clark and her husband had presided over the South African Mission.

A few lucky young men and women also were permitted to work beside these great men and women and to breathe the rarified air of Temple Square daily. Summers, made vibrant by the increased tourist traffic, meant information clerk positions were opened to LDS college students seeking summer jobs. Where could a young Latter-day Saint committed to fulfilling President McKay's "every member a missionary" find a position where the job description read: serve graciously, dress in a modest, attractive fashion, school yourself in the principles of the gospel so you are able to answer investigators' questions accurately, cheerfully assist guides and hosts, send thank-you notes [the script of the movie *Man's Search for Happiness*] to registered guests, spend your working hours sharing the gospel of Jesus Christ? It sounded like a posting for full-time missionaries; yet undoubtedly, missionaries never had it this good! No tracting necessary; investigators actually stood in line waiting to speak to an information clerk. Inquiring guests included Norman Vincent Peale, the DuPonts, visiting ambassadors to the United States, and other recognizable dignitaries. Each day Mormon Who's Who designates, General Authorities accompanying their guests; Tabernacle organists, Alexander Schreiner, Robert Cundick, Roy M. Darley, and newcomer John Longhurst, who played daily half hour noon organ recitals; Tabernacle Choir director Gerald Ottley; and stake presidents and ward bishops i.e. President Andrew Renfrew of the Belfast Ireland Stake, visiting from around the world for General Conference, and others walked among the tourists to their posts.

If people thought being hired to work on Temple Square was the best job available in either Church or secular employment, they were absolutely right, and they were unaware of many of the benefits of employment: the Snelgrove ice cream sandwiches available in the lunchroom, the marathon thank-you-note-typing sessions, the late night summer canyon parties after the Square closed at ten-thirty p.m., the Christmas firesides in the visitors' center theater, the underground tunnels leading to the Tabernacle, the shared letters written from people whose lives had been changed because they spent a few hours on Temple Square, and the forever friendships forged on this ten acre plot of ground. In addition to all these privileges and fun, and unlike full-time missionaries, the supervisors and information clerks collected a regular pay-check, which after President Garner's suggestion, contained a few more dollars than it had previously.

Not only this happily invested group greeted President Garner, but also the specters of glorious traditions past. In the program for "Devotional Services Honoring Former Temple Square Directors" at the Assembly Hall, November 14, 1984, President Garner's name is preceded by Richard L. Evans, Marion D. Hanks, Russell C. Harris, and Theodore C. (Ted) Jacobsen. On Temple Square B. M. T. had almost a reverenced meaning. Even the name Temple Square touched emotions felt about the very beginnings of honored pioneer heritage and industry. Stepping into revered shoes in these renowned surroundings, President Garner initiated historic firsts, building on the past and foreshadowing the future and leaving at his departure his own very large shoes to fill.

From the moment he set foot on Temple Square, President Garner took off running. As he reconnoitered the Square for the first time as its president, finding it as he had described to the *Church News* reporter, President Garner may have stopped at the "Old Log Cabin" which was built in September of 1847 by Osmyn M. and William H. Deuel, sold to Albert Carrington in 1849, used as an office by Captain Howard Stansbury of the Topographical Engineers of the U.S. Army while surveying the Great Salt Lake during the winter of 1849-50, and, unbeknownst to any histori-ans, designated by Elder Garner in 1939-42 as the secure depository for the Book of Mormon gold plates. Of course, since Keith's designation was completely fictional, the Deuels, Mr. Carrington, and Captain Stansbury made no mention of the cabin ever being used for this lofty purpose, but had they known, they may have enjoyed Keith's fanciful selection of their "Old Log Cabin" as his setting for gold deposits.

Perhaps he whimsically walked over to the log cabin, smiling at the memory and wondering if he might happen upon one of the many individuals to whom years before in Hawaii he had told the Joseph Smith story embellished with gold plates locked in a vault in this log cabin. The details of how he would have reacted to such a visitor is unknown, but among his many friends and acquaintances from his years as a missionary in Hawaii who did greet him, the unexpected visit to Temple Square by an unselfish couple who had years before given to Elder Garner and his companion their house key, President Garner met with joyful surprise.

In Salt Lake City, President Garner met many generous gospel workers. Two of these he immediately put to good use. Gerald G. Smith and Clyde J. Summerhays were named in the *Church News*, week ending February 8, 1975, as Temple Square

Temple Square presidency; l to r: Gerald G. Smith, Keith E. Garner, Clyde J. Summerhays

counselors. Like President Garner, both men had served as mission presidents; Brother Smith in the Eastern States Mission and Brother Summerhays in the Ireland Belfast Mission. Like President Garner both were successful in their careers; Brother Smith as an executive with Zions Cooperative Mercantile Institution [ZCMI] and Brother Summerhays as an executive with Beneficial Life Insurance Company. Like President Garner married to Marilynn Ressel and the father of four children, they both were family men. Brother Smith who was married to Olive Lunt was the father of three children, and Brother Summerhays, married to Sarah Dixon, was the father of five children.

President Garner quickly gave each one of these men assignments where they were free to magnify their callings and draw on their own experiences and strengths. He describes Brother Smith as a very capable administrator and Brother Summerhays as quiet, humble, and always responsive. In the weekly presidency meeting, they would report and counsel together.

In addition, as the number of visitors grew necessitating more frequent tours, President Garner asked Dr. Burtis R. Evans, a prominent internist and the doctor for the University of Utah athletic teams, to assist in interviewing tour guides.

With such able men available, he relished the possibilities. Even the Utah weather seemed milder than anticipated. Having left California again and having survived the dreary months of January and February in Utah, he looked out his visitors' center office window and viewed the early signs of the spring of 1975. He even thought this beautiful array of blossoms deserved the title he had reserved for Menlo Park, the Garden of Eden.

When the Salt Lake Temple was dedicated, President Wilford Woodruff petitioned the Lord "to bless and sanctify the whole of this block…with the surrounding walls, the walks, paths, and ornamental beds, also the trees, plants, flowers, and shrubbery that grow in its soil; may they bloom and blossom and become exceedingly beautiful and fragrant;" he further asked that the Lord's "spirit dwell in the midst thereof, that this plot of ground may be a place of rest and peace, for holy meditation and inspired thought."

President Woodruff's dedicatory supplication to the Lord seemed fulfilled in the gardens of Temple Square. Peter Lassig, the Church gardener, and Irvin Nelson who served in this capacity before him, made sure this was the case. Brother Lassig has an artist's perfect love of nature in all its spontaneity and a worker's embrace of the Lord's admonition "By the sweat of thy brow…" He will tell you, while acknowledging the Lord's hand, that it is the "sweat of many brows" which produces the landscaping that never fails to dazzle the world.

In a November 26, 1976, letter to President Garner, Peter expresses his poignant thoughts about Temple Square.

> Bro. Garner:
> You asked me for some of my feelings about Temple Square. My most profound impressions of Temple Square are of its sanctity. These grounds are made holy by diligent workers, doing their duty, by sacred buildings fulfilling the measure of their intent, and by water, sustaining the life of the gardens.
> In my twenty years of service here, I have met many sincerely dedicated workers, some dominant, some humble; most who if put to it would say, 'Better to be a door keeper in my Father's house than to….' These kind of selfless workers have sanctified Temple Square with their toil.
> The edifices that grace these gardens speak for themselves.
> It may come as a surprise that I list water as a third sanctifying entity for these grounds. But Mother Nature has never let me forget how transitory would be these gardens were it not for the water we depend on. In spring, early watering carries fertilizer in solution to plants that are rousing, hastening their good looks in time for April Conference when most of the gardens of the Wasatch Front still look dormant. In summer continual watering assures a lush oasis here when Ensign Peak only a mile away stands tinder dry, a parched example of

how things would be but for water. And in fall we depend on water to sustain our newly planted pansies, 55,000 of them, so that they might weather the winter and be in good condition for next Spring's Show.

Next, my heart is with the trees of Temple Square. On the outside southeast corner of Temple Square next to the Old Folks monument stands an aged Ailanthus Altissima. The Chinese called it the tree of heaven. Some unknown pioneer planted it there when Salt Lake streets were dirt. He must have been inspired to put it there for when they paved the street, built the wall, and cemented the sidewalks, by rights the tree should have died for they cut off all possibility of watering it. Any other tree would have died, but the Ailanthus Altissima is one of the few trees in the world that can survive happily growing in asphalt or concrete. In my twenty years here, we have never watered it, but the tree remains, as always, lush and green. I wonder if the pioneer who planted it chose it for its position there, knowing that it would be neglected.

Along the same sidewalk on the outside south side of Temple Square are some old ash trees in a narrow strip of grass between the curb and the sidewalk. The ash is the only large street tree I know of after a bachelor's degree and three years of graduate study that will grow in so narrow a planting space without lifting the sidewalk. What wise pioneer plantsman chose these trees?

A line of beautiful London plane trees grow on the west side of Temple Square where the width of the parking is a generous seventeen plus feet. The London plane is one of the world's longest lived trees. It is disease resistant, pollution resistant and will tolerate most soils. You can't even carve a lasting imprint in it because the bark is "liquid." It flows over every blemish, seals it, the new bark forms beneath the blemish, and as it expands, casts off the old bark with the blemish leaving not a trace. It was under a London plane that the first Hippocratic oath was administered. That tree survived ancient Greek times till the nineteenth century. At the time of its death, its girth was equal to the circumference of a small Greek house. The pioneer who planted these trees must have wanted to plant a tree that would last through the millennium.

Within the Square too are some important trees. Near

the Relief Society campanile are, appropriately, two white weeping birch symbolizing grace and purity, two "expected" virtues of Mormon womanhood. An old blue spruce stands guard at the Seagull monument. The hand cart monument is flanked with Utah natives, the Rocky Mountain Douglas fir, quaking aspen, Utah juniper, and native shrubs, Yucca, Manzineta, Dogwood and of course, sage brush.

The main walk between the north and south gates is probably my favorite. This promenade is lined with magnificent elms, two kinds, English and American. These trees were among the first planted in this valley. I imagine that English converts wanted to place their mark on the Utah Deseret with the English elm. They are beautiful! Somehow the decision for English elm was tempered with a little American nationalism because two of the group are American elms.

It is easy to take the trees on Temple Square for granted. They've always been here, haven't they? But every time I break in a new gardener and see him through the usual quota of first year mistakes and skip a watering or two, and I see one or two of the elms show their displeasure with a telltale early leaf drop, I am humbled and reminded that were it not for diligent, trustworthy men and life giving water, only the buildings here would remain and the spirit of this holy place would be just a memory.

Horticulturally,
Peter Lassig

Peter also had definite impressions of President Garner as president of Temple Square. He thought Keith personified his own definition of a spiritual leader, "One who gets things done NOW." In a well-remembered incident, President Garner, at the Tabernacle baptistery accompanied by Dr. Evans, reacted with shock at finding old, dusty plastic flowers still in the planter boxes inside the door. He had already lodged his dissatisfaction. Who was responsible for this substandard display is not known; certainly not Peter. Keith immediately displaced the fake flowers, throwing them in the trash. Alarmed by the incident, an uninformed witness called security. After Church security discovered the identity of the vandal, Keith Garner, president of Temple Square, Peter was notified. Peter commended President Garner's quick solution and replaced the eyesore with beautiful beds in keeping with the rest of the magnificence of the Square.

In a luncheon tribute to President Garner decades later, Peter good-humoredly described his job when they worked together on Temple Square as "To never let any grass grow under Keith's feet." He also said it was an easy task since he found Keith never relaxed long enough for such a happening to take place.

It would be interesting to know how Peter with his training and Keith with his innovative handling of problems might have dealt with the situation the pioneers faced as told by the guides in front of the Seagull Monument. Histories recount that President Brigham Young led the main pioneer company from Nauvoo, Illinois, into the Salt Lake Valley on July 24, 1847. By the next spring, 5,000 acres were plowed, planted, and sown. In late May-early June, hordes of Rocky Mountain crickets infested the valley. Their crops in peril, the pioneers with every method possible worked to eradicate this menace but met with little success. Turning to a loving and concerned Heavenly Father, they prayed for help. In answer to these supplications, flocks of seagulls flew into the valley and gorged themselves on crickets for a period of three weeks, saving enough crops for the pioneers to endure the winter. The Seagull Monument was "erected in grateful remembrance of the mercy of God to the Mormon pioneers." Schooled in hard work which had been incorporated into their life patterns, Peter and Keith, no doubt, would have acted in the same way their ancestors had with faith that God lives and that He hears and answers prayers as the catalyst for their actions.

Joe Osmond, the building engineer for Temple Square, exhibited the same much appreciated qualities of service and skill as Peter Lassig. In a thankfully unique incident one Sunday night, an embittered young man threw a stone into the Visitors' Center North, breaking one of the large windows and damaging a priceless sculpture. The sculpture was a copy of the original done by the Danish sculptor Thorvaldsen in the 1800s. The *Christus* stands in the visitors' center rotunda surrounded by walls depicting the heavens.

When he heard of this incident, Joe called President Garner to see what was to be done about it. Keith told him that since this copy had been done in Florence and was made of Italian white marble, that it had been suggested that the talents of an Italian expert be employed to repair the chip. Joe said to President Garner, "Well, before you do anything, let me give it a try." Knowing the magnitude of the job, Keith with some reluctance told Joe to go ahead. Joe crushed the fragments of white marble that had been recovered into a powder. Because the visitors' center was open from seven a.m. to ten-thirty p.m., he, under the cover of darkness with only a flashlight held by President Garner, used his mix to plaster over the chip. President Garner, pleased with the job, told Joe, "It is impossible to spot." This statement holds true for everyone with the possible exception of a small number who actually viewed the damage done, and even they have to look very closely to find a blemish.

As part of a radio broadcast, Diane Dunford related this little known story in order to illustrate selfless service. "Joe Osmond's caring for the building and for people just carried over into doing anything he could to help," she lovingly stated.

This well-taken-care-of building and other buildings on Temple Square presented Keith with more intriguing possibilities than the Log Cabin for fanciful housing of gold plates. Neither he nor Temple Square tour guides could substantiate the existence of gold plates by producing them, but they could point to the majestic Salt Lake Temple and Tabernacle to evidence the devotion and faith of the Mormon pioneers and their testimonies of the Book of Mormon. Keith read the brief histories of these buildings available at the visitors' center, and like the visitors to the Square, marveled at the innovation and the attention to detail.

Driving down Main Street from his home near Capitol Hill to Temple Square, he could not miss seeing atop the east central spire of the Salt Lake Temple the gold-leafed, hammered copper statue of the angel Moroni, the embodiment of the prophecy that an angel would bring the restored gospel to the earth in this latter-day dispensation. President Garner marveled at the patience and persistence of the pioneers in building the Salt Lake Temple as he thought of the forty year construction time-frame, 1853-1893, and the twenty mile trip to Little Cottonwood Canyon granite quarry using three to four yoke of oxen requiring about four days to make a round trip to procure one block of foundation stone.

Often as he walked the promenade from the south to the north gate on his way to his office, he would hear the Tabernacle Choir recording of "Come, Come Ye Saints" wafting from within the Tabernacle. President Garner mingled on a few occasions with the guests being led inside through the large double doors. The elliptical shaped Tabernacle, built between 1863-1867, fascinated him. Indeed, the massive roof, supported only by great wooden arches spanning the width of the building is a remarkable nineteenth century engineering feat, a modification of "Remington lattice-truss." The roof rests like a great inverted bowl on forty-four pillars of cut sandstone masonry. The interior pillars are expertly painted to appear as marble.

Keith, in his element since Temple Square is a gold mine of various architectural designs and superior craftsmanship, satisfied his innate curiosity and climbed into the Tabernacle dome and viewed the wooden pegs, pins and rawhide wrappings, and the amazingly few bolts used by the pioneers to hold the roof together. Having acquired from necessity a cursory knowledge of organ construction in connection with the Menlo Park Chapel, he found the Tabernacle organ, equally as famous as the building, a masterpiece. The story is told that Brigham Young asked Joseph Ridges, an expert organ builder who had joined the Church in Australia, to construct an instrument that would be a fitting complement to the Tabernacle. Considerable difficulty was experienced in finding suitable timber, but finally a tall, straight-grained pine was found some 300 miles south, hauled to the valley by ox team, and laboriously shaped by skilled artisans. The organ had by 1975 been renovated and enlarged several times. As rebuilt in 1948, there were eight divisions in the organ, comprising almost 11,000 pipes and 189 ranks.

President Garner would have heartily agreed with President Young when he said in 1867, at the time when both the Tabernacle and its organ were nearing completion, "We cannot preach the gospel unless we have good music. I am waiting patiently for the organ to be finished; then we can sing the gospel into the hearts of the people."

Seated among the tourists, Keith would have witnessed one of the drawing cards that had undoubtedly brought many of the curious visitors to the Tabernacle. A Temple Square employee dropped a pin at the front of the 6,500 seat auditorium which could be heard by tour groups seated on the back benches. This much talked about demonstration confirmed the building's magnificent acoustical qualities. However, the more stirring confirmation in Keith's mind came at the noon organ recitals, which had been inaugurated in 1900 at the request of the First Presidency, and the Thursday night choir rehearsals and Sunday morning broadcasts when the approximately 325 voice Mormon Tabernacle choir, which had its beginnings in the Bowery in 1847, sang filling every nook of the famous building with harmonious anthems of praise.

The Mormon initiative embodied in brick and mortar sprang from the doctrines of salvation. For most of President Garner's tenure, January 1, 1975, to December 31, 1978, with the Bureau of Information no longer standing, travelers requesting tours were directed into the Assembly Hall, a semi-Gothic structure made of the granite remaining from the construction of the Temple. Here after visitors were greeted warmly, they were invited to watch a slide presentation prepared under President Garner's supervision informing them of other points of historic interest also built from faith and testimony. A few lines of this presentation follow.

> *Since Salt Lake City is the world headquarters of the Church, the new twenty-eight story Church Office Building serves the 3.5 million members worldwide. This building consolidated the many departments of the Church which prior to then were housed in buildings in downtown Salt Lake. Emphasizing particular aspects of the gospel, tours take you to the genealogical, historical, missionary, and translation departments. The genealogical library is the largest of its kind in the world. Birth, death, and marriage records, family group sheets, and much more information is located there. The historical department functions under Joseph Smith's admonition to the saints when the Church was organized in 1830 to be a record keeping people as the Lord's people have always been. The missionary department supervises the more than one hundred missions of the Church wherein over 24,000 full-time missionaries serve for two years at their own expense. The translation department provides full Church programs in sixteen languages and portions of the Church materials in twenty-eight other languages. The beautiful mural on the ground level entitled "Go ye therefore, and teach*

all nations" depicting the Savior commissioning His Apostles to preach
the gospel in all the world summarizes one of the major purposes of the
work which goes on in the Church Office Building.

Incidentally, as one of his unique opportunities, President Garner worked with Tom Daniels of the genealogy department in organizing a conference where Alex Haley, the author of Roots, was the keynote speaker.

The slide presentation continues:

On the corner of Main and North Temple stands the Relief Society
Building. Relief Society is the woman's organization of the Church.
The woman holds an honored position in the LDS family. One of the
current projects of this organization is the erecting of a park to women
in Nauvoo, Illinois. This series of monuments commemorates the organ-
ization of the Relief Society under Joseph Smith in 1842, depicts a
woman's many roles, and the circle of a woman's influence.

The Lion House and the Beehive House at the corner of South Temple
and State Street were the official residences of Brigham Young while he
was the President of the Church and Governor of the Territory of
Deseret. The Lion House was named after the epithet "Lion of the
Lord" given by his people to their beloved leader.

The Beehive House completed in 1854 just seven years after the
pioneers came to the valley stands as a monument to the culture and
the home life of the Mormon pioneers. Brigham Young, anticipating
the now formally organized Family Home Evening program of the
Church, each evening rang a prayer bell and the children gathered for
their family hour of visiting, singing, and praying with their father.

At the mouth of Emigration Canyon stands This Is The Place
Monument and the recently relocated Brigham Young Farm Home.
It was at this spot that Brigham Young announced to the saints he had
led from Nauvoo that this would be their home. As they looked over
this valley it is reported that a person could count on one hand the
number of trees growing here. Jim Bridger believing it an impossibility
told Brigham Young that he would give him $1000 for the first bushel
of grain grown in the Salt Lake Valley. Later in response to the
murmurings of some of the saints Brigham Young said, "We have been
kicked out of the frying pan into the fire, and out of the fire into the
middle of the floor, and here we are and here we will stay. God has

*shown me that this is the spot to locate his people, and here is where
they will prosper; he will temper the elements for the good of
his Saints; he will rebuke the frost and sterility of the soil and the land
shall become fruitful." The fulfillment of Brigham Young's prophetic
statement that the valley would blossom as the rose
can be viewed today from this monument.*

*Forty miles south of Salt Lake is located Church-owned and
operated Brigham Young University. One of the basic precepts of the
gospel is that "the glory of God is Intelligence or light and truth." Karl
G. Maeser, then president of the University, was cautioned by Brigham
Young that "neither the alphabet nor the multiplication
tables were to be taught without the Spirit of God."*

Ending this presentation, the tour host or hostess would declare, "The gospel of Jesus Christ is a full-time seven-days-a-week philosophy of life. It ennobles, uplifts, provides direction and answers in every aspect of life, and brings happiness and peace to faithful adherents. Brigham Young prophesied in 1849 from these grounds that the great and wise and noble of the earth would visit. Your very presence along with over two million other people who visit Temple Square yearly is literal fulfillment of his words."

Touring Temple Square in the late seventies, few visitors or for that matter Church members imagined the growth the Church would experience over the next twenty-five years. If a similar presentation were given today, the correct statistics would be raised from 3.5 million members to 11.6 million; sixteen operating temples to 114; 24,000 full-time missionaries to 60,850 serving in 335 missions; and the Book of Mormon available in sixty-eight different languages rather than sixteen.

Of course, the basic beliefs presented on Temple Square remain unchanged, but President Garner changed the presentation of those truths into simple scriptural statements of testimony. He instructed tour guides that they were missionaries and as such they should be prayerfully prepared to accompany their guests. In his enthusiasm for the work, President Garner repeatedly cautioned all workers on Temple Square to be "bold but not overbearing."

He established a fruitful referral system which involved a direct, straight forward approach by the tour host whereby the visitor who signed the Temple Square referral card understood that by so doing there was a possibility that two Mormon missionaries would call on him to make an appointment.

He reminded these committed volunteer hosts that a testimony put into words was the most important gift they could give a visitor to Temple Square.

Remembering the great sister missionaries he had valued so highly in the Southern Far East Mission, he invited women to participate in the Temple Square experience, including as tour guides, an assignment previously filled only by Priesthood holders. Marcia Smith Merrill recalls President Garner as her mission president encouraging the sisters in matters of personal hygiene including hair coloring, which may have been classified by others as excessive. She heard President Garner as president of Temple Square create a similar atmosphere and repeat to Temple Square guides what he had told sister missionaries years before, "You are working for the Lord; you have got to look good!"

President Garner participated in opening Temple Square for stake nights. Just like the person who lives within a mile of Disneyland yet never goes unless accompanied by an out-of-town guest, every Mormon feels a rapport with Temple Square but rarely visits unless he is taking a guest along. Stake leaders were encouraged to incorporate the obvious, a visit to Temple Square, into their missionary programs. During the months when Temple Square tourists came less frequently, members of neighboring stakes were invited on particular nights to accompany their non-member friends and less active members to enjoy the physical and spiritual beauties of the square.

Along with all of these firsts for President Garner came a last, the final visit to Temple Square of newly called missionaries. Elder Carlos E. Asay, executive director of the missionary department, wrote to President Garner with the news.

> On June 8, 1978, the First Presidency and the Quorum of the Twelve approved the closing of the Salt Lake Missionary Home, the amalgamation of training at Provo, and the change of the name of the Language Training Mission to the Missionary Training Center... The last date that missionaries from the Salt Lake Missionary Home will tour the Visitors' Center will be Sunday, October 15, 1978.
>
> We are so grateful, Brother Garner, for your excellent support and cooperation in providing the missionaries with such a choice experience and such an important contribution to their missionary training and preparation. Would you please express our personal appreciation to the members of your staff.
>
> May the Lord continue to bless and sustain you in your great work.

This truly was the end of an era and the beginning of another. J. Martell Bird, president of the Salt Lake Missionary Home, expressed his feelings to President Garner in a letter dated October 16, 1978.

> It is with heartfelt appreciation that I express to you my sincere thanks for the many blessings realized by the newly

called missionaries who have passed through the Visitors' Center these past three and one half years. They have certainly enjoyed the experience and especially the love and courtesies extended by your entire staff.

Sister Bird, my counsellors, and I, have been abundantly blessed as we have been privileged to bring some thirty-four thousand new missionaries to the Visitors' Center. We owe to you, your counsellors and your entire staff a debt of gratitude for the many personal inconveniences which have been necessitated because of our very early attendance at the Visitors' Center each Sunday morning. You and your associates have always made us feel so welcome, and we have enjoyed the cheerful, friendly, and gracious treatment which has always been extended to us.

Yesterday, Sunday October 15, 1978 brings to a close an era in the missionary preparation. The nearly three hundred missionaries who were blessed in the Visitors' Center yesterday is the last group to come to the Missionary Home, and that of course means it is the last group to come to the Visitors' Center. It is with much personal sadness that I realize that hereafter the missionaries will miss that great blessing; however, I realize that progress must take place and that there will be compensating features under the new program in Provo.

President Johnson, President Osborn, Sister Bird, and I want you to know of our personal love and appreciation for you, your counsellors, and your entire staff at the Visitors' Center. We sustain you in your great calling and shall always pray for your continued success, happiness, and welfare."

Ironically, though visits to Temple Square by full-time missionaries before leaving for world-wide mission fields had been discontinued, in only a few years full-time missionaries would be called to serve on Temple Square.

The need for such a change became more and more obvious. The number of visitors to Temple Square increased substantially from an already numerous 1.5 million when President Garner arrived, and among these were welcomed international travelers speaking numerous languages. As an immediate but temporary solution to this problem, Latter-day Saints working across the street in the Church Office Building or downtown Salt Lake City who possessed various language skills were summoned and appeared within minutes when non-English speaking groups presented themselves. The increase in these tourists meant linguistically proficient men and women were called more and more frequently with shorter notice, taking them away from their regular employment. In order to more expeditiously resolve this wonderful inconvenience, President Garner supplemented the information clerks hired each summer with young men and women, returned missionaries, who spoke Spanish, French, German, or Japanese. He even proposed reassigning to Temple Square for the last three months of their missions a small number of assistants to the president assigned to countries requiring these language skills. A select number of full-time missionaries from the Salt Lake Mission did serve on Temple Square prior to President Garner's release. Keith always seemed to be a few years ahead of everybody else, and that was the case in this instance. Visiting Temple Square a few years later, President Garner would find Temple Square staffed by full-time lady missionaries, whose home towns dotted the globe.

The globe seemed to be getting smaller. Returning in 2002 while visiting with a sister missionary assigned to Temple Square, President Garner discovered that the sister's companion was from Vietnam. Keith had talked extensively on previous occasions about how the Lord uses even the worst of circumstances, war, to open doors for the presentation of the gospel. Here standing in front of him was the product of a war he knew well. In his interesting take on World War II, Keith concluded that we won the war because we were less confused than the enemy; that condition made possible because we had less bureaucracy. He observes about both World War II and Vietnam, "Hitler took away power from his generals; presidents ran the war in Vietnam rather than the generals." Echoing Elder Widtsoe, Keith's proximity to war caused him to utter, "War opens up countries for the preaching of the gospel." Perhaps the missionary effort of Latter-day Saints stationed around the world incident to WWII, Korea, and Vietnam qualifies as the "sleeping giant" the Japanese and later the Chinese Communists awakened.

This same missionary spirit to which he was referring, and which had defined Keith since his youth, revealed itself again as he formatted the tour of the North Visitors' Center into simple statements of basic beliefs. He had had some experience with this before. In August 1966, always open to new ideas and trying new ways, he had heard about the opening to tourists of a new visitors' center on Temple Square; in fact, it was the very one in which he now had his office. The 2003 *Church Almanac* reads, "While this would be the most elaborate center, it represented a trend of building visitors' centers at historic sites and temples and at various other locations during the 1960s and 1970s."

Mission President Garner copied the visitors' center concept, okaying a store front below the second floor chapel in Chu Wan to be decorated with pictures illustrating Mormon beliefs, inviting passers-by to enter for more exposure and announcing open houses at particular times. A temporary visitors' center was created at Kam Tong Hall offering film presentations. Keith did not stop there. He tapped into President Young's feeling that the gospel could be sung into the hearts of inquiring, in this case, Chinese by utilizing the talents of elders like E. Winston Elton to organize choirs, perhaps not as great in number as the Tabernacle Choir, but made up of individuals who were just as talented and devoted.

Undeniably, President Garner had the crown jewel of Church visitors' center exhibits with which to work, but the truths presented played just as well on the old "Fulness of Times" records he carried in Hawaii as they did when illustrated by the paintings of artists Harry Anderson, Sidney King, John Scott, or by the statues of sculptors Torliof Knaphus, Mahonri Young, Avard Fairbanks, Dennis Smith, and Cyrus Dallin.

Along with these available artistic vehicles, President Garner's use of pithy, profound declarations of doctrine caught the eye and heart of many visitors who took the hour necessary to hear them enunciated. Beginning the tour at the Visitors' Center North, groups standing in front of the Adam and Eve statue were introduced to the following points.

1. "So God created man in his own image, in the image of God created he him; male and female created he them."[49]

2. Adam and Eve were our first parents and were created in the image and likeness of God.

3. Christ is in the express image of the Father. [50]

4. We are created in the image of God and are literally his spirit children.

Visitors looking down the row of Old Testament paintings of Noah, Abraham, Jacob, Moses, Aaron, Samuel, and Isaiah, were told the following facts.

1. God loves His children.

2. God reveals His will to His children through living prophets. "Surely the Lord God will do nothing, but he revealeth his secret unto his servants the prophets."[51]; "…God hath spoken by the mouth of all his holy prophets since the world began." [52]

3. Adam through Isaiah communicated the Father's will to his children and bore witness of the reality of the Father and the Son.

4. Our message is the same as the prophets of old depicted in these paintings. WE ARE THE LITERAL SPIRIT SONS AND DAUGHTERS OF A LOVING FATHER IN HEAVEN WHO REVEALS HIS GOSPEL TO US TODAY AS HE DID ANCIENTLY THROUGH A LIVING PROPHET.

---

[49] Genesis 1:27

[50] Hebrews 1;1-5

[51] Amos 3:7

[52] Acts 3:20-21

In the Rotunda with the group looking up at the *Christus*, the tour host explained.

1. Jesus Christ, under the direction of God, the Father, created this world and all things that are in it. [53]

2. We accept Him without question as the Only Begotten of the Father in the flesh, that He lived a sinless life, that He was the atoning sacrifice, that He rose from the dead, that He rules and reigns in the heavens.

3. He is the central being in our belief.

4. He stands at the head of His church today and directs its affairs through a living prophet.

Moving along the corridor, consideration was given to the successive oil paintings depicting events in the Savior's life as recorded in the New Testament.

1. "The Boy Jesus in the Temple"

Jesus realized at an early age who he was and the mission he was here to perform. "…wist ye not that I must be about my Father's business?" [54]

2. "Jesus Baptized"

John the Baptist was the forerunner of the Savior. Jesus said of him, "This is he, of whom it is written, Behold, I send my messenger before thy face, which shall prepare thy way before thee. For I say unto you, Among those that are born of women there is not a greater prophet than John the Baptist…" [55]

John the Baptist testifies of the Savior. [56]

3. "Calling of the Fisherman"

The calling of an Apostle is "to be a special witness of the name of Christ in all the world." [57]

4. "The Sermon on the Mount"

"I am the light of the world…" [58]

"I am the bread of life…" [59]

Acceptance of the dead prophets but rejection of the living [60]

---

[53] John 1:1-5

[54] Luke 2:49

[55] Luke 7:27-28

[56] Matthew 3:11-12, Mark 1:7-8, Luke 3:15-18

[57] Doctrine and Covenants 107:23

[58] John 8:12

[59] John 6:35, 48

[60] John 6:22-71

"If ye believe not that I am He..."[61]

"I am the way, the truth, and the life: no man cometh unto the Father, but by me.:"[62]

5. "The Triumphant Entry"

6. "Gethsemane"

The Atonement provides for universal resurrection and individual exaltation. The first is granted unconditionally; the second is conditional based on our faith in Christ, our exercising the principle of repentance, and our living in accordance with His gospel. Christ assumes our guilt on that basis.[63]

7. "Crucifixion"

The Savior was put to death because He would not deny His Sonship.

8. "Resurrection"

The Savior broke the bands of death assuring us all that we will live again after death. Mary was the first witness of the reality of the literalness of the Resurrection.

9. "Jesus Shows His Wounds"

Created in the image of His Father the Savior is a glorified personage of flesh and bones. "Behold my hands and my feet, that it is I myself: handle me, and see; for a spirit hath not flesh and bones, as ye see me have."[64]

10. "Jesus Teaches the Five Hundred"

11. "Commissions Disciples"

They are called to be witnesses to all the world that the Savior lives and are to take His message to all people.

12. "Leaves the Disciples"

The Savior promises to return again. "Ye men of Galilee, why stand ye gazing up into heaven? this same Jesus, which is taken up from you into heaven, shall so come in like manner as ye have seen him go into heaven."[65]

President Garner pronounced the central idea of the Restoration Room: THE GOSPEL OF JESUS CHRIST HAS BEEN RESTORED TO THE EARTH IN ITS FULNESS IN THESE LATTER DAYS.

1. Christ organized His Church during his earthly ministry.

2. Before the second coming of the Savior, two events were to take place:

---

[61] John 8:24

[62] John 14:6

[63] Helaman 14

[64] Luke 24:39

[65] Acts 1:11

a falling away and a restoration. The Savior indicated, "For I know this, that after my departing shall grievous wolves enter in among you, not sparing the flock. Also of your own selves shall men arise, speaking perverse things, to draw away disciples after them." [66]

3. In 1820 in Palmyra, New York, a fourteen year old boy confused by the religious rivalry between churches for membership and desiring to know which church was right read in James "If any of you lack wisdom, let him ask of God, that giveth to all men liberally, and upbraideth not; and it shall be given him." [67] Following this admonition, Joseph Smith retired to a grove of trees where he offered up the feelings of his heart. Directly over his head appeared a pillar of light which gradually descended. When the light rested upon him, Joseph saw two personages whose brightness and glory defied all description. One of them spoke to him calling him by name and said pointing to the other "This is My Beloved Son, Hear Him." Joseph inquired of the Lord which church was right and which he should join and was told to join none of them.

Joseph emerged from the grove knowing who he was--a son of God, created in His image.

Subsequent to this glorious event, the Lord through a living prophet Joseph Smith, organized His church with all the priesthood keys, authority, and power to act in God's name in these last days.

Like the prophets of old, Joseph Smith bore record: "And now, after the many testimonies which have been given of him, this is the testimony, last of all, which we give of him: That he lives! For we saw him, even on the right hand of God; and we heard the voice bearing record that he is the Only Begotten of the Father--That by him, and through him, and of him, the worlds are and were created, and the inhabitants thereof are begotten sons and daughters unto God." [68]

Joseph Smith, by the power of God, translated the Book of Mormon which like the Bible, a record of the Lord's dealings through living prophets with his people on the Eastern continent, is an account of his dealings with his children on this the American continent.

President Garner, not unlike Temple Square volunteers, wished to make the presentation of the vital message of the gospel of Jesus Christ easily understandable, intriguing, accessible, and life changing. His persistence, persuasion, and performance won over those already serving on Temple Square, and he quadrupled the number of

---

[66] Acts 20:29-30

[67] James 1:5

[68] Doctrine and Covenants 76:22-24, Pearl of Great Price, Joseph Smith 1:25

volunteer guides and hosts from 260 when he arrived to 1050 when he was released four years later.

On May 31, 1977, following President Garner's "personal expression of congratulations" on his call as Young Men's president, Neil D. Schaerrer wrote to President Garner of his time spent on Temple Square.

"After seventeen years of being a guide on Temple Square, it was with sadness that I called to ask to be released from this precious assignment. I have had many letters and several converts as a result of this tremendous privilege that has been mine over these many years. I remember following a tour directed by Marion D. Hanks in the early days of my service, and I learned a great deal from his approach. During that period of time, I have served under several presidents of the Temple Square Mission, and even had the opportunity to help determine through committee assignment the rooms and the type of visual aids that would be used in the new Visitors' Center. I will miss this calling very much, but I hope to substitute a few times each year.

President Garner, I must say that under your administration, there has been a stronger accent on actually teaching people and getting solid referrals than at any other time. Though I have had many people from Temple Square in our home after my tours in the past and had many teaching opportunities, I was more effective and more successful under your administration and direction than I was at any other time. I obtained more referrals and after so doing, personally wrote each family a letter as well as the Mission President that was to send missionaries to them. I received letters from missionaries who taught them and letters from the investigators themselves. My success was higher than ever before. The changes you requested the guides to make were difficult for the older guides I am sure, because it was for me. But I knew that you were the president of this mission, and you were entitled to the inspiration and revelation after having analyzed and evaluated all the circumstances involved. What I am saying is that the course you have taken is the right one for this particular time, and I am certain that Temple Square in its pure missionary effort has never been greater. I wish to thank you for your excellent leadership and for the wonderful opportunity I had to work under your direction.

And as noted in a May 14, 1975, letter from Macoy A. McMurray, an associate director to President Jacobsen, Keith's acceptance for some did not take very long.

> Dear President:
>   Congratulations! You just "quarterbacked" the finest meeting I have ever attended on Temple Square. It was superb. Thank you so much for an inspiring evening that prompts all of us to be better hosts and more committed to our work. I sustain you and the wonderful brethren who work with you. I cannot tell you how much I appreciate the privilege of serving on Temple Square.
>   May the Lord continue to bless you.

Keith shared this poignant letter with President Hinckley, adding a couple of postscripts.

>   We met with 200 tour hosts and Visitors' Center Hosts on May 13 and 14. Special 'talking' slides (much like the presentation for stake leaders) were given as guidelines.
>   In all modesty the meetings were terrific. The 400 hosts all equally great. Keith
>   P.S. Considering the source, this memo was touching.

Diane Dunford, out of her loyalty, a quality always respected by President Garner, and affection for President Jacobsen and his long-established manner, came to a vocalized appreciation for the new kid on the block later than some. "Thank you for your patience, endurance, long suffering, and many kindnesses in my behalf. I have learned much these past few years. Unfortunately, my understanding came too late for me to be of any service to you, but I have you to thank for my well being at this time."

As much as her admiration for President Jacobsen would remain constant, the gift she suggested when President Garner expressed his desire to give her something for her new home brings her lots of fond memories of Temple Square and Keith Garner. "I knew President Garner had money and when he asked what I'd like for my new home I thought drapes, carpeting, and a few other quite expensive things. I knew I couldn't really ask for those, so I asked for a ladder so I could care for the fruit trees I'd planted."

He no doubt viewed her request with admiration. It had what could have been his middle name written all over it--PRACTICAL.

"President Garner brought me a ladder; it was no cheapy either. Over the years I have replaced my carpeting, my drapes, my car, but not my ladder. Every time I put it up, I think of Keith Garner."

Other Temple Square employees had also enjoyed qualities in President Garner which they found quite unique and exemplary. One experience involved supervisor Kay Garff. Keith had asked her to manage the annual Christmas buffet. She had prepared and mailed invitations to all the Temple Square volunteers and a long list of Church leaders. She had arranged with a local company to cater the event. On the day of the party as the beginning hour drew near and early party guests began to arrive, she called the caterer in a panic, "Where is the food?!" Making it known that somehow the dates had been confused, the voice on the other end of the line stated, "We are scheduled for a week from today." Embarrassed by the error, though it is doubtful it was Kay's fault, she went to President Garner with her distressing news. She found it was not disturbing in the least to him. He simply took center stage as the guests arrived inviting everyone to stay and enjoy visiting one with another and to return the following week for refreshments. Kay would never forget his unsolicited kindness. President Garner did, however, after three years of these highly successful Christmas festivities, decide that because of the significantly increased numbers of hosts and hostesses and in deference to the Church coffers to forgo this event.

While working on Temple Square, I had my own experience with President Garner's kindly reproof and tutoring. While stationed as a supervisor at the Bureau of Information, I was approached by a family from Salt Lake City who, having seen the display of Book of Mormon in other languages, inquired about purchasing a copy of the Book of Mormon in Chinese. The details are hazy, and I cannot remember why they wished one, but I do remember clearly refusing to sell them one with the explanation that we only made them available to native speakers visiting Temple Square. Unsatisfied, they tracked down President Garner who sent them back to me. He had called me from his office with instructions to sell the Chinese copy to them. Mortified that I and the long standing policy had been overruled, I did as directed with less than a happy heart. Of course, at that time I was unaware of his prolific distribution of Chinese Book of Mormons during his mission presidency, but if I had been, I would have thought, "No wonder the first printing of the Chinese Book of Mormon, 3000 copies, were disbursed so quickly while he was mission president in Hong Kong." That same afternoon President Garner sought me out and instructed me about humility, the predominance of the spirit over the letter of the law, all the while bringing to my memory the words in the Doctrine in Covenants, "We have learned by sad experience that it is the nature and disposition of almost all men, as soon as they get a little authority, as they suppose, they will immediately begin to exercise unrighteous dominion."[69] In this instance it applied to a woman having the power, "as she supposed," to tell someone no. President Garner was not thinking about power; he must have been remembering the joy he felt at the delivery to him of those precious

---

[69] Doctrine and Covenants 121:39

books in Hong Kong. I would benefit from many more of his tutorials over many more years.

In a spirit of humility and joy, he prepared his speech for deliverance at the completion of the Visitors' Center South and, he with a recognized thoughtfulness, secured tickets not previously specified for workers on Temple Square to attend the dedication.

When Keith began his service as president of Temple Square, plans for a new visitors' center to replace the old Bureau of Information at the south gate were already on the drawing board. During his tenure, the old bureau would be leveled, a new visitors' center at the south gate would stand in its place, and President Garner as always would move the missionary work forward in a spirited way. The culmination of this effort occurred when on June 1, 1978, the dedication of the Visitors' Center South took place. A significant part of that program included a speech given by President Garner. Elder Hanks communicates in the following letter to Keith his feelings about his address.

June 2, 1978

Dear Keith:

I've been thinking again this morning of yesterday's experience on Temple Square and wish to put in writing my statements of appreciation and pride, expressed personally after the meeting.

Your talk was forthright, strong, full of meaning, and full of feeling. I am sure there was anxiety, as there would be with any person under the circumstances, but none of it came through. What did come through was the finest statement of the heart and spirit of Temple Square that I have heard since Richard Evans' time, and it was expressed in by far the outstanding statement made at that meeting.

The Lord bless you in this highly important calling. It seems to me to be as significant as any missionary and teaching opportunity could be, and certainly the finest in the Church. I am personally proud of what you have done to make the most of it.

Very sincerely,
Marion D. Hanks

Keith gave the speech to which Elder Hanks refers as one of the invited speakers at the Visitors' Center South Dedication. He spoke along with such luminaries as Governor of Utah Scott M. Matheson, Elder Gordon B. Hinckley, and President Nathan L. Tanner. President Spencer W. Kimball offered the dedicatory prayer. As

President Garner visiting LDS troops stationed at DaNang in May 1968

President Garner's last trip to Vietnam in June 1968

Plaque presented to President Garner

Hong Kong Temple

Peter Lassig told Keith "Plant flowers like life is lived"

Dedicatory Program of Visitors' Center South

President Gordon B. Hinckley, Major Allen C. Rozsa and President Keith Garner traveling in Vietnam in 1966

The International Mission Committee relaxing in Heber; l to r: Reed Reeve, Floyd Stoker, Gary Schwendeman, Keith Garner, Carlos Asay

Llew and Margaret Leigh in Israel

International Mission couples Frank A. and Clora Martin (left) and Edwin Q (Ted) and Janeth Cannon (right) welcome visitors Oscar and Judy McKonkie to Nigeria

The City on the Hill-Erik Ostling

International Mission presidency: l to r: Keith E. Garner, Carlos E. Asay, Gary Schwendeman

Robert W. Wilcoxen with Keith

noted by Elder Hanks, President Garner's speech encapsulated the purpose and spirit of Temple Square, the Church's most visited site.

President Kimball, Brothers and Sisters, it is appropriate that this new addition to Temple Square be dedicated on this special day, the 177th birthday of President Brigham Young. For on July 28, 1847, 111 years ago, four days after the arrival of the pioneers in the Salt Lake Valley, President Young while walking over the ground with some of his associates, suddenly stopped and striking the point of his cane into the parched soil exclaimed 'Here we will build the Temple of our God.' That evening the ten acres selected for the Temple Block were marked out, and it was decided that the future city should surround the square.

Forty-six years later on April 6th, President Wilford Woodruff dedicated the completed Salt Lake Temple. In his dedicatory prayer, he petitioned the Lord to sanctify the whole of this block upon which these buildings stand and further asked that His spirit would dwell in the midst thereof that this plot of ground would be a place of inspiration and meditation.

Set in the beauty of these grounds, the gospel of Jesus Christ is taught to tens of thousands who visit Temple Square every year. The pattern of teaching here was set by the Savior as recorded in Luke Chapter 4. Jesus had returned to Nazareth, the home of his childhood, and as was his custom attended the synagogue service on the Sabbath Day. In attendance, no doubt, were members of his family, friends, and neighbors. He stood and read from our Isaiah the sixty-first chapter. Quote.

The Spirit of the Lord is upon me, because he hath
anointed me to preach the gospel to the poor; he hath sent me
to heal the broken hearted, to preach deliverance to the captives,
and recovering of sight to the blind, to set at liberty them that
are bruised, to preach the acceptable year of the Lord.

This scripture was recognized by all the congregation as specifically referring to the long awaited Messiah. It was customary for the speaker to be seated if he wished to expound or interpret the text. The eyes of all the synagogue were fastened upon him. Luke records. He took his seat and made the fol-

lowing electrifying declaration. "This day is this scripture fulfilled in your ears." It was decisive for all time. He declared
his Sonship with dignity, strength, and conviction. They rejected him, repudiated his message, and even attempted to take his
life. And yet Luke reports and an equally significant thing I
want to emphasize today is that they marveled at the gracious
words which proceeded out of his mouth. He stood before his
associates as the "resurrection and the life." Knowing his eternal role, he testified if they did not accept him, they would die
in their sins. His commission was clear. He had to testify to
them because their very lives depended upon it.

Today we have a similar mandate. The spirit and message
of Temple Square is the same because the message is the same.
The profound events of the Restoration must be proclaimed to
all mankind. They have become commonplace, but the events
are real and urgent for all the world. It is reliably recorded
that the best blood of the nineteenth century had been spilt to
bring forward this marvelous restoration. Such great events
must never be viewed with complacency or indifference.
Joseph Smith saw the Father and the Son. John, the Baptist,
Moses, Moroni, and others appeared on earth with divine messages. Joseph Smith in writing of Moroni's visit said, "He
called me by name and said unto me that he was a messenger
sent from the presence of God." He told Joseph of a record
that he had deposited in a hill one thousand years before
Columbus sailed which was written on gold tablets and which
contained the fulness of the gospel. We possess the translation
of these records and concur and affirm with King Benjamin's
testimony as recorded in the Book of Mormon.

> *I would that you should remember, my sons, that these*
> *sayings are true, and also that these records are true.*
> *And also the plates of Nephi…and we can know of*
> *their surety because we have them before our eyes.*

Yes, we have that book. We know of its verity because we
have it before our eyes. The Lord said, "Whether it be by my
own voice or the voice of my servants it is the same." There
are approximately 1200 devoted members of the Church who
in addition to their ward and stake callings serve on Temple
Square, and this is their testimony. In following the Master's

example, we must be forthright in our proclamation of truth yet always gracious, kind, and sensitive. Alma counseled his missionary sons to be "bold but not overbearing." In this dispensation the Lord has instructed us to "let our preaching be the warning voice; every man to his neighbor in mildness and meekness." Each year we receive hundreds of letters from visitors expressing their gratitude for the peace and love that abounds on this square. May I share two or three with you.

This first one is a letter written by a Catholic nun with the Sisters of Notre Dame in Wisconsin. She said, "Dear Sir, about a month ago, I had the privilege of visiting Temple Square. I was truly impressed not only by the beauty of the buildings, the magnificent sound of the organ and choir but also by the way you people SPEAK (and she printed it) the presence of Christ. You are real witnesses for Him; your enthusiasm for spreading His message can put some other Christians to shame. I pray that some of our fellow Christians can become more eager to witness for His sake as you seem to." And then in the letter, the reason she wrote it, she'd been humming a little tune that she'd heard on Temple Square, and she wanted to know if we'd send her the words, and that tune was "Come, Come Ye Saints."

We have another typical letter written from a lady in New York. She said, "Dear Sir, Recently we visited Temple Square and were impressed, not only with the beauty and extent of same, but with the inner peace and look of happiness and serenity that was evident in the faces and manner of each and every guide. It was quite obvious who were and were not Mormons. We realized that you have something that we do not have and would appreciate further information about the Mormon way of life."

And then last. This is a great letter written to Mr. Garner. She said, "I just finished a note of appreciation to a Tour Hostess and wanted to express to you also my heartfelt and sincere thanks for a tour that changed my life. As a matter of background, I have been a Christian for many years...I'd come to the conclusion that the LDS doctrine had merit for its members but not for me. And then a return trip from California to South Dakota included a visit to Temple Square...As my friend and I were part of a tour group in the Visitors' Center, my heart was 'strangely warmed' by the witness of the Holy Spirit to my spirit that said 'THIS IS TRUE, AND IT IS FOR YOU.' I found out only this week who the tour guide was. She had a wonderful testimony and her face radiated her love for Christ...I observed her in an attitude of prayer while the film was being shown. But the witness to my spirit was so personal it still brings tears when I think of it...Thanks to all of you for your part in this wonderful thing that has come into my life."

I bear testimony that this great work is true, that Jesus is the Christ, and that we have a divine mission to bring these sacred truths, and especially the Atonement, into the lives of our brothers and sisters, and I bear it humbly in the name of Jesus Christ, Amen.

C h a p t e r

T W E L V E

A Mission Without Borders

*...those to whom these commandments were given, might have power
to lay the foundation of this church, and to bring it forth out
of obscurity and out of darkness, the only true and living church
upon the face of the whole earth,...*
— D & C 1:30

"A gentleman asked the Prophet Joseph once if he believed that all other sects and parties would be damned excepting the Mormons. Joseph Smith's reply was 'Yes, sir, and most of the Mormons too unless they repent.'"

A gentleman asked Keith on his way to Church "Is yours the only true Church?" Keith's reply was, "Yes, sir."

This man had watched Keith as he walked the few blocks to the Menlo Park Ward Chapel every Sunday morning. He inquired further, "How many members of your Church?" Keith's answer given in 1970 was "Oh, three to four million." Incredulous, the neighbor stated, "There are billions of people who live on the earth," and then asked, "Your God is that discriminatory? Why do you have it and not me?" Keith said, "I've been instructed to bring it to you."

In farewell words to his Apostles, the Savior commands, "...Go ye into all the world, and preach the gospel to every creature."[70] Since his missionary call to Hawaii in 1939, Keith had been "anxiously engaged" in response to both specific assignments

---

[70] Mark 16:15

from those authorized and the general directive from President David O. McKay, "Every member a missionary." He preached the gospel, crying repentance across the world, not as a perfected man, but as a man filled with the expediency and magnitude of the message.

Concurrent with his assignment on Temple Square and following his release, Keith served as a counselor in the International Mission presidency first under President James E. Faust and then under Elder Carlos Asay. He would draw on the lessons learned in his previous assignments to advance the goals of the International Mission. He would also enjoy his association with these two good men and the others who served with him.

On August 16, 1977, as recorded in International Mission Committee minutes, Elder James E. Faust, acting in his capacity as president of the International Mission, introduced Keith Garner as his second counselor to the committee. The rest of the committee was made up of first counselor Edwin Q. [Ted] Cannon, mission clerk Floyd Stoker, administrative and advisory committee member Reed Reeve, executive secretary Lynn A. Sorensen, and secretary Melba Erwin.

The International Mission, an administrative entity, was created because the tag "world-wide Church" became a reality with members scattered around almost every part of the world. This mission functioned from November 9, 1972, until August 15, 1987. Its primary duty was to serve what was designated "unattached members."

As president of the Southern Far East Mission, Keith's duty to keep in contact with these isolated, small groups in Southeast Asia preceded the establishment of the International Mission and his call to its presidency. Mission President Garner had known then, as he knew when he served in each of his positions from Regional and Mission Representative, to bishop, to home teacher, the importance of not losing track of the individual Church member. When that individual lived in an area without Church structure, the need to identify other members in the region and establish a way for the blessings of association and activity to come to them became even more vital.

In an effort to accomplish this, President Garner had requested from small groups throughout his mission field reports and photographs for publication in the October 1967 edition of *The Orientor*. Ever mindful of the few, he had written introductory and concluding words which were placed among these published reports and photographs:

> Dear Companions:
>   Living in this Mission which is on the frontier of the
> Church, and traveling into India, Pakistan, Thailand, Vietnam,
> Malaysia, Indonesia, and Taiwan, meeting with large and small
> groups of Latter-day Saints, the full impact of Nephi's vision

twenty-six centuries ago regarding our times is literally fulfilled before our eyes. He saw that this Church of the Lamb of God would be upon the earth. Its members would be all over the world in every nation. Its numbers would be few, and its dominion would be small because of the influence and power of the great and abominable church. But the members of the Church would be armed with righteousness and with the power of God in great glory.

Now, we know of the following groups:

Kuala Lumpur, Malaysia . . . . Fred J. Bonney
Molacco, Malaysia . . . . Sgt. R.J. Pearson
Singapore, Malaysia . . . . . . Roger Deeley
Vietnam, South . . . . Capt. Louis T. Bowring
Vietnam, Central . . . . Capt. Donald L. Greenhalgh
Vietnam, North . . . . Lt. Preston N. Kearsley
Saigon Branch . . . . L.M. Newberger
Thailand District . . . . Eugene P. Till
Bangkok Branch . . . . Hollis A. Hunt
Vientiane, Laos . . . . Bert W. Foote
Ramna Dacca, East Pakistan . Max G. Williams
Peshawar, West Pakistan . . . . W. Kenneth Bach
New Dehli, India . . . . Miller F. Shurtleff
Bombay, India . . . . William Pettersson
Taiwan . . . . Maj. Lafayette L. Hoke
Rangoon, Burma . . . . George E. Burke

Thus we can plainly see that this great people possessing the gifts and blessings of the restored Church are literally fulfilling prophecy.

Furthermore, we learn to appreciate the joy and peace and satisfaction that comes to members of the Church as they seek out and find brothers and sisters--even one or two--in remote parts of the world and meet together and partake of the sacrament, renew their covenants, and mutually bless and edify each other.

This "meeting oft" is an indispensable part of the plan of God and illustrates the truth that Jesus taught, paradoxical as it might sound, that "he...that loseth his life for my sake shall find it."[71]

If President Garner had thought of it, he might have included a comment by one of his favorite authors, Rabbi Heschel, on the company of believers, for it certainly could be applied to the LDS sacrament meeting. "To attain a degree of spiritual security one cannot rely upon one's own resources. One needs an atmosphere, where the concern for the spirit is shared by a community. We are in need of students and scholars, masters and specialists. But we need also the company of witnesses, of human beings who are engaged in worship, who for a moment sense the truth that life is meaningless without attachment to God."[72]

President Garner witnessed the importance of this attachment while traveling in 1966 with Elder and Sister Hinckley to India. "November fourth found us in Bombay. Such a lamentable city with its teeming masses, poverty, begging, disease, deformity, and tragedy. We stayed in the home of Brother and Sister Robert B. Evans. Brother Evans works with the American Consulate in India and is our group leader in India."

The Evans' were not alone. Between 1965 and 1968, members of the Church living in these far-flung areas of the world included an NCO in charge of the Marine Security Guard at an American Embassy, Peace Corps volunteers, an Executive Officer for the National Science Foundation of the United States, employees of Air America, USAID, and Engineering Consultants, Inc., and teachers with a Texas A & M teaching exchange group. In the ensuing years, many more members of the Church living and working in these outposts would be added to the ranks. Through their efforts and example combined with International Mission representatives, some of these areas of limited numbers and thus activity would blossom into strongholds of missionary success.

As part of worldwide supervision, the International Mission, under the direction of the International Missionary Committee, was responsible for isolated members, groups, and branches living in Iron Curtain and other countries, including Africa. In accordance with its purpose to identify and strengthen, Keith's initial assignments covered "administration and leadership of groups and branches and survey of resources of individuals and computerizing of records of members living away from home." This surely was a momentous task. By 1980, individual members or small groups of members of the Church had been found in Algeria, Bahrain, Bangladesh, Botswana, Brunei, Bulgaria, China, Crete, Cyprus, Diego Garcia, Republique de

---

[71] *The Orientor Gazette of the Southern Far East Mission*, II:10, October 1967, 2-3, 26

[72] Abraham J. Heschel, *The Insecurity of Freedom* (New York: The Noonday Press, 1967), 243.

Djibouti, Egypt, Faroe Islands, Gabon, The Gambia, Ghana, Greece, Greenland, French Guiana, Guinea, Guinea Ecuatorial, Guyana, India, Iran, Iraq, Ile de la Reunion, Israel, Ivory Coast, Jordan, Kenya, Kuwait, Lebanon, Liberia, Libya, Malaysia, Mali, Morocco, Nepal, New Guinea, Niger, Nigeria, Oman, Pakistan, Poland, Russia, Rwanda, Saudi Arabia, Senegal, Sierra Leone, Somalia, Sri Lanka, Sudan, Surinam, Swaziland, Tanzania, Togo, Turkey, United Arab Emirates, Upper Volta, Yemen, Yugoslavia, Zaire, and Zambia.

President Garner had generally found bureaucracies less than praiseworthy by their very nature, but much of the work, and especially his work in the International Mission presidency, relied on the ability to enhance communication with and between Church departments and use the resources available. In this position, that meant enlisting the help of stake and mission presidents in identifying members living and working abroad. Significantly helpful were the efforts of men such as President Dallin Oaks at Brigham Young University and Jeffrey Holland of the Church Education System and their associates in addressing the needs of international students and sponsoring athletic and entertainment groups on tours abroad. Other major contributors to this monumental effort included Arch Madsen at Bonneville Communications in providing media coverage, consultant David Kennedy in international relations, Oscar McKonkie in legal matters including gaining recognition in countries behind the Iron Curtain, and Tom Daniels of the genealogical department in microfilming vital statistic records in foreign countries. The translation department made Church literature available in native languages, and the Church magazine department made print media accessible. Keith marveled at the resources and expertise of people and their willingness to address every necessity in every part of the world.

The experience gained by President Garner on Temple Square, especially working with the new visitors' center's layout, scripting the Temple Square tour, and designing a slide presentation for the Assembly Hall, made him particularly effective. He worked with Tom Lasko of the Church exhibits department in developing portable visitors' centers for cities in the Middle East and elsewhere. He demonstrated the slide show used in the Assembly Hall to the committee, and his presentation received high marks accompanied by the directive that it should be made available to every International Mission representative. His first-hand knowledge of the world also came to bear as he briefed the committee on Singapore and Vietnam.

One event of particular interest for him took place in Iran when the Shah's regime was overturned by religious militants in 1979. Concern for the missionaries assigned to the Tehran Iran Mission and for Church-owned property stimulated Keith's wonderment about the safety of ancient records he had beheld and handled in the museum in Tehran. As it happened, missionaries, members, property, and ancient records were unharmed.

Since the International Mission covered all the areas of the world where the Church did not yet have established missions due to restrictions on proselyting or other circumstances, a significant part of Keith's assignment included recommending couples to serve in these unique settings. The particular qualifications of Keith's friends Frank and Clora Martin and Lewellyn and Margaret Leigh suggested that they be sent to prime pioneering places in Africa and Israel. They had fervent testimonies, friendly personalities, and financial ability. However, the creature comforts they fully enjoyed in their own homes were less procurable, if not completely missing from the more physically challenging surroundings the Martins would call home for a year in Nigeria and the Leighs for eighteen months in Israel.

Keith's acquaintance with the Martins went back to at least 1939. Frank, after a lifetime of association, recalls, "Keith was always a very good friend, always solid in the gospel. We spent many, many hours together, some of them meant nothing, just friends."

In those early days in San Francisco, the Church was family. Clora recalls, "We were called the faithful forty."

Clora was Keith's sister LaVon's best friend, and according to Clora, "Keith was LaVon's baby, a baby brother she really loved." In fact, Vaughn, LaVon's husband, used to say "Keith is my only competition."

Frank tells Keith, "I remember you and I coming from San Francisco in a new Chrysler that you had bought. I remember how much I admired it. Here was a young man who was successful in life. There wasn't anything really he couldn't have if he wanted it. He was financially well-off and doing well for a young man. I used to say Keith is just someone who puts his whole heart into what he's doing and he's successful."

Clora piped in, "And I said how did a kid get a car like that?!"

Recalling Keith's enjoyment of cars, they rehearsed one particularly outrageous yet true tale, punctuated with laughter. The story goes that driving by a dealership in Palo Alto one morning, Keith spotted a car on the showroom floor which aroused his interest. He stopped and inquired. At the end of a very brief visit, made so by an appointment to which he was already late, he tersely instructed the bewildered salesman to have the car he had selected ready for pick up the next morning. The following day when he returned, the car was not ready; the dumbfounded salesman confessed he had thought because of Keith's highly unusual instruction that Keith was an escaped patient from the nearby mental hospital. Needless to say, Keith's check was accepted, the car was readied, and everyone, mostly Keith, had a good laugh.

Keith quickly saw an opening and used the car references to suggest in practical, pragmatic terms his view of the celestial kingdom. "If you do not gain eternal life, you will be walking rather than driving a Mercedes." Keith can be pretty sure his friend Robert Garff, the Mercedes dealer in Salt Lake City, would appreciate such an advertisement for his product. He added, "As much as I think asphalt is the greatest invention of our time and makes driving so smooth, I'm counting on Joseph Smith's description of the roads in the celestial kingdom given in an 1836 meeting in the Kirtland Temple. '…the beautiful streets of that kingdom, had the appearance of being paved with gold.'" Even though celestial glory has no earthly comparable the Martins understood Keith's words.

The ties of friendship existing in 1979 that were undiminished by distance and strengthened by small thoughtful acts of kindness during the refining experiences of a lifetime prompted Keith to turn to Frank and Clora in his search for qualified missionary couples. Frank had worked for the global food company, H. J. Heinz, for thirty-four years, but the experiences he and Clora would have in Nigeria in a single year would demand just as many pages in the family album. Of necessity they carried water bottles with them at all times. They traversed mud roads. Clora taught the sisters the basics of personal hygiene and the arts of bread baking and sewing.

A little over a year before the Martins left for Nigeria, President Spencer W. Kimball on June 9, 1978, announced that every worthy male member of the Church age twelve and over would enjoy the blessings of the Priesthood. The International Mission presidency rejoiced in this proclamation and then began the necessary work to make this privilege available to members in Africa. This meant by November 1978 the Rendell N. Mabeys were in Nigeria. They were soon joined by the Martins and later by the Edwin Q. Cannons who labored in both Nigeria and Ghana. These and other capable International Mission couples assigned to African nations were dealing with an explosion of interest, the changing legal status of the Church in West African countries, and limited hours in a day to accomplish the almost overwhelming tasks that lay before them. A month after their arrival, Keith received the Martin's August 2, 1979, letter.

> Dear Keith:
>
> First let me say although this is a very difficult mission in many respects, it is still a very rewarding and spiritual experience. There are many hardships, but I am sure no more than those who first went out into the mission field when the Church came into being. Some of ours are just a bit different, but I'm sure require the same amount of faith and trust that the Lord will take care of us. Clora and I have both been very well, and other than the usual aches and pains that come even when we are home and under normal living conditions, we are getting along just fine. The work is going forward under Bro. Mabey's direction, and I appreciate his great knowledge of things and his ability to get things done with the authorities. His knowledge of the law and his former experience as a mission president has been a great asset. I feel confident he was the man for the job, and those who come after will have a

much easier time because of his efforts. I have now had a month to get some idea of things and can only concur in what Bro. Mabey has written to you regarding the mission. We cannot possibly do the things we need to do because of the great distances and the lack of additional missionaries. There are branches and groups that need supervision and training, and it is just impossible to get to them. We know there are many people who would like to be baptized, but there has to be a stopping point somewhere along the line and time spent in training. Nigeria has a project of building new roads, but unless you see them, you can't believe the condition some of them are in. I'm sure Bishop Brown can tell you of his ride down to one of the branches. Our last trip south because of the rains was hazardous. We were the last car across one bridge, as it was so bad they had stopped cars and were tearing it apart. It is a good thing we can keep our sense of humor. We have not had water in the house for 22 days. We've gone to the water dept every day without fail, and they give us the excuse that the pipe is clogged up. Every morning Ren and I take our Jerry cans and go hunting water, and this takes an hour or so. The girls, bless their hearts, are holding up very well in about two inches of bath water. Yesterday it rained very hard, and Ren and I wrapped a towel around us and went out in the back yard and took a bath in the rain. These experiences will long be remembered, I can assure you of that. The joy though of being able to have gospel conversations in the stores, banks, on the street, and in the markets is really a thrill. I have never been in a place where it is so easy to start up a gospel conversation. The early Christian missionaries did a good job in getting these people prepared for the restored gospel. The Mabeys plan on leaving here in October, so be sure and get a real choice couple to come and be with us, someone who is good at finances. This mission is so expensive; I can hardly believe what it costs to live and maintain ourselves. Whoever is coming over next give them a few suggestions on what to bring in the way of clothes. Many things we brought just are not practical. Tell them to bring all permanent press, wash and wear, short sleeve shirts, light weight dresses, thin socks, plenty of handkerchiefs, good shoes, sandals, knock around pants, sport shirts, and if they use razor blades, bring plenty. I could mention other things, but those are the most important. The

> most important thing I can write to you is to send more cou-
> ples. The work just cannot progress like it should unless we
> can get more help. Our southern branches need guidance and
> assistance, and the distance is so far we just can't get down
> there to help them. It is hundreds of miles, and when you get
> there, there is no place to stay, and letters take almost as long
> to reach places in Nigeria as it does to Salt Lake. Most mail
> from S.L. takes around seventeen days. Well, good brother, in
> spite of it all, I love you. You're a good man, and I know the
> Lord appreciates all you do and is blessing you. We hope
> you'll come over and visit us, but if you decide not to come
> with all the problems, we will certainly understand. Let me
> assure you, this is not the place to come for a vacation, unless
> one is used to roughing it. Please give our kindest regards to
> the Brethren and let us hear from you. God bless you.
> PS Whoever comes over next I would certainly appreciate if
> they would get hold of Carlene [a daughter] and have her give
> them a pair of white pants. The ones I brought are knit and
> just not suitable for river baptizing and take too long to dry.

In fact, a trip to Africa for Keith and Ted Cannon was already in the planning
stage. It would never occur, as Keith reported in a letter to Frank and Clora dated
February 28, 1980.

> I just returned from a two week sabbatical away from the
> world and found your letter of January 24th waiting. I am
> always pleased to hear from you. Upon returning I learned
> that Ted's and my proposed trip to Nigeria has been cancelled
> (great things are planned for your part of the world which will
> be forthcoming and which will more than offset what good we
> may have done by our visit.)
> I regret I did not have the chance to visit you in your
> plush surroundings but know of them. I am always reminded
> that the Lord compensates for our devotion and service.
> We think of you and pray for your success. We esteem
> you as always our dear friends.

The "great thing" to which President Garner referred was the creation of
the African West Mission on July 1, 1980, with Bryan A. Espenschied as mission
president.

Frank remembered that at the Martins' missionary farewell at which both

Elder Asay and President Garner spoke, someone familiar with the heat they would soon experience saying, "You have been called to serve in heck!" While visiting with Keith in 2000, Frank looked at him and summarized, "During that year in Africa, there were days I thought of you and said, 'That bounder!' but I think of it now as the best experience in the world."

Llew and Margaret Leigh's experiences as International Mission representatives in Israel replicated in less dramatic ways the Martins' sojourn in Nigeria. President Garner states, "During this period of time, Israel was struggling to survive. The government enforced an austerity program which meant Margaret and Llew ended up in a little living compound in Tel Aviv with a common bath and shower shared by a number of families. For Margaret, a past 'Days of '47 Queen,' and Llew, a prominent dentist from Palo Alto, it was a call only the strong in heart and the humble in spirit could survive, and they did."

President Garner recommended his friends the Leighs to the International Mission Committee with the utmost confidence. Llew had served as Keith's counselor in the Menlo Park bishopric. He was also the expert dentist who Keith had trusted to cap all of his teeth. In all his dealings with the Leighs, Keith had discovered and reconfirmed two qualities he admired and valued greatly in Llew. The qualities, loyalty and trust, Keith extolled in the speech he gave at Llew's funeral years later.

This mutually shared trust and bond of friendship between Keith and Llew can be felt as he recounts the following incident. "I've forgotten the year, but I was a well-known developer and contractor in the Palo Alto/Menlo Park area. Being that prominent in the area I found caused sellers/brokers to charge me more than they would someone less well-known. So on occasion I would buy property for my account in another person's name. This one time I saw a piece of property I wanted to make an offer on, so I made an offer through a broker and put it in Llew Leigh's name. I signed it, and they told me they needed a deposit. I left with every intention of discussing this transaction with Llew. Either I was called out-of-town or became involved and a few days later received a call from the broker to inform me that they'd accepted the offer. I said, 'Well, I never gave you a check for the deposit.' The broker said Dr. Leigh gave it to us. Llew didn't know anything about it, but they just said that Keith Garner had negotiated a deal for him on a piece of property and that they needed a $5000 deposit. Llew gave it to them! Amazing!"

Llew compared Keith to Apostle Matthew Cowley and repeatedly expressed to him his gratitude for giving him opportunities for Church service. Keith explains how the opportunity to serve in Israel was a little more challenging than most. "This assignment was especially revealing because of the nature of their assignment. Dr. Leigh and his wife Margaret were called to Israel with instructions not to proselyte. I told Llew to take his golf clubs and to join Rotary wherever he was assigned."

Some days were filled with discouragement for the couple, and Keith, sensing this from a few of their letters, began calling them weekly. When Llew or Margaret answered, instead of a cheerful hello, he'd greet them by singing:

> *I walked today where Jesus walked--In days of long ago;*
> *I wandered down each path He knew,--With rev'rent step and slow.*
> *Those little lanes, they have not changed--A sweet peace fills the air.*
> *I walked today where Jesus walked,--And felt His presence there.*
> *My pathway led through Bethlehem,--Ah! memories ever sweet;*
> *The little hills of Galilee,--That knew those childish feet;*
> *The Mount of Olives: hallowed scenes--That Jesus knew before;*
> *I saw the mighty Jordan roll--As in the days of yore.*
> *I knelt today where Jesus knelt,--Where all alone He prayed;*
> *The Garden of Gethsemane--My heart felt unafraid!*
> *I picked my heavy burden up--And with Him by my side,*
> *I climbed the Hill of Calvary, I climbed the Hill of Calvary,*
> *I climbed the Hill of Calvary,Where on the Cross He died!*
> *I walked today where Jesus walked and felt Him close to me!* [73]

After hearing Keith intone these wonderful words, Llew and Margaret could not help cheering up and rejoicing in their calling.

Keith continues, "Only a short time before they departed for home, the assigned speaker for Rotary couldn't make it, so they asked Llew if he would pinch hit. Llew had that speech written and memorized! It was the story of the restoration of the gospel with Joseph Smith, the gold plates, the visitation of Moroni, and their relationship to the Jews taking center stage. Had he tracted every home in the proceeding eighteen months, it would never have equalled this captive audience of Jewish leaders in the community."

When Llew and Margaret returned home, they graciously and certainly with some sense of accomplishment sent to Keith the speech, "The Mormon Community" given by Llewellyn Leigh at Rotary Club in Tel Aviv, Israel, on August 7, 1980. After receiving this speech, Keith readily shared Llew's extraordinary opportunity in both the conversations he had and in the speeches he was asked to deliver.

On one such occasion, Keith was invited to speak to the Temple Square volunteers by his successor President Dale L. Curtis; Keith in 1981 drew upon his service in the International Mission, and that always meant telling of Llew.

Dear Brethren and Sisters.

It is my privilege and choice opportunity to be here again.

---

[73] Geoffrey O'Hara, *I Walked Today Where Jesus Walked*, poem by Daniel S. Twohig (New York: G. Schirmer, Inc., 1937).

There is no place in the world or the Church for that matter like Temple Square.

Impressions made here coupled with faithful performance by Church members and effective proselyting by dedicated missionaries complete the eternal life package.

I've been asked to talk about the unreached peoples of the world with some special emphasis on Asia since I spent many years there.

The Lord says in the Doctrine and Covenants 133:37, "And this gospel shall be preached unto every nation, and kindred, and tongue, and people." His commission to Joseph Smith recorded in Doctrine and Covenants 5:10 is "But this generation shall have my word through you."

Consider the monumental nature of this task by putting it into perspective.

On our globe there are 221 countries. Nations range in size from the large with estimated populations of eight hundred fifty million, to the medium with ninety million, to the small with one hundred twenty thousand. That tremendous variation shows how difficult it is to talk about world proselyting and conversions. It is one thing to proselyte Taiwan but quite another to reach the one hundred forty million people on the islands of Indonesia, or India, or China.

The numbers of people increase daily. Look at today's world population. The explosion has been startling. When Jesus was born it is estimated that the world's population was two hundred fifty million. Fifteen hundred years later or by the time Martin Luther posted his ninety-five Theses at Wittenberg, it doubled to five hundred million. Two hundred fifty years later it doubled, and by 1914 it had doubled again. It then stood at two billion. In the next sixty-seven years, it doubled, and it continues at the same rate. Today we have four billion, and by the year 2000, world population will be somewhere between six and seven billion people.

Think of that in terms of just one country. India, almost as populous as China, adds 35,000 per day. Ten days of that? Three times ten days? ONE MILLION PLUS EVERY MONTH. A recent newspaper article indicates the rate is double this estimation--or twenty-five million a year! It's beyond human comprehension.

Look at languages. According to the translation department

there are between 2500 and 5000 tongues spoken in the world if dialects are included. The complexities in communication can be noted when one realizes that in some languages intonation can change the meaning of a word. India has seventeen major languages and 840 mother tongues. Over ninety-six languages are heard in Bombay; the government is conducting school in ten languages.

To date, the Church has nineteen "established languages," Fuijian and Indonesian having just recently been added. An established language is defined by the translation department as one in which the basic Church pamphlets, Book of Mormon, and selected lesson manuals are available. At the present time the Church also classifies seventy-nine languages as "emerging languages" or ones in the process of translation and publication. Seven of these have been added since August.

Now think of the world in terms of its religions. Christians number approximately one billion, Muslims seven hundred million, Hindus six hundred million, Markists five hundred million, Buddhists two hundred fifty million, traditional Chinese five hundred million, Animists two hundred million, traditional Japanese sixty million, Jews fifteen million, and all others one hundred million. Members of the Church comprise approximately 4.7 million.

In these religious divisions, Christians include those who accept Jesus Christ. Accordingly, one billion people may have heard of Him; two billion have probably heard His name. Most of the unreached people of the world fall into this latter category. Our audience is a large one. If we allowed two feet for each person and lined them up circling the circumference of the earth, it would take roughly thirteen loops to accommodate one billion individuals. Most of the people of the world, our audience, is the same as Paul describes in the powerful language of Acts 17:22-23.

> *Then Paul stood in the midst of Mars' hill, and said, Ye men*
> *of Athens, I perceive that in all things ye are too superstitious.*
> *For as I passed by, and beheld your devotions, I found*
> *an alter with this inscription, TO THE UNKNOWN GOD.*
> *Whom therefore ye ignorantly worship, him declare I unto you.*

We speak of two billion plus people for whom the name

Jesus Christ has no meaning. It is one thing to choose to be without Christ and quite another to be without knowledge or understanding of Him. Life is sad indeed, for there is no hope in the resurrection, nor the joy that comes from a relationship with the Master.

This review of population explosions, numbers of countries, languages, and religions gives us a rather comprehensive view of the difficulty and amount of gospel presentation still to be accomplished.

Satan delays and hampers the spreading of the gospel message by every means available. No Christian missionaries are allowed in India, Sri Lanka, China, Egypt, Malaysia, Islamic countries, or nations behind the Iron Curtain. Laws prohibit the preaching of the gospel. In some countries violation of religious suppression laws is on penalty of death. In a few where Christian missionaries are admitted, proselyting is prohibited or severely restricted. These restrictions coupled with poverty, tradition, cultural bias, customs, education, and religion slow the work.

We see the fulfillment of the vision of Nephi when he saw the Church in our day.

And it came to pass that I beheld the church of the Lamb of God, and its numbers were few, because of the wickedness and abominations of the whore who sat upon many waters; nevertheless, I beheld that the church of the Lamb, who were the saints of God, were also upon all the face of the earth; and their dominions upon the face of the earth were small, because of the wickedness of the great whore whom I saw. [74]

The Church struggles to meet these challenges but with difficulty and in removed corners of the earth--far from Salt Lake City. In India with its seven hundred million people, seventeen languages, 400 castes and laws prohibiting the entrance of foreign missionaries, we have isolated groups struggling for survival without leadership or basic understanding of the gospel. A few hundred members in all of India. This is not to say that there are not others desirous of the blessings of baptism, yet we say WAIT for fear we send them to the waters of baptism and leave them alone without guidance and teachers.

---

[74] I Nephi 14:12

"Perhaps baptism, in three month, or so when we return, when we can somehow provide teachers and continuity, when there is more than one of a village and two of a family." In the newly created West African Mission, there are 800 desirous souls in Ghana on a baptismal waiting list.

Paul questions in Romans 10:13-15: "For whosoever shall call upon the name of the Lord shall be saved. How then shall they call on him in whom they have not believed? and how shall they believe in him of whom they have not heard? and how shall they hear without a preacher? And how shall they preach, except they be sent? as it is written, How beautiful are the feet of them that preach the gospel of peace, and bring glad tidings of good things!"

The difficulties do not all lie outside the Church. And perhaps it is really with our own attitudes that we must start. President J. Reuben Clark admonishes: "We must give up this idea too many of us have that our way of life and living is not only the best, but often the only true way of life and living in the world, that we know what everybody else in the world should do and how they should do it. We must come to realize that every race and every people have their own way of doing things, their own standards of life, their own ideals, their own kinds of food and clothing and drink, their own concepts of civil obligation and honor, and their own views as to the kind of government they should have. It is simply ludicrous for us to try to recast all of these into our mold."

I recently listened to a Billy Graham television crusade in which he stirringly called upon his thousands of listeners to confess Christ, to come forward publicly, and acknowledge Him as their personal Savior. He asked them to incorporate these declarations into personal actions--to attend their Church each Sunday.

This task of world-wide conversion is great, and we must open-mindedly accept and acknowledge works of righteousness from all sources. Joseph Smith declared that we must embrace truth wherever it is found.

In the Lord's plan of salvation and eternal life--even sanctification--is found in eternal progress through daily application of gospel principles--through participation and ordinances.

We must not despair. The task before us is not insurmountable with the Lord. Recall the missionary story of

Ammon, Aaron, and King Lamoni. These servants of the Lord
through preparation and righteous living were instrumental in
the conversion of the royal household and the proclamation of
religious freedom through the land.

> *O God, Aaron hath told me that there is a God; and if there is a God,*
> *and if thou art God, wilt thou make thyself known unto me, and I will*
> *give away all my sins to know thee, and that I may be raised from*
> *the dead, and be saved at the last day. And now when the king*
> *had said these words, he was struck as if he were dead.* [75]

Not all missionary experiences are this striking, but missionary results today are no less dramatic. In the Philippines, a
people blessed with religious freedom and a Christian background, the gospel flourishes. In 1965 there were 350 members
of the Church. Today there are thirty thousand.

> *And it came to pass that I, Nephi, beheld the power of the Lamb*
> *of God, that it descended upon the saints of the church of the*
> *Lamb, and upon the covenant people of the Lord, who were*
> *scattered upon all the face of the earth; and they were armed*
> *with righteousness and with the power of God in great glory.* [76]

Man will hear the message if we prepare ourselves to
deliver it. One of our fine International Mission couples was
sent to Israel for eighteen months. The letters I received from
them were full of frustration at their inability to proselyte
because of government regulations and what they perceived to
be the lack of any gains for the cause because of their having
been there.

One month prior to their coming home this good brother
was asked by the Rotary Club of Tel Aviv, which he had joined,
to address their club. He began by relating the exchange
between Count Leo Tolstoy and Andrew D. White, the U.S.
foreign minister to Russia in 1892, when he inquired about the
American religion, commonly known as the Mormon Church.
Discovering that White knew little concerning Mormons,

---

[75] Alma 22:18

[76] I Nephi 14:14

Tolstoy rebuked the ambassador. "Dr. White, I am greatly surprised and disappointed that a man of your great learning and position should be so ignorant on this important subject. Their principles teach the people not only of heaven and its attendant glories, but how to live so that their social and economic relations with each other are placed on a sound basis. If the people follow the teachings of this Church, nothing can stop their progress--it will be limitless." Tolstoy continued, "There have been great movements started in the past but they have died or been modified before they reached maturity. If Mormonism is able to endure, unmodified, until it reaches the third and fourth generation, it is destined to become the greatest power the world has ever known."[77]

This missionary told of the Book of Mormon, the Jerusalemic origin of the people, the fulfillment of the prophecy of Ezekiel regarding the stick of Judah and the stick of Joseph. And from the Book of Mormon, he read to them promises made to their ancestors. "Hated of all nations the Jews will yet be remembered of the Lord."[78] "They shall be gathered in from their long dispersion, from the four corners of the Earth and 'from the isles of the sea' and in their aid, 'nations of the gentiles shall be great in the eyes' of the Lord."[79] "After they are restored they shall no longer be confounded. Neither shall they be scattered again."[80]

He recapped the organization of the Church, the Nauvoo period of temple building, the Saints persecution, and their journey to the Rocky Mountains.

Explaining the deep interest The Church of Jesus Christ of Latter-day Saints has always felt for the House of Israel, he taught them of Joseph Smith's dispatching Orson Hyde in 1840 to the land of Palestine to dedicate it for the return of the descendants of Judah--an Apostolic dedication which occurred fifty years before Theodor Herzel.

---

[77] Thomas J. Yates, "Count Tolstoi and the 'American Religion,'" *Improvement Era*, February 1939, 94.

[78] I Nephi 19:13-15

[79] II Nephi 10:8

[80] I Nephi 15:19-20

Today this prayer is enshrined in bronze and centered on a wall in a garden east of Jerusalem on the Mount of Olives--a park landscaped and maintained by a million dollar donation from the Orson Hyde Foundation.

His concluding thoughts proclaimed our concern and interest is one of kinship.

Two hundred influential men listened to the message of the Restoration. If this missionary brother and his wife had tracted every day of their mission, they would not have reached the numbers or had the influence for good for the Savior that he had in that one afternoon.

O that I were an angel, and could have the wish of mine heart, that I might go forth and speak with the trump of God, with a voice to shake the earth, and cry repentance unto every people! But behold, I am a man, and do sin in my wish; for I ought to be content with the things which the Lord hath allotted unto me. Why should I desire that I were an angel, that I could speak unto all the ends of the earth?
For behold, the Lord doth grant unto all nations, of their own nation and tongue, to teach his word, yea, in wisdom, all that he seeth fit that they should have; therefore we see that the Lord doth counsel in wis-dom, according to that which is just and true...and this is my glory, that perhaps I may be an instrument in the hands of God to bring some soul to repentance; and this is my joy. [81]

We must desire to share the precious message with which we have been entrusted. We must prepare. We must be exemplary in our own spheres of influence. As we are prepared, willing, and trust in the Lord the opportunities will come.

This promise was not conjectural or wishful thinking on President Garner's part; he knew of what he spoke. Over a lifetime the opportunities had come for him to serve. This was also true among all the members of the International Mission presidency. President Cannon, well prepared by having participated in the fact-finding mission with Merrill Bateman in 1978, returned to Africa as an International Mission representative. Floyd Stoker, with more than a willing heart, accepted an assignment to Malaysia. Elder Faust in October of 1978 became a member of the Quorum of the Twelve. Elder Carlos E. Asay of the First Quorum of the Seventy became president of

---

[81] Alma 29:1, 3, 7, 8, 9

the International Mission. President Garner, second counselor to Elder Faust, became President Asay's first counselor. Gary Schwendeman became second counselor, and Arthur Casper became mission clerk. Secretaries Jennifer Pratt and Joan Kingsley also aided the committee at different times.

During his tenure with the International Mission, President Garner visited the Middle East and accompanied Elder Asay to the Far East. On a glorious trip to the Middle East from among a wealth of possible speakers, including Jim and Elaine Cannon, Ken Gardner, Daniel Ludlow, Richard Gunn, and Robert Taylor, Keith was asked to speak at a sacrament meeting held aboard ship docked off the coast of Egypt. A week later Keith records, "I was asked to conduct a special sacrament service in the amphitheater in the ruins of Ephesus where Paul preached over 2000 years ago." President Garner, holding the necessary keys to do so, presided at and conducted the October 23, 1977, sacrament meeting. It was quietly reflective of the implementation in modern times of Paul's pronouncements and Joseph Smith's 1842 statement of beliefs, known as *The Articles of Faith*, written in reply to *Chicago Democrat* editor John Wentworth's inquiry, especially articles five and six.

> We believe that a man must be called of God, by prophecy,
> and by the laying on of hands by those who are in authority, to
> preach the Gospel and administer in the ordinances thereof.
> We believe in the same organization that existed in the
> Primitive Church, namely, apostles, prophets, pastors, teachers,
> evangelists, and so forth.

These LDS sacrament meetings were being held in the same reverent manner on every continent.

In addition to his assignment in Ephesus during these years, Keith enjoyed the privilege of speaking at sacrament meetings held in such hallowed spots as the Sacred Grove in Palmyra, New York, and the Hill Cumorah, the very places where the spectacular events which began the Restoration of the gospel of Jesus Christ in the nineteenth century had taken place. Keith also joyfully accompanied Elder Asay to the Far East, thousands of miles from Palmyra, where he, having participated in the beginnings of Church growth in the Southern Far East, delighted in meeting with the expanding congregations. President Garner who had traveled the world found his greatest joy not in seeing the seven wonders of the world or the works of men, but in seeing the gospel of Jesus Christ fill the earth as the Old Testament Daniel, prophesied.

> The keys of the kingdom of God are committed unto man
> on the earth, and from thence shall the gospel roll forth unto
> the ends of the earth, as the stone which is cut out of the

mountain without hands shall roll forth, until it has filled the whole earth. [82]

One travel adventure in which he displayed an expressed curiosity he did not pursue. This time his interest did not include another search for the sword of Laban in Central America, but it did date back to the days when Lehi left Jerusalem. As a gift on his seventy-first birthday, he received the Scot Facer Proctor and Maurine Jensen Proctor book *Light from the Dust: A Photographic Exploration into the Ancient World of the Book of Mormon*. In their search for the possible location from which Lehi and his family set sail, the Proctors photographed and wrote of their challenging, difficult journey and their hypotheses that a remote inlet on the coast of Oman offered real possibilities of being the authentic site of Lehi's departure from the "old world" for the "promised land." If Keith could have rounded up the same group who accompanied him to Tehran in 1961, he would have been off thirty years later headed for the Arabian Peninsula on this new adventure, outfitted with the same enthusiasm he had taken on that earlier trip of a lifetime.

Keith would not travel the world on assignment again like he had over the fifteen years between 1965 and 1980, but a much shorter, less exotic trip taken in 2001 ranked among his most memorable. When President Hinckley called Keith to extend an invitation to accompany him to the funeral of Allen Rozsa, their friend from days spent together in Vietnam, he gladly accepted. What a tribute to Colonel Rozsa, who had after his tour in Vietnam served as president of the Los Angeles Temple. Here sat Elder Hinckley, now President of the Church, and Keith Garner, the man Rozsa had piloted and protected during his visits into Vietnam for almost a year of his three year assignment. This time they rode together to attend Colonel Rozsa's final send-off not in the armed helicopter *Here After*, but in a car making the two hour drive to Hyrum, Utah.

They may have reflected on the feelings President Garner had expressed in a letter to Elder Hinckley dated June 3, 1966.

> To date, we have found some seven hundred Latter-day Saint service men, and now that transportation is more available and our District and Group organizations better organized, we'll find the other one thousand odd that they estimate are serving in the country.
> At our Zone Conference last Sunday, all of our District Presidencies of the various Districts or their counsellors were in attendance, and I've never attended a more spiritual meeting.

---

[82] Doctrine and Covenants 65:2

The hall was filled to capacity, and there were very few dry
eyes through the entire proceedings.

They treat me with the same deference that royalty merits,
and I have to keep reminding them that I'm just a mission president. I had to swear on the Book of Mormon that I'd visit them
every four to six weeks, and now that transportation will be
available to visit the outlying groups, I'm looking forward to
each return trip because it's such a great privilege and blessing."

President Garner, filled with the nostalgic reflections of their discussion,
reports, "It was a wonderful drive; we talked about traveling the whole world and
how the Church is in the whole world."

Keith supplemented the conversation with the observation that people of
differing cultures greet each other in defining ways. "We talked about cultures being
the product of how well the people eat and how much peace they have in their lives.
The thought came. In Asia they struggle for meals to eat because overpopulated their
production does not equal their consumption. In Asia, reflective of the concern that
food sufficient to feed millions is not a certainty, the Chinese greeting is 'Have you
eaten yet?' To them that's the most significant thing. The same is true in India.
I quoted again Ghandi's saying that when he meets the Lord they'll dine first, and
talk before, during, and after the meal.

I mentioned Israel where the scriptures say they will never have peace, so
their greeting 'Shalom' is heard in the marketplaces, schools, and neighborhoods of
Israeli cities. For them, the illusive state of peace is a fervent desire that seems almost
without the possibility of fulfillment."

Keith continued, "It's interesting that the American greeting is 'good morning,' a declared optimism for the day ahead. I said that among the Mormons if we
really understood and appreciated what we have, our greeting should be 'Have you
had a revelation today?'"

In actuality, President Garner's signature greeting really is "Have you had any
revelations lately?" Even though the question is generally asked with a twinkle in his
eye, he is not even a little surprised to have it answered in the affirmative. In Keith's
universe, personal and continuing revelation is fundamental to the gospel message and
our relationship to the Master. Even the words he uses in his farewells reflect this tenant of faith. "If you have any revelations, call me. I'll do the same. I'm always looking for them, fighting for them, repenting constantly so I'll be a candidate for them."

During those hours together, Keith was invited by President Hinckley to share
the lesson he had been preparing for one of his teaching opportunities. He happily
accepted and began by quoting the Prophet Joseph Smith, "Every man who has a calling to minister to the inhabitants of the world was ordained to that very purpose

in the Grand Council of heaven before this world was."[83]

Then he quoted Abraham. "Now the Lord had shown unto me, Abraham, the intelligences that were organized before the world was; and among all these there were many of the noble and great ones; And God saw these souls that they were good, and he stood in the midst of them, and he said: These I will make my rulers; for he stood among those that were spirits, and he saw that they were good; and he said unto me: Abraham, thou art one of them; thou wast chosen before thou wast born."[84]

Keith supported the prophet Abraham's point by quoting from a modern patriarchal blessing, "You are one of the honored and highly favored sons of God. Your noble spirit once dwelt in His presence, and your eyes beheld the beauties of the Eternal World, and you understood the principles of life and salvation, even before coming to this earth…He will require at thy hands much service in this Church and Kingdom. You are of the chosen lineage of Ephraim, one born under the New and Everlasting Covenant, and your testimony will be made strong and your voice will be heard in other lands besides this. The Lord will call you to go out as one of His messengers to proclaim the gospel to the nations."

Keith continued by asserting, "Studying and searching the scriptures opens the floodgates of our illustrious and glorious past where we lived in the presence of God, saw the beauties of the eternal world, and committed our lives to God--to live and preach and teach the gospel of Christ. For it is Christ who said, "This is my work and my glory – to bring to pass the immortality and eternal life of man."[85] Is it any wonder that Joseph Smith declared, "After all that has been said the greatest and most important duty of man is to preach the gospel"[86]?

He concluded with his own words, "The gospel is a heart matter, exclusively designed to rekindle in us the memories and commitments we made before coming to this mortal sphere."

Keith thought of the friend of his youth, Grant Foulger, and himself at age sixteen presenting themselves to patriarch Adam A. Bingham in Ogden for their patriarchal blessings. He looked at his friend seated beside him sixty-six years after that event and stated, "President Hinckley, through you that patriarchal blessing has been fulfilled."

Indeed, Keith thanks President Hinckley for giving him many of his opportu-

---

[83] Joseph Smith, *History of the Church*, vol. 6 (Salt Lake City: Deseret Book Company, 1967) 364.

[84] Abraham 3:22-23

[85] Moses 1:39

[86] Joseph Smith, *Teachings of the Prophet Joseph Smith*, comp. by Joseph Fielding Smith (Salt Lake City: Deseret Book, 1965) 113.

nities to serve. Why would President Hinckley extend such vital missionary assignments to the man from Sugar City, Idaho? Elder Hanks in describing his and Keith's friendship sheds some light on a possible answer to this question. "I've been honored by Keith's occasional exaltations about our kind of friendship. It is so well-founded on the sharing of eternal subjects of conversation and interest that we don't have to be in stride, left, right, left, right, all the way or feeling exactly the same about everything.

I've never known Keith to really aspire to anything except to be found worthy, and so he attracts friendships with people who really care about him, who are his friends, who receive and share inspiration, comfort, and encouragement."

Another chapter of Keith's designated missionary service came to a close on October 10, 1980, when a letter of release from President Benson arrived.

> Dear President Garner:
>
> With deep appreciation for the valuable services rendered by you, we hereby extend to you an honorable release as the first counselor in the International Mission Presidency. Your release will take effect immediately.
>
> You retire from your present position with our utmost confidence, goodwill and appreciation. We are grateful for your faithful administration and are confident that many of our Father's children have been blessed by your labors in the International Mission.
>
> We trust that throughout your life you will have the abiding satisfaction of knowing that you have contributed to the advancement of the Lord's kingdom on the earth.
>
> We earnestly pray that you may be greatly blessed of the Lord in all your future labors.
>
> Faithfully your brother,
Ezra Taft Benson
President

Perhaps even more significant because of their close association since December 22, 1978, when Elder Faust introduced Elder Asay to the Committee as its new president and when Keith became his first counselor, were the words President Carlos E. Asay wrote in a letter dated October 22, 1980.

> Dear Keith:
>
> Before memories become too dim, I want to thank you for all that you have shared with me these past several months, as we have associated together in the International Mission Presidency. You have been most supportive and willing to

assume your share and more of the load. For this and other expressions of kindness, I extend heartfelt thanks.

Among your many virtues, I have learned to appreciate and rely upon your sound judgment. Always, when important decisions were to be made, your counsel was solid. Another thing, I have appreciated the genuine interest which you have shown in people. Too often, I fear, we are prone to become program oriented at the expense of people. You helped us maintain a balance of perspective between programs and people.

May the Lord bless you always as you serve in other callings in the Church. Please know of my love and deep respect. Do call by when you have time. Don't become too involved again in your multiple enterprises.

Blessings to you.

His handwritten postscript read, "Please keep in touch!"

Keith had brought counsel to the committee often-repeated in diverse situations that "we need to be very wise because of the difficulties and differences manifest in the countries we oversee." He stressed the need for a simple approach and for timely responses so essential to successful programs.

Combined with President Ted Cannon's words "I miss your smiling face and gentle touch," Elder Asay's mention of Keith's talents, his "sound judgment," and "balance of perspective between programs and people," seem significant as one looks over his years of dedicated service to the Lord's Church. Serving the individual with sound judgment, a smiling face, and a gentle touch is the demarcation of Keith's day-to-day role in the building of the Lord's kingdom.

C h a p t e r

THIRTEEN

In the Refiner's Fire

An injury can grieve us only when remembered.
The noblest revenge is to forget.
Those who spiritually arrive are forgetters.
— Sunday, April 23, 1963, Mexico City Church meeting

While president of the Southern Far East Mission, President Garner snapped individual pictures of his missionaries. As he traveled to his mission assignments, he studied the snapshots connecting names to distinct, good-looking faces.

Changing roles did not lessen Keith's desire to acknowledge others with a personal salutation and a firm handshake. As bishop of the Menlo Park Ward, he mentally opened the camera's shutter. Visiting every member of his ward, he associated the faces with the names. While president of Temple Square Mission, he had photos taken of the tour guides and the Visitors' Center hosts and hostesses numbering more than a thousand. He attempted to retain each one in his memory.

His efforts in this regard led to his phenomenal retention of names. In the mission field where a last name is preceded by "elder" or "sister" or in his ward or on Temple Square where everyone responds to the simple appellation "brother" or "sister," his use of the one word titles saved him embarrassment on the rare occasion when the name escaped him.

Keith has always known how important an individual's name is to him. His greeting a person by name evidences a genuine regard. However, the heightened relevance Keith places on this precept is not based on behavioral science but on the heavenly template that the Lord knows each of us, His children, individually and by name. Accepting such a wonder-filled truth is tantamount to our acknowledgement of His interest in us and applied as Keith does elevates relationships with others.

When glancing through newspapers, he found a few names and faces for whom he had little regard. He jokingly suggested that he ought to extend his picture taking practice so he would have images to hang on his wall, not under the title "My Seminary Students" or "The Elite of Our Generation" or "Menlo Park Ward Members" or "Temple Square Volunteers," but under the pejorative title "Rogue's Gallery" or the applicable Book of Mormon phrase "The Slow of Heart." Of course, he did not create that kind of picture board because he was uninterested in remembering those names and faces, and having never gained much enjoyment from throwing darts, Mr. Garner had little use for a dart board.

His disappointment in the actions of people who in his estimation should have behaved better is simply a part of man's reaction to the human condition. One of my nieces wrote home from her mission in a letter received the day after Keith had expressed the same sentiment, "I tell you, the missionary work is the easy part of a mission. The most difficult part for me has been dealing with members, leaders, and companions." Perhaps they were both echoing Brigham Young, who reportedly wrote:

> To live with Saints in Heaven is bliss and glory.
> To live with Saints on Earth is another story" [87]

Keith is more specific. He comments on the necessity for members of the Church to sublimate unfriendly feelings, though entirely justified towards one another, by remembering that "the keeper of the gate is the Holy One of Israel." [88] He sadly states, "Sometimes we have to walk over the bishop's body to attend sacrament meeting. Maybe some of my ward members felt they had to walk over mine. I hope not."

He was intrigued by the response of an apparently trusting contractor to the question he posed, "Are you sure you will get paid?" The reply came quickly. "I know you are an active Mormon. If I don't get paid, I'll show up at your fast and testimony meeting."

Keith echoing other wise men's council states, "Among members of the Lord's Church who possess understanding minds and hearts, repenting and forgiving should be ceaseless."

Living in this repentant state necessitates a decency, courage, humility, and good sense that none of us robustly and consistently exercises. Confounded by the

---

[87] Richard Neitzel Holzapel and Jeni Broberg, *Women of Nauvoo* (Salt Lake City: Bookcraft, 1992), 69.

[88] II Nephi 9:41

actions of Church members, several of whom held Church leadership positions, a city employee, who is also a member of the Church, at the conclusion of a Board of Adjustment meeting, volunteered this strong suggestion. "Those people should read President Gordon B. Hinckley's *Standing for Something*, paying particular attention to the chapters on civility and integrity."

Keith is certainly not singling out members of the Church, only to the extent that they fall into the category of those to whom the Lord refers when he said, "For of him unto whom much is given much is required; and he who sins against the greater light shall receive the greater condemnation."[89] The problem is universal. During the days when the television series *Dallas* monopolized conversation around the water cooler, Keith, dealing with a lack of integrity in others, could be heard paraphrasing a line uttered by Larry Hagman, the actor portraying the fictional character, the sly, the ruthless J. R. Ewing. "Once you've lost your integrity, everything else is easy."

Perhaps as a substitute for the previously mentioned rogue's gallery, a 30" X 30" framed picture of an innocent looking, dimpled, pleasantly smiling man's face with a very long nose hangs on a wall in Keith's office; it is an obvious reference to the classic fairy tale *Pinocchio*, where the wooden puppet's nose grows longer when he tells a lie. Keith has tucked in the bottom of the frame a newspaper article written by Marc Lacey headlined **"Big Tobacco Grew Long Noses, but It's Not a Crime."** Personifying the headline is a picture of eight executives each holding his right hand to the square as they appear at a 1994 Congressional hearing. They each swear under oath, "I believe that nicotine is not addictive."

Referring to another headline, this one on the cover of a 1950s *Life* magazine, "America Is Great Because America Is Good," Keith shakes his head and utters a barely less than unequivocal, "No more."

He is not alone in these feelings. As a guest of Elder Hanks, Keith attended the Sixth Annual Board of Governors' Luncheon of Enterprise Mentors International held April 7, 2003, at the Joseph Smith Memorial Building. Following lunch and unable to gracefully excuse himself, he was reconciled to an afternoon of reports, remarks, and speakers as outlined on the program. Never comfortable sitting for any length of time, he surprised himself when the founder Menlo F. Smith's remarks completely captured him. Impressed by what he heard, he asked Mr. Smith if he had a copy of the words which he had so stirringly spoken. In the course of the conversation, Keith invited him to visit one of his Salt Lake ventures, the Garner Funeral Home. Mr. Smith accepted with the words, "What are you doing this afternoon?" The two spent the rest of a delightful afternoon together. When their visit concluded, he had been introduced to the unique history of the Salt Lake Mausoleum, had received a tutorial on the funeral business, and had witnessed firsthand the splendor of the facili-

---

[89] Doctrine and Covenants 82:3

ty now known as the Garner Funeral Home. He wrote to Keith the same week, "That was a most enjoyable hour or so I spent with you this past Monday. I'm grateful for the opportunity to get better acquainted with you and to visit one of Utah's great landmark buildings. It is truly impressive and unique! Thanks so much for the opportunity."

Keith received Mr. Smith's thanks in addition to a copy of his outstanding speech. Parts of the speech make him laugh, although it is certainly debatable whether one should laugh or cry. Keith chooses to chuckle rereading it, almost as energetically as he did at the initial hearing, probably because it brings to mind for him and obviously for other builders a few of his own battles.

NOAH IN THE YEAR 2003

It is the year 2003 and Noah lives in the United States.

The Lord speaks to Noah and says, "In one year I am going to make it rain and cover the whole earth with water until all is destroyed. But I want you to save the righteous people and two of every kind of living thing on the earth. Therefore, I am commanding you to build an Ark."

In a flash of lightning, God delivered the specifications for an Ark.

Fearful and trembling, Noah took the plans and agreed to build the Ark.

"Remember," said the Lord, "You must complete the Ark and bring everything aboard in one year."

Exactly one year later, a fierce storm cloud covered the earth and all the seas of the earth went into a tumult. The Lord saw Noah sitting in his front yard weeping.

"Noah," He shouted, "Where is the Ark?"

"Lord please forgive me!" cried Noah. "I did my best but there were big problems. First, I had to get a permit for construction and your plans did not comply with the codes. I had to hire an engineering firm and redraw the plans.

"Then I got into a fight with OSHA over whether or not the Ark needed a firesprinkler system and floatation devices.

"Then my neighbor objected, claiming I was violating zoning ordinances by building the Ark in my front yard, so I had to get a variance from the city planning commission.

"I had problems getting enough wood for the Ark, because there was a ban on cutting trees to protect the Spotted Owl. I finally convinced the U.S. Forest Service that I needed the wood to save the owls. However, the Fish and Wildlife Service won't let me catch any owls. So, no owls.

"The carpenters formed a union and went out on strike. I had to negotiate a settlement with the National Labor Union. Now I have 16 carpenters on the Ark, but still no owls.

"When I started rounding up the other animals, I got sued by an animal rights group. They objected to me only taking two of each kind aboard. Just when I got the suit dismissed, the EPA notified me that I could not complete the Ark without filing an environmental impact statement on your proposed flood. They didn't take very kindly to the idea that they had no jurisdiction over the conduct of the Creator of the universe.

"Then the Army Corps of Engineers demanded a map of the proposed new flood plain. I sent them a globe.

"Right now, I am trying to resolve a complaint filed with the Equal Employment Opportunity Commission that I am practicing discrimination by not taking godless, unbelieving people aboard.

"The IRS has seized all my assets, claiming that I am building the Ark in preparation to flee the country to avoid paying taxes.

"I just got a notice from the State that I owe some kind of user tax and failed to register the Ark as a recreational water craft.

"Finally, the ACLU got the courts to issue an injunction against further construction of the Ark, saying that since God is flooding the earth, it is a religious event and therefore unconstitutional.

"I really don't think I can finish the Ark for another 5 or 6 years!" Noah wailed. The sky began to clear, the sun began to shine and the seas began to calm. A rainbow arched across the sky. Noah looked up hopefully.

"You mean Lord, you are not going to destroy the earth?"

"No" said the Lord sadly. "The government already has."

AMEN [90]

Keith quotes Solon of Athens' rather discouraging yet real commentary on the earthly experience given centuries ago. "Like gaping fools we amuse ourselves with

---

[90] Menlo F. Smith adapted from an Internet transmission; source unknown.

empty dreams. Do not doubt it. Insecurity follows all the works of man. One man trying to do the right thing steps right into ruin and disaster because he cannot see ahead, while another behaves like a rascal and not only escapes the penalty of his own follies but is blessed with all kinds of success."

Life is not fair. Keith purchased a red Ferrari identical to the one driven by Tom Selleck on the *Magnum P.I.* series. "After playing a round of golf, I drove home." Keith remembers, "My route took me past a high school. I stopped to let some students cross the street. One young lady stopped right in the middle of the road, glared at me, truculently put her hands on her hips, and loudly informed me, 'Life isn't fair!'

Keith Garner, Senior, Sparks High School, Sparks, Nevada

I said with understanding, 'And don't you forget it, dear.'"

Solon's and this young woman's factual assertion does not excuse inaction or justify a dour outlook. Keith observes, "In mortality if the sun shines on you, great. If it rains on you, you still have to fight the battle. Rarely in matters of this world do you know with certainty how things will turn out."

Within the same discussion, he offers this comforting comment, "To believe in God is to know that all the rules will be fair, and that there will be wonderful surprises."

Keith, like the rest of us, has watched the inexplicable happen, lending credence to Solon's appraisal. During the depression years, he learned from a safe distance about the importance of hedging his bets. He observed a man whose inheritance had given him "deep pockets" wager thousands of dollars at the crap tables in Reno while just a few feet away outside on the street unemployed men begged for work so they could feed their families.

Keith always found work, even as a teenager, and when he found a job, he worked! In Sparks, Nevada he worked for his brother-in-law Clemence B. Waltz at the meat market after school and on Saturdays cleaning the cases with ammonia, washing down the walls and floors, leaving the premises spotless and ready for the next day's beef, mutton, pork, and poultry. Not too many years later, he returned the favor by taking Clem from Piggly Wiggly and setting him up in his own butcher shop in San Carlos, California.

Years after Clem's retirement, Keith invited him and his wife, Keith's sister Beatrice, to move to Utah. Clem helped out by making bank deposits, dropping off the mail, hiring maintenance workers, keeping secretaries entertained, and customers amused. Keith relates, "Occasionally I look up toward heaven and say, 'Clem, I've replaced you; I'm running messages now.' I have to call various other people to remind myself I'm Keith Garner and not Clem Waltz."

Neither would be mistaken for the other, but frankly Clem and Keith both possess an endearing charm. Each has been heard in his own way cajoling, captivating, and engaging bankers, contractors, waitresses, and others in unexpected topics of conversation unusual for normal customers. Each one could also be counted on to rush to another's aid. Of course, they never participated in the LDS Church's Young Women's Mutual Improvement program, but no Laurel ever was a better example of the class motto, "Serve gladly," than Keith and Clem. In doing so, Clem, like Keith, built enormous friendships. For example, when Clem was recovering from an operation, Keith's secretary went down to the bank to purchase a needed cashier's check. The only face the teller associated with Keith's account was Clem's. Even though one of the signers on the account, the secretary, was standing right in front of her, she insisted on calling Clem at home for his authorization. The smiling secretary thought the teller had made this outrageous demand because she'd missed their banter when Clem dropped off bank deposits. But back in 1936 Sparks, those memories were still to be made.

At Sparks High School some distance from the butcher shop, Keith's participation in the drama club immersed him in Shakespeare's *Merchant of Venice*, a play replete with quotes schooling the reader in "business" and "life" practices: letter of the law versus spirit of the law and mercy versus justice. Chosen by Richard Hillman, the drama teacher, to play Antonio, Keith and his taller, good looking friend Bill Casey exchanged parts.

Bill was smart, handsome, and honorable, and he came from an affluent family able to provide him with many advantages. After high school, he attended university and fought in World War II. Aboard a train taking him and other soldiers home and only a short distance from his destination, he, in his exuberance, leaned out the window and was struck by a yardarm. It killed him. It was a tragic twist to a life of promise. The only part Keith was allowed to exchange with this friend was his Antonio for Bill's Bassanio.

Keith and Bill explored together the twists and turns of life as the curtain rose on "The Trial Scene from The Merchant of Venice." As Bassanio, Keith rebuked

Shylock, played by Louis Quinn, in the following exchange between Bassanio, Shylock, and Antonio.

> Bassanio: This is no answer, thou unfeeling man, To excuse the current of thy cruelty."
> Shylock: I am not bound to please thee with my answers."
> Bassanio: Do all men kill the things they do not love?"
> Shylock: Hates any man the thing he would not kill?
> Bassanio: Every offense is not a hate at first.
> Antonio: I pray you, think you question with the Jew. You may as well go stand upon the beach and bid the main flood bate his usual height, you may as well use question with the wolf why he hath made the ewe bleat for the lamb, you may as well forbid the mountain pines to wag their high tops and to make no noise when they are fretten with the gusts of heaven, you may as well do anything most hard as seek to soften that--than which what's harder?--His Jewish heart. Therefore, I do beseech you make no more offers, use no farther means, but with all brief and plain conveniency let me have judgment and the Jew his will.
> Bassanio: For thy three thousand ducats here is six.
> Shylock: If every ducat in six thousand ducats
> Were in six parts and every part a ducat,
> I would not draw them. I would have my bond.
> Duke: How shalt thou hope for mercy, rendering none?
> Shylock: What judgment shall I dread, doing no wrong?...

Drawing from his own natural optimism and courageous independence, he had no trouble voicing Bassanio lines:

> Good cheer, Antonio! What, man, courage yet! The Jew shall have my flesh, blood, bones, and all Ere thou shalt lose for me one drop of blood.

These many years later Keith may not be able to quote unaided every word of Portia's well-known "quality of mercy" speech, but he has always known the less than well-practiced idea is worth assimilating.

> *The quality of mercy is not strained,*
> *It droppeth as a gentle rain from heaven*
> *Upon the place beneath. It is twice blest;*

The Merchant of Venice, Sparks High School, 1937; l to r: Shylock: Louis Quinn, Portia: Jean Cowles, The Duke: Vincent Keele, Antonio: Bill Casey, Bassanio: Keith Garner

It blesseth him that gives and him that takes.
'Tis mightiest in the mightiest. It becomes
The throned monarch better than his crown.
His scepter shows the force of temporal power,
The attribute to awe and majesty
Wherein doth sit the dread and fear of kings.
But mercy is above this sceptered sway,
It is enthroned in the hearts of kings,
It is an attribute to God himself,
And earthly power doth then show likest God's
When mercy seasons justice. Therefore, Jew,
Though justice be thy plea, consider this,
That in the course of justice none of us
Should see salvation. We do pray for mercy,
And that same prayer doth teach us all to render
The deeds of mercy...

In 1983, Lily Venton Simpson, one of Keith's classmates, graciously provided the Sparks Year Book for 1937 with the salutation, "I hope that this book can be helpful and will have pleasant memories for Keith." Glancing through the pages eliciting recollections, he spotted a picture. Titled "Trial Scene from *The Merchant of Venice*," the caption read, "With this familiar scene we won 2nd place and Jean Cowles again won the award for best Shakespearean actress in the state. Cast: Bassanio, Keith Garner; Antonio, Bill Casey; Portia, Jean Cowles; Shylock, Louis Quinn; The Duke, Vincent Keele."

Shakespeare provided the script; Keith spoke Bassanio's lines. As he memorized his lines and attended rehearsals, he quickly came to the conclusion that Shakespeare's powerful written words gave voice to some of his most cherished Mormon beliefs, beliefs he drew on as he dealt with others. Whatever talents Keith retained from his theatrical participation, it is unlikely that any casting director screentesting for a convincing pound-of-flesh Shylock would have given Keith a second glance. His peers in trying to characterize Keith may have found Portia's words and her cleverness in bringing about the final outcome perfectly reflective of their friend.

Keith's participation in other trial scenes had not stimulated any memories of Portia's prudence. As the invited speaker at the 1998 Hong Kong Missionary Reunion, he was asked to reminisce about his life since leaving the mission field. As he looked out over this group all these years later, he still saw in their now mature faces the "elite of their generation." Though he and they were not perfect, there were no places reserved in his imaginary rogue's gallery for these associates.

He began his speech the same way he had signed his correspondence to them, his missionaries, "My Companions."

> When Jerry James called and asked if I would say a few words at a thirty year reunion of the Hong Kong missionaries, I said yes. I'm delighted to participate. In the last few days since his invitation, I have thought and pondered and marvelled at the rapidity of "time gone by." Thirty years! I was only forty-nine then and seventy-nine today. Jacob of old wrote of his and their feelings, "The time passed away with us, and also our lives passed away like as it were unto us as a dream."[91]
>
> The time spent in the mission field was crowded with rich and rewarding experiences. And we, missionaries who did our duty, can look back and know that we did live after the manner of happiness. Basically that means we were sharing and testifying gospel truths and as the Prophet Joseph declared, "After all that is said and done, the greatest and most important duty is to teach the gospel." A worthy goal for us is to desire to be as

---

[91] Jacob 7:26

Enos and share his conviction when he writes, "I have declared it in all my days, and have rejoiced in it above that of the world."[92]

If we have carried that same spirit of the missionary out of the mission field into our lives, we would be following the truth enunciated by Marley as he tried to convey to Scrooge that being good in business is not the primary role of man, exclaiming, "Mankind is my business."

When I received my call to preside over the Southern Far East Mission, my friends in California who were not members of the Church couldn't believe that there was a Chinese Mormon and expressed so a number of times. In fact, one of them was called to do construction work in Viet Nam and came to Hong Kong to investigate the role of the Mormon Church and whether we were really converting Chinese.

We could outline the miracles of the kingdom in Hong Kong. Imagine living in #2 Cornwall Street, a mission home many hundreds of missionaries passed through on their way to assignments in all parts of Asia. Today on that spot stands a miracle of miracles, a Mormon Temple to the Most High God. The British have gone, the Communist Chinese rule, and the Church flourishes.

Having traveled the world many times and visited the exciting cities of the world, there is no place that equals Hong Kong. So what a great privilege we had having been called to serve there and having touched the lives of many great and wonderful people. Each of you tonight if called upon to add your testimony and recollections would buoy us up with renewed enthusiasm for teaching the gospel.

In spite of all the wonderful things that happened during our years spent in missionary service in the Southern Far East Mission, when it is time to return home, we're anxious to do that as well. It actually reminded me of a statement made by a young Mormon captain in Viet Nam when his eleven months of duty were up and he was giving his farewell to his brethren. His statement has stayed with me all these years.

He said, "I approach this moment with mixed emotions, joy intermingled with happiness."

After I returned home, I am pleased to say my opportuni-

---

[92] Enos 1:26

ties to do missionary work continued. I was called as a Regional Representative of the Twelve in northern California, then as a Mission Representative of the Twelve over Southeast Asia, the very areas I presided over as a mission president.

When we were there, the Southern Far East Mission covered half the world. When I went back as a Mission Representative, there were a number of missions in this area. It was gratifying to find faithful saints in Bangkok, Calcutta, Singapore. It brought to my mind the vision an angel gave to Nephi when he showed him the events that would transpire in the world in the latter-days. Nephi said he saw the Church of the Lamb of God was all over the world. They were few in numbers but armed with righteousness.

In 1974, I was called to return to Utah to preside over Temple Square. It was a wonderful opportunity for a missionary; I thoroughly enjoyed the challenges. I initiated bringing missionaries from French, Japanese, German, and Spanish speaking missions to serve their last few months at Temple Square. I brought women to the Square to conduct tours. We changed the tours from not only encompassing the marvelous history lessons but including testimony-bearing and gospel principle teaching. I am so pleased to see Temple Square a full-time mission with missionaries at their posts.

In the ensuing years, I was called to the presidency of the International Mission. I had the choice opportunity of recommending to the President of the Church many of my friends to serve in areas of the world not organized into formal missions such as Africa, Sri Lanka, and Israel…

How many times in the past thirty years when opportunities have come have we looked back on our mission experiences in Hong Kong as a graduate school for our life experiences.

My patriarchal blessing states, in my own words, I can live as long as I desire. I always mentally set up age seventy-two as my departure time based on the Lord having referred to the "age of man" as seventy-two. Well, seventy-two came and went, and during these past seven years I met Mr. Waterloo. What an experience! I understand things I never knew before and am grateful now I have tarried a little longer.

Will Durrant wrote in his *Lessons of History*, "Animals eat one another without qualm; civilized men consume one another by due process of law." I must have had a premonition this was going to happen to me because I quoted it often. I understand now what due process of law means.

I sat through some tough trials thinking, "For every good deed there's a punishment."

In a infinitesimal measure, I understand the life trials and struggles of the Prophet Joseph, and so when I read these great and wonderful revelations that were received by the prophet in Liberty Jail, etc, they have a full impact in my heart.

As I said before, I am glad I lived through these tests, for today I stand a bearer of the witness that God does empower and preserve us.

In Nephi's vision he referred to this Church as the Church of the Lamb of God. And I believe that. Our leaders today are endowed with the same power and authority that the Savior gave to his Apostles in the days of old. The Atonement of Christ is the most significant truth that has ever come into the world. And the companionship of the Holy Spirit should be the quest of all men. "For men are free to choose liberty and eternal life, through the great Mediator of all men, or to choose captivity and death, according to the captivity and power of the devil; for he seeketh that all men might be miserable like unto himself." [93]

Not present at this missionary reunion, but present in 2003 at a missionary gathering in Hawaii, Albert John Aki was reunited with four former Hong Kong missionaries. It was an occasion similar to the one described in the scripture he cited as he addressed President Garner on tape. "I remember one of the really important things in my life was that closing interview with you where you talked about Alma Chapter 17, about Alma meeting with the sons of Mosiah. Usually when anyone quotes that scripture, he goes right into the fasting and waxing strong and so on, but you brought out one point that I think a lot of people miss. Alma was so glad, so happy to see the sons of Mosiah after fourteen years on their missions, but what added more to his joy was that they were still his brethren in the gospel.

When I was mission president in Hong Kong, that is the same scripture that I used when the missionaries returned home. The thought was that one day if we meet again, of course we'll be happy to see each other but what will add more joy to us will be to know that we are still active in the gospel. I learned that from you. I sit around the dinner table tonight saying, 'I've never heard that point of view from anyone

---

[93] II Nephi 2:27

except from you.' It's been these many, many years that it has stuck in my memory. Sometimes I kind of wonder if it was because I came from a non-member family that you really wanted to make a strong point that I needed to remain active in the Church when I returned home. I really appreciated that closing interview."

President Garner concluded his remarks at this thirty year mission reunion with the same parting words he had given these and all his missionaries as they departed for home from the mission field. "It is great to be in your company. As I've greeted you this evening, it brings to my mind the feelings of Alma upon his reunion with the sons of Mosiah. "Alma did rejoice exceedingly to see his brethren; and what added more to his joy, they were still his brethren in the Lord." [94]

Those closing words and their "endure to the end" subtext is echoed in the closing joyous words found in the book of Job, words that convey comfort and solace to those who though bruised by life's trials tighten rather than loosen their trusting grip around the gospel of Jesus Christ.

Keith is not the Old Testament Job, but it is interesting how everyone relates to Job in some way. Job's story is the story of man's life in mortality. "Although affliction cometh not forth of the dust, neither doth trouble spring out of the ground; Yet man is born unto trouble, as the sparks fly upward." [95]

Deanne Greene and her husband Skip, along with others who had served with President Garner on Temple Square, attended a monthly fireside which he taught on the Book of Mormon for a decade following his release. During the days when some of the darts of his adversaries hit their mark and stung him, she sent to him a letter that elicited his responding with, "Young lady, you are indeed a poet!...insightful, con-soling. I was humbled by such kind words of understanding and solace. Thank you for the beautiful letter and for yours and Skip's friendship." Though his feelings remained cloistered and for the most part unshared, she and others speculated that if they had been in Keith's shoes they would have felt "Why me?" They considered the good he had done for others. They thought that his whole life had been devoted to declaring the Savior and Him crucified. They wondered if the Lord had withdrawn the protec-tive arms, apparent to all, which had encircled him for years. "Hast not thou made an hedge about him, and about his house, and about all that he hath on every side? thou hast blessed the work of his hands, and his substance is increased in the land." [96]

In fact, she wrote, "I don't think that I can even come close to imagining what you must be feeling...I cannot imagine that Job suffered any more than you must be."

Being such a pragmatic, practical optimist, Keith was unable to relate to any such dramatic description. His trials compared to Job's seemed minor to him, but

---

[94] Alma 17:2

[95] Job 5:6-7

[96] Job 1:10

only to him.

However, the dichotomy of suffering explained in Job did find utterance in Keith in this respect. He, too, increased in testimony and prospered. Job writes, "I have heard of thee by the hearing of the ear: but now mine eye seeth thee."[97] And if that was not more than sufficient, "...the Lord gave Job twice as much as he had before."[98]

Today Keith, in concert with the rest of the human family, looks over his shoulder for the next test, maybe even knocking on wood now and then. Having been delayed by his necessary attendance at a longer than usual Temple Square presidency meeting, he arrived late for the Capitol Hill Second Ward sacrament meeting. He quietly seated himself on the back row. He noticed a friend seated a row in front and to his left. Closing the meeting with prayer, the petitioner asked the Lord for trials in order to make them stronger. Almost startled by the request, both President Garner and his friend raised their bowed heads. She was shaking her head as if to say, "Please, no more, we have sufficient." Keith, catching her eye, nodded his concurrence with what he perceived to be her thoughts while whispering "Amen."

On a casual inspection in 2003 as the owner of the Garner Funeral Home and Salt Lake Mausoleum, Keith's gaze rested on his favorite Tiffany style stained glass window "City on a Hill," an allusion to the Biblical reference interpreted by Mormons to refer to Jerusalem and Independence, Missouri, sometimes even to Salt Lake City. Never free of strengthening trials, Keith surely had been tested in Salt Lake. It is not hard to imagine the rush of memories with which he was flooded as his eyes followed the curving stream bordered by colorful iris and tulips in bloom to the majestic building which always took him back to the University of San Francisco and his days spent in that city. Keith thought of Bishop Nalder, a mortician by trade, and wondered how surprised he would have been to know that the teenager he had tutored in the gospel all those years ago now owned a mortuary and mausoleum. He smiled as he thought of Bishop Nalder and his counselor in the San Francisco Ward bishopric, Dr. Vincent, a pediatrician. They embodied the slogan "From the womb to the tomb."

Keith knew another statement, "Truth is stranger than fiction," pertained to him when he was introduced as the local mortician. Owner of a funeral home, Keith Garner!?

Maybe it was not so unbelievable. In a notation Keith made in his journal on Saturday, the 13th of February 1971, he wrote, "Mother died 7:05 this morning-- really should have written graduated." So in Keith's case, acquiring and refurbishing a 1929 building used for "graduation" celebrations may not have been predictable but

---

[97] Job 42:5

[98] Job 42:10

maybe should have been expected. Who better to own a funeral home than someone with this hopeful, enlightened view of death?

Californian Cecil Bryan, who built over one hundred mausoleums in his life-time including ones in the famous Forest Lawn Cemetery, and nationally known architect Clarence Jay, if judged by words they'd had engraved in the French brown marble at the Salt Lake Mausoleum, agreed with Mr. Garner.

> *Oh, why these tears, these doubts, and fears?*
> *Why dread the fate of coming years?*
> *Day follows night - Hope's star is bright.*
> *Faith rends the clouds and heaven's in sight.*

In the same spirit that Bishop Garner had elevated the work on the Menlo Park Chapel, these men had, paying attention to timeless detail, constructed a masterful work which reflected a harmonious embrace of Gladstone's words, "Show me the manner in which a community cares for its dead, and I will measure with mathematical exactness the tender sympathies of its people, their respect for the laws of the land and their loyalty to high ideals." When Keith acquired the building, he accepted the premise and added in that same tradition beautiful, gated garden pavilions, niches, and crypt walls.

Walking these majestic halls and adorned grounds, Keith found images which produced memories of his own history. Over three dozen stained glass windows, which tradition holds were created at the famed New York City studio of Louis Comfort Tiffany, chronicle the natural beauty and pioneer heritage of Utah and beyond.

A window depicting a stagecoach full of adventurers headed for California invited memories of Keith's business ventures and his advice to California entrepreneurs in search of financial gains to "just jump out of an airplane with a good parachute, and wherever you land buy it, and you'll become rich."

Another window portraying a farmer tilling the ground summoned the recollection of having taken the young men and women from his ward to Oasis Burgers for milk shakes and telling them the following story defining the goal of work. "There were two farmers, one located in the San Joaquin Valley of California and one from Vermont. The farmer from Vermont visits his friend in California. He is taken on a tour. He sees fruits, vegetables, and flowers which grow year round with little effort. The California farmer visits his friend in Vermont. Upon his arrival he finds the farmer working in his garden, and so he picks up a shovel to help. He fights the Vermont soil, finding his shovel loaded with rocks rather than dirt ready for planting. Finally, sweating, he looks up at his friend and asks, 'By the way, what do you grow up in this country?' The Vermont farmer replies, 'Men.'"

Keith only has to walk down the corridor to a window commemorating the laying of the Golden Spike to have the message that hard work builds men reinforced. The 1896 vintage steam engine takes him to the days when his father worked for the railroad. Adjacent to this stained glass window are windows showing pioneers in a covered wagon, Indians sitting in front of tepees, and buffalo herds on the prairie. These likenesses take him back to the stories he has heard of his ancestors crossing the plains, speaking to the Indians in their native tongue, and helping to settle the West.

Likewise, reminders of Temple Square hover throughout the halls. Images of seagulls reminiscent of the Seagull Monument rouse memories of Keith's leaving California and coming to Utah. The brethren had called, and, of course, he had answered. A raft of people retained in their memories one of his most frequently spoken unconditional declarations. Patrick Abernathy voices it for all. "I related, probably as recently as ten days ago, a statement President Garner made all the time that I've carried with me all these years. It is a statement that stuck in my mind and will be there forever. He would say, 'Every good thing that has come in my life has come through The Church of Jesus Christ of Latter-day Saints.'"

As Keith reconnoitered the area, he glanced at the model crypt, a crypt without the marble facing, used to explain above ground entombment. His thoughts never lingered here long, except as he thought of the Savior's clean, dry entombment. He had heard that morning from President Charlie Goo. "I'll always remember you, President Garner, especially your knowledge of the Book of Mormon and the lessons we learned at your feet as missionaries. When I was a mission president in Hong Kong, I always wondered how you did so much: Taiwan, Philippines, Thailand, and also Hong Kong. I had a hard time with just Hong Kong alone.

A scripture I'll always remember that you stressed and that I memorized too is Alma talking to one of his sons Shiblon in Alma 38, verse 5, where he said, 'And now my son, Shiblon, I would that ye should remember, that as much as ye shall put your trust in God even so much ye shall be delivered out of your trials, and your troubles, and your afflictions, and ye shall be lifted up at the last day.'"

Wherever Keith looked, he saw the exquisite marble embellishing the Mediterranean architectural style: Italian white Carrera, Spanish black marble, called black gold, and Mexican coral. Turning the solid brass handles and opening one of the mahogany doors, he continued on his reminiscent journey through the funeral home.

The splendid handcrafted wood doors brought to mind a meeting with an expert and a missive from a craftsman. Keith had been introduced to Dr. Herbert A. Schroeder, a professor of Wood Chemistry at Colorado State University. When the topic turned to wood, he was the authority; his business cards made of wood were embossed with his name, address, telephone, and the type of wood. The craftsman's letter came from Jack Stuart, a Church convert who laid all the hardwood floors in the chapel in Menlo Park. His account was memorable as he told of the Vikings' use of wood, examples of which were still available for viewing one thousand years later.

As the funeral director Robert W. Wilcoxen, an affable, highly skilled professional, passed him in the hall, Keith might have thought, "What a good substitute for Bishop Nalder."

The sun's rays streaming through the glass picture window of the mountain peaks of the Wasatch front led Keith outside. The panoramic views of the Salt Lake valley below were breathtaking. Keith's favorite window "City on a Hill" is nearly replicated on the grounds of the funeral home. Walking up the path bordered by a stream edged with an array of flowering bushes and bulbs, Keith ascended to the pavilion at the top of the slope. He could see his home as he looked farther northeast. He had told many of his associates that he intended to install a slide from his house to the funeral home, and when he died, he wanted to be dropped down the chute.

On this memory-filled walk Keith could have bid any of his many friends to accompany him. Had he invited Senator Orrin Hatch, he would have heard him say, remembering his 1976 election to the Senate, "Keith worked so hard. He called all of his friends and told them they had to vote for me. Most of them didn't even know who I was; I had zero name recognition when I filed on the last day. He was a whirling dervish on my behalf. Keith during the election gave the maximum donation he could and he helped to raise funds for me. I used to go visit him during the campaign in the Kearns, McIntyre Building. He had a really interesting office. We would sit there and chat; he was always ebullient and always uplifting and always building me so that I had the emotional and physical strength to do what I did. It was wonderful to have a good friend like him helping me, to have somebody of his capacity, his decency, his influence, his reputation, his dedication back me.

We had a dear friendship even before that but ever since for sure. He's always been there ever since too.

He invited me to his beautiful home up there on the avenues. A while after I was elected, he called me and said, 'You've got to come to a fireside at our house.' I was pretty busy but I didn't want to turn Keith down so Elaine and I went and, lo and behold, the speaker was none other than Gordon B. Hinckley. It was a marvelous thing but the second speaker was Orrin Hatch; he didn't tell me I was going to be one of the speakers. To follow President Hinckley was not exactly an easy thing to do, but I had a great time and I did my best. It was one of the uplifting things of my life to be there, not only with Keith but to listen to President Hinckley.

Keith is a very strong member of our faith, always given and done his best to promulgate the gospel. He has a friend for eternity in me."

The night of the election and the following morning, the telephones at Temple Square were flooded with calls to President Garner congratulating him on Senator Hatch's victory. One would have thought he was the candidate, but then he always worked as hard for others as he did for himself. Keith says, "The best thing about Senator Hatch is his wife Elaine." To which the senator responds, "She is." Keith continues, "He is articulate, intelligent, conservative, the kind of senator the state of Utah should have."

There was nothing conservative about the experience Keith afforded to another associate, Sandra Rushforth, who invited to walk with him would have told him, "It didn't really surprise me at all when Susan told me that Keith Garner, her boss, was offering us his VIP tickets to the 1997 NBA Finals between the Utah Jazz and the Chicago Bulls in Salt Lake City. We could have them if we wanted. Never mind that they were on the second row about mid-court and that he had a boat load of high-level friends he could have invited or to whom he could have given the tickets. Never mind that he could have sold them for four times their face value. (Is it legal in Utah?)

Even though he always seemed to have the best, he really never seemed that tied to things. They never really seemed that important to him. I happily accepted the opportunity to see a finals game and treated it like the once-in-a-lifetime event it was for me. We bought Jazz shirts and come game day we enjoyed the pre-game buffet dinner, then went to our seats.

One of my nephews came down to see what the view of the floor was from our seats and was impressed with how close we were to the players and the media personnel who were on the sidelines. I spent my pre-game time collecting autographs from Chris Tunis, Gail Miller, Steve Young, Larry Miller, Ruth Todd, Hot Rod Hudley, Roger Davis, and Gretchen Carr. I appreciated very much his generosity in giving us the tickets because that experience that night could not be duplicated, but it didn't surprise me."

Sandra did surprise Keith when the morning of the game she showed up at his office with a large basket overflowing with Jazz memorabilia: a watch, a shirt, a pennant, a cap, a key chain, taffy...as her way of saying, "Thank you."

At Keith's side at Jazz games, sailing or boating on Lake Tahoe, walking the beaches in LaJolla, riding dune buggies in Heber, cruising the oceans (no wonder he was tapped to accept a position on the board of the Utah Travel Council working alongside director Alton V. Fraiser, who took him to dinosaur country in Moab and to other Utah destinations) might have been any number of friends from his days in the mission fields of Hawaii and Southeast Asia, in the bishopric and seminary class in Menlo Park, on the grounds at Temple Square, in the ventures of building, developing, and selling.

One of those friends Richard Peery, a seminary student of Bishop Garner, and himself now the bishop of a Stanford student ward, might have found more fascinating a walk through the funeral home with his former seminary teacher as he took in the beauty of the surroundings and reminisced.

"My memories mostly consist of my admiration for him at the time I was growing up and in high school. I will always remember him for his ability to inspire and to get people to reach to a higher level and the way he got to know each of us individually. He had boundless energy in every respect with everything and everyone whether building a building, teaching the gospel, pursuing anything that interested him, or anything that was needed. When our stake center was built, he was in charge of the construction and design, and I know it was built to a whole different quality standard because of his leadership.

Seminary he led with gusto. He knew everybody individually and his strengths, weaknesses and what he needed to grow. I was not a serious seminary student at the time, but at least I was showing up everyday. I showed up because he always had good stories and kept us entertained. He slipped the gospel in there at the same time. I've always admired him and his dedication and his abilities to accomplish. Our ward, our youth, and the stake moved to new levels of excellence when Keith Garner was there. There wasn't anybody that didn't know him or that he didn't know. He knew their spirit and their heart, and his friendship and love were a great blessing for us at that time.

Every place he's been, from his mission to Temple Square, and throughout his life, he's tried to do what the Lord wanted him to do with the best abilities he had at the time. If problems arose in his life, and those happened from time to time, he's been resilient and been able to take those on and learn from his mistakes, and come out on top in the end."

Not available for a walk with his former mission president, Kent Watson e-mailed him from Taiwan the following summary of his memories, "I was privileged to serve as the mission president's assistant in Taiwan from before his arrival until my departure in April of 1966. Looking back, I now appreciate more the trust and confidence that President Garner placed in me. His mission covered a huge geographic area that now includes the ten missions comprising the Asia Area, plus all of the missions comprising the Philippines. Viet Nam and the many servicemen's groups during wartime were also a part of his stewardship. It was also a time of significant growth, publishing of the Book of Mormon in Chinese, and opening new territories. He was so busy and had such a large area of the world to cover we only saw him in Taiwan on two or three occasions. On those occasions, he instilled in us the faith and enthusiasm to be actively engaged on our own in his absence. I recall with some clarity how he enthused us about the Book of Mormon by citing various passages by heart and relating story after story to our work in a vigorous manner that instilled excitement, faith and testimony. Currently serving as a mission president for the second time, I can now appreciate more than ever his outstanding contribution in establishing the Church in Asia and touching the lives of so many missionaries, members and peoples of all different languages, cultures and persuasions.

We were recently instructed by Elder L. Tom Perry and Elder Earl C. Tingey that you could only judge the effectiveness of a mission president after time in determining what manner of men his missionaries and their children became. Using this as a measure, one better understands President Garner's service. In Taiwan alone which comprised only one small zone of his very large mission, I am aware of at least eight mission presidents--Larry Chen, Harvey Horner, Karl Koerner, Kent Larkin, Pat

Price, Richard Stamps, Larry White, Kent Watson--who I think were previously his missionaries. Perhaps there are more. This is just a small example. If one could inventory the accomplishments of his many many missionaries (professional accomplishments, Church service, families, children, and grandchildren) a book of volumes could be written about how his service and mentoring affected the lives of perhaps thousands."

Keith's response to the question, "Who are you?" is an emphatic "I'm a struggling sinner." J. Kent Larkin volunteered, "Keith is a saint." Both are true, and so perhaps the answer should be "He is a struggling saint."

During one of his resonant conversations, this time on the topic of the judgment, Keith, trying to justify his position that there really won't be a judgment per se, was quoting the scripture "Ye cannot say, when ye are brought to that awful crisis, that I will repent, that I will return to my God. Nay, ye cannot say this; for that same spirit which doth possess your bodies at the time that ye go out of this life, that same spirit will have power to possess your body in that eternal world."[99] Keith concludes, "We will already be judged."

Merrill Osmond shared with Keith a poignant dream he had experienced relating to "the judgment." Keith remembers, "In his dream, Merrill was awakened, and he saw a beautiful half-moon curving staircase. At the bottom of the staircase there were chairs. The chairs were occupied by individuals. At the top of the staircase, there were three thrones and a table in front with crowns. On each side of the staircase were bleachers. The individuals seated on the chairs below were called by name. When called, the person summoned ascended the staircase towards the thrones. As he ascended the stairs, the bleachers miraculously filled with people. Merrill indicated to me that these were the supporters of the person climbing up to the throne, the recipients of the good deeds performed by the person being judged. Before the throne he was crowned with a crown of glory. The brilliance of his crown was in direct proportion to the acclaim given to him by those in the bleachers. After that was done, another person was called. All those in the bleachers vanished away, and another group took over their seats. I thought 'Merrill is recounting Matthew 25.'

Merrill said this dream was accompanied by beautiful background music. He said upon waking he wrote down the music as he remembered it. With his melodious voice, he sang the heavenly music to me."

Keith referenced the scripture, "And if it so be that you should labor all your days in crying repentance unto this people, and bring, save it be one soul unto me, how great shall be your joy with him in the kingdom of my Father!

And now, if your joy will be great with one soul that you have brought unto me into the kingdom of my Father, how great will be your joy if you should bring

---

[99] Alma 34:34

many souls unto me!"[100]

After hearing Merrill's depiction of the judgment, a knowledgeable listener proffered, "If that's the way it works, when it is Keith's turn, Peter's army of angels will be assigned to crowd control."

In his attempt to put together an advertising plan for the Garner Funeral Home, Keith became acquainted with Emmy Award winning Michael Dunn. Mike, a creative, imaginative writer/producer, was well-known for his life/death experience in the mountains near Jackson Hole, which he had shared across the country and finally recorded under the title *Bears and Prayers*. Keith hired Mike to create a brochure, web site, and logo for the Garner Funeral Home and Salt Lake Mausoleum. His brochure won *Print Magazine*'s Western Regional Design Award for outstanding brochure. Words from the pamphlet expressed Keith's now realized vision for the five acres in the foothills of Salt Lake City. "Here, on a hillside, is a refuge of rest. Within this respite from the world, there are meandering walkways, gently spilling waterfalls, majestic marble corridors, sprawling native plant life, and elegant tributes to life engraved upon brass plaques. It is truly a rare combination of elements which have combined to create a gentle aura of peace and tranquility."

Mike appreciated the recognition from *Print Magazine*, but more significant to him were President Hinckley's expressions of appreciation in a letter to Keith.

> November 4, 1998
>
> Dear Keith:
>
> I have looked over the brochure which you sent. It is a beautiful piece of work. The layout is artistic. The typography is excellent.
>
> The photo of the chapel is particularly impressive. You have done a wonderful work up there.
>
> Everything you touch becomes attractive. You have a wonderful sense of artistry.
>
> My very best wishes to you.

President Hinckley's support of his friend never seems to diminish.

The image Mike incorporated into the logo and Keith selected from the six or seven concepts presented to him is the international sign for Resurrection. It appears as a man rising and as used in the Garner Funeral Home logo is placed above the outline of a spring flower, the tulip.

Keith's selection, a picture that could hang anywhere, is certainly an appropriate symbol. Whether in life or in death, everything that really matters leads right to

---

[100] Doctrine and Covenants 18:15-16

the redeeming and atoning sacrifice of the Savior of the world. "In this world you shall have tribulation: but be of good cheer; I have overcome the world."[101]

---

[101] John 16:33

Chapter

FOURTEEN

Pressing on in the Work of the Lord

*"People grow old only by deserting their ideals. Years may wrinkle the
skin, but to give up interest wrinkles the soul. You are as young as your
faith, as old as your doubt; as young as your self-confidence, as old
as your fear; as young as your hope, as old as your despair. In the
central place of every heart there is a recording chamber; so long as
it receives messages of beauty, hope, cheer and courage, so long are
you young. When...your heart is covered with the snows of pessimism
and the ice of cynicism, then and then only are you grown old--
and then, indeed, as the ballad says, you just fade away."* [102]
— General Douglas MacArthur

Keith's life has not been boring. His personality bubbles with the energy of a
healthy body, an inquisitive yet practical intellect, and a generous spirit. His is a life
full of a wide variety of experiences. And, oh, yes, he stumbles into unanticipated
adventures and undeserved difficulties. He stubs his toe on his own impatience and
slips on trust he has given unreservedly to others.

Keith's testimony of the gospel of Jesus Christ is his immovable rock, the
defining quality of his life. It presses him to seize his innovative urges and push forward. It allows him to dare to be himself in challenging situations. It requires him to

---

[102] William Manchester, *American Caesar* (Boston: Little, Brown, and Company, 1978),
702.

Keith E. Garner in front of a life full of memories

accept assignments to move the Lord's work along from those with the authority to issue such calls. It turns duty into a cheerful lifestyle. It transforms the heat of the refiner's fire into the gold of mastering the trials the Lord promises to those he loves. And most importantly, it keeps the gift he desires the most, the greatest of all the gifts of God, eternal life, at the center of his world.

The present embraced both the past and the future as Keith rang the outer entry bell at the South Temple condominium of Elder David B. Haight and Sister Ruby Haight. Sister Haight answered the buzzer, told Keith she had tried to reach him to delay his coming for an hour, and asked if he would indulge her and return in a half an hour for their visit. Keith, cognizant of Ruby's age, 92, thought the delay might be ascribed to her advanced age, that she might need extra time to be, as he described it, "up and moving." Keith even felt a rush of guilt at having asked her to make the effort to allow this visit.

Nonetheless, spurred on by uncertain assurances that Sister Haight was well and absolutely certain pledges that she was eager to see him, he returned forty-five minutes later, purposely having given her a few extra minutes. Sister Haight greeted Keith enthusiastically with a warm embrace, ushered him into her inviting home, and apologized for the postponement. Keith received her explanation with delight. She said that her morning activity, reading the Book of Mormon with a lovely younger lady, had extended longer than normal. Together Ruby and this bright, inquisitive non-member were reading one of Keith's favorite books, Jacob, and they had not wanted to stop.

After her explanation, Ruby's first comment to Keith was "Who are you teaching?" She asked believing he, too, at eighty-three would still be involved in spreading the good news contained in the gospel of Jesus Christ. She looked unsurprised when he answered that sharing the truths of the Book of Mormon with several interested families appeared on his mental appointment book each week. In fact, he had scheduled a "cottage meeting," a term prevalent in his days as a missionary in Hawaii, that very evening.

Here sat friends of over fifty years reminiscing in fond terms of past associations, but more consequentially sharing the present wrapped in their common embrace of the principles of the gospel. The Book of Mormon prophet Mosiah wrote, "And for a testimony that the things that they had said are true they have brought twenty-four plates which are filled with engravings, and they are of pure gold." [103] The wealth of the world cannot compete with friendships fired by the truths of this record written on "pure gold" plates.

In this atmosphere of remembering, Sister Haight smiled as she heard that on a prior occasion Elder Haight had volunteered that Sister Haight knew which casseroles were Keith's favorites. In those halcyon days of Menlo Park when Elder Haight was President Haight and Keith was Bishop Garner, the stake officers and bishoprics used to enjoy each other's company at frequent dinner parties. Watching these two friends discuss shared topics of interest, it seemed almost ordinary to hear Ruby say, "I liked to sit by Keith at dinner parties because he always talked about the scriptures." Keith rejoiced in what he accepted as the most laudatory of compliments and thought about his days as a mission president. He hoped his missionaries had scrambled over each other to sit by him at meals, not just because he never finished anything on his plate and shared his abundance with those seated next to him, but because they felt as Sister Haight did.

The scriptural substance of these dinner conversations often could be found in the first book of the Book of Mormon in which Lehi writes of the most priceless principle of the restored gospel:

> *Wherefore, how great the importance to make these things*
> *known unto the inhabitants of the earth, that they*
> *may know that there is no flesh that can dwell in the*
> *presence of God, save it be through the merits, and mercy,*

---

[103] Mosiah 8:9

and grace of the Holy Messiah, who layeth down his life
according to the flesh, and taketh it again by the power
of the Spirit, that he may bring to pass the resurrection
of the dead, being the first that should rise. [104]

Thus, not surprisingly, Keith is a man who takes personally Rabbi Abraham Joshua Heschel's observation. "The greatest problem is not how to continue but how to exalt our existence. The cry for a life beyond the grave is presumptuous, if there is no cry for eternal life prior to our descending to the grave. Eternity is not perpetual future but perpetual presence. He has planted in us the seed of eternal life. The world to come is not only a hereafter but also a herenow." [105]

In a sentinel moment in his life in Tehran, forty-one year old Keith Garner held in his hands gold plates. Almost daily in his personal study time in nearly every part of the globe, he has held in his hands the product of gold plates given to Joseph Smith for translation by a messenger from the presence of God, the Book of Mormon. In so doing he has felt the companionship of the Book of Mormon prophets as they speak from the grave. He has known the companionship of modern day prophets as he has walked the earth with them, preaching the revealed word and building the kingdom of God in these latter days.

Now, even as this attempt to share golden moments, memories, and musings is concluded, Keith E. Garner begins new hours secure in "pure gold" doctrine as he lives a life of duty, discovery, and destiny.

---

[104] II Nephi 2:8

[105] Abraham Joshua Heschel, *Man is Not Alone* (New York: Harper & Row, 1951), 295.

ACKNOWLEDGEMENTS

My heartfelt thanks is extended to all who assisted in making this book possible. Four require particular mention. Elder Marion D. Hanks, my sister Kathleen Goodwin, and my friend Suzette Kinzer, who read the manuscript with an editor's eye, and Elaine Cannon, who though she did not live to see the last completed chapters made me promise to see this story through to the book shelves.

Everyone was generous and graciously available; their names follow in alphabetical order. Patrick B. Abernathy, Albert John Aki, Borge B. Anderson, Sherman F. Anderson, Edwin K. Andrus, Kathy Andrus, Roy Avondet, David Bacon, Sidney Badger, Peter W. Basker, Beverly S. Beasley of the City of Menlo Park, Kathy Beilfus, Judge Jerome T. Benson, David L. Bird, Mike Blackmore, Marvin Brinkerhoff, Donald P. Brown, Donna Brown, George E. Brown, Douglas R. Buck, William J. Christiansen, Linda Dalley, Colonel LaVoi B. Davis, Samuel Davis, James R. Derrick, Jr., Diane Dunford, Michael Dunn, Chester H. Elliott, Gordon F. Esplin, Roger Evans, Patrick Farrell, Thomas Stuart Ferguson, Dorothy Fielding of the Church Missionary Department, Arnold B. Fluckiger, Grant Foulger, C. W. Freston, Alan V. Funk, Bette A. Gardnber, Kay Garff, Kent Garner, Susan B. Garner, Worth B. George, Jamie Glenn, Lynne Garner Godfrey, Charles W. H. Goo, Carl Ben Goodwin, Jr., David D. Goodwin, Jonathan S. Goodwin, Rachel Ann Goodwin, Deanne Greene, Randi Greene, David Bruce Haight, Jr., Angela Bowen Haight, Ruby Olsen Haight, Clark Hamblin, Richard Harris, Dr. Leon R. Hartshorn, Bea Hartshorn, Linda Haslam of the Church Historical Department, Senator Orrin Hatch, Sidney B. Henderson, Alan H. Hess, Dr. Ray C. Hillam, Richard Hillman, Donald Ray Hinton, Carla C. Hosein of the Oriental Institute Museum in Chicago, Illinois, Dorothy Hintze, Wayne Hintze, Proctor Hug, Mitchell W. Hunt, Julie G. Isaacson, Jerry W. James, Newell K. Johnson, Barbara Jones, Gloria L. Kelly, Eugene L. Kimball, Karl R. Koerner, Ronald Lam, Richard Lambert, J. Kent Larkin, Peter Lassig, Fred Latu, Joan Latu, Duane A.

Lee, Dr. Llewelyn Leigh, Margaret Young Leigh, Agnes Farnsworth Lindsay, Gary Little, Erlyn Gould Madsen, Clora Martin, Frank Martin, Stan Mattson, Elder Neal A. Maxwell, Marcia Crofts McLain, Douglas McOmber, John J. McSweeney, Aubin J. Meizel, Cliunt Merrell, Marcia Smith Merrill, Jenet Mills, Kevin Mills, NaConna Millward, Ruth Montoya, Craig Morrison, Robert G. Mouritsen, Clark R. Nielsen, Robert M. Ord, Jennett Osmond, Merrill Osmond, Jennifer Peery, Mimi Peery, Richard Peery, Barbara Grimmer Pennington, Kathryn Phillips, David E. Poulsen, Charles Pollei, L. P. Quinn, Dr. C. Elliott Richards, John D. Richards, Stephen L. Richey, Kristina Rodriguez of The Church Missionary Department, JoAnne Rogers, Craig Rushforth, Sandra Rushforth, Kathryn Ruzicka, Leo Sant, Maralynn V. Sant, Eva C. Scarselli, Gayle Garner Schenk, Herman J. Schlesselmann, Blanche Wycoff Scranton, Lilly Venton Simpson, Earl C. Sloan, Gerald G. Smith, Menlo F. Smith, Rita Smith, Mary Ann Soong, John G. Southerland, Don H. Staheli, Seth Layton Stewart, Alexia Nelson Stewart, Judge Stephen J. Swift, Nita Sloan Taylor, Dee Tolles, Lee H. Van Dam, Phyllis P. Warnick, Kent Watson, Franklin L. West, Hugh S. West, Sue West, Karl H. Wheatley, Larry R. White, "Tip" Whitehead, E. V. (Red) Wolford, Ken Woolley.

Without a doubt inadvertent omissions have occurred. Please forgive any oversights; such imperfection seems synonymous with life.

And finally to all secretaries who at their posts behind-the-scenes play important supporting roles.

INDEX

A ROOKIE BIOGRAPHY

L. FRANK BAUM

Author of
The Wonderful Wizard of Oz

By Carol Greene

CHILDRENS PRESS®
CHICAGO

This book is for Diane Babb.

L. Frank Baum (1856-1919)

Library of Congress Cataloging-in-Publication Data

Greene, Carol.
    L. Frank Baum: author of the Wonderful Wizard of OZ / by Carol
Greene.
      p.   cm. — (A Rookie biography)
    Includes index.
    ISBN 0-516-04264-5
    1. Baum. L. Frank (Lyman Frank), 1856-1919—Juvenile literature.
    2. Authors, American—20th century—Biography—Juvenile literature.
    3. Oz (Imaginary place)—Juvenile literature. [1. Baum. L. Frank (Lyman
Frank), 1856-1919. 2. Authors, American.] I. Title. II. Series: Greene,
Carol. Rookie biography.
PS3503.A923Z67   1995   94-37514
                                           CIP
                                           AC

L. Frank Baum
was a real person.
He lived from 1856 to 1919.
Frank wrote many
books for children,
including *The Wonderful
Wizard of Oz*.
This is his story.

TABLE OF CONTENTS

Chapter 1

Scary Things and Secret Places

There it hung in the field,
big and spooky and still.
But wait! It moved!
It was getting down
from its post.

Its long, long legs
brought it closer, closer.
It was going to get him!

Little Frank Baum
woke up screaming.
He'd had the nightmare again,
the scarecrow nightmare.

"He reads too many fairy tales,"
said Frank's parents.
"And he's not very healthy."

Frank *did* love fairy tales
and he *wasn't* healthy.
He had angina pectoris,
a heart problem
that made his chest hurt.

A street in Syracuse, New York, as it looked when L. Frank Baum was born

But Frank still had fun
with his brothers and sisters.
They lived on a farm, Rose Lawn,
near Syracuse, New York.

The children played croquet,
baseball, and other games.
They had friends over
and went for carriage rides.

Frank's parents, Cynthia and Benjamin Baum

They didn't even have to leave
Rose Lawn to go to school.
Mr. and Mrs. Baum hired
teachers to come to them.

Frank couldn't play rough games
because of his heart.
But his mind got
plenty of exercise.

Frank liked to hide in
secret places with his toys
and make-believe friends.
There he made up stories.
He wanted to write
fairy tales someday.

But Frank knew how much
witches and goblins scared him.
So he promised himself
that he wouldn't put
scary things in *his* tales.

Frank didn't keep that promise.

Peekskill Academy (below) was located in
the beautiful Hudson River valley (above).

Chapter 2

From School to Axle Grease

~~~~~~~~~~~~~~~~~~~~~~~~~~~~~~~~~~~~~

When Frank was twelve,
his doctor said he could
go away to boarding school.
Frank's parents chose
Peekskill Academy
in Peekskill, New York.

Peekskill was a military school.
Boys there learned to march
and shoot a gun.
They played rough games.

Peekskill Academy as it looked in the 1930s

Frank hated it.
He hated always being busy.
He hated the way
teachers hit students.
He hated the rough games
and the guns and the marching.

12

The main building at Peekskill Academy. Frank was not happy there. He left after two years.

Frank stayed at Peekskill
for two long years.
Then something happened.
No one knows just what.
Maybe Frank had a heart attack.
Maybe he just fainted.

But Frank's parents let him
come home at last.

For his fourteenth birthday,
Frank's father gave him
a little printing press.
It was the perfect gift.

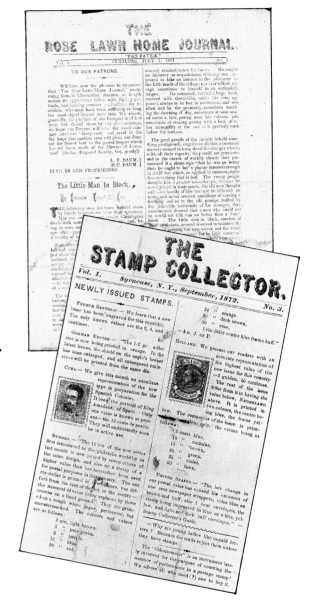

Frank and his brother Harry published newspapers (right) and a magazine for stamp collectors (below right).

Frank and his brother Harry started a newspaper for their neighborhood. Then, when Frank was seventeen, he started another paper and a magazine for stamp collectors.

Later, Frank raised fancy chickens with his father and Harry. So he started a magazine about raising chickens.

Frank at age 21 (above).
He acted the part of
a young artist (left)
in a play called
The Maid of Arran.

As time passed, Frank went
from one job to another.
He was an actor for a while.
Then he began to write a musical.

Maud Gage Baum in 1900

Frank was
still working
on the musical
when he met
Maud Gage.
Soon he wanted
to marry her.

Maud's mother said Maud
would be "a darned fool"
to marry Frank.
Maud decided to be
"a darned fool."
They were married in 1882.

This ad is for the Castorine Axle Oil that Frank sold in the 1880s.

For a while, Frank acted
in his musical and
he and Maud traveled.
Then they rented a house in
Syracuse and Frank sold
axle grease for wagon wheels.

In 1883, Frank, Jr., was born.
Robert came along in 1886.
Now Frank was a family man.

Top left: Frank opened a store in this building in Aberdeen, South Dakota. Top right: Frank Baum in the 1890s. Below: Frank acted in plays with this theater group in Aberdeen.

Chapter 3

Oz!

The next few years brought
more moves and changes.
First the Baums moved to
Aberdeen, South Dakota,
and opened a store.

When the store
closed, Frank ran
a newspaper.
Two more little
boys, Harry and
Kenneth,
were born.

Frank's sons Kenneth (left)
and Harry. Frank had
many costumes and wigs
that the boys used
when they played "actor."

State Street in Chicago, Illinois, looked like this in the early 1890s.

In the living room of the Baums' house in Chicago: (left to right)
Frank, Jr., Robert, Harry (holding the cat), Kenneth, and Frank

At last, the Baums moved
to Chicago and Frank found
a job selling dishes.
But when he wasn't working,
he loved to tell stories
to his boys and their friends.

Sometimes Frank made up
stories about the characters
in nursery rhymes.
Maud's mother thought
those stories were good.

She made Frank send
them to a publisher.
Mother Goose in Prose
came out in 1897.

Then Frank's heart began
to bother him again.
His doctor said he shouldn't
sell dishes anymore.
So Frank wrote full-time.

William Denslow at work on his drawings

Frank had a whole stack of
funny poems he had written.
He showed them to
an artist, William Denslow.

Denslow drew pictures
to go with the poems,
and *Father Goose, His Book*,
came out in 1899.

Till then, most pictures
in children's books were
in black and white.
But Frank and Denslow
wanted color on every page.

That was a good idea.
Father Goose became the
best-selling children's book
of the year.

One day, Frank was telling
a story to his boys
and their friends.
It was about a girl who
is blown by a cyclone
to a magic land.

All at once, something
clicked in Frank's mind.
He shooed the children away
and began to write
as fast as he could.

The Wonderful Wizard of Oz was Frank Baum's most famous story.

The story was about
Dorothy and her dog, Toto,
who traveled to the land of Oz.
They had adventures with
the Scarecrow, the Tin Woodsman,
and the Cowardly Lion.

Denslow painted pictures
with plenty of color,
and in 1900, *The Wonderful
Wizard of Oz* came out.

"Where did you get the name 'Oz'?"
people asked Frank.

He said he was looking
at his file drawers.
The first was labeled A-G.
The second said H-N.
The third said O-Z and
that's where he got the name.

Frank's sense of humor is shown in this portrait photo.

That *might* be true.
Or it might be another story
that Frank made up.
Sometimes he couldn't stop himself.

Frank didn't want to put
scary things in his story,
and he didn't think he had.
But some children thought
the cyclone and the Wicked Witch
of the West were pretty scary.

They didn't mind, though.
They loved the book.
The Wonderful Wizard of Oz
was the best-selling
children's book for 1900.

The Scarecrow and the Tin Woodsman from *The Wizard of Oz*,
as they looked in a stage production of the early 1900s

Chapter 4

More Oz

Soon Frank and Denslow
began work on a musical
of *The Wizard of Oz*.
Paul Tietjens wrote the music.

**Paul Tietjens
wrote the music
for the stage
musical of
The Wizard of Oz.**

A poster advertises the stage show *The Wizard of Oz.*

The three men worked
at Frank's house.
They sang, danced,
and acted silly.
The musical was good,
though, and did well.

That was fine
with Frank's readers.
But they really wanted
more books about Oz.
And Frank wouldn't write them.

He thought he'd told
the whole story of Oz.
So he wrote books about
other magic lands.
He even wrote a book
about Santa Claus.

But, at last, Frank
gave in and wrote
The Marvelous Land of Oz.

In *The Marvelous Land of Oz*, the Woggle-Bug and his friends (left) are prisoners in a palace. They bring materials to the roof so they can build a flying machine to escape. Below, the Woggle-Bug sits down on the grass to tell his story.

Some characters from the first book are in it. So is a wonderful new character, the Woggle-Bug. It's a people-sized insect.

John Neill drew
the pictures for
thirteen of Baum's
fourteen Oz books.

Frank and Denslow had
a fight about money.
So John Neill drew the
pictures for the new book.
he ended up doing the art
for thirteen Oz books in all.

Frank wrote other books too.
Some weren't very good.
But they earned money and
Frank always needed money.

The boys were
grown up, so
Frank and Maud
could travel—
and they did.
In 1906, they went
to Europe and
northern Africa.

But Frank still couldn't
stop writing Oz books,
even when he wanted to.
Almost every year,
he wrote a new one.

And still his readers cried,
"More!"

Chapter 5

Ozcot

In 1911, Frank and Maud
built a house
in Hollywood, California.
Frank called it Ozcot.

Ozcot was big and comfortable.
Outside were a huge birdcage,
a chicken yard, goldfish ponds,
and a beautiful garden.

Frank (above) in the rose garden at Ozcot with Maud and her sister Julia. Frank loved to work in the Ozcot garden (right)

Frank loved that garden.
There he dug and planted.
He wrote books there too.
Sometimes children visited
him in his garden and
Frank told them stories.

38

Frank liked to tell his Oz stories
to the children who visited him.

Thanksgiving Day — 1918

Frank and Maud surrounded by their family on Thanksgiving Day, 1918

But as time went by,
Frank's health grew worse.
He had to have an operation.
That made his heart weaker.
Soon he had to stay in bed.

On May 5, 1919,
Frank Baum had a stroke.
It took away most of
his power to speak.

But on May 6, he opened
his eyes for just a moment.
"Now we can cross
the Shifting Sands," he said.
Then, quietly, he died.

The cast of the 1939 film *The Wizard of Oz*: Dorothy,
the Cowardly Lion, the Tin Woodsman, and the Scarecrow

Twenty years after Frank died,
MGM brought out its film,
The Wizard of Oz.
Frank would have loved it.

The Wizard of Oz is one of the best-loved children's films of all time.

THE WONDERFUL WIZARD of OZ
BY L. FRANK BAUM PICTURES BY W.W. DENSLOW

MOTHER GOOSE IN PROSE
L. FRANK BAUM
PICTURES by MAXFIELD PARRISH

DOT AND TOT OF MERRYLAND
BY L. FRANK BAUM
PICTURES BY W.W. DENSLOW

L. FRANK BAUM

THE ARMY ALPHABET
PICTURES by HARRY KENNEDY
By L. FRANK BAUM

THE NAVY ALPHABET
PICTURES BY HARRY KENNEDY
By L. FRANK BAUM

AND HIS POPULAR Books FOR CHILDREN

FATHER GOOSE HIS BOOK
VERSE BY L. FRANK BAUM
PICTURES BY W.W. DENSLOW

AMERICAN FAIRY TALES
AMERICAN FAIRY TALES
BY L. FRANK BAUM

THE SONGS OF FATHER GOOSE
FOR THE KINDERGARTEN THE NURSERY AND THE HOME.
The George M. Hill Company, NEW YORK. CHICAGO. 1900

GEO. M. HILL COMPANY.
CHICAGO. PUBLISHERS. NEW YORK.

44

L. Frank Baum
in 1914

Today, some adults say
the Oz books are no good.
But children know better
and Frank wrote for *them*.

"I would much rather be
your story-teller," he wrote
to his young readers,
". . . than to be the President."

Important Dates

1856 May 15—Born in Chittenango, New York, to Cynthia and Benjamin Baum

1868 Went to Peekskill Academy, Peekskill, New York

1870 Returned home

1882 Married Maud Gage

1888 Moved to Aberdeen, South Dakota

1891 Moved to Chicago, Illinois

1897 *Mother Goose in Prose* published

1899 *Father Goose, His Book*, published

1900 *The Wonderful Wizard of Oz* published

1911 Moved to Hollywood, California

1919 May 6—Died at Ozcot, Hollywood, California

INDEX

Page numbers in boldface type indicate illustrations.

ABOUT THE AUTHOR

Carol Greene has degrees in English literature and musicology. She has worked
in international exchange programs, as an editor, and as a teacher of writing.
She now lives in Webster Groves, Missouri, and writes full-time. She has
published more than 100 books, including those in the Childrens Press Rookie
Biographies series.

ABOUT THE ILLUSTRATOR

Of Cajun origins, Steven Gaston Dobson was born and raised in New Orleans,
Louisiana. He attended art school in the city and worked as a newspaper artist
on the New Orleans Item. After serving in the Air Force during World War II,
he attended the Chicago Academy of Fine Arts in Chicago, Illinois. Before
switching to commercial illustration, Mr. Dobson won the Grand Prix in
portrait painting from the Palette and Chisel Club. In addition to his
commercial work, Steven taught illustration at the Chicago Academy of Fine
Arts and night school classes at LaGrange High School. In 1987, he moved to
Englewood, Florida, where he says "I am doing something that I have wanted
to do all of my 'art life,' painting interesting and historic people."